2274C: Managing a Microsoft® Windows Server™ 2003 Environment

X11-46557

1 2 3 4 5 6 7 8 9 QWE 9 8 7 6 5

Course Number: 2274C
Part Number: X11-46557
Released: 08/2005

END-USER LICENSE AGREEMENT FOR OFFICIAL MICROSOFT LEARNING PRODUCTS - STUDENT EDITION

PLEASE READ THIS END-USER LICENSE AGREEMENT ("EULA") CAREFULLY. BY USING THE MATERIALS AND/OR USING OR INSTALLING THE SOFTWARE THAT ACCOMPANIES THIS EULA (COLLECTIVELY, THE "LICENSED CONTENT"), YOU AGREE TO THE TERMS OF THIS EULA. IF YOU DO NOT AGREE, DO NOT USE THE LICENSED CONTENT.

1. GENERAL. This EULA is a legal agreement between you (either an individual or a single entity) and Microsoft Corporation ("Microsoft"). This EULA governs the Licensed Content, which includes computer software (including online and electronic documentation), training materials, and any other associated media and printed materials. This EULA applies to updates, supplements, add-on components, and Internet-based services components of the Licensed Content that Microsoft may provide or make available to you unless Microsoft provides other terms with the update, supplement, add-on component, or Internet-based services component. Microsoft reserves the right to discontinue any Internet-based services provided to you or made available to you through the use of the Licensed Content. This EULA also governs any product support services relating to the Licensed Content except as may be included in another agreement between you and Microsoft. An amendment or addendum to this EULA may accompany the Licensed Content.

2. **GENERAL GRANT OF LICENSE.** Microsoft grants you the following rights, conditioned on your compliance with all the terms and conditions of this EULA. Microsoft grants you a limited, non-exclusive, royalty-free license to install and use the Licensed Content solely in conjunction with your participation as a student in an Authorized Training Session (as defined below). You may install and use one copy of the software on a single computer, device, workstation, terminal, or other digital electronic or analog device ("Device"). You may make a second copy of the software and install it on a portable Device for the exclusive use of the person who is the primary user of the first copy of the software. A license for the software may not be shared for use by multiple end users. An "Authorized Training Session" means a training session conducted at a Microsoft Certified Technical Education Center, an IT Academy, via a Microsoft Certified Partner, or such other entity as Microsoft may designate from time to time in writing, by a Microsoft Certified Trainer (for more information on these entities, please visit www.microsoft.com). WITHOUT LIMITING THE FOREGOING, COPYING OR REPRODUCTION OF THE LICENSED CONTENT TO ANY SERVER OR LOCATION FOR FURTHER REPRODUCTION OR REDISTRIBUTION IS EXPRESSLY PROHIBITED.

3. DESCRIPTION OF OTHER RIGHTS AND LICENSE LIMITATIONS

3.1 *Use of Documentation and Printed Training Materials.*

3.1.1 The documents and related graphics included in the Licensed Content may include technical inaccuracies or typographical errors. Changes are periodically made to the content. Microsoft may make improvements and/or changes in any of the components of the Licensed Content at any time without notice. The names of companies, products, people, characters and/or data mentioned in the Licensed Content may be fictitious and are in no way intended to represent any real individual, company, product or event, unless otherwise noted.

3.1.2 Microsoft grants you the right to reproduce portions of documents (such as student workbooks, white papers, press releases, datasheets and FAQs) (the "Documents") provided with the Licensed Content. You may not print any book (either electronic or print version) in its entirety. If you choose to reproduce Documents, you agree that: (a) use of such printed Documents will be solely in conjunction with your personal training use; (b) the Documents will not republished or posted on any network computer or broadcast in any media; (c) any reproduction will include either the Document's original copyright notice or a copyright notice to Microsoft's benefit substantially in the format provided below; and (d) to comply with all terms and conditions of this EULA. In addition, no modifications may made to any Document.

Form of Notice:

Copyright undefined.

© 2005. Reprinted with permission by Microsoft Corporation. All rights reserved.

Microsoft and Windows are either registered trademarks or trademarks of Microsoft Corporation in the US and/or other countries. Other product and company names mentioned herein may be the trademarks of their respective owners.

3.2 *Use of Media Elements.* The Licensed Content may include certain photographs, clip art, animations, sounds, music, and video clips (together "Media Elements"). You may not modify these Media Elements.

3.3 *Use of Sample Code.* In the event that the Licensed Content include sample source code ("Sample Code"), Microsoft grants you a limited, non-exclusive, royalty-free license to use, copy and modify the Sample Code; if you elect to exercise the foregoing rights, you agree to comply with all other terms and conditions of this EULA, including without limitation Sections 3.4, 3.5, and 6.

3.4 *Permitted Modifications.* In the event that you exercise any rights provided under this EULA to create modifications of the Licensed Content, you agree that any such modifications: (a) will not be used for providing training where a fee is charged in public or private classes; (b) indemnify, hold harmless, and defend Microsoft from and against any claims or lawsuits, including attorneys' fees, which arise from or result from your use of any modified version of the Licensed Content; and (c) not to transfer or assign any rights to any modified version of the Licensed Content to any third party without the express written permission of Microsoft.

3.5 *Reproduction/Redistribution Licensed Content.* Except as expressly provided in this EULA, you may not reproduce or distribute the Licensed Content or any portion thereof (including any permitted modifications) to any third parties without the express written permission of Microsoft.

4. **RESERVATION OF RIGHTS AND OWNERSHIP.** Microsoft reserves all rights not expressly granted to you in this EULA. The Licensed Content is protected by copyright and other intellectual property laws and treaties. Microsoft or its suppliers own the title, copyright, and other intellectual property rights in the Licensed Content. You may not remove or obscure any copyright, trademark or patent notices that appear on the Licensed Content, or any components thereof, as delivered to you. **The Licensed Content is licensed, not sold.**

5. **LIMITATIONS ON REVERSE ENGINEERING, DECOMPILATION, AND DISASSEMBLY.** You may not reverse engineer, decompile, or disassemble the Software or Media Elements, except and only to the extent that such activity is expressly permitted by applicable law notwithstanding this limitation.

6. **LIMITATIONS ON SALE, RENTAL, ETC. AND CERTAIN ASSIGNMENTS.** You may not provide commercial hosting services with, sell, rent, lease, lend, sublicense, or assign copies of the Licensed Content, or any portion thereof (including any permitted modifications thereof) on a stand-alone basis or as part of any collection, product or service.

7. **CONSENT TO USE OF DATA.** You agree that Microsoft and its affiliates may collect and use technical information gathered as part of the product support services provided to you, if any, related to the Licensed Content. Microsoft may use this information solely to improve our products or to provide customized services or technologies to you and will not disclose this information in a form that personally identifies you.

8. **LINKS TO THIRD PARTY SITES.** You may link to third party sites through the use of the Licensed Content. The third party sites are not under the control of Microsoft, and Microsoft is not responsible for the contents of any third party sites, any links contained in third party sites, or any changes or updates to third party sites. Microsoft is not responsible for webcasting or any other form of transmission received from any third party sites. Microsoft is providing these links to third party sites to you only as a convenience, and the inclusion of any link does not imply an endorsement by Microsoft of the third party site.

9. **ADDITIONAL LICENSED CONTENT/SERVICES.** This EULA applies to updates, supplements, add-on components, or Internet-based services components, of the Licensed Content that Microsoft may provide to you or make available to you after the date you obtain your initial copy of the Licensed Content, unless we provide other terms along with the update, supplement, add-on component, or Internet-based services component. Microsoft reserves the right to discontinue any Internet-based services provided to you or made available to you through the use of the Licensed Content.

10. **U.S. GOVERNMENT LICENSE RIGHTS**. All software provided to the U.S. Government pursuant to solicitations issued on or after December 1, 1995 is provided with the commercial license rights and restrictions described elsewhere herein. All software provided to the U.S. Government pursuant to solicitations issued prior to December 1, 1995 is provided with "Restricted Rights" as provided for in FAR, 48 CFR 52.227-14 (JUNE 1987) or DFAR, 48 CFR 252.227-7013 (OCT 1988), as applicable.

11. **EXPORT RESTRICTIONS**. You acknowledge that the Licensed Content is subject to U.S. export jurisdiction. You agree to comply with all applicable international and national laws that apply to the Licensed Content, including the U.S. Export Administration Regulations, as well as end-user, end-use, and destination restrictions issued by U.S. and other governments. For additional information see <http://www.microsoft.com/exporting/>.

12. **TRANSFER.** The initial user of the Licensed Content may make a one-time permanent transfer of this EULA and Licensed Content to another end user, provided the initial user retains no copies of the Licensed Content. The transfer may not be an indirect transfer, such as a consignment. Prior to the transfer, the end user receiving the Licensed Content must agree to all the EULA terms.

13. **"NOT FOR RESALE" LICENSED CONTENT.** Licensed Content identified as "Not For Resale" or "NFR," may not be sold or otherwise transferred for value, or used for any purpose other than demonstration, test or evaluation.

14. **TERMINATION.** Without prejudice to any other rights, Microsoft may terminate this EULA if you fail to comply with the terms and conditions of this EULA. In such event, you must destroy all copies of the Licensed Content and all of its component parts.

15. **DISCLAIMER OF WARRANTIES. TO THE MAXIMUM EXTENT PERMITTED BY APPLICABLE LAW, MICROSOFT AND ITS SUPPLIERS PROVIDE THE LICENSED CONTENT AND SUPPORT SERVICES (IF ANY) *AS IS AND WITH ALL FAULTS*, AND MICROSOFT AND ITS SUPPLIERS HEREBY DISCLAIM ALL OTHER WARRANTIES AND CONDITIONS, WHETHER EXPRESS, IMPLIED OR STATUTORY, INCLUDING, BUT NOT LIMITED TO, ANY (IF ANY) IMPLIED WARRANTIES, DUTIES OR CONDITIONS OF MERCHANTABILITY, OF FITNESS FOR A PARTICULAR PURPOSE, OF RELIABILITY OR AVAILABILITY, OF ACCURACY OR COMPLETENESS OF RESPONSES, OF RESULTS, OF WORKMANLIKE EFFORT, OF LACK OF VIRUSES, AND OF LACK OF NEGLIGENCE, ALL WITH REGARD TO THE LICENSED CONTENT, AND THE PROVISION OF OR FAILURE TO PROVIDE SUPPORT OR OTHER SERVICES, INFORMATION, SOFTWARE, AND RELATED CONTENT THROUGH THE LICENSED CONTENT, OR OTHERWISE ARISING OUT OF THE USE OF THE LICENSED CONTENT. ALSO, THERE IS NO WARRANTY OR CONDITION OF TITLE, QUIET ENJOYMENT, QUIET POSSESSION, CORRESPONDENCE TO DESCRIPTION OR NON-INFRINGEMENT WITH REGARD TO THE LICENSED CONTENT. THE ENTIRE RISK AS TO THE QUALITY, OR ARISING OUT OF THE USE OR PERFORMANCE OF THE LICENSED CONTENT, AND ANY SUPPORT SERVICES, REMAINS WITH YOU.**

16. **EXCLUSION OF INCIDENTAL, CONSEQUENTIAL AND CERTAIN OTHER DAMAGES. TO THE MAXIMUM EXTENT PERMITTED BY APPLICABLE LAW, IN NO EVENT SHALL MICROSOFT OR ITS SUPPLIERS BE LIABLE FOR ANY SPECIAL, INCIDENTAL, PUNITIVE, INDIRECT, OR CONSEQUENTIAL DAMAGES WHATSOEVER (INCLUDING, BUT NOT**

LIMITED TO, DAMAGES FOR LOSS OF PROFITS OR CONFIDENTIAL OR OTHER INFORMATION, FOR BUSINESS INTERRUPTION, FOR PERSONAL INJURY, FOR LOSS OF PRIVACY, FOR FAILURE TO MEET ANY DUTY INCLUDING OF GOOD FAITH OR OF REASONABLE CARE, FOR NEGLIGENCE, AND FOR ANY OTHER PECUNIARY OR OTHER LOSS WHATSOEVER) ARISING OUT OF OR IN ANY WAY RELATED TO THE USE OF OR INABILITY TO USE THE LICENSED CONTENT, THE PROVISION OF OR FAILURE TO PROVIDE SUPPORT OR OTHER SERVICES, INFORMATION, SOFTWARE, AND RELATED CONTENT THROUGH THE LICENSED CONTENT, OR OTHERWISE ARISING OUT OF THE USE OF THE LICENSED CONTENT, OR OTHERWISE UNDER OR IN CONNECTION WITH ANY PROVISION OF THIS EULA, EVEN IN THE EVENT OF THE FAULT, TORT (INCLUDING NEGLIGENCE), MISREPRESENTATION, STRICT LIABILITY, BREACH OF CONTRACT OR BREACH OF WARRANTY OF MICROSOFT OR ANY SUPPLIER, AND EVEN IF MICROSOFT OR ANY SUPPLIER HAS BEEN ADVISED OF THE POSSIBILITY OF SUCH DAMAGES. BECAUSE SOME STATES/JURISDICTIONS DO NOT ALLOW THE EXCLUSION OR LIMITATION OF LIABILITY FOR CONSEQUENTIAL OR INCIDENTAL DAMAGES, THE ABOVE LIMITATION MAY NOT APPLY TO YOU.

17. <u>LIMITATION OF LIABILITY AND REMEDIES</u>. NOTWITHSTANDING ANY DAMAGES THAT YOU MIGHT INCUR FOR ANY REASON WHATSOEVER (INCLUDING, WITHOUT LIMITATION, ALL DAMAGES REFERENCED HEREIN AND ALL DIRECT OR GENERAL DAMAGES IN CONTRACT OR ANYTHING ELSE), THE ENTIRE LIABILITY OF MICROSOFT AND ANY OF ITS SUPPLIERS UNDER ANY PROVISION OF THIS EULA AND YOUR EXCLUSIVE REMEDY HEREUNDER SHALL BE LIMITED TO THE GREATER OF THE ACTUAL DAMAGES YOU INCUR IN REASONABLE RELIANCE ON THE LICENSED CONTENT UP TO THE AMOUNT ACTUALLY PAID BY YOU FOR THE LICENSED CONTENT OR US$5.00. THE FOREGOING LIMITATIONS, EXCLUSIONS AND DISCLAIMERS SHALL APPLY TO THE MAXIMUM EXTENT PERMITTED BY APPLICABLE LAW, EVEN IF ANY REMEDY FAILS ITS ESSENTIAL PURPOSE.

18. **APPLICABLE LAW.** If you acquired this Licensed Content in the United States, this EULA is governed by the laws of the State of Washington. If you acquired this Licensed Content in Canada, unless expressly prohibited by local law, this EULA is governed by the laws in force in the Province of Ontario, Canada; and, in respect of any dispute which may arise hereunder, you consent to the jurisdiction of the federal and provincial courts sitting in Toronto, Ontario. If you acquired this Licensed Content in the European Union, Iceland, Norway, or Switzerland, then local law applies. If you acquired this Licensed Content in any other country, then local law may apply.

19. **ENTIRE AGREEMENT; SEVERABILITY.** This EULA (including any addendum or amendment to this EULA which is included with the Licensed Content) are the entire agreement between you and Microsoft relating to the Licensed Content and the support services (if any) and they supersede all prior or contemporaneous oral or written communications, proposals and representations with respect to the Licensed Content or any other subject matter covered by this EULA. To the extent the terms of any Microsoft policies or programs for support services conflict with the terms of this EULA, the terms of this EULA shall control. If any provision of this EULA is held to be void, invalid, unenforceable or illegal, the other provisions shall continue in full force and effect.

Should you have any questions concerning this EULA, or if you desire to contact Microsoft for any reason, please use the address information enclosed in this Licensed Content to contact the Microsoft subsidiary serving your country or visit Microsoft on the World Wide Web at <u>http://www.microsoft.com</u>.

Si vous avez acquis votre Contenu Sous Licence Microsoft au CANADA :

DÉNI DE GARANTIES. Dans la mesure maximale permise par les lois applicables, le Contenu Sous Licence et les services de soutien technique (le cas échéant) sont fournis *TELS QUELS ET AVEC TOUS LES DÉFAUTS* par Microsoft et ses fournisseurs, lesquels par les présentes dénient toutes autres garanties et conditions expresses, implicites ou en vertu de la loi, notamment, mais sans limitation, (le cas échéant) les garanties, devoirs ou conditions implicites de qualité marchande, d'adaptation à une fin usage particulière, de fiabilité ou de disponibilité, d'exactitude ou d'exhaustivité des réponses, des résultats, des efforts déployés selon les règles de l'art, d'absence de virus et d'absence de négligence, le tout à l'égard du Contenu Sous Licence et de la prestation des services de soutien technique ou de l'omission de la 'une telle prestation des services de soutien technique ou à l'égard de la fourniture ou de l'omission de la fourniture de tous autres services, renseignements, Contenus Sous Licence, et contenu qui s'y rapporte grâce au Contenu Sous Licence ou provenant autrement de l'utilisation du Contenu Sous Licence. PAR AILLEURS, IL N'Y A AUCUNE GARANTIE OU CONDITION QUANT AU TITRE DE PROPRIÉTÉ, À LA JOUISSANCE OU LA POSSESSION PAISIBLE, À LA CONCORDANCE À UNE DESCRIPTION NI QUANT À UNE ABSENCE DE CONTREFAÇON CONCERNANT LE CONTENU SOUS LICENCE.

<u>EXCLUSION DES DOMMAGES ACCESSOIRES, INDIRECTS ET DE CERTAINS AUTRES DOMMAGES</u>. DANS LA MESURE MAXIMALE PERMISE PAR LES LOIS APPLICABLES, EN AUCUN CAS MICROSOFT OU SES FOURNISSEURS NE SERONT RESPONSABLES DES DOMMAGES SPÉCIAUX, CONSÉCUTIFS, ACCESSOIRES OU INDIRECTS DE QUELQUE NATURE QUE CE SOIT (NOTAMMENT, LES DOMMAGES À L'ÉGARD DU MANQUE À GAGNER OU DE LA DIVULGATION DE RENSEIGNEMENTS CONFIDENTIELS OU AUTRES, DE LA PERTE D'EXPLOITATION, DE BLESSURES CORPORELLES, DE LA VIOLATION DE LA VIE PRIVÉE, DE L'OMISSION DE REMPLIR TOUT DEVOIR, Y COMPRIS D'AGIR DE BONNE FOI OU D'EXERCER UN SOIN RAISONNABLE, DE LA NÉGLIGENCE ET DE TOUTE AUTRE PERTE PÉCUNIAIRE OU AUTRE PERTE

DE QUELQUE NATURE QUE CE SOIT) SE RAPPORTANT DE QUELQUE MANIÈRE QUE CE SOIT À L'UTILISATION DU CONTENU SOUS LICENCE OU À L'INCAPACITÉ DE S'EN SERVIR, À LA PRESTATION OU À L'OMISSION DE LA 'UNE TELLE PRESTATION DE SERVICES DE SOUTIEN TECHNIQUE OU À LA FOURNITURE OU À L'OMISSION DE LA FOURNITURE DE TOUS AUTRES SERVICES, RENSEIGNEMENTS, CONTENUS SOUS LICENCE, ET CONTENU QUI S'Y RAPPORTE GRÂCE AU CONTENU SOUS LICENCE OU PROVENANT AUTREMENT DE L'UTILISATION DU CONTENU SOUS LICENCE OU AUTREMENT AUX TERMES DE TOUTE DISPOSITION DE LA U PRÉSENTE CONVENTION EULA OU RELATIVEMENT À UNE TELLE DISPOSITION, MÊME EN CAS DE FAUTE, DE DÉLIT CIVIL (Y COMPRIS LA NÉGLIGENCE), DE RESPONSABILITÉ STRICTE, DE VIOLATION DE CONTRAT OU DE VIOLATION DE GARANTIE DE MICROSOFT OU DE TOUT FOURNISSEUR ET MÊME SI MICROSOFT OU TOUT FOURNISSEUR A ÉTÉ AVISÉ DE LA POSSIBILITÉ DE TELS DOMMAGES.

LIMITATION DE RESPONSABILITÉ ET RECOURS. MALGRÉ LES DOMMAGES QUE VOUS PUISSIEZ SUBIR POUR QUELQUE MOTIF QUE CE SOIT (NOTAMMENT, MAIS SANS LIMITATION, TOUS LES DOMMAGES SUSMENTIONNÉS ET TOUS LES DOMMAGES DIRECTS OU GÉNÉRAUX OU AUTRES), LA SEULE RESPONSABILITÉ 'OBLIGATION INTÉGRALE DE MICROSOFT ET DE L'UN OU L'AUTRE DE SES FOURNISSEURS AUX TERMES DE TOUTE DISPOSITION DEU LA PRÉSENTE CONVENTION EULA ET VOTRE RECOURS EXCLUSIF À L'ÉGARD DE TOUT CE QUI PRÉCÈDE SE LIMITE AU PLUS ÉLEVÉ ENTRE LES MONTANTS SUIVANTS : LE MONTANT QUE VOUS AVEZ RÉELLEMENT PAYÉ POUR LE CONTENU SOUS LICENCE OU 5,00 $US. LES LIMITES, EXCLUSIONS ET DÉNIS QUI PRÉCÈDENT (Y COMPRIS LES CLAUSES CI-DESSUS), S'APPLIQUENT DANS LA MESURE MAXIMALE PERMISE PAR LES LOIS APPLICABLES, MÊME SI TOUT RECOURS N'ATTEINT PAS SON BUT ESSENTIEL.

À moins que cela ne soit prohibé par le droit local applicable, la présente Convention est régie par les lois de la province d'Ontario, Canada. Vous consentez Chacune des parties à la présente reconnaît irrévocablement à la compétence des tribunaux fédéraux et provinciaux siégeant à Toronto, dans de la province d'Ontario et consent à instituer tout litige qui pourrait découler de la présente auprès des tribunaux situés dans le district judiciaire de York, province d'Ontario.

Au cas où vous auriez des questions concernant cette licence ou que vous désiriez vous mettre en rapport avec Microsoft pour quelque raison que ce soit, veuillez utiliser l'information contenue dans le Contenu Sous Licence pour contacter la filiale de succursale Microsoft desservant votre pays, dont l'adresse est fournie dans ce produit, ou visitez écrivez à : Microsoft sur le World Wide Web à http://www.microsoft.com

Contents

Module 5: Implementing Printing

Module 6: Managing Printing

Module 7: Managing Access to Objects in Organizational Units

Module 8: Implementing Group Policy

Module 9: Managing the User Environment by Using Group Policy

Module 10: Implementing Administrative Templates and Audit Policy

Index

About This Course

This section provides you with a brief description of the course, audience, suggested prerequisites, and course objectives.

Description

This five-day, instructor-led course provides students with the knowledge and skills to manage accounts and resources in a Microsoft® Windows Server™ 2003 environment. The course is intended for systems administrator and systems engineer candidates who are responsible for managing accounts and resources. These tasks include managing user, computer, and group accounts; managing access to network resources; managing printers; managing an organizational unit (OU) in a network based on Active Directory® directory service; and implementing Group Policy to manage users and computers.

Audience

This is the first course in the systems administrator and systems engineer tracks for Windows Server 2003, and it serves as the entry point for other courses in the Windows Server 2003 curriculum.

Student prerequisites

This course requires that students meet the following prerequisites:

- A+ certification or equivalent knowledge and skills
- Network+ certification or equivalent knowledge and skills

Course objectives

After completing this course, the student will be able to:

- Create and populate OUs with user and computer accounts.
- Manage user and computer accounts.
- Create and manage groups.
- Manage access to resources.
- Implement printing.
- Manage printing.
- Use OUs to manage access to objects.
- Implement Group Policy.
- Use Group Policy to manage the user and computer environment.
- Implement administrative templates and audit policy in Windows Server 2003.

Student Materials Compact Disc Contents

The Student Materials compact disc contains the following files and folders:

- *Autorun.inf.* When the compact disc is inserted into the compact disc drive, this file opens StartCD.exe.
- *Default.htm.* This file opens the Student Materials Web page. It provides you with resources pertaining to this course, including additional reading, review and lab answers, lab files, multimedia presentations, and course-related Web sites.
- *Readme.txt.* This file explains how to install the software for viewing the Student Materials compact disc and its contents and how to open the Student Materials Web page.
- *StartCD.exe.* When the compact disc is inserted into the compact disc drive, or when you double-click the **StartCD.exe** file, this file opens the compact disc and allows you to browse the Student Materials DVD.
- *StartCD.ini.* This file contains instructions to launch StartCD.exe.
- *Addread.* This folder contains additional reading pertaining to this course.
- *Appendix.* This folder contains appendix files for this course.
- *Flash.* This folder contains the installer for the Macromedia Flash browser plug-in.
- *Fonts.* This folder contains fonts that might be required to view the Microsoft Office Word documents that are included with this course.
- *Media.* This folder contains files that are used in multimedia presentations for this course.
- *Mplayer.* This folder contains the setup file to install Microsoft Windows Media® Player.
- *Webfiles.* This folder contains the files that are required to view the course Web page. To open the Web page, open Windows Explorer, and in the root directory of the compact disc, double-click **StartCD.exe**.
- *Wordview.* This folder contains the Word Viewer that is used to view any Word document (.doc) files that are included on the compact disc.

Document Conventions

The following conventions are used in course materials to distinguish elements of the text.

Convention	Use
Bold	Represents commands, command options, and syntax that must be typed exactly as shown. It also indicates commands on menus and buttons, dialog box titles and options, and icon and menu names.
Italic	In syntax statements or descriptive text, indicates argument names or placeholders for variable information. Italic is also used for introducing new terms, for book titles, and for emphasis in the text.
Title Capitals	Indicate domain names, user names, computer names, directory names, and folder and file names, except when specifically referring to case-sensitive names. Unless otherwise indicated, you can use lowercase letters when you type a directory name or file name in a dialog box or at a command prompt.
ALL CAPITALS	Indicate the names of keys, key sequences, and key combinations—for example, ALT+SPACEBAR.
`monospace`	Represents code samples or examples of screen text.
[ ]	In syntax statements, enclose optional items. For example, [*filename*] in command syntax indicates that you can choose to type a file name with the command. Type only the information within the brackets, not the brackets themselves.
{ }	In syntax statements, enclose required items. Type only the information within the braces, not the braces themselves.
|	In syntax statements, separates an either/or choice.
▶	Indicates a procedure with sequential steps.
...	In syntax statements, specifies that the preceding item may be repeated.
. . .	Represents an omitted portion of a code sample.

THIS PAGE INTENTIONALLY LEFT BLANK

Microsoft®

Introduction

Contents

Introduction

- Name
- Company affiliation
- Title/function
- Job responsibility
- Systems administration experience
- Windows Server operating systems experience
- Expectations for the course

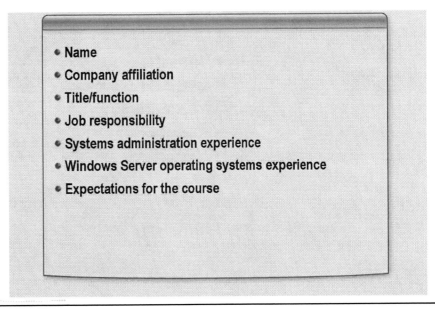

Course Materials

- Name card
- Student workbook
- Student Materials compact disc
- Course evaluation
- Assessments

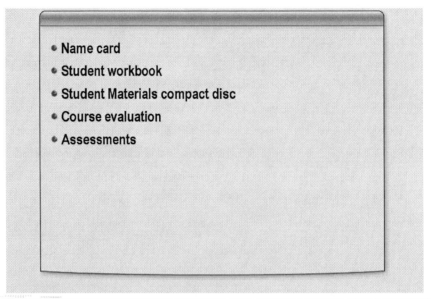

The following materials are included with your kit:

- *Name card.* Write your name on both sides of the name card.
- *Student workbook.* The student workbook contains the material covered in class, in addition to the hands-on lab exercises.
- *Student Materials compact disc.* The Student Materials compact disc contains Web page that provides you with links to resources pertaining to this course, including additional readings, review and lab answers, lab files, multimedia presentations, and course-related Web sites.

  Note To open the Web page, insert the Student Materials compact disc into the CD-ROM drive, and then in the root directory of the compact disc, double-click **StartCD.exe**.

- *Course evaluation.* Near the end of the course, you will have the opportunity to complete an online evaluation to provide feedback on the course, training facility, and instructor.

  To provide additional comments or feedback on the course, send e-mail to support@mscourseware.com. To inquire about the Microsoft Certified Professional program, send e-mail to mcphelp@microsoft.com.

Prerequisites

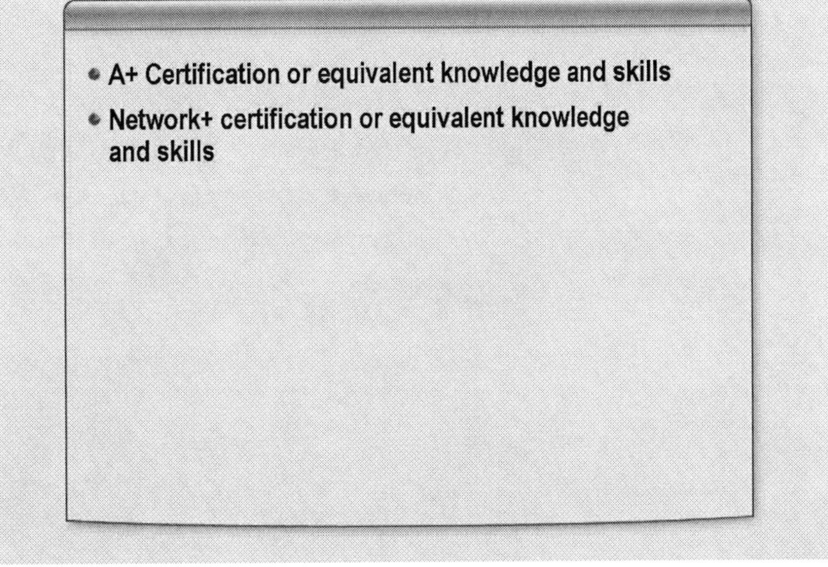

This course requires that you meet the following prerequisites:

- A+ certification or equivalent knowledge and skills
- Network+ certification or equivalent knowledge and skills

Course Outline

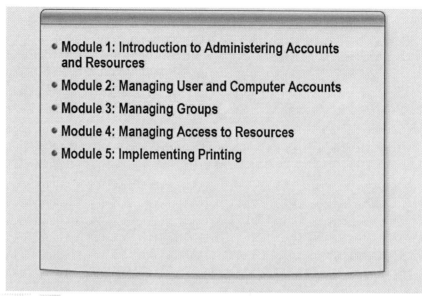

- Module 1: Introduction to Administering Accounts and Resources
- Module 2: Managing User and Computer Accounts
- Module 3: Managing Groups
- Module 4: Managing Access to Resources
- Module 5: Implementing Printing

Module 1, "Introduction to Administering Accounts and Resources," introduces the Microsoft® Windows Server™ 2003 family of operating systems and the tasks and tools for administering accounts and resources on computers running Windows Server 2003 in a networked environment.

Module 2, "Managing User and Computer Accounts," explains how to create and modify user and computer accounts on computers running Windows Server 2003 in a networked environment.

Module 3, "Managing Groups," explains how to use groups to simplify domain administration.

Module 4, "Managing Access to Resources," explains how permissions enable resource access. You also learn how to use NT file system (NTFS) permissions to manage access to files and folders, use special permissions to manage access to files and folders, and manage permission inheritance.

Module 5, "Implementing Printing," explains how to install, configure, and manage printers.

Course Outline *(continued)*

- Module 6: Managing Printing
- Module 7: Managing Access to Objects in Organizational Units
- Module 8: Implementing Group Policy
- Module 9: Managing the User Environment by Using Group Policy
- Module 10: Implementing Administrative Templates and Audit Policy

Module 6, "Managing Printing," explains how to set up a network-wide printing strategy to meet the needs of users and how to troubleshoot installation or configuration problems.

Module 7, "Managing Access to Objects in Organizational Units," explains the permissions available for managing access to objects in Active Directory® directory service. You also learn how to move objects between organizational units in the same domain and how to delegate control of an organizational unit.

Module 8, "Implementing Group Policy," explains the purpose and function of Group Policy in a Windows Server 2003 environment. It also explains how to implement and manage Group Policy objects (GPOs).

Module 9, "Managing the User Environment by Using Group Policy," explains how to use Group Policy to configure folder redirection, Microsoft Internet Explorer connectivity, and the desktop.

Module 10, "Implementing Administrative Templates and Audit Policy," explains how to manage security in an Active Directory domain and how to audit events to ensure the effectiveness of a security strategy.

In addition to these modules, the student CD also includes the following appendices located in the Appendix folder.

Appendix A, "Differences Between Microsoft Windows 2000 Server and Microsoft Windows Server 2003," explains the differences between the operating systems in the context of the tasks in each module. This appendix is provided for students who are familiar with Windows 2000 Server.

Appendix B, "Administering Microsoft Windows Server 2003 by Using Scripts," provides information about using scripts to perform the administration tasks taught in this course.

Setup

- The virtual environment is configured as one Windows Server 2003 domain: Contoso.msft
- DEN-DC1 is the domain controller
- DEN-SRV1 is a member server and is used as a remote computer for student labs
- DEN-CL1 is a workstation running Windows XP Professional, Service Pack 2
- Server computers are running Windows Server 2003, Enterprise Edition, Service Pack 1

Classroom setup

Each student machine has Microsoft Windows® XP Professional installed and is running Microsoft Virtual PC 2004.

The name of the domain is contoso.msft. The domain is named after Contoso, Ltd., a fictitious company that has offices worldwide.

The domain controller is named DEN-DC1, and there is a member server, named DEN-SRV1. Both computers are running Windows Server 2003 Enterprise Edition with Service Pack 1 (SP1). The workstation computer is named DEN-CL1 and is running Windows XP Professional with Service Pack 2 (SP2).

The domain has been populated with users, groups, and computer accounts for each administrator to manage.

Demonstration: Using Microsoft Virtual PC

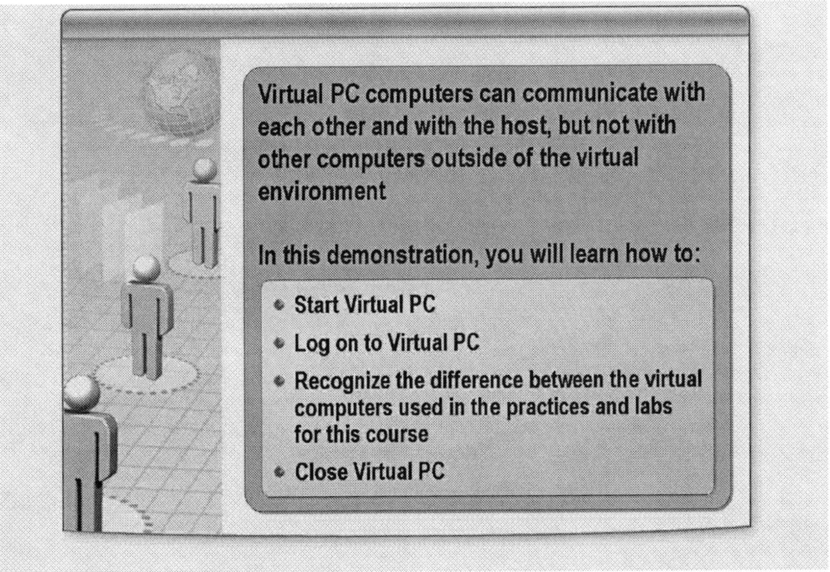

In this demonstration, your instructor will help familiarize you with the Virtual PC environment in which you will work to complete the practices and labs in this course. You will learn:

- How to open Virtual PC.
- How to start Virtual PC.
- How to log on to Virtual PC.
- How to switch between full screen and window modes.
- How to tell the difference between the virtual machines that are used in the practices for this course.
- That the virtual machines can communicate with each other and with the host, but they cannot communicate with other computers that are outside of the virtual environment. (For example, no Internet access is available from the virtual environment.)
- How to close Virtual PC.

Keyboard shortcuts

While working in the Virtual PC environment, you might find it helpful to use keyboard shortcuts. All Virtual PC shortcuts include a key that is referred to as the HOST key or the RIGHT-ALT key. By default, the HOST key is the ALT key on the right side of your keyboard. Some useful shortcuts include:

- ALT+DELETE to log on to the Virtual PC
- ALT+ENTER to switch between full screen mode and window modes
- ALT+RIGHT ARROW to display the next Virtual PC

For more information about Virtual PC, see Virtual PC Help.

Microsoft Learning

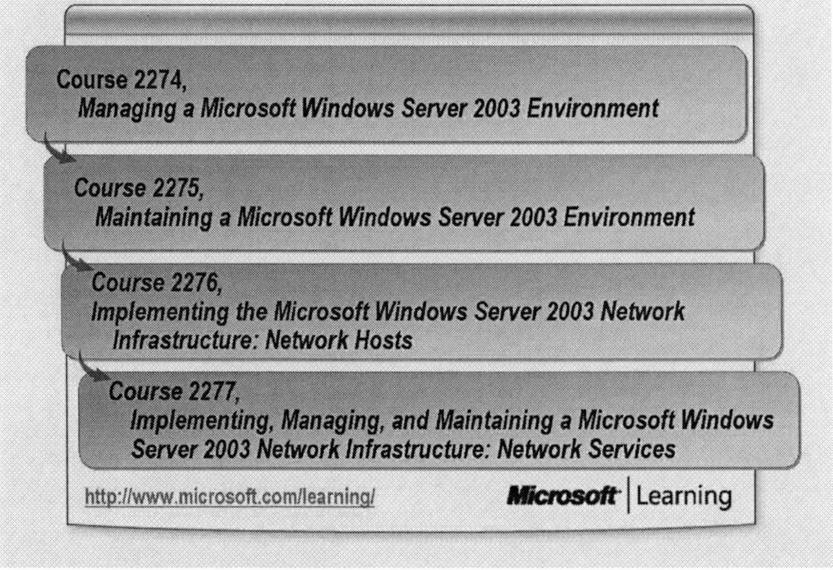

Microsoft Learning develops Official Microsoft Learning Products for computer professionals who design, develop, support, implement, or manage solutions by using Microsoft products and technologies. These learning products provide comprehensive, skills-based training in instructor-led and online formats.

Additional recommended learning products

Each learning product relates in some way to other learning products. A related product might be a prerequisite; a follow-up course, clinic, or workshop in a recommended series, or a learning product that offers additional training.

It is recommended that you take the following courses in this order:

- Course 2274: *Managing a Microsoft Windows Server 2003 Environment*
- Course 2275: *Maintaining a Microsoft Windows Server 2003 Environment*
- Course 2276: *Implementing a Microsoft Windows Server 2003 Network Infrastructure: Network Hosts*
- Course 2277: *Implementing, Managing, and Maintaining a Microsoft Windows Server 2003 Network Infrastructure: Network Services*
- Course 2278: *Planning and Maintaining a Microsoft Windows Server 2003 Network Infrastructure*
- Course 2279: *Planning, Implementing, and Maintaining a Microsoft Windows Server 2003 Active Directory Infrastructure*

Other related learning products might become available in the future, so for up-to-date information about recommended learning products, visit the Microsoft Learning Web site.

Microsoft Learning information

For more information, visit the Microsoft Learning Web site at http://www.microsoft.com/learning/.

Microsoft Learning Product Types

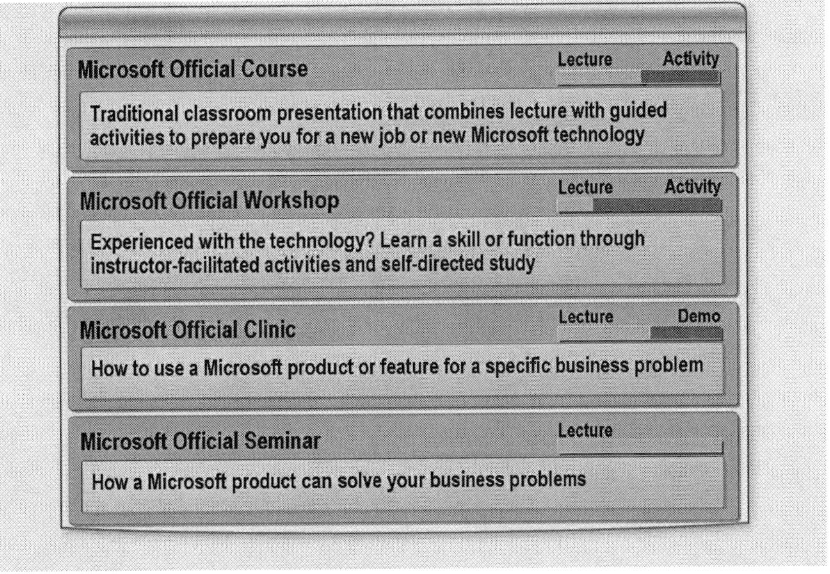

Microsoft Learning offers four types of instructor-led products type. Each is specific to a particular audience type and level of experience. The different product types also tend to suit different learning styles. These types are as follows:

- Microsoft Official Courses are for information technology (IT) professionals and developers who are new to a particular product or technology and for experienced individuals who prefer to learn in a traditional classroom format. Courses provide a relevant and guided learning experience that combines lecture and practice to deliver thorough coverage of a Microsoft product or technology. Courses are designed to address the needs of learners engaged in planning, design, implementation, management, and support phases of the technology adoption lifecycle. They provide detailed information by focusing on concepts and principles, reference content, and in-depth hands-on lab activities to ensure knowledge transfer. Typically, the content of a course is broad, addressing a wide range of tasks necessary for the job role.
- Microsoft Official Workshops are for knowledgeable IT professionals and developers who learn best by doing and exploring. Workshops provide a hands-on learning experience in which participants use Microsoft products in a safe and collaborative environment based on real-world scenarios. Workshops are the learning products where students learn by doing through scenario and through troubleshooting hands-on labs, targeted reviews, information resources, and best practices, with instructor facilitation.

- Microsoft Official Clinics are for IT professionals, developers and technical decision makers. Clinics offer a detailed "how to" presentation that describes the features and functionality of an existing or new Microsoft product or technology, and that showcases product demonstrations and solutions. Clinics focus on how specific features will solve business problems.
- Microsoft Official Seminars are for business decision makers. Through featured business scenarios, case studies, and success stories, seminars provide a dynamic presentation of early and relevant information on Microsoft products and technology solutions that enable decision makers to make critical business decisions. Microsoft Official Seminars are concise, engaging, direct-from-the-source learning products that show how emerging Microsoft products and technologies help our customers serve their customers.

Microsoft Certified Professional Program

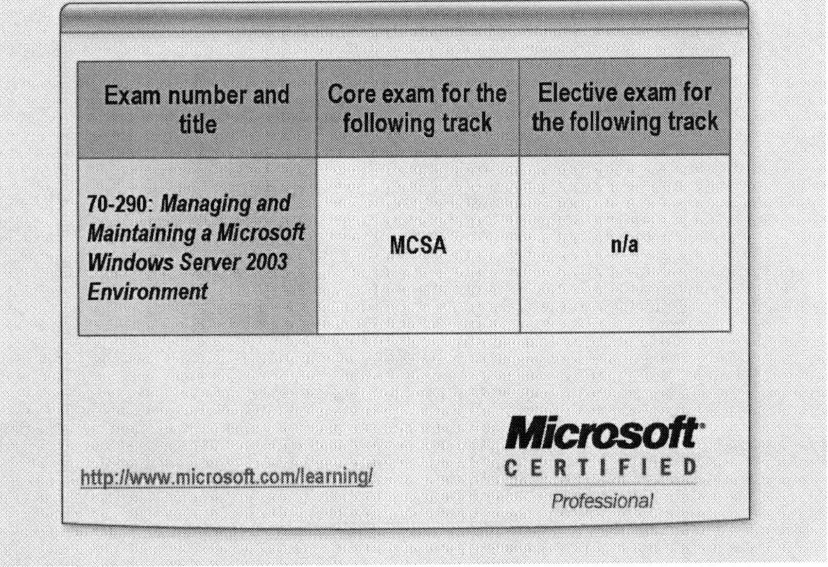

Exam number and title	Core exam for the following track	Elective exam for the following track
70-290: *Managing and Maintaining a Microsoft Windows Server 2003 Environment*	MCSA	n/a

Microsoft Learning offers a variety of certification credentials for developers and IT professionals. The Microsoft Certified Professional (MCP) program is the leading certification program for validating your experience and skills, keeping you competitive in today's changing business environment.

Related certification exams

This course, in combination with Course 2275: *Maintaining a Microsoft Windows Server 2003 Environment*, helps students to prepare for Exam 70-290: *Managing and Maintaining a Microsoft Windows Server 2003 Environment.* To prepare for the exam, you should complete both courses.

Exam 70-290 is a core exam for the Microsoft Certified Systems Administrator certification.

MCP certifications

The MCP program includes the following certifications:

- MCDST on Windows XP

  The Microsoft Certified Desktop Support Technician (MCDST) certification is designed for professionals who successfully support and educate end users and troubleshoot operating system and application issues on desktop computers running the Windows operating system.

- MCSA on Windows Server 2003

  The Microsoft Certified Systems Administrator (MCSA) certification is designed for professionals who implement, manage, and troubleshoot existing network and system environments based on the Windows Server 2003 platform. Implementation responsibilities include installing and configuring parts of systems. Management responsibilities include administering and supporting systems.

- MCSE on Windows Server 2003

  The Microsoft Certified Systems Engineer (MCSE) credential is the premier certification for professionals who analyze business requirements and design and implement infrastructure for business solutions based on the Windows Server 2003 platform. Implementation responsibilities include installing, configuring, and troubleshooting network systems.

- MCAD

  The Microsoft Certified Application Developer (MCAD) for Microsoft .NET credential is appropriate for professionals who use Microsoft technologies to develop and maintain department-level applications, components, Web or desktop clients, or back-end data services, or who work in teams developing enterprise applications. The credential covers job tasks ranging from developing to deploying and maintaining these solutions.

- MCSD

  The Microsoft Certified Solution Developer (MCSD) credential is the premier certification for professionals who design and develop leading-edge business solutions with Microsoft development tools, technologies, platforms, and the Microsoft Windows DNA architecture. The types of applications MCSDs can develop include desktop applications and multi-user, Web-based, N-tier, and transaction-based applications. The credential covers job tasks ranging from analyzing business requirements to maintaining solutions.

- MCDBA on Microsoft SQL Server™ 2000

  The Microsoft Certified Database Administrator (MCDBA) credential is the premier certification for professionals who implement and administer SQL Server databases. The certification is appropriate for individuals who derive physical database designs, develop logical data models, create physical databases, use Transact-SQL to create data services, manage and maintain databases, configure and manage security, monitor and optimize databases, and install and configure SQL Server.

- MCP

  The Microsoft Certified Professional (MCP) credential is for individuals who have the skills to successfully implement a Microsoft product or technology as part of a business solution in an organization. Hands-on experience with the product is necessary to successfully achieve certification.

- MCT

  Microsoft Certified Trainers (MCTs) demonstrate the instructional and technical skills that qualify them to deliver Official Microsoft Learning Products through a Microsoft Certified Partner for Learning Solutions.

Certification requirements

Requirements differ for each certification category and are specific to the products and job functions addressed by the certification. To become a Microsoft Certified Professional, you must pass rigorous certification exams that provide a valid and reliable measure of technical proficiency and expertise.

For More Information See the Microsoft Learning Web site at http://www.microsoft.com/learning/.

You can also send e-mail to mcphelp@microsoft.com if you have specific certification questions.

Acquiring the skills tested by an MCP exam

Official Microsoft Learning Products can help you develop the skills that you need to do your job. They also complement the experience that you gain while working with Microsoft products and technologies. However, no one-to-one correlation exists between Official Microsoft Learning Products and MCP exams. Microsoft does not expect or intend for the courses to be the sole preparation method for passing MCP exams. Practical product knowledge and experience is also necessary to pass MCP exams.

To help prepare for MCP exams, use the preparation guides are available for each exam. Each Exam Preparation Guide contains exam-specific information such as a list of topics on which you will be tested. These guides are available on the Microsoft Learning Web site at http://www.microsoft.com/learning/.

Multimedia: Job Roles in Today's Information Systems Environment

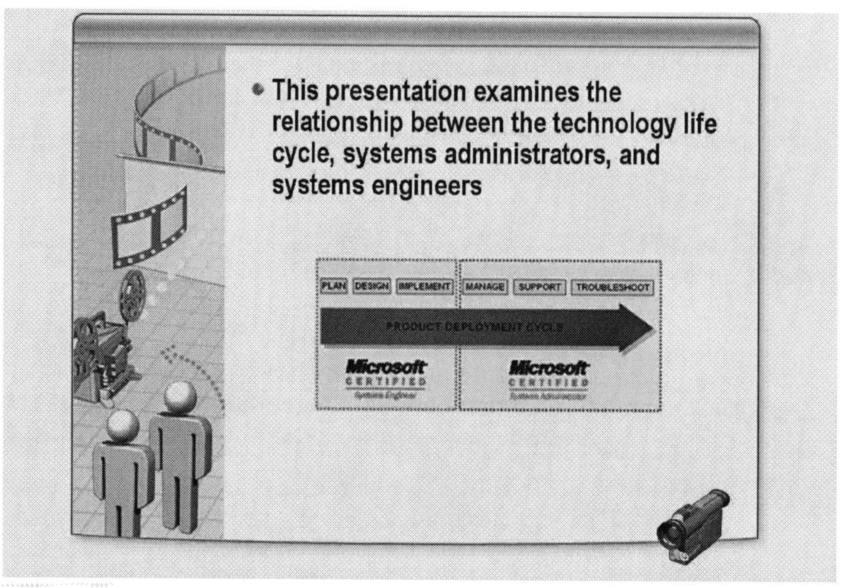

File location

To view the *Job Roles in Today's Information Systems Environment* presentation, open the Web page on the Student Materials compact disc, click **Multimedia**, and then click the title of the presentation. Do not open this presentation unless your instructor tells you to do so.

Facilities

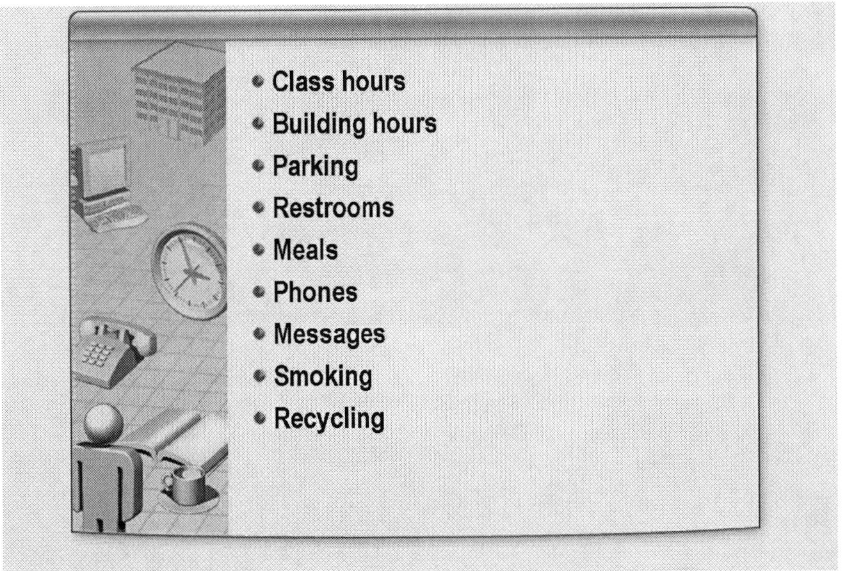
Class hours
Building hours
Parking
Restrooms
Meals
Phones
Messages
Smoking
Recycling

THIS PAGE INTENTIONALLY LEFT BLANK

Module 1: Introduction to Administering Accounts and Resources

Contents

Overview

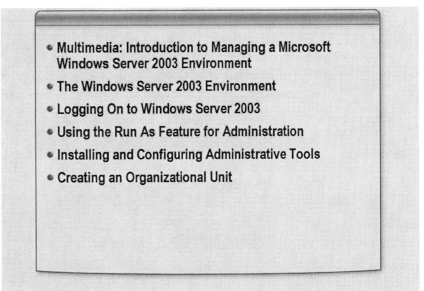

- Multimedia: Introduction to Managing a Microsoft Windows Server 2003 Environment
- The Windows Server 2003 Environment
- Logging On to Windows Server 2003
- Using the Run As Feature for Administration
- Installing and Configuring Administrative Tools
- Creating an Organizational Unit

Introduction

In this module, you will learn the skills that you need to administer accounts and resources on computers running Microsoft® Windows Server™ 2003 software in a networked environment. These lessons provide information and procedures that you will use throughout the course.

Objectives

After completing this module, you will be able to:

- Describe the Windows Server 2003 environment.
- Log on to a computer running Windows Server 2003.
- Use the **Run as** feature to perform administrative tasks.
- Install and configure the administrative tools.
- Create an organizational unit.

Multimedia: Introduction to Managing a Microsoft Windows Server 2003 Environment

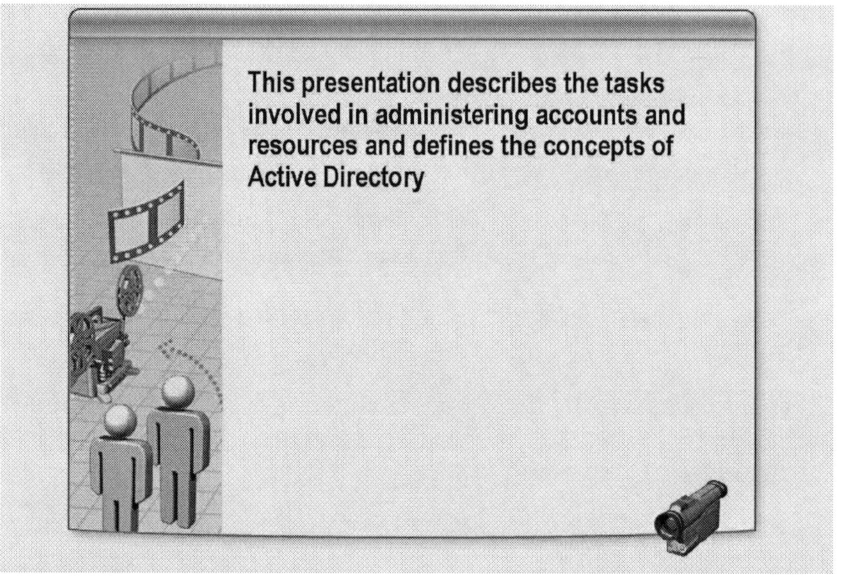

This presentation describes the tasks involved in administering accounts and resources and defines the concepts of Active Directory

Introduction

In this presentation, you are introduced to the tasks involved in administering accounts and resources in a Windows Server 2003 environment. The tasks and concepts in this presentation are explained in more detail throughout the course.

File location

To view the *Introduction to Managing a Microsoft Windows Server 2003 Environment* presentation, open the Web page on the Student Materials compact disc, click **Multimedia**, and then click the title of the presentation. Do not open this presentation unless the instructor tells you to.

Objective

After completing this lesson, you will be able to describe some common tasks for administering accounts and resources.

Lesson: The Windows Server 2003 Environment

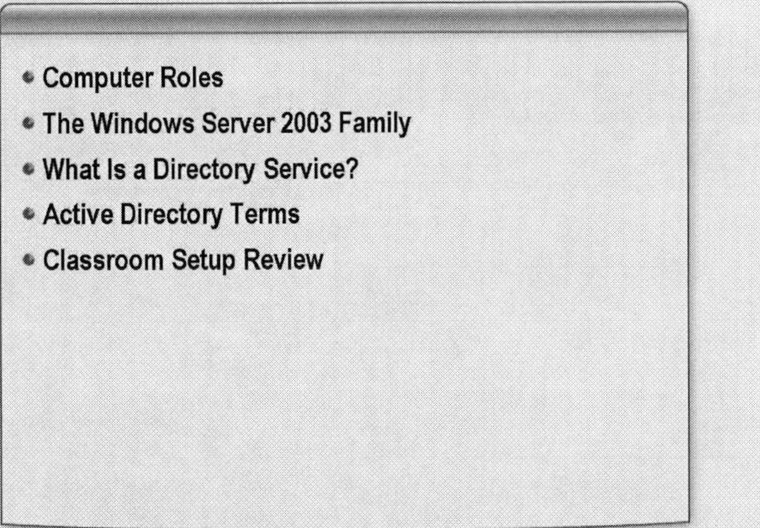

Computer Roles
The Windows Server 2003 Family
What Is a Directory Service?
Active Directory Terms
Classroom Setup Review

Introduction

To manage a Windows Server 2003 environment, you must understand which operating system edition is appropriate for different computer roles. You must also understand the purpose of a directory service and how Active Directory® directory service provides a structure for the Windows Server 2003 environment.

Lesson objectives

After completing this lesson, you will be able to:

- Describe the different computer roles in a Windows Server 2003 environment.
- Describe the uses of the different editions of Windows Server 2003.
- Explain the purpose of a directory service.
- Differentiate between the components of an Active Directory structure.

Computer Roles

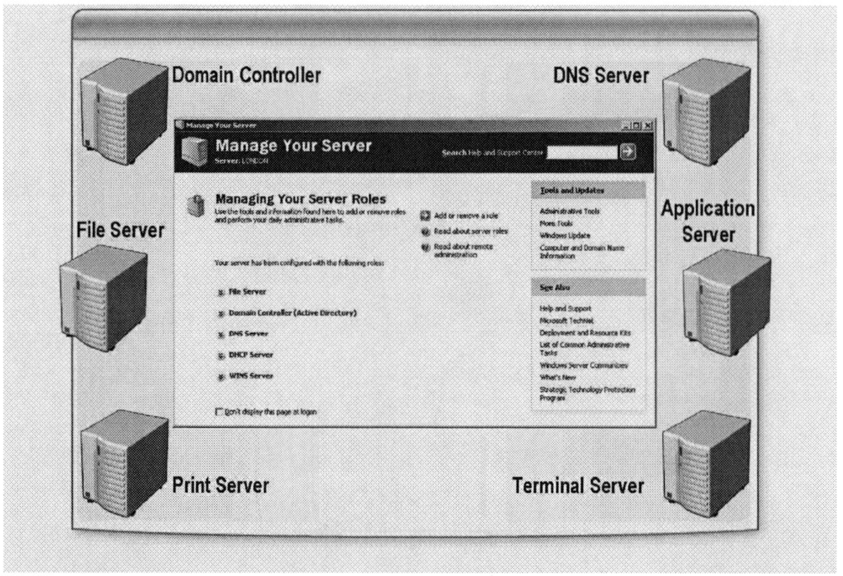

Introduction

Servers play many roles in the client/server networking environment. Some servers are configured to provide authentication, and others are configured to run applications. Some provide network services that enable users to communicate with other servers and resources in the network. As a systems administrator, you are expected to know the primary types of servers and what functions they perform in your network.

Domain controller (Active Directory)

Domain controllers store directory data and manage communication between users and domains, including user logon processes, authentication, and directory searches. When you install Active Directory on a computer running Windows Server 2003, the computer becomes a domain controller.

Note In a Windows Server 2003 network, all servers in the domain that are not domain controllers are called *member servers*. Servers not associated with a domain are called *workgroup servers*.

File server

A file server provides a central location on your network where you can store and share files with users across your network. When users require an important file such as a project plan, they can access the file on the file server instead of passing the file between their separate computers.

Print server

A print server provides a central location on your network where users can print documents. The print server provides clients with updated printer drivers and handles all print queuing and security.

DNS server

Domain Name System (DNS) is an Internet and TCP/IP standard name service. The DNS service enables client computers on your network to register and resolve DNS domain names. A computer configured to provide DNS services on a network is a DNS server. You must have a DNS server on your network to implement Active Directory.

Application server

An application server provides key infrastructure and services to applications hosted on a system. Typical application servers include the following services:

- Resource pooling (for example, database connection pooling and object pooling)
- Distributed transaction management
- Asynchronous program communication, typically through message queuing
- A just-in-time object activation model
- Automatic Extensible Markup Language (XML) Web Service interfaces to access business objects
- Failover and application health detection services
- Integrated security

Microsoft Internet Information Services (IIS) provides the tools and features necessary to easily manage a secure Web server. If you plan to host Web and File Transfer Protocol (FTP) sites with IIS, configure the server as an application server.

Terminal server

A terminal server provides access to Microsoft Windows®–based programs to remote computers running Windows Server 2003, Standard Edition; Windows Server 2003, Enterprise Edition; or Windows Server 2003, Datacenter Edition. With a terminal server, you install an application at a single point on a single server. Multiple users can then access the application without installing it on their computers. Users can run programs, save files, and use network resources all from a remote location, as if these resources were installed on their own computer.

The Manage Your Server tool

When Windows Server 2003 is installed and a user logs on for the first time, the Manage Your Server tool starts automatically. You use this tool to add or remove server roles. When you add a server role to the computer, the Manage Your Server tool adds this server role to the list of available, configured server roles. After the server role is added to the list, you can use various wizards that help you to manage the specific server role. The Manage Your Server tool also provides Help files specific to the server role that provide checklists and troubleshooting recommendations.

The Windows Server 2003 Family

Windows Server 2003 Edition	Usage Scenario	Sample Roles: Web server	File and infrastructure server	Domain controller	Scalable, business-critical applications
Web	Application server	✓			
Small Business Server	Small business with one server	✓	✓	✓	
Standard	Small business or department	✓	✓	✓	
Enterprise	Medium or large organizations	✓	✓	✓	✓
Datacenter	Large organizations	✓	✓	✓	✓

Microsoft Windows Server System

Introduction

Windows Server 2003 is available in five editions. Each edition is developed to be used in a specific server role. This enables you to select the operating system edition that provides only the functions and capabilities that your server needs.

Web Edition

Windows Server 2003, Web Edition, is designed to be used specifically as a Web server. It is available only through selected partner channels and is not available for retail. Although computers running Windows Server 2003, Web Edition, can be members of an Active Directory domain, you cannot run Active Directory on Windows Server 2003, Web Edition.

Small Business Server Edition

Windows Server 2003, Small Business Server Edition, delivers a complete business server solution for small businesses with up to 75 workstations and is available in two editions: Standard and Premium. Windows Small Business Server 2003 provides technologies and tools, including e-mail, shared documents and calendars, security-enhanced Internet access and data storage, reliable printing and faxing, and remote administration on a single server.

Standard Edition

Windows Server 2003, Standard Edition, is a reliable network operating system that delivers business solutions quickly and easily. This flexible server is the ideal choice for small businesses and departmental use. Use Windows Server 2003, Standard Edition, when your server does not require the increased hardware support and clustering features of Windows Server 2003, Enterprise Edition.

Enterprise Edition

Windows Server 2003, Enterprise Edition, has all the features in Windows Server 2003, Standard Edition. It also provides features not included in Standard Edition that enhance availability, scalability, and dependability.

Windows Server 2003, Enterprise Edition, is designed for medium to large businesses. It is the recommended operating system for applications, XML Web services, and infrastructure, because it offers high reliability, performance, and superior business value.

The major difference between Windows Server 2003, Enterprise Edition, and Windows Server 2003, Standard Edition, is that Enterprise Edition supports high-performance servers. Windows Server 2003, Enterprise Edition, is recommended for servers running applications for networking, messaging, inventory and customer service systems, databases, and e-commerce Web sites. Also, you can cluster servers running Enterprise Edition to handle larger loads.

Datacenter Edition

Windows Server 2003, Datacenter Edition, is designed for business-critical and mission-critical applications that demand the highest levels of scalability and availability.

The major difference between Windows Server 2003, Datacenter Edition, and Windows Server 2003, Enterprise Edition, is that Datacenter Edition supports more powerful multiprocessing and greater memory. In addition, Windows Server 2003, Datacenter Edition, is available only through the Windows Datacenter Program offered to Original Equipment Manufacturers (OEMs).

Additional reading

For detailed information about each edition's capabilities, see the Windows Server 2003 Product Overviews page on the Microsoft Web site.

What Is a Directory Service?

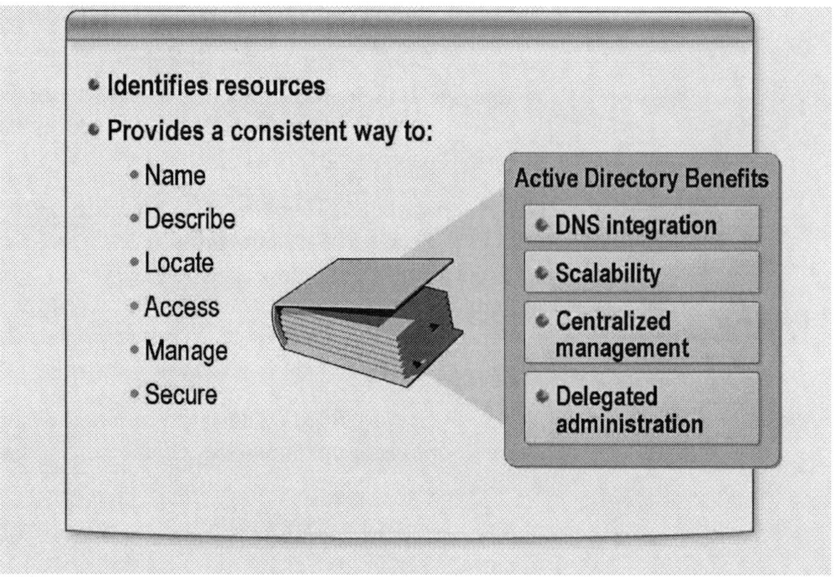

Introduction

As a user logged on to a network, you might need to connect to a shared folder or send a print job to a printer on the network. How do you find that folder and printer and other network resources?

Definition

A directory service is a network service that identifies all resources on a network and makes that information available to users and applications. Directory services are important, because they provide a consistent way to name, describe, locate, access, manage, and secure information about these resources.

When a user searches for a shared folder on the network, it is the directory service that identifies the resource and provides that information to the user.

Active Directory

Active Directory is the directory service in the Windows Server 2003 family. It extends the basic functionality of a directory service to provide the following benefits:

- Domain Name System integration

  Active Directory uses DNS naming conventions to create a hierarchical structure that provides a familiar, orderly, and scalable view of network relationships. DNS also functions to map host names, such as www.microsoft.com, to numeric TCP/IP addresses, such as 192.168.19.2.

- Scalability

  Active Directory is organized into sections that can store a large number of objects. As a result, Active Directory can expand as an organization grows. An organization that has a single server with a few hundred objects can grow to thousands of servers and millions of objects.

- Centralized management

  Active Directory enables administrators to manage distributed desktops, network services, and applications from a central location, while using a consistent management interface. Active Directory also provides centralized control of access to network resources by enabling users to log on only once to gain full access to resources throughout Active Directory.

- Delegated administration

  The hierarchical structure of Active Directory enables administrative control to be delegated for specific segments of the hierarchy. A user authorized by a higher administrative authority can perform administrative duties in their designated portion of the structure. For example, users might have limited administrative control over their workstation's settings, and a department manager might have the administrative rights to create new users in an organizational unit.

Additional reading

For more information about Active Directory, see *White Paper: Technical Overview of Windows Server 2003 Active Directory* at the Microsoft Web site.

LDAP - LOCATE/NAME OBJECTS

Active Directory Terms

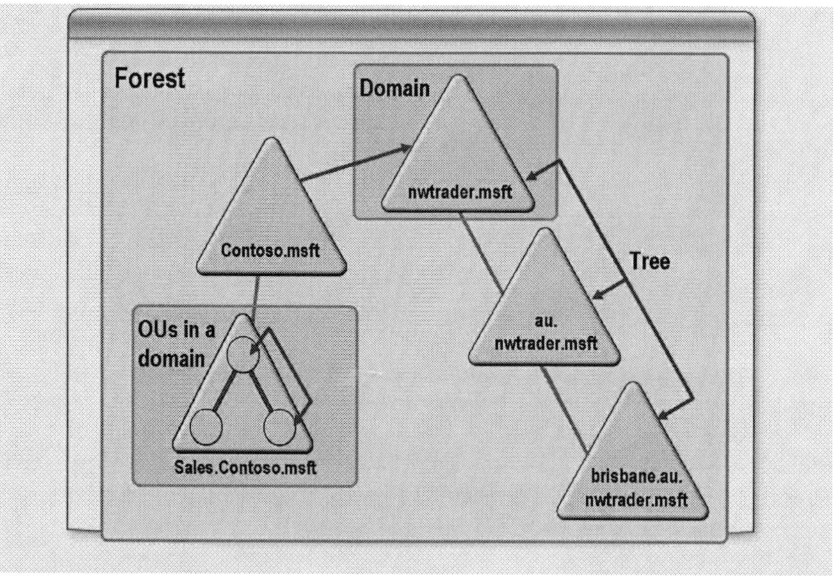

Introduction

The logical structure of Active Directory is flexible and provides a method for designing a hierarchy within Active Directory that is comprehensible to both users and administrators.

Logical components

The logical components of the Active Directory structure include the following:

- *Domain.* The core unit of the logical structure in Active Directory is the domain. A domain is a collection of security principals such as user and computer accounts and other objects like printers and shared folders. The domain objects are defined by an administrator and share a common directory database and a unique name.
- *Organizational unit.* An organizational unit is a type of container object that you use to organize objects within a domain. An organizational unit might contain objects such as user accounts, groups, computers, printers, and other organizational units.
- *Forest.* A forest is one or more domains that share a common configuration, schema, and global catalog.
- *Tree.* A tree consists of domains in a forest that share a contiguous DNS namespace and have a two-way transitive trust relationship between parent and child domains.

Classroom Setup Review

- The virtual environment is configured as one Windows Server 2003 domain: Contoso.msft
- Den-DC1 is the domain controller
- Den-SRV1 is a member server and is used as a remote computer for student labs
- Den-CL1 is a workstation running Windows XP Professional, Service Pack 2
- Server computers are running Windows Server 2003, Enterprise Edition, Service Pack 1

Introduction

Now that you have been introduced to the basic components of an Active Directory structure, you have a better understanding of the setup of the classroom.

Classroom setup

Each student machine has Microsoft Windows XP Professional installed and is running Microsoft Virtual PC 2004.

The name of the domain is contoso.msft. The domain is named after Contoso, Ltd., a fictitious company that has offices worldwide.

The domain controller is named DEN-DC1, and there is a member server, named DEN-SRV1. Both computers are running Windows Server 2003 Enterprise Edition with Service Pack 1. The workstation computer is named DEN-CL1 and is running Windows XP Professional with Service Pack 2.

The domain has been populated with users, groups, and computer accounts for each administrator to manage.

DOMAIN: USERS PC'S OU'S AND OTHER OBJECTS THAT SHARE A COMMON AD DATABASE. SECURITY BOUNDARY: PASSWORDS
ACCT LOCKOUT

DOMAIN TREE - ONE OR MORE DOMAINS SETUP IN A PARENT-CHILD RELATIONSHIP W/ TRANSITIVE TRUST RELATIONSHIP BETWEEN PARENT AND CHILD. COMMON NAME SUFFIX

OU'S SUBDIVISION OF A DOMAIN FOR 3 REASONS: STRUCTURE A DOMAIN
DELEGATE ADMIN CTRL
TARGET GP.

Lesson: Logging On to Windows Server 2003

- Multimedia: Logon and Authentication
- Logon Dialog Box Options
- What Are User Principal Names?
- Practice: Logging On to Windows Server 2003

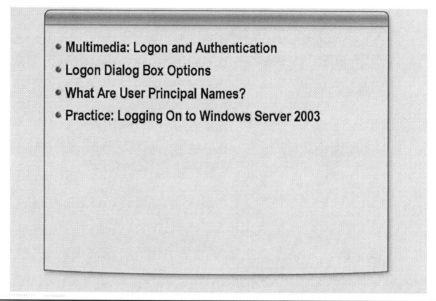

Introduction

Windows Server 2003 authenticates a user during the logon process to verify the identity of the user. This mandatory process ensures that only valid users can access resources and data on a computer or the network.

Lesson objectives

After completing this lesson, you will be able to:

- Explain the difference between a local and a domain logon.
- Identify logon dialog box options.
- Describe the function of the user principal name.
- Log on to a local computer and a domain.

Multimedia: Logon and Authentication

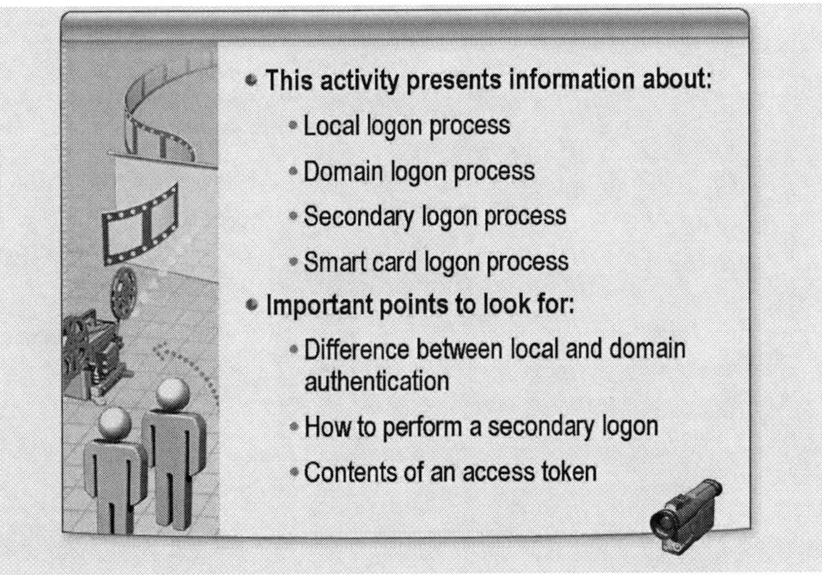

File location

To start the *Logon and Authentication* activity, open the Web page on the Student Materials compact disc, click **Multimedia**, and then click the title of the activity.

Logon Dialog Box Options

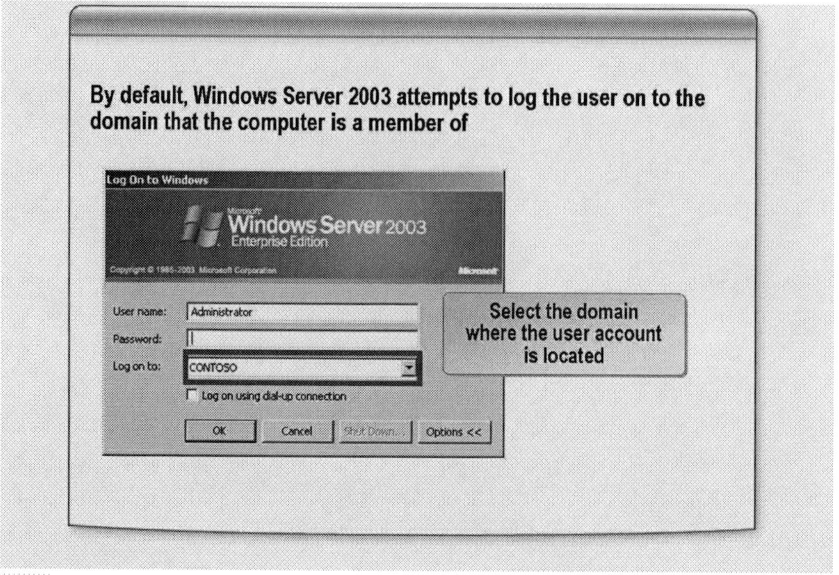

Introduction

The Windows Server 2003 logon dialog box provides an **Options** button for users that are logging on. Clicking the **Options** button displays the **Log on to** dialog box. The **Log on to** list includes the names of all trusted domains and the local machine. The user then has the option of logging on to the local machine by using a local user account or logging on to the domain where that user's account is located. By default, Windows Server 2003 does not show the **Log on to** dialog box at the initial logon but will remember the status of the **Log on to** dialog box from the last logon for subsequent logons.

The logon dialog box

The following table describes all the options in the logon dialog box.

Option	Description
User name	A unique user logon name that is assigned by an administrator. To log on to a domain, this user account must reside in the directory database in Active Directory.
Password	The password that is assigned to the user account. Users must enter a password to prove their identity. Passwords are case sensitive. The password appears on the screen as dots (●) to protect it from onlookers. To prevent unauthorized access to resources and data, users must keep passwords secret.

(*continued*)

Option	Description
Log on to	Specifies whether a user logs on to a domain or logs on locally. The user can choose one of the following: • **Domain name**: The user must select the domain that that user's account is in. This list contains all of the domains available in the forest and through trust relationships. • **Computer name**: The name of the computer that the user is logging on to. The user must have a local user account on the computer. The option to log on locally is not available on a domain controller.
Log on using dial-up connection	Permits a user to connect to a server in the domain by using a dial-up network connection. Dial-up networking enables a user to log on and perform work from a remote location.
Shut Down	Closes all files, saves all operating system data, and prepares the computer so that a user can safely turn it off. On a computer running Windows Server 2003, the **Shut Down** button is disabled. This prevents an unauthorized user from using this dialog box to shut down the server. To shut down a server, a user must be able to log on to it.
Options	Switches between the two versions of the **Enter Password** dialog box. One of these two dialog boxes provides the **Log on to** option, which enables the user to select a domain or the local computer.

What Are User Principal Names?

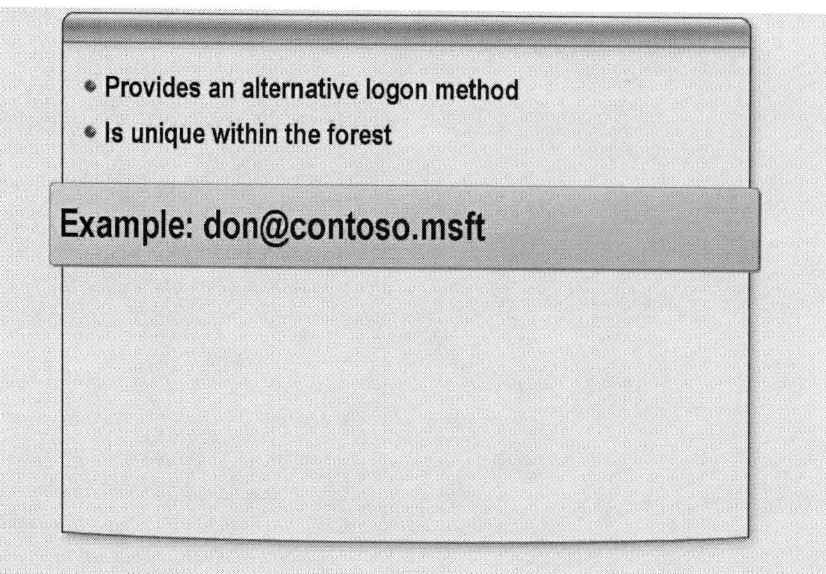

Provides an alternative logon method
Is unique within the forest
Example: don@contoso.msft

Introduction

Users can log on to a Windows 2003 domain using two different logon names. For example, you can use your user logon name—for example, **don**—or your User Principal Name (UPN)—for example, Don@Contoso.msft.

Alternative logon

The UPN consists of a logon name and the UPN suffix that must be appended to the name (the text following the @ symbol).

By default, the user has a UPN suffix of @domain_name. When an account is created, it can be assigned a UPN suffix other than the domain name to simplify logon. For example, the user Joe in the Northwest.America.Contoso.msft domain might prefer to use a UPN of **Joe@contoso.msft.**

Why use User Principal Names?

In a multiple-domain environment, users must supply the domain name to log on—for example, **Contoso\Don**. A UPN already includes the domain name, making logon easier. In many cases, the UPN will be the same as the user's e-mail address so that users do not have to remember one name to log on to the network and a different name for e-mail.

Unique within the forest

The UPN must be unique within the forest. A global catalog resolves the UPN if the authentication domain controller does not have knowledge of the account. This happens when a mobile user is logging on to a computer in an office that uses a different domain in the same forest. For the logon to be successful, a global catalog server must be available for the UPN logon to succeed.

Practice: Logging On to Windows Server 2003

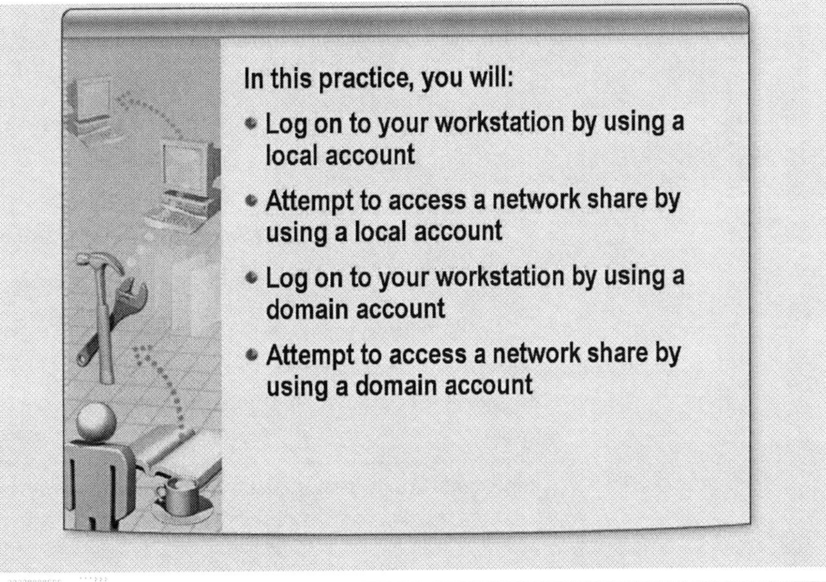

Objective

In this practice you will:

- Log on to your workstation by using a local account.
- Attempt to access a network share by using a local account.
- Log on to your workstation by using a domain account.
- Attempt to access a network share by using a domain account.

Instructions

Ensure that the DEN-DC1 and DEN-CL1 virtual machines are running.

Practice

► **Log on to your workstation by using a local account**

1. Make sure that the DEN-CL1 virtual machine is the active window. Press RIGHT ALT+DEL.
2. In the **Log on to Windows** dialog box, in the **User name** text box, type **Paul.**
3. In the **Password** box, type **Pa$$w0rd** (the 0 is a zero).
4. In the **Log on to** box, select **DEN-CL1 (this computer)**, and then click **OK.**

► **Attempt to access a network share** by **using a local account**

1. Click **Start** and then click **Run.**
2. In the **Run** dialog box, type **\\den-dc1\sales_data** and then click **OK.** You should see a logon dialog box asking you to provide credentials to access the domain resource.
3. Provide the credentials of Don Hall, a valid domain user, in the form **contoso\don.** In the **Password** box, type **Pa$$w0rd.** You should see the contents of the shared folder displayed.
4. Close all windows and log off the local computer.

▶ Log on to your workstation by using a domain account

1. Press RIGHT ALT+DEL.
2. In the **Log On to Windows** dialog box, in the **User name** box, type **don**.
3. In the **Password** box, type **Pa$$w0rd**.
4. In the **Log on to** box, verify that the **CONTOSO** domain name is displayed, and then click **OK**.

▶ Attempt to access a network share by using a domain account

1. Click **Start** and then click **Run**.
2. In the **Run** dialog box, type **den-dc1\sales_data** to attempt to connect. You should see the contents of the shared folder displayed.
3. Close all windows and log off the domain.

Important Do not shut down the virtual machines.

Lesson: Using the Run As Feature for Administration

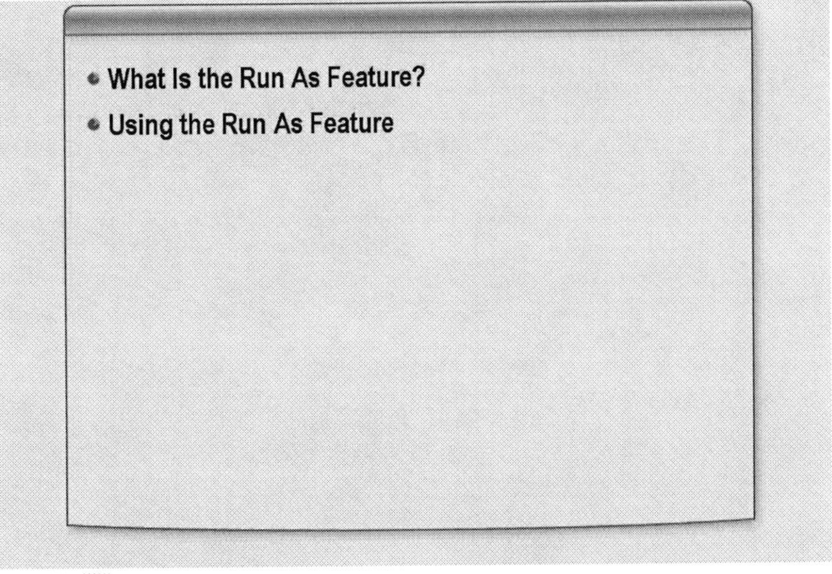
What Is the Run As Feature?
Using the Run As Feature

Introduction

In an Active Directory environment, users should not be logged on to workstations with administrative credentials. Instead, users should be logged on with a nonadministrative account and perform administrative tasks using the **Run as** feature. In this lesson, you will learn the function and use of the **Run as** feature.

Lesson objectives

After completing this lesson, you will be able to:

- Describe the function of the **Run as** feature.
- Use the **Run as** feature for administrative tasks.

What Is the Run As Feature?

- Allows a user to run specific tools and programs at any workstation with different permissions than the user's current logon provides
- Can be used in troubleshooting scenarios to perform administrative tasks at the client's workstation without logging off the current user

Introduction

It is a security best practice for administrators to perform routine, nonadministrative tasks using an account with only those permissions that are required to accomplish those tasks. In this way, administrators can reserve the use of accounts with administrative permissions to perform tasks that require administrative privileges. You could accomplish this temporary elevation of privileges by logging off the user account and then logging back on using the administrative account. You can also remain logged on to the user account and then use the **runas** command. This command allows you to exercise privileges associated with an account that is different from the account you are currently logged in as. The **runas** command provides a quick and secure way to run the tools that require the administrative permissions from an account with a reduced set of privileges.

When to use the Run as feature

The use of the **Run as** feature is not restricted to administrator accounts, although that is the most common use. Any user with knowledge of alternative credentials can use the **runas** command to run a program, an MMC console, or a Control Panel item using those credentials. For example, help desk personnel might use the feature to troubleshoot client issues without having to log off the client.

With the **runas** command, you can run programs (.exe), saved MMC consoles (.msc), shortcuts to programs and saved MMC consoles, and Control Panel items. You can run them as an administrator while you are logged on to your computer as a member of another group, such as the Users or Power Users group.

You can use the **runas** command if you provide the appropriate user account and password information and that user account has the ability to log on to the computer, and if the program, MMC console, or Control Panel item is available on the system and to the user account.

Important Not every administrative task can be accomplished by using the **runas** command. For example, property dialog boxes such as network adapter TCP/IP properties or the Printers folder cannot be accessed as a different user.

Using the Run As Feature

- The Run as feature can be invoked from a shortcut menu
- A desktop shortcut can be configured to use the Run as feature
- The Run as feature can be used from the command line

runas /user:domain\domainadmin "mmc %windir%\system32\compmgmt.msc"

Introduction

The **Run as** feature can be employed by using various methods. It can be used from the shortcut menu of an executable or MMC. It can be configured as a parameter of a desktop shortcut, or it can be invoked from the command line.

Using Run as from a shortcut menu

To start a program as an administrator from a shortcut menu:

1. From the program's executable or a **Start** menu item, right-click the program icon, and then click **Run as**.
2. In the **Run as** dialog box, type the administrator account name and password that you want to use.

Configuring a desktop shortcut

To configure a desktop shortcut to always use the **Run as** feature:

1. Create a new shortcut that points to the executable.
2. Open the property sheet for the shortcut, and then click the **Shortcut** tab.
3. Click the **Advanced** tab, and then select the **Run with different credentials** check box.

Using the command line

To use the command line to invoke the **Run as** feature, open a command prompt window and use the following syntax:

runas [{*/profile*|*/noprofile* [*/smartcard*] */user*:UserAccountName program

The following table defines the **runas** command-line parameters.

Parameter	Description
/profile or */noprofile*	Specifies whether or not the user profile should be loaded. The default is **/profile.**
/smartcard	Use if credentials are being supplied by a smartcard.
/user	The name of the user whose credentials will be used by the **runas** command. The user name should be in the form *user@domain* or *domain\user*.
program	The path to the executable program that will be started by the **runas** command.

For a complete list of available options, type **runas /?** at a command prompt. For example, to run the Computer Management console as the domain administrator in the Contoso domain, the command would be:

runas /user: Contoso\administrator "mmc %windir%\system32\compmgmt.msc"

Lesson: Installing and Configuring Administrative Tools

- What Are Administrative Tools?
- What Is MMC?
- Practice: Configuring the Administrative Tools
- Guidelines for Resolving Problems with Installing and Configuring Administrative Tools

Introduction

In this lesson, you will learn how to install and configure administrative tools. This lesson also introduces the different types of user accounts and shows how to create them.

Lesson objectives

After completing this lesson, you will be able to:

- Describe the administrative tools.
- Describe the Microsoft Management Console (MMC).
- Configure the administrative tools.
- Resolve problems with installing and configuring administrative tools.

What Are Administrative Tools?

- Commonly used administrative tools:
  - Active Directory Users and Computers
  - Active Directory Sites and Services
  - Active Directory Domains and Trusts
  - Computer Management
  - DNS
  - Remote Desktops
- Install to perform remote administration

Introduction

Administrative tools enable network administrators to add, search, and change computer and network settings and Active Directory objects. You can install the administrative tools for managing a Windows Server 2003 environment on computers running Microsoft Windows XP Professional and Windows Server 2003 to remotely administer Active Directory and network settings.

Administrative tools

Some of the more commonly used tools include the following:

- Active Directory Users and Computers
- Active Directory Sites and Services
- Active Directory Domains and Trusts
- Computer Management
- DNS
- Remote Desktops

Installing administrative tools

You must install administrative tools on the computer running Windows XP Professional when you want to remotely manage network resources such as Active Directory or network services such as Windows Internet Name Service (WINS) or Dynamic Host Configuration Protocol (DHCP) from a workstation. If you want to install the administrative tools on a computer running Windows XP Professional, Service Pack 1 or a hotfix from Microsoft Knowledge Base article 329357 must be installed.

Tip Administrative tools are not displayed by default on the **Start** menu on a computer running Windows XP Professional. You can customize the **Start Menu** advanced properties to display them.

Windows Server 2003 includes all the administrative tools as snap-ins that can be added to a custom MMC. This includes all the tools for managing Active Directory but does not include management tools for services that are not installed on the server, such as WINS or DHCP. If you must remotely manage a network service from a computer running Windows Server 2003 and the service is not installed on the computer, you must install the administrative tools.

To install the Windows Server 2003 Administration Tools Pack on a computer running Windows XP Professional, you must have administrative permissions on the local computer. If the computer is joined to a domain, members of the Domain Administrator group are able to perform this procedure. You must have access to the adminpak.msi file. This file is available on the Windows Server 2003 compact disc and in the %windir%/systerm32 folder on any computer running Windows Server 2003.

Note As a security best practice, do not install Windows Server 2003 Administration Tools Pack if someone who is not an administrator is going to use the computer running Windows XP Professional.

What Is MMC?

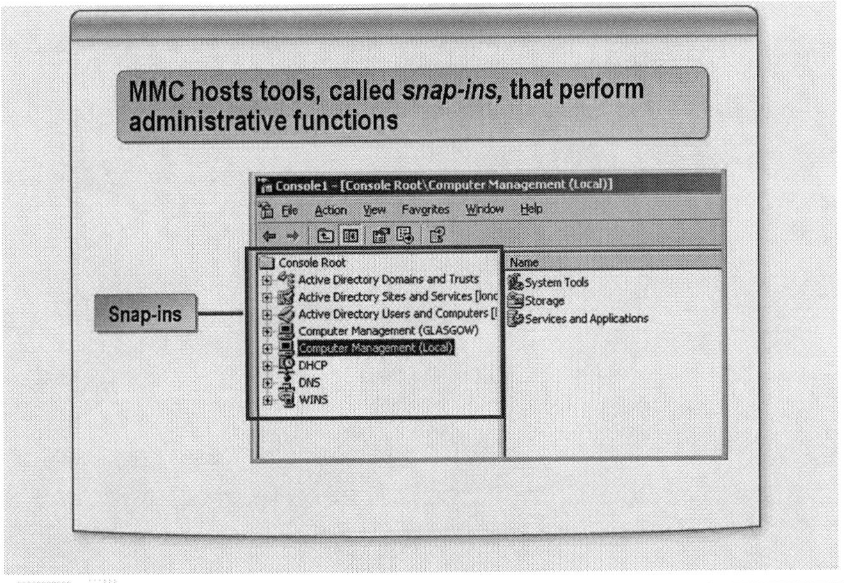

Definition

You use Microsoft Management Console (MMC) to create, save, and open administrative tools, called consoles, which manage the hardware, software, and network components of your Microsoft Windows operating system. MMC runs on all client operating systems that are currently supported.

Creating a custom MMC

You can use MMC to create custom tools and distribute these tools to users. With both Windows XP Professional and Windows Server 2003, you can save these tools so that they are available in the **Administrative Tools** folder. To create a custom MMC, you will use the **runas** command.

What are snap-ins?

A snap-in is a tool that is hosted in MMC. MMC offers a common framework in which various snap-ins can run so that you can manage several services by using a single interface. MMC also enables you to customize the console. By picking and choosing specific snap-ins, you can create management consoles that include only the administrative tools that you need. For example, you can add tools to manage your local computer and remote computers.

Additional reading

For more information about MMC, see *Step-by-Step Guide to the Microsoft Management Console* at the Microsoft Web site.

Practice: Configuring the Administrative Tools

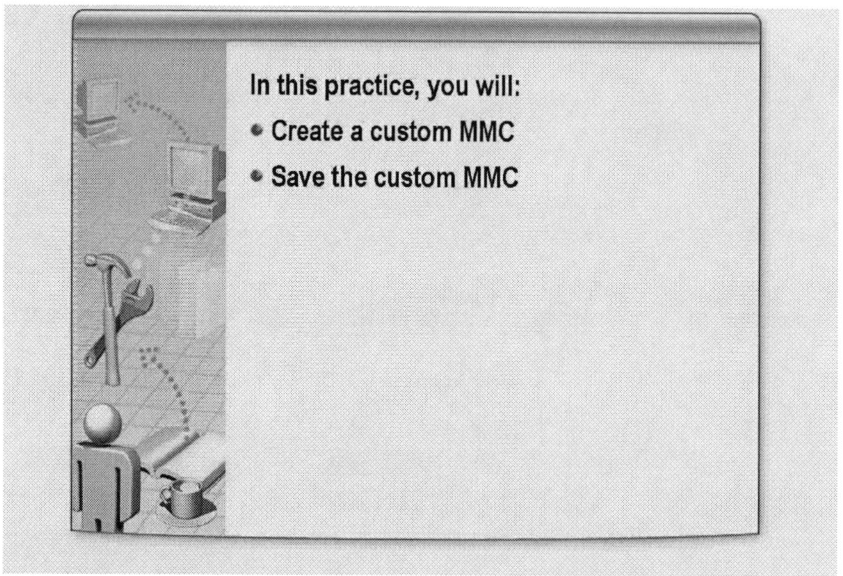

Objective

In this practice, you will:

- Create a custom MMC.
- Save the custom MMC.

Note This practice focuses on the concepts in this lesson and as a result might not comply with Microsoft security recommendations. For example, this practice does not comply with the recommendation that users log on with a nonadministrative account and use the **runas** command when performing administrative tasks.

Instructions

Ensure that the DEN-DC1 and DEN-CL1 virtual machines are running.

Practice

► **Create a custom MMC**

1. Log on to DEN-DC1 as the **Administrator** with the password **Pa$$w0rd.**
2. Click **Start**, click **Run.**
3. In the **Run** dialog box, type **MMC** and then click **OK.**
4. In the Console1 window, click the **File** menu, and then click **Add/Remove Snap-in.**
5. In the **Add/Remove Snap-in** dialog box, click **Add.**
6. In the **Add Standalone Snap-in** dialog box, double-click the items to add as follows.
   a. Add the **Computer Management** snap-in. Ensure that **Local computer** radio button is selected.
   b. Add the **Computer Management** snap-in again and select the **Another computer** radio button, and type **DEN-CL1.**
   c. Add the **Active Directory Users and Computers** snap-in.

7. In the **Add Standalone Snap-in** dialog box, click **Close**.
8. Click **OK**.

► **Save the custom MMC**

1. Click the **File** menu and then click **Save As**.
2. Save the MMC on the desktop as **CustomMMC.msc**.
3. Close all open windows.

Important Do not shut down the virtual machines.

Guidelines for Resolving Problems with Installing and Configuring Administrative Tools

Symptom	Cause	Resolution
Cannot install the administrative tools	Insufficient permissions	You must have administrative permissions on the local computer
	Incorrect operating system	You can install the Windows Server 2003 Administration Tools Pack only on supported operating systems
Broken links in Help files	Both server and client Help systems are required	You can install the Help files for Windows Server 2003 Administration Tools Pack

Introduction

Two common problems that you might encounter when installing and configuring administrative tools are that you cannot install the administrative tools properly and that the Help files contain broken links.

Cannot install

If you have problems installing or configuring administrative tools in Windows Server 2003, verify that you have administrative permissions on the local computer.

Another reason you might not be able to install the administrative tools is that the incorrect operating system is installed. You can install the Windows Server 2003 Administration Tools Pack only on computers running Windows XP Professional or Windows Server 2003.

Broken Help links

When the Windows Server 2003 Administration Tools Pack is installed on a computer running Windows XP Professional, some Help links might appear to be broken. This happens because you must have both server and client Help files for the Windows Server 2003 Administration Tools Pack on Windows XP Professional.

To resolve the problem, you must integrate the server and client Help files for the Windows Server 2003 Administration Tools Pack by installing the server Help files on Windows XP Professional. This is fairly easy to do and should be done after the Windows Server 2003 Administration Tools Pack is installed on Windows XP Professional.

Install Help files

To install Help files from another computer running Windows, or from a CD or disk image:

1. On the **Start** menu, click **Help and Support**.
2. In the **Help and Support Center** window, on the navigation bar, click **Options**.
3. In the left pane, click **Install and share Windows Help**.
4. In the right pane, depending where you want to install Help from, click the link **Install Help content from another Windows computer** or **Install Help content from a CD or disk image**.
5. Type the location of the computer, CD, or disk image, and then click **Find**.

   If you are installing from a CD or disk image, you can click **Browse** to locate the disk containing Help files.
6. When the available Help files appear, click the version of Help that you want, and then click **Install**.

   When the installation is complete, you can switch to the new Help files.

Lesson: Creating an Organizational Unit

- Multimedia: The Organizational Unit Structure
- What Is an Organizational Unit?
- Organizational Unit Hierarchical Models
- Names Associated with Organizational Units
- Practice: Creating an Organizational Unit

Introduction

In this lesson, you will learn how to create an organizational unit.

Lesson objectives

After completing this lesson, you will be able to create an organizational unit, including:

- Describe the organizational unit structure.
- Explain the purpose of an organizational unit.
- Describe organizational unit hierarchical models.
- Identify the names associated with organizational units.
- Create an organizational unit.

Multimedia: The Organizational Unit Structure

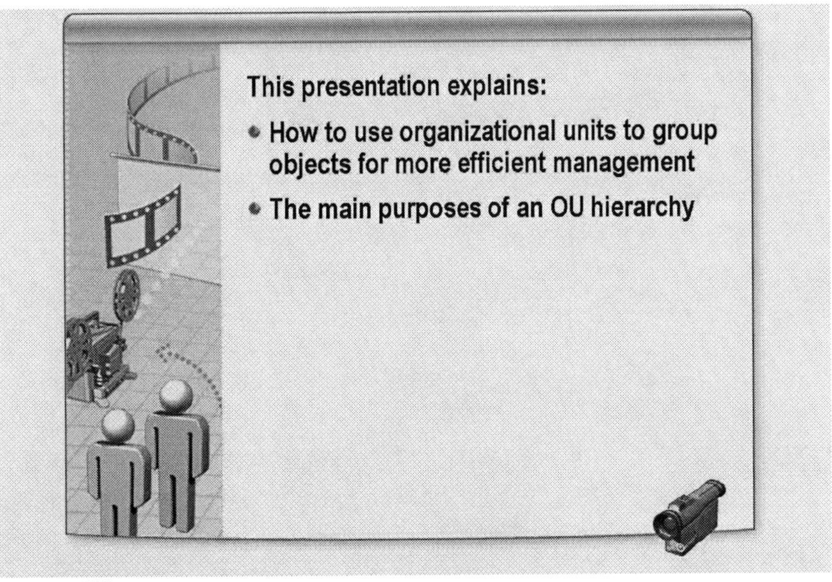

File location

To view this presentation, open the Web page on the Student Materials compact disc, click **Multimedia**, and then click the title of the presentation. Do not open this presentation until the instructor tells you to.

What Is an Organizational Unit?

- Organizes objects in a domain
- Allows you to delegate administrative control
- Simplifies the management of commonly grouped resources

Definition

An organizational unit is a particularly useful type of Active Directory object contained in a domain. You can use organizational units to organize hundreds of thousands of objects in the directory into manageable units. You use an organizational unit to group and organize objects for administrative purposes, such as delegating administrative rights and assigning policies to a collection of objects as a single unit.

Benefits of using organizational units

You can use organizational units to:

- Organize objects in a domain.

  Organizational units contain domain objects, such as user and computer accounts and groups. File and printer shares that are published to Active Directory are also found in organizational units.

- Delegate administrative control.

  You can assign either complete administrative control, such as the Full Control permission, over all objects in the organizational unit, or limited administrative control, such as the ability to modify e-mail information, over user objects in the organizational unit. To delegate administrative control, you assign specific permissions on the organizational unit and the objects that the organizational unit contains for one or more users and groups.

- Simplify the management of commonly grouped resources.

  Using organizational units, you can create containers in a domain that represent the hierarchical or logical structures in your organization. You can then use Group Policy settings to manage the configuration of user and computer settings based on your organizational model.

Organizational Unit Hierarchical Models

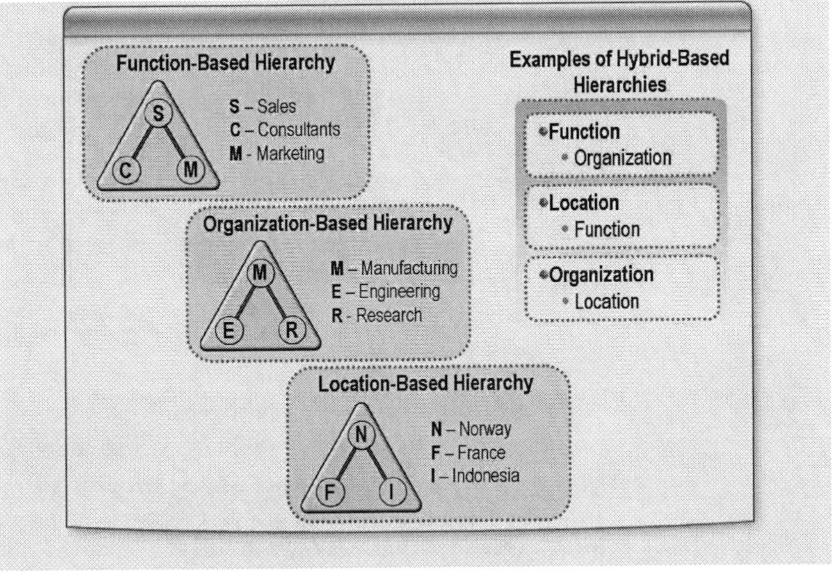

Introduction

As a systems administrator, you do not select the design of the Active Directory structure for your organization. However, it is important to know the characteristics and ramifications of each structure. This knowledge might be critical to you when performing systems administrator tasks within the Active Directory structure. This topic describes the four basic hierarchy designs.

Function-based hierarchy

The function-based hierarchy is based on only the business functions of the organization, without regard to geographical location or departmental or divisional barriers. This approach is chosen only if the IT function is not based on location or organization.

When deciding whether to organize the Active Directory structure by function, consider the following characteristics of function-based designs:

- *Not affected by reorganizations*. A function-based hierarchy is not affected by corporate or organizational reorganizations.
- *Might require additional layers*. When using this structure, you might need to create additional layers in the organizational unit hierarchy to accommodate the administration of users, printers, servers, and network shares.

This structure is appropriate only in small organizations, because functional departments in medium and large organizations are often diverse and cannot be effectively grouped into broad categories.

Organization-based hierarchy

The organization-based hierarchy is based on the departments or divisions in your organization. If the Active Directory structure is organized to reflect the organizational structure, it might be difficult to delegate administrative authority because the objects in Active Directory, such as printers and file shares, might not be grouped in a way that facilitates delegation of administrative authority. Because users rarely see the Active Directory structure, the design should accommodate the administrator instead of the user.

Location-based hierarchy

If the organization is centralized and network management is geographically distributed, you should use a location-based hierarchy. For example, you might decide to create organizational units for New England, Boston, and Hartford in a single domain, such as contoso.msft.

A location-based organizational units or domain hierarchy has the following characteristics:

- *Not affected by reorganizations.* Although divisions and departments might change frequently, location rarely changes in most organizations.
- *Accommodates mergers and expansions.* If an organization merges with or acquires another company, it is simple to integrate the new locations into the existing organizational units and domain hierarchy structure.
- *Might compromise security.* If a location includes multiple divisions or departments, an individual or a group with administrative authority over that domain or over organizational units might also have authority over any child domains or organizational units.

Hybrid-based hierarchy

A hierarchy based on location and then by organization, or any other combination of structure types, is called a hybrid-based hierarchy. The hybrid-based hierarchy combines strengths from several areas to meet the needs of the organization. This type of hierarchy has the following characteristics:

- Accommodates additional growth in geographic, departmental, or divisional areas.
- Creates distinct management boundaries according to department or division.
- Requires cooperation between administrators to ensure the completion of administrative tasks if they are in the same location but in different divisions or departments.

DSADD.EXE

BULK ADDITIONS TO AD

FROM CMD PROMPT

Names Associated with Organizational Units

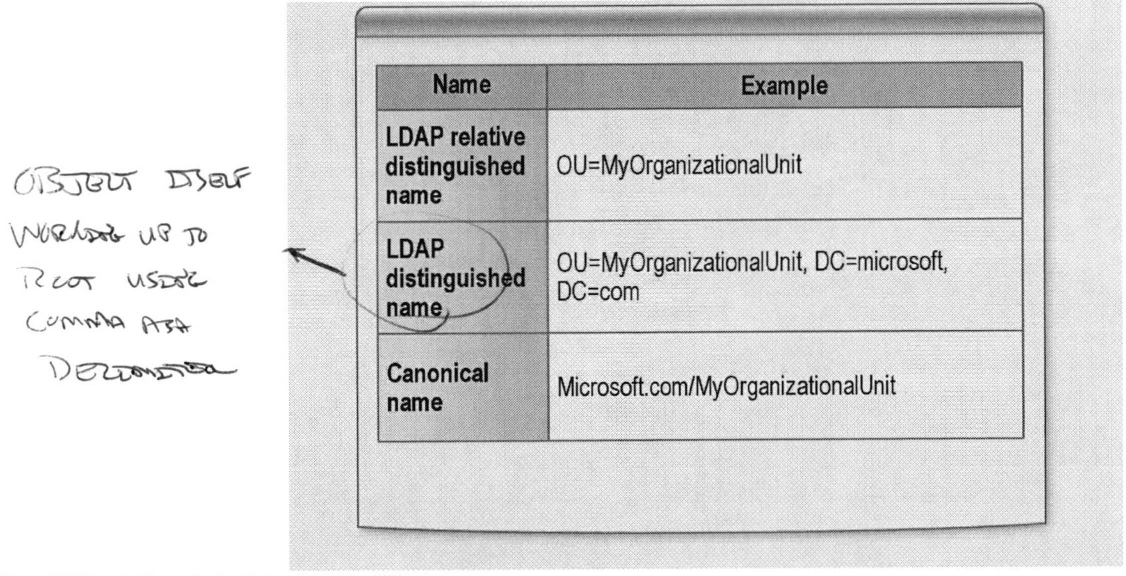

Name	Example
LDAP relative distinguished name	OU=MyOrganizationalUnit
LDAP distinguished name	OU=MyOrganizationalUnit, DC=microsoft, DC=com
Canonical name	Microsoft.com/MyOrganizationalUnit

Introduction

Each object in Active Directory can be referenced by several types of names that describe the location of the object. Active Directory creates a relative distinguished name, a distinguished name, and a canonical name for each object, based on information that is provided when the object is created or modified.

LDAP relative distinguished name

The Lightweight Directory Access Protocol (LDAP) relative distinguished name uniquely identifies the object in its parent container. For example, the LDAP relative distinguished name of an organizational unit named MyOrganizationalUnit is OU=MyOrganizationalUnit. Relative distinguished names must be unique in an organizational unit. It is important to understand the syntax of the LDAP relative distinguished name when using scripts to query and manage Active Directory.

LDAP distinguished name

Unlike the LDAP relative distinguished name, the LDAP distinguished name is globally unique. An example of the LDAP distinguished name of an organizational unit named MyOrganizationalUnit in the microsoft.com domain is OU=MyOrganizationalUnit, DC=microsoft, DC=com. Systems administrators use the LDAP relative distinguished name and the LDAP distinguished name only when writing administrative scripts or during command-line administration.

Canonical name

The canonical name syntax is constructed in the same way as the LDAP distinguished name, but it is represented by a different notation. The canonical name of the organizational unit named myOrganizationalUnit in the microsoft.com domain is Microsoft.com/MyOrganizationalUnit. Administrators use canonical names in some administrative tools. A canonical name is used to represent a hierarchy in the administrative tools.

Practice: Creating an Organizational Unit

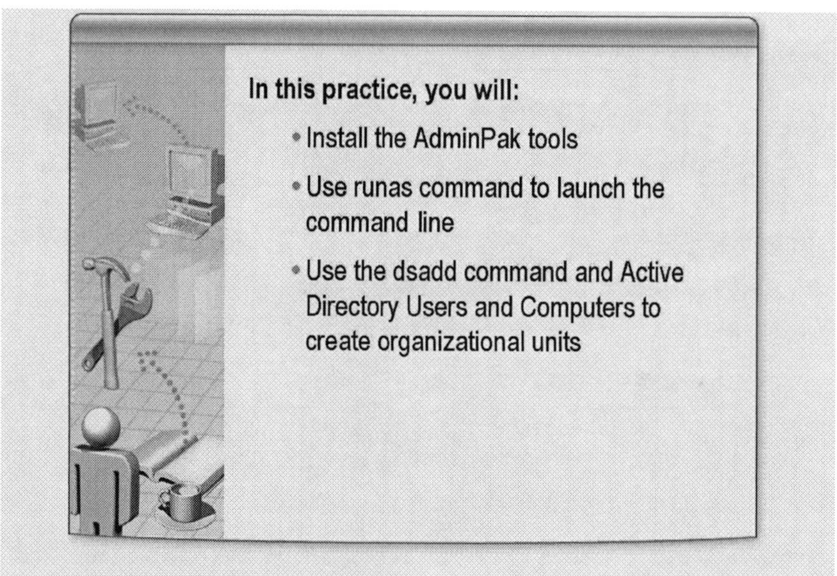

Objective

In this practice you will:

- Install the AdminPak tools.
- Use the **runas** command to launch the command line.
- Use the **dsadd** command and Active Directory Users and Computers to create organizational units.

Instructions

Ensure that the DEN-DC1 and DEN-CL1 virtual machines are running.

Practice: Using a command line

► **Install the AdminPak tools**

1. Log on to the domain from the DEN-CL1 machine as the **Administrator** with the password of **Pa$$w0rd**.
2. Click **Start**, and then click **Run**.
3. In the **Run** box, type **\\DEN-DC1\Admin_Tools**.
4. Double-click **adminpak.msi**, and accept all the default settings.
5. Log off as the **Administrator**.

► **Create an organizational unit by using dsadd**

1. Log on to the domain from the DEN-CL1 machine as **Judy** with a password of **Pa$$w0rd**.
2. Click **Start**, and then click **Run**.
3. In the **Open** box, type **runas /user:contoso*administrator* cmd** and then click **OK**.
4. When prompted for the password, type **Pa$$w0rd** and then press ENTER.

5. At the command prompt, type the following command and then press ENTER:

   dsadd ou "ou=Finance,dc=contoso,dc=msft"

   You should get a **dsadd** succeeded message.

6. Close the command prompt window.
7. Log off of DEN-CL1.

Tip Although double quotation marks are required around the distinguished name only when the name includes spaces, it is a good practice to always use double quotation marks.

Practice: Using Active Directory Users and Computers

► **Create an organizational unit by using Active Directory Users and Computers**

1. If necessary, log on to DEN-DC1 as **Administrator** with a password of **Pa$$w0rd.**
2. Click **Start**, point to **Administrative Tools**, and click **Active Directory Users and Computers.**
3. Right-click **contoso.msft**, point to **New**, and then click **Organizational Unit.**
4. In the **New Object – Organizational Unit** dialog box, type **Test OU** in the **Name** field.
5. Click **OK.**
6. Close **Active Directory Users and Computers.**
7. Log off of DEN-DC1.

Important Do not shut down the virtual machines.

Lab: Creating Organizational Units

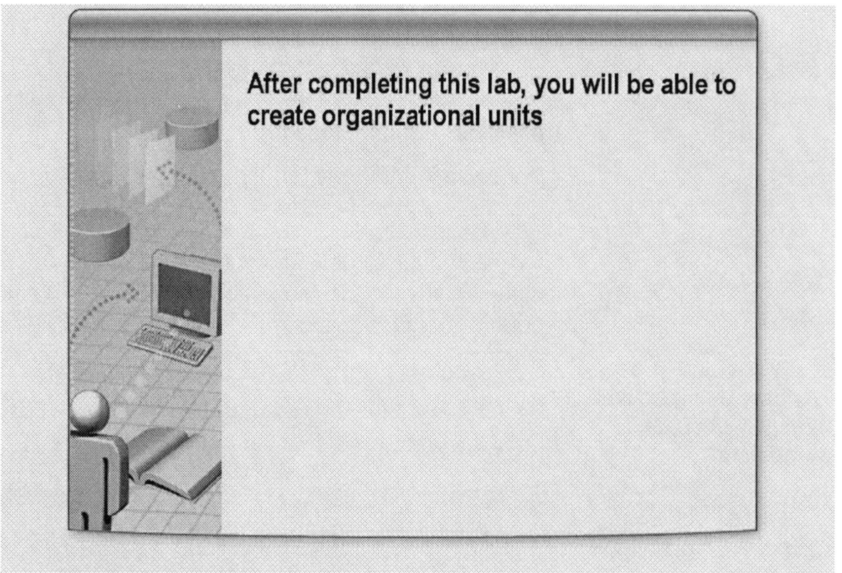
After completing this lab, you will be able to create organizational units

Objective

After completing this lab, you will be able to create organizational units.

Prerequisites

To complete this lab, you must have the following virtual machines:

- DEN-DC1
- DEN-CL1

Lab setup

This section lists the tasks that you must perform before you begin the lab. To complete this lab, you must have reviewed the procedures in the module and successfully completed each practice.

Estimated time to complete this lab: 20 minutes

Exercise 1
Creating Organizational Units from the Workstation

In this exercise, you will log on with a nonadministrative account and create a custom MMC. You will create a desktop shortcut that points to the MMC and uses the **Run as** feature to perform administrative tasks.

Scenario

As a systems administrator for Contoso, Ltd., you have been given the task of creating an organizational unit hierarchy designed by the Contoso Ltd. design team. The organizational unit hierarchy will use a hybrid design that separates business functions by region. You will create the organizational unit hierarchy for the marketing team.

Tasks	Specific Instructions
1. Log on as **Judy Lew**.	▪ On DEN-CL1, log on to the CONTOSO domain as **Judy** with the password of **Pa$$w0rd**.
2. Create a custom MMC with a desktop shortcut that uses the **Run as** feature to launch Active Directory Users and Computers.	**a.** Create a custom MMC. **b.** Add the **Active Directory Users and Computers** snap-in. **c.** Save the custom MMC as **AD_Admin.msc** in the **My Documents** folder. **d.** Create a desktop shortcut that will launch **AD_Admin.msc.** **e.** Right-click the **Shortcut to AD_Admin**, and click **Properties.** On the **Shortcut** tab, click **Advanced**, and then select the check box next to **Run with different credentials.** **f.** Double click **Shortcut to AD_Admin**, to open the AD_Admin console. Provide the domain administrator's credentials: **Contoso\administrator** and a password of **Pa$$w0rd.**
3. Create a Marketing organizational unit and two nested organizational units for the eastern and western regions.	**a.** Create a new organizational unit named **Marketing** at the domain level. **b.** Create an organizational unit named **Western Region** inside the Marketing organizational unit. **c.** Create an organizational unit named **Eastern Region** inside the Marketing organizational units. **d.** Close the **AD_Admin** console. Do not save changes.
4. Complete the lab exercise.	**a.** Close all programs and shut down all computers. Do not save changes. **b.** To prepare for the next module, start the DEN-DC1 and DEN-CL1 virtual computers.

Module 2: Managing User and Computer Accounts

Contents

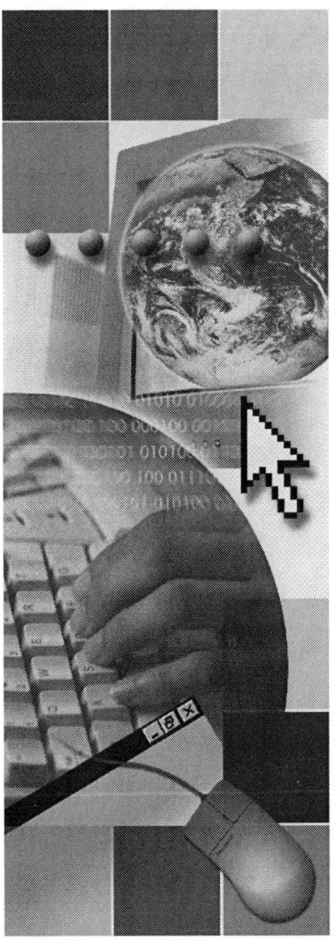

Overview

- Creating User Accounts
- Creating Computer Accounts
- Modifying User and Computer Account Properties
- Creating a User Account Template
- Managing User and Computer Accounts
- Using Queries to Locate User and Computer Accounts in Active Directory

Introduction

One of your functions as a systems administrator is to manage user and computer accounts. These accounts are Active Directory® directory service objects, and you use these accounts to enable individuals to log on to the network and access resources. In this module, you will gain the skills and knowledge that you need to modify user and computer accounts on computers running Microsoft® Windows Server™ 2003 in a networked environment.

Objectives

After completing this module, you will be able to:

- Create user accounts.
- Create computer accounts.
- Modify user and computer account properties.
- Create a user account template.
- Enable and unlock user and computer accounts.
- Manage user and computer accounts.
- Use queries to locate user and computer accounts in Active Directory.

Lesson: Creating User Accounts

- What Is a User Account?
- Names Associated with Domain User Accounts
- Guidelines for Creating a User Account Naming Convention
- User Account Placement in a Hierarchy
- User Account Password Options
- When to Require or Restrict Password Changes
- Tools to Create User Accounts
- Practice: Creating User Accounts
- Best Practices for Creating User Accounts

Introduction

As a systems administrator, you give users access to various network resources. To do this, you will need to know how to create and configure user accounts and how to establish these accounts within your organization's system. With this knowledge, you will ensure that your Windows Server 2003 network identifies and authenticates users before granting them access to the network.

Lesson objectives

After completing this lesson, you will be able to:

- Explain the purpose of user accounts.
- Describe the types of names associated with domain user accounts.
- Explain guidelines for creating a convention for naming user accounts.
- Describe user account placement in an Active Directory hierarchy.
- Describe user account password options.
- Determine when to require password changes on domain user accounts.
- Describe the tools to create user accounts.
- Create local and domain user accounts.
- Apply best practices when creating user accounts.

What Is a User Account?

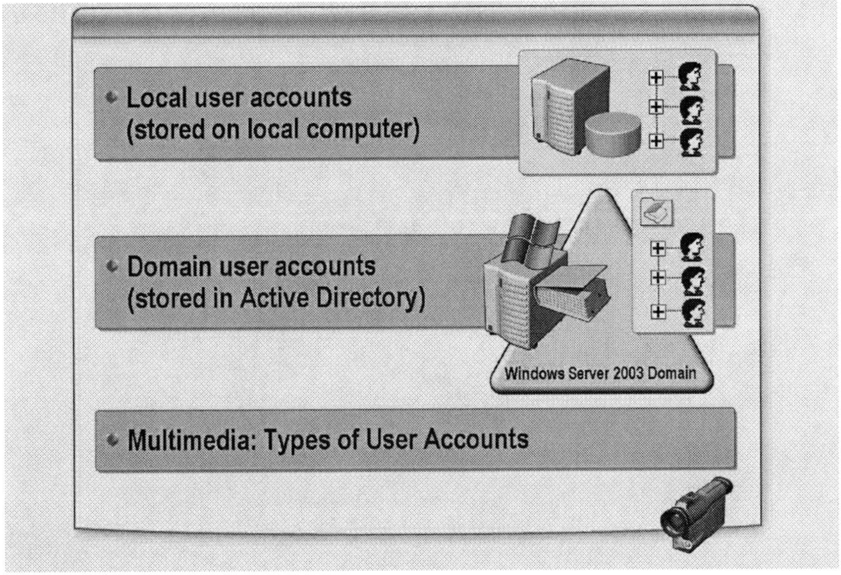

Definition

A user account is an object that consists of all the information that defines a user in Windows Server 2003. The account can be either a local or a domain account. A user account includes the user name and password as well as group memberships.

You can use a user account to:

- Enable someone to log on to a computer based on a user account's identity.
- Enable processes and services to run under a specific security context.
- Manage a user's access to resources such as Active Directory objects and their properties, shared folders, files, directories, and printer queues.

Multimedia: Types of User Accounts

To view the *Types of User Accounts* presentation, open the Web page on the Student Materials compact disc, click **Multimedia**, and then click the title of the presentation.

The *Types of User Accounts* presentation explains how using accounts that grant different levels of access to the network meets the requirements of network users.

Names Associated with Domain User Accounts

Name	Example
User logon name	Tadams
Pre-Windows 2000 logon name	contoso\Tadams
User principal logon name	Tadams@contoso.msft
LDAP distinguished name	CN=terry adams,ou=sales,dc=contoso,dc=msft
LDAP relative distinguished name	CN=terry adams

Introduction

Five types of names are associated with domain user accounts. In Active Directory, each user account consists of a user logon name, a pre–Windows 2000 user logon name (Security Accounts Manager account name), a user principal logon name, a Lightweight Directory Access Protocol (LDAP) distinguished name, and a LDAP relative distinguished name.

User logon name

When creating a user account, an administrator types a user logon name. User logon names must be unique in the forest in which the user account is created. Users use this name only during the logon process. The user enters the user logon name, a password, and the domain name in separate fields on the logon screen.

User logon names can:

- Contain up to 20 uppercase and lowercase characters. (The name can be more than 20 characters, but Windows Server 2003 recognizes only 20.)
- Include a combination of special and alphanumeric characters, except the following: " / \ [ ] : ; | = , + * ? < >
- Have any combination of uppercase and lowercase letters. User logon names are case-retained, but not case-sensitive. For example, the user TAdams can enter any combination of uppercase and lowercase letters when logging on.

Some examples of user logon names are **Terryadams** and **Tadams**.

Pre–Windows 2000 logon name

You can use the pre-Windows 2000 network basic input/output system (NetBIOS) user account to log on to a Microsoft Windows® domain from computers running pre-Windows 2000 operating systems by using a name with the *DomainName\UserName* format. You can also use this name to log on to Windows domains from computers running Microsoft Windows 2000 or Microsoft Windows XP or servers running Windows Server 2003. The pre–Windows 2000 logon name must be unique in the domain. Users can use this logon name with the **runas** command or on a secondary logon screen. This name is limited to 15 characters.

User principal logon name

The user principal name (UPN) consists of the user logon name and the user principal name suffix, joined by the at sign (@). The UPN must be unique in the forest.

The second part of the UPN is the user principal name suffix. The user principal name suffix can be the Domain Name System (DNS) domain name, the DNS name of any domain in the forest, or an alternative name that an administrator creates only for logon purposes. Users can use this name to log on with the **runas** command or on a secondary logon screen.

An example of a UPN is **Tadams@contoso.msft.**

LDAP distinguished name

The LDAP distinguished name uniquely identifies the object in the forest. Users never use this name, but administrators use this name to add users to the network from a script or command line. All objects use the same LDAP naming convention, so all LDAP distinguished names must be unique in the forest.

The following are examples of an LDAP distinguished name:

- **CN= terry adams,ou=sales,dc=contoso,dc=msft**
- **CN=computer1,ou=sales,dc=contoso,dc=msft**

LDAP relative distinguished name

The LDAP relative distinguished name uniquely identifies the object within its parent container. The following are examples of an LDAP relative distinguished name:

- **CN= terry adams**
- **CN=computer1**

How names are assigned

From the information provided when a security principal object is created, Windows Server 2003 generates a security ID (SID) and a globally unique ID (GUID) used to identify the security principal. If the object is created using Active Directory Users and Computers, Active Directory also creates an LDAP relative distinguished name, based on the security principal full name. Therefore, the full name must be unique in the container in which the user account is created. An LDAP distinguished name and a canonical name are derived from the relative distinguished name and the names of the domain and container contexts in which the security principal object is created. If an object is created from a script or command line, the LDAP distinguished name is provided and the relative distinguished name and canonical name are derived from it.

If your organization has several domains, you can use the same user name or computer name in different domains. The SID, GUID, LDAP distinguished name, and canonical name generated by Active Directory will uniquely identify each user, computer, or group in the forest. If the security principal object is moved to a different domain, the SID, LDAP relative distinguished name, LDAP distinguished name, and canonical name will change, but the globally unique ID generated by Active Directory will not change.

Guidelines for Creating a User Account Naming Convention

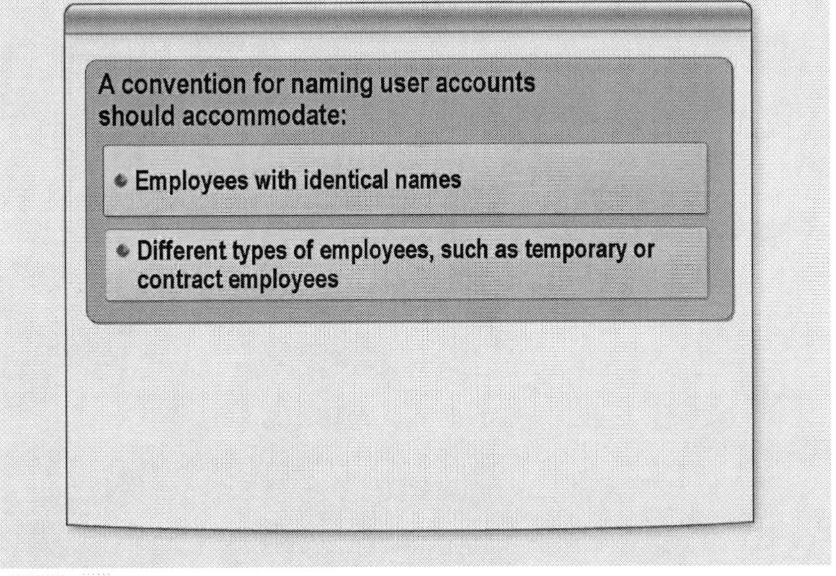

Introduction

A naming convention establishes how user accounts are identified in the domain. A consistent naming convention makes it easier for you to remember user logon names and locate them in lists. It is a good practice to adhere to the naming convention already in use in an existing network that supports a large number of users.

Guidelines

Consider the following guidelines for creating a naming convention:

- Maintain a consistent corporate standard for user names. Accounts adhering to a standard are easier to understand, search for, and create. For example, if your company uses *firstname.lastname* (judy.lew) as the standard, an account created using *firstinitiallastname* (jlew) is confusing.
- If you have a large number of users, your naming convention for user logon names should accommodate employees with identical names. A method to accomplish this is to use the first name and the last initial, and then add additional letters from the last name to accommodate duplicate names. For example, for two users named Judy Lew, one user logon name can be **Judyl** and the other can be **Judyle**.
- In some organizations, it is useful to identify temporary employees by their user accounts. To do so, you can add a prefix to the user logon name, such as a **T** and a hyphen. An example is **T-Judyl**.
- User logon names for domain user accounts must be unique in the forest. Full names for domain user accounts must be unique in the container in which you create the user account.

User Account Placement in a Hierarchy

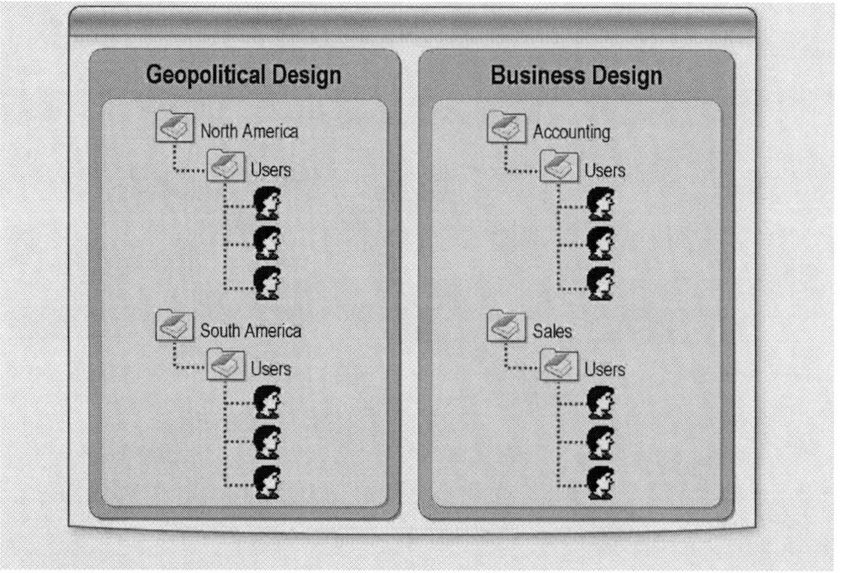

Introduction

You can place domain user accounts in any domain in the forest and any organizational unit in the domain. Typically, account hierarchies are based on geopolitical boundaries or business models.

Place user accounts in an Active Directory hierarchy based on the way the user accounts are managed. For example, security principals that will have similar security requirements, will have the same Group Policy settings, or will be managed by the same administrative personnel can be placed in the same organizational unit hierarchy.

Note The Users container is not an organizational unit. It is a system container that houses the administrative accounts and groups. More importantly, Group Policy objects cannot be directly assigned to the Users container, and the Users container cannot contain any child organizational units. Although you can create user accounts in the Users container, as a best practice the Users container should be reserved for administrative groups and service accounts.

Geopolitical design

In a geopolitical design, you place users in organizational units that match their physical location. You can create an organizational unit hierarchy using parent containers based on city or region.

Business design

When the hierarchy of organizational units is based on business models, you place your sales personnel in a Sales organizational unit and manufacturing personnel in a Manufacturing organizational unit.

Note In many cases, one domain will work for a corporate environment. You can still separate administrative control of users by placing them into organizational units.

User Account Password Options

Account options	Description
User must change password at next logon	Users must change their passwords the next time they log on to the network
User cannot change password	Users do not have the permissions to change their own password
Password never expires	Users' passwords will not expire and do not need to be changed
Account is disabled	Users cannot log on by using the selected account

Introduction

As a systems administrator, you can manage user account password options. These options can be set when the user account is created or in the **Properties** dialog box of a user account.

Password options

The administrator can choose from the following password options to protect access to the domain or a computer:

- **User must change password at the next logon.** Use this option when a new user logs on to a system for the first time or when the administrator resets forgotten passwords for users. This is the default for new user accounts.
- **User cannot change password.** Use this option when you want to prevent a user from changing his or her account password.
- **Password never expires.** This option prevents the password from expiring. To maintain security best practice, do not use this option.
- **Account is disabled.** This option prevents the user from logging on to the selected account.

Default password settings

By default, passwords in a Windows 2003 Active Directory domain must meet several minimum requirements.

- Must not contain all or part of the user's account name.
- Must be at least seven characters in length.
- Must contain characters from three of the following four categories:
  - English uppercase characters (A through Z)
  - English lowercase characters (a through z)
  - Base 10 digits (0 through 9)
  - Nonalphabetic characters (for example, !, $, #, %)

If an administrator changes the password complexity requirements, the new requirements will be enforced the next time passwords are changed or created.

These requirements are not enforced on stand-alone servers for local accounts but are still recommended practices.

HOLD DOWN SHIFT R-CLICK TO SHOW RUN-AS

When to Require or Restrict Password Changes

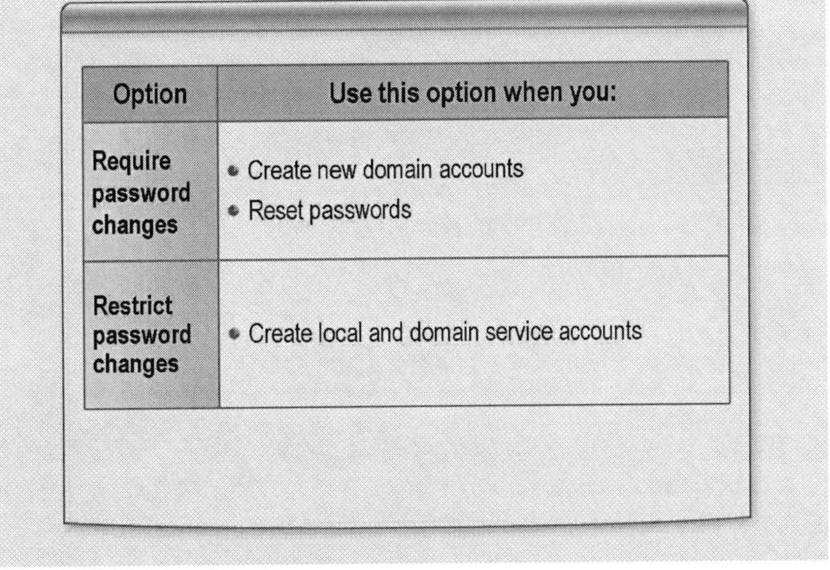
Option
Use this option when you:
Require password changes
Create new domain accounts
Reset passwords
Restrict password changes
Create local and domain service accounts

Introduction

To create a more secure environment, require password changes on user accounts and restrict password changes on service accounts. The following table describes when you need to restrict or require password changes.

Password modifications options

Option	Use this option when you:
Require password changes	• Create new domain user accounts. Select the check box that requires the user to change the password the first time the user logs on to the domain. • Reset passwords. This option enables the administrator to reset a password when the password expires or if the user forgets it.
Restrict password changes	• Create local or domain service accounts. Service accounts typically have many dependencies on them. As a result, you might want to restrict the password change policy so that service account passwords are changed by the administrator who is responsible for the applications that depend on the service account.

Additional reading

For more information about service accounts, see "Services permissions" on the Microsoft TechNet Web site.

For more information about changing passwords, see:

- Article 324744, "How to Prevent Users from Changing a Password Except When Required in Windows Server 2003," in the Knowledge Base on the Microsoft Help and Support Web site.
- Article 320325, "User May Not Be Able to Change Their Password If You Configure the 'User Must Change Password at Next Logon' Setting," in the Knowledge Base on the Microsoft Help and Support Web site.

Tools to Create User Accounts

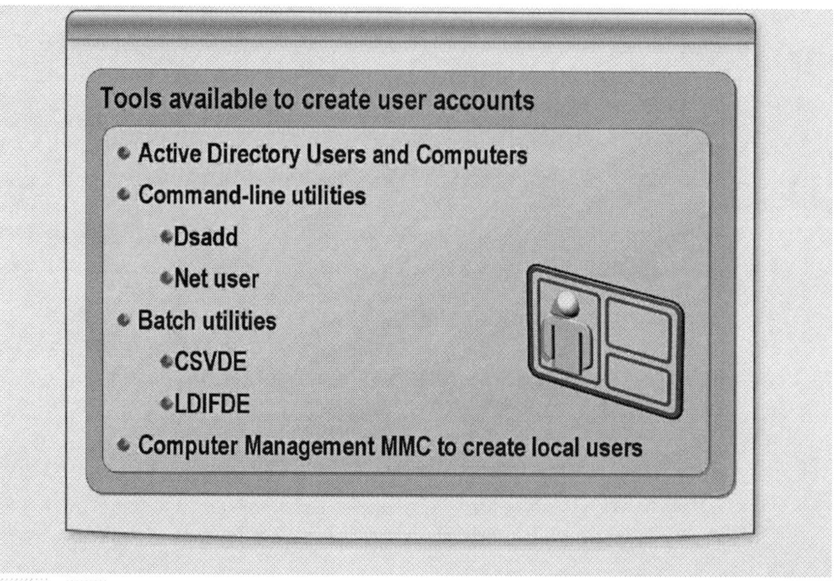

Tools available to create user accounts
Active Directory Users and Computers
Command-line utilities
Dsadd
Net user
Batch utilities
CSVDE
LDIFDE
Computer Management MMC to create local users

Introduction

Domain user accounts enable users to log on to a domain and access resources anywhere on the network. Local user accounts enable users to log on and access resources only on the computer on which you create the local user account. As a systems administrator, you must create domain and local user accounts to manage your network environment. A number of tools are available for the creation of user accounts, including legacy tools such as User Manager for Domains and command-line and batch utilities.

Using Active Directory Users and Computers

Active Directory Users and Computers is the primary tool used for day-to-day administration of Active Directory. Similar to the file system displayed in Windows Explorer, Active Directory Users and Computers displays Active Directory by using the left pane for a tree view of the domain and the right pane to display the detailed view. You can use Active Directory Users and Computers to create new objects, such as user, group, and computer accounts, and to manage existing objects.

Using a command line

Another way to create a domain user account is to use the **dsadd** command. The **dsadd user** command adds a single user to the directory from a command prompt or batch file.

Type:

dsadd user *UserDN* [**-samid** *SAMName*]
[**-upn** *UPN*] [**-fn** *FirstName*] [**-ln** *LastName*] [**-display** *DisplayName*]
[**-pwd** {*Password*|*}]

Use " " if there is a space in any variable.

Note For the complete syntax of the **dsadd user** command, at a command prompt, type **dsadd user /?**.

An example of **dsadd user** is shown here:

```
dsadd user "cn=test user,cn=users,dc=contoso,dc=msft" -samid
testuser -upn testuser@contoso.msft -fn test -ln user -display
"test user" -pwd Pa$$w0rd
```

Another way to create a user account is to use **net user** command.

For example, to create a new user named Greg Weber with a password of **Pa$$w0rd**, you would type the following command:

net user "Greg Weber" Pa$$w0rd /add

The following example shows the syntax of the **net user** command:

```
net user [username [password | *] [options]] [/domain]
username {password | *} /add [options] [/domain] username
[/delete] [/domain]
```

Important Legacy tools such as **User Manager for Domains** and **net** commands will place newly created user accounts in the Users container by default. Also, Microsoft Windows NT® 4.0 domains that have been upgraded to Windows 2003 Active Directory will place the upgraded user accounts in the Users container. This default location can be modified by using the **Redirusr** command. For more information, see article 324949, "Redirecting the users and computers containers in Windows Server 2003 domains," on the Microsoft Help and Support Web site.

Using batch utilities

Batch utilities can be used to import user accounts from input files. The CSVDE utility uses comma-delimited input files and the LDIFDE utility uses line-delimited files as input to create user accounts and other types of Active Directory objects.

Note For more information about the CSVDE and the LDIFDE utilities refer to Course 2279, *Planning, Implementing, and Maintaining a Microsoft Windows Server 2003 Active Directory Infrastructure.*

Using the Computer Management MMC

You can use the Local Users and Groups snap-in in the Computer Management Microsoft Management Console (MMC) to create local user accounts.

Important You cannot create local user accounts on a domain controller.

Important A local user name cannot be identical to any other user or group name on the computer being administered. A local user name can contain up to 20 uppercase or lowercase characters, except for the following:

" / \ [ ] : ; | = , + * ? < >

A user name cannot consist solely of periods or spaces.

Practice: Creating User Accounts

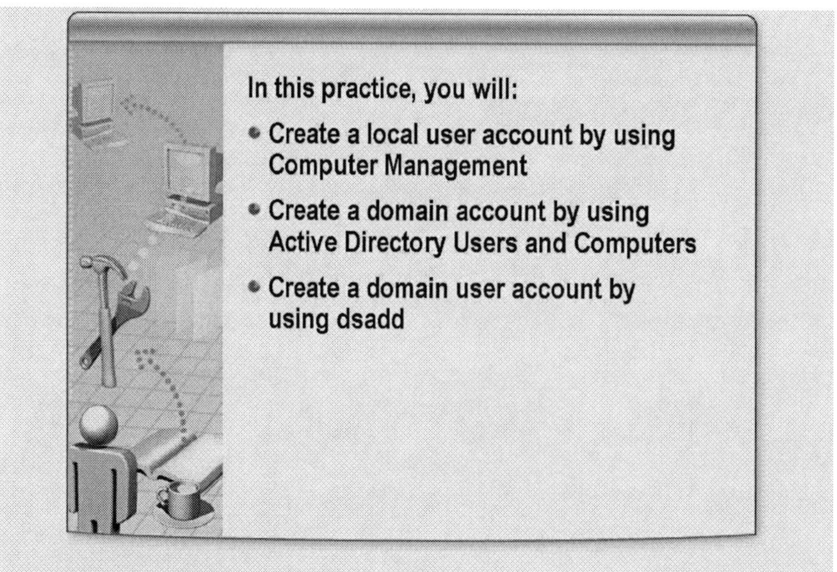

Objectives

In this practice, you will:

- Create a local user account by using Computer Management.
- Create a domain account by using Active Directory Users and Computers.
- Create a domain user account by using **dsadd**.

Instructions

Ensure that the DEN-DC1 virtual machine and the DEN-CL1 virtual machine are running.

Practice

► **Create a local user account by using Computer Management**

1. Log on to DEN-CL1 as **Judy** with the password of **Pa$$w0rd**.
2. Click **Start** and then click **Control Panel**.
3. Click **Performance and Maintenance**, and then click **Administrative Tools**.
4. Right-click **Computer Management** and then click **Run as**.
5. Select **The Following user** check box. Log on using **DEN-CL1\administrator** with a password of **Pa$$w0rd**.
6. In **Computer Management**, expand **Local Users and Groups**.
7. Right-click the **Users** folder, and then click **New User**.

8. In the **New User** dialog box, create an account using the following parameters:
   - User name: **Service_Backup**
   - Description: **Service Account for Backup Software**
   - Password: **Pa$$w0rd** (where 0 is zero)
   - Confirm password: **Pa$$w0rd**
   - User must change password at next logon: **Cleared**
   - Password never expires: **Selected**
9. Click **Create** and then click **Close**.
10. Close **Computer Management**, and then close **Administrative Tools.**
11. Log off from DEN-CL1.

► Create a domain account by using Active Directory Users and Computers

1. Log on to DEN-DC1 as **Administrator** with a password of **Pa$$w0rd.**
2. Click **Start,** point to **Administrative Tools,** and then click **Active Directory Users and Computers.**
3. Right-click the **IT Admin** OU, point to **New** and then click **User.**
4. In the **New Object – User** dialog box, enter the following parameters:
   - First name: **Kerim**
   - Last name: **Hanif**
   - Full name: **Kerim Hanif**
   - User logon name: **Kerim**
5. Click **Next.**
6. In the **Password** and **Confirm password** fields, enter **Pa$$w0rd.**
7. Clear the **User must change password at next logon** check box.
8. Click **Next.**
9. Click **Finish.**
10. Close **Active Directory Users and Computers.** Do not log off.
11. Test the user account that you just created by logging on to DEN-CL1 as **Kerim**, with a password of **Pa$$w0rd.**
12. Log off of DEN-CL1.

► **Create a domain user account by using dsadd**

1. On DEN-DC1 open a command prompt window.
2. At the command prompt, type the following command and then press ENTER:

   dsadd user "cn=Luis Bonifaz,ou=it admin,dc=contoso,dc=msft" -samid luis -pwd Pa$$w0rd –desc Administrator

   You should see a "dsadd succeeded" message.
3. Close all windows and log off of DEN-DC1. Do not shut down the virtual machines.

Important If the **dsadd** command does not specify a password and the domain policy requires a password, the account will be created but will be disabled until the password requirements are met. If the Security Accounts Manager (SAM) name (**samid**) is not specified, **dsadd** will use up to the first 20 characters of **CN** to create the SAM account name.

Best Practices for Creating User Accounts

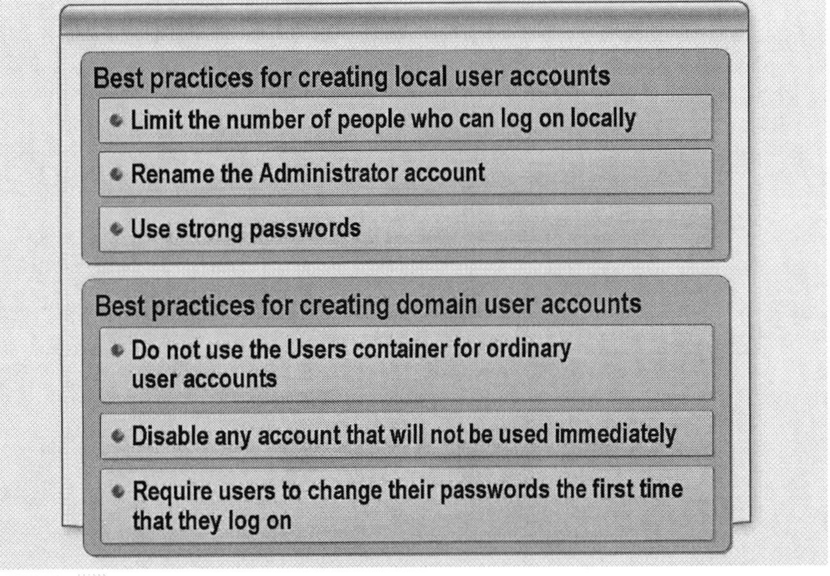

Introduction

Several best practices for creating user accounts reduce security risks in the network environment. Software products change, however, so be sure to review current best practices at www.microsoft.com/security.

Local user accounts

Consider the following best practices when creating local user accounts:

- Do not enable the Guest account.
- Limit the number of people who can log on locally.
- Rename the Administrator account.
- Use strong passwords.

Domain user accounts

Consider the following best practices when creating domain user accounts:

- Avoid using the Users container for ordinary user accounts. The Users container is a system container and should be used to hold administrative groups or accounts and service accounts.
- Disable any account that will not be used immediately.
- Require users to change their passwords the first time that they log on. This will prevent administrators from having access to user passwords. This is the default setting for new user accounts.
- As a security best practice, it is recommended that you do not log on to your computer with administrative credentials.
- When you are logged on to your computer without administrative credentials, it is recommended that you use the **runas** command to accomplish administrative tasks.
- Rename or disable the Administrator and Guest accounts in each domain to reduce the attacks on your domain.
- By default, all traffic on Active Directory administrative tools is signed and encrypted while in transit on the network. Do not disable this feature.

Lesson: Creating Computer Accounts

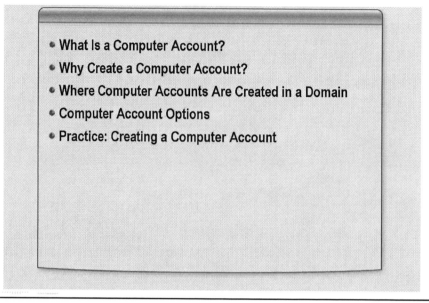

- What Is a Computer Account?
- Why Create a Computer Account?
- Where Computer Accounts Are Created in a Domain
- Computer Account Options
- Practice: Creating a Computer Account

Introduction

The information in this lesson presents the skills and knowledge that you need to create a computer account.

Lesson objectives

After completing this lesson, you will be able to:

- Define a computer account.
- Describe the purpose of computer accounts.
- Describe where computer accounts are created in a domain.
- Describe the various computer account options.
- Create a computer account.

What Is a Computer Account?

- Identifies a computer in a domain
- Provides a means for authenticating and auditing computer access to the network and to domain resources
- Is required for every computer running:
  - Windows Server 2003
  - Windows XP Professional
  - Windows 2000
  - Windows NT

Introduction

Every computer running Microsoft Windows NT, Windows 2000, Windows XP, or Windows Server 2003 that joins a domain has a computer account. Similar to user accounts, computer accounts provide a means for authenticating and auditing computer access to the network and to domain resources.

What does a computer account do?

In Active Directory, computers are security principals, just like users. This means that computers must have accounts and passwords. To be fully authenticated by Active Directory, a user must have a valid user account, and the user must also log on to the domain from a computer that has a valid computer account.

Note You cannot create computer accounts for computers running Microsoft Windows 95, Microsoft Windows 98, Microsoft Windows Millennium Edition, and Windows XP Home Edition, because their operating systems do not adhere to Active Directory security requirements.

Why Create a Computer Account?

- Security
  - Authentication
  - Auditing
- Management
  - Software deployment
  - Desktop management
  - Hardware and software inventory through Systems Management Server

Introduction

Computers access network resources to perform key tasks such as authenticating user logons, obtaining an IP address, and receiving security policies. To have full access to these network resources, computers must have valid accounts in Active Directory. The two main functions of a computer account are performing security and management activities.

Authentication

A computer account must be created in Active Directory for users to take full advantage of Active Directory features. When a computer account is created, the computer can use advanced authentication processes such as Kerberos authentication. For each workstation or server running Windows 2000, Windows 2003, or Windows XP that is a member of a domain, there is a discrete communication channel, known as the security channel, with a domain controller. The security channel's password is stored along with the computer account on all domain controllers. The default computer account password change period is every 30 days.

Auditing

The computer also needs a computer account to dictate how auditing is applied and recorded.

Management

Computer accounts help the systems administrator manage the network structure. The systems administrator uses computer accounts to manage the functionality of the desktop environment, automate the deployment of software by using Active Directory, and maintain a hardware and software inventory by using Microsoft Systems Management Server. Computer accounts in the domain are also used to control access to resources.

Where Computer Accounts Are Created in a Domain

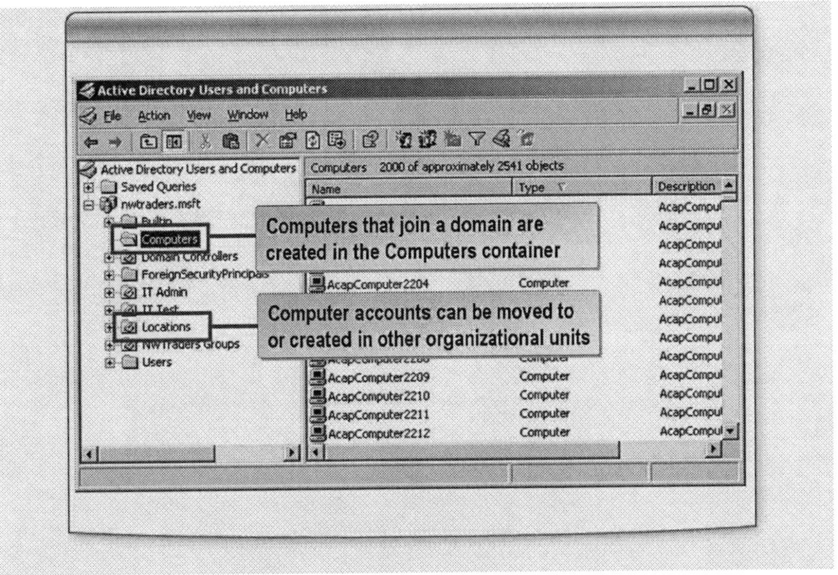

Introduction

When systems administrators create a computer account, they can choose the organizational unit in which to create that account. If a computer joins a domain, the computer account is created in the Computers container, and the administrator can move the account to its proper organizational unit as necessary.

Tip You can change the default location for computers joining the domain by using the **redircmp** command. For more information, see article 324949, "Redirecting the users and computers containers in Windows Server 2003 domains," Microsoft Help and Support Web site.

Who can create computer accounts?

By default, administrators can create computer accounts in any container except the System and NTDS Quotas containers. Computer accounts cannot be created in those containers. The Account Operators group can create computer accounts in the Computers container and in new organizational units. However, they cannot create computer accounts in the Builtin, Domain Controllers, ForeignSecurityPrincipals, LostAndFound, Program Data, System, or Users containers. Also, anyone who has been delegated authority to create computer objects in an organizational unit can create computers accounts in that container.

Users adding computers to the domain

When a user joins a computer to the domain, the computer account is added to the Computers container in Active Directory. This is accomplished through a service that adds the computer account on behalf of the user. The system account also records how many computers each user has added to the domain.

By default, Active Directory users can add up to 10 computers to the domain with their user account credentials. This default configuration can be changed. If the systems administrator pre-creates a computer account in Active Directory, a user can join a computer to the domain without using any of the 10 allocated computer accounts.

Pre-staged computer accounts

Adding a computer to the domain by using a previously created account is called pre-staging, which means that computers are added to any organizational unit for which the systems administrator has permissions to add computer accounts. Usually, users do not have the appropriate permissions to pre-stage a computer account, so as an alternative they join a computer to the domain by using a pre-staged account. You can designate which user or group has the right to join the computer to the domain during the creation of the computer account by clicking the **Change** button in the **New Object – Computer** dialog box.

Additional reading

For more information about users adding computer accounts to a domain, see article 251335, "Domain Users Cannot Join Workstation or Server to a Domain," on the Microsoft Help and Support Web site.

Computer Account Options

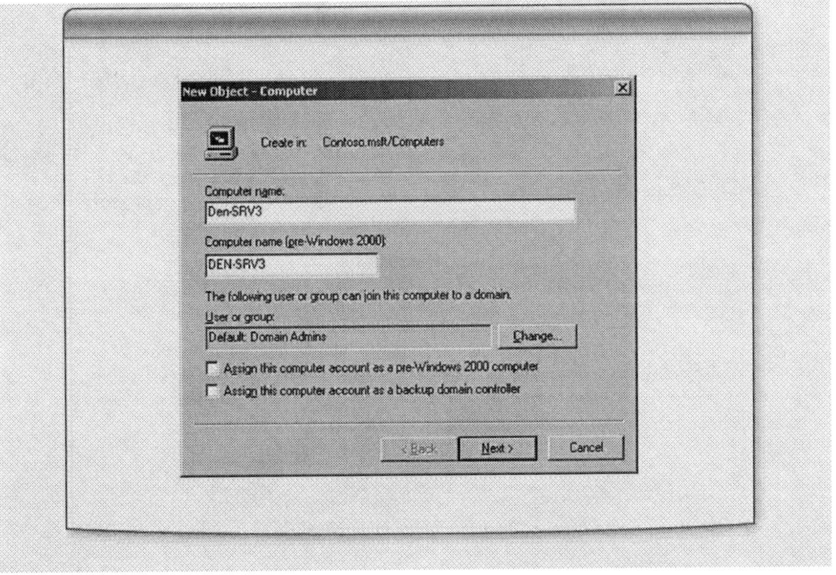

Introduction

You can enable two optional features when creating a computer account. You can assign a computer account as a pre–Windows 2000 computer or as a backup domain controller (BDC).

Pre–Windows 2000

Select the **Assign this computer account as a pre-Windows 2000 computer** check box to assign a password based on the computer name. If you do not select this check box, a random password is assigned as the initial password for the computer account. The password automatically changes every five days. This option guarantees that a pre–Windows 2000 computer will be able to interpret whether the password meets the password requirements.

Backup domain controller

Select the **Assign this computer as a backup domain controller** check box if you intend to use the computer as a backup domain controller. You should use this feature if you are still in a mixed environment with a Window Server 2003 domain controller and Windows NT 4.0 BDC. After the account is created in Active Directory, you can then join the BDC to the domain during the installation of Windows NT 4.0.

Practice: Creating a Computer Account

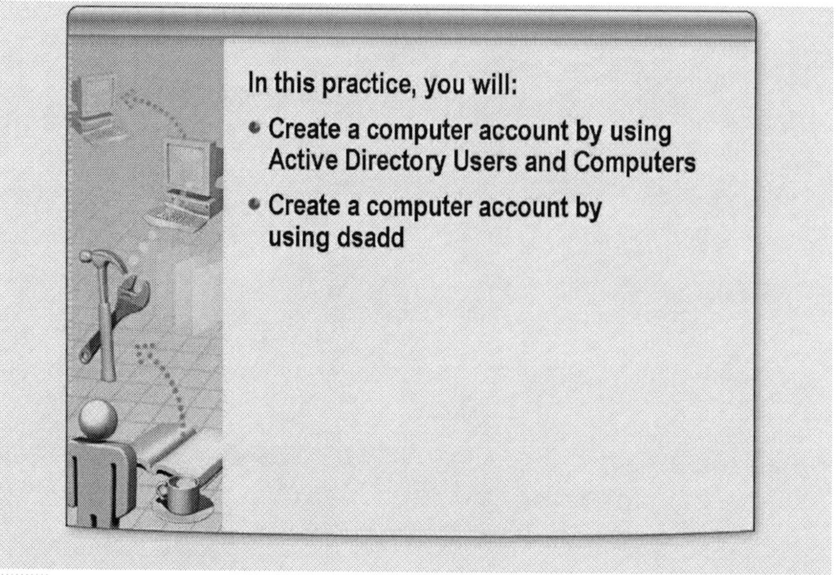
In this practice, you will:
Create a computer account by using Active Directory Users and Computers
Create a computer account by using dsadd

Objectives

In this practice, you will

- Create a computer account by using Active Directory Users and Computers.
- Create a computer account by using **dsadd**.

Instructions

Ensure that the DEN-DC1 virtual machine and the DEN-CL1 virtual machine are running.

Practice

► **Create a computer account by using Active Directory Users and Computers**

1. Log on to DEN-DC1 by using the **Administrator** account, with a password of **Pa$$w0rd.**
2. Click **Start**, point to **Administrative Tools**, and then click **Active Directory Users and Computers.**
3. Right-click the **Sales** organizational unit, point to **New**, and then click **Computer.**
4. In the **New Object-Computer** dialog box, enter **Sales2** in the **Computer name** field.
5. Under **The following user or group can join this computer to a domain**, click **Change.**
6. In the **Select User or Group** dialog box, type **Judy**, and then click **Check Names**. Click **OK**.
7. Click **Next** twice.
8. Click **Finish.**
9. Close **Active Directory Users and Computers.**

► Create a computer account by using dsadd

1. Open a command prompt window.
2. At the command prompt, type the following command and then press ENTER:

   dsadd computer "cn=Sales3,ou=sales,dc=contoso,dc=msft" –loc downtown

   You should see a "dsadd succeeded" message.
3. Close all windows and log off of DEN-DC1.

Note To perform this procedure, you must be a member of the Account Operators group, the Domain Admins group, or the Enterprise Admins group in Active Directory, or you must be delegated the appropriate authority. As a security best practice, consider using **runas** to perform this procedure.

Important Do not shut down the virtual machines.

Lesson: Modifying User and Computer Account Properties

- When to Modify User and Computer Account Properties
- Properties Associated with User Accounts
- Renaming a User Account
- Properties Associated with Computer Accounts
- Practice: Modifying User and Computer Account Properties

Introduction

This lesson presents the skills and knowledge that you need to modify user and computer accounts.

Lesson objectives

After completing this lesson, you will be able to:

- Determine when to modify user and computer account properties.
- Describe the properties associated with user accounts.
- Describe how to rename user accounts.
- Describe the properties associated with computer accounts.
- Modify user and computer account properties.

When to Modify User and Computer Account Properties

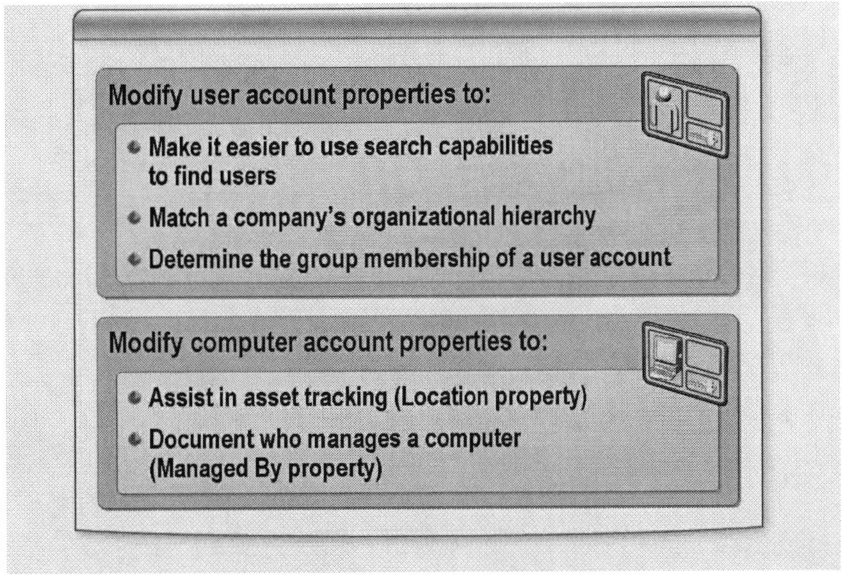

Modify user account properties to:
Make it easier to use search capabilities to find users
Match a company's organizational hierarchy
Determine the group membership of a user account
Modify computer account properties to:
Assist in asset tracking (Location property)
Document who manages a computer (Managed By property)

Introduction

As a systems administrator, you might be responsible for creating user and computer accounts in Active Directory. You also might be responsible for maintaining those user and computer accounts. To complete these tasks, you must be very familiar with the various properties for each user and computer account.

User account properties

It is critical that systems administrators are familiar with user account properties so that they can manage the network structure. Users might use the user account properties as a single source of information about other users, like a telephone book, or to search for users based on items such as office location, supervisor, or department name. The systems administrator can use the properties of a user account to determine how the user account behaves in a terminal server session or how the user can gain access to the network through a dial-up connection.

Computer account properties

To maintain computers, you must find the physical location of the computers. The most commonly used properties for computer accounts in Active Directory are the **Location** and **Managed by** properties. The **Location** property can be used to document the computer's physical location in your network. The **Managed By** property lists the individual responsible for the computer. This information can be useful when you have a data center with servers for different departments and you need to perform maintenance on the server. You can call or send e-mail to the person who is responsible for the server before you perform maintenance on the server.

Properties Associated with User Accounts

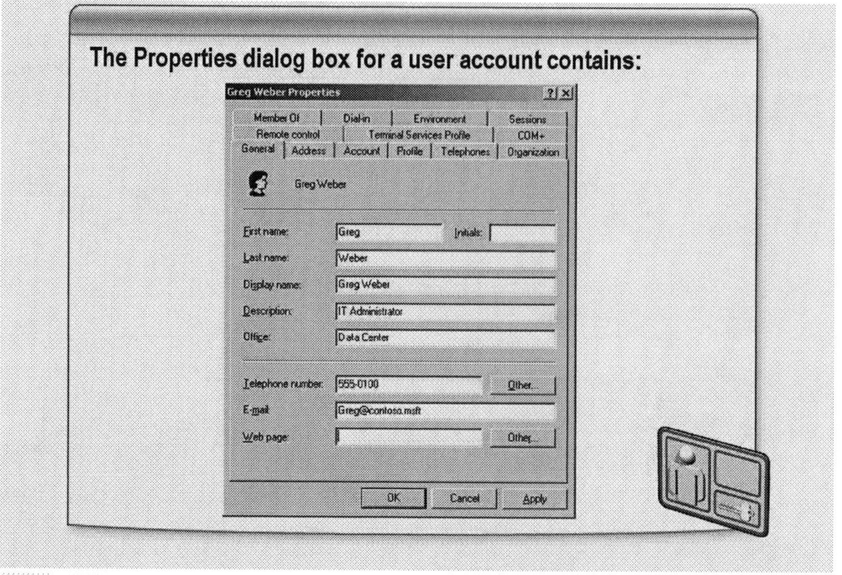

Introduction

The **Properties** dialog box for a user account contains information about each user account that is stored in Active Directory. The more complete the information in the **Properties** dialog box, the easier it is to search for users in Active Directory.

User account properties

The following table lists the most commonly used properties for user accounts.

Tab	Properties
General	Name, job description, office location, telephone number, e-mail address, and home page information
Address	Street address, city, state or province, postal zip code, and country
Account	Logon name, account options, unlock account, and account expiration
Profile	Profile path, logon scripts, and home folder
Telephone	Home, pager, mobile phone, fax, and IP telephone numbers
Organization	Title, department, company, manager, and direct reports
Member Of	Groups to which the user belongs
Dial-in	Remote access permissions, callback options, and static IP address and routes
Environment	One or more applications to start and the devices to connect to when a Terminal Services user logs on
Sessions	Terminal Services settings
Remote control	Terminal Services remote control settings
Terminal Services Profile	The user's Terminal Services profile

Renaming a User Account

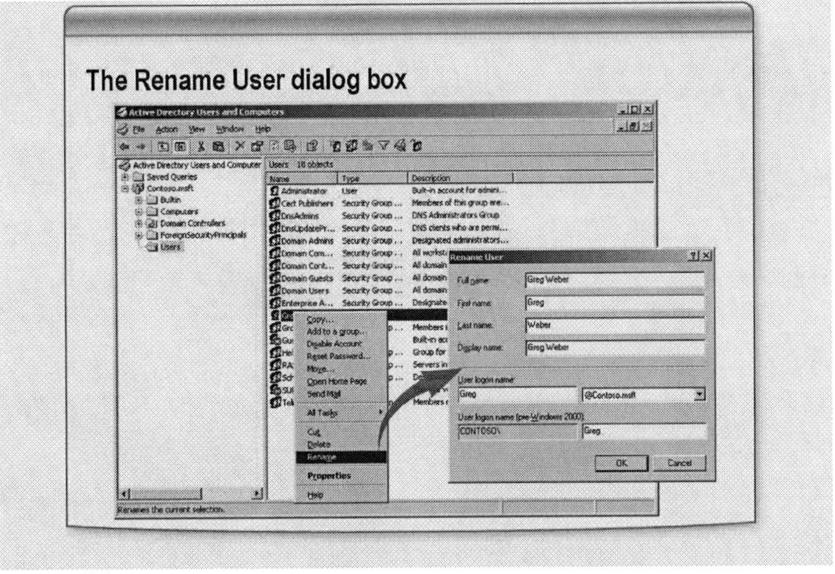

Introduction

Occasionally, employees in your organization will need to change their user name for personal or legal reasons. For example, employees who get married and legally change their surnames will need their user account names updated. Instead of deleting the old account and creating a new user, you can rename the original account. Use the following procedure to rename a user account.

Renaming a user account

1. Open **Active Directory Users and Computers**.
2. Right-click the user name that you need to change, and click **Rename** on the shortcut menu.
3. Type the new user name, and then press **Enter**.
4. In the **Rename User** dialog box, change the appropriate fields.

The renamed user account will maintain the same security descriptors, properties, rights, and permissions that were associated with the old account name.

Properties Associated with Computer Accounts

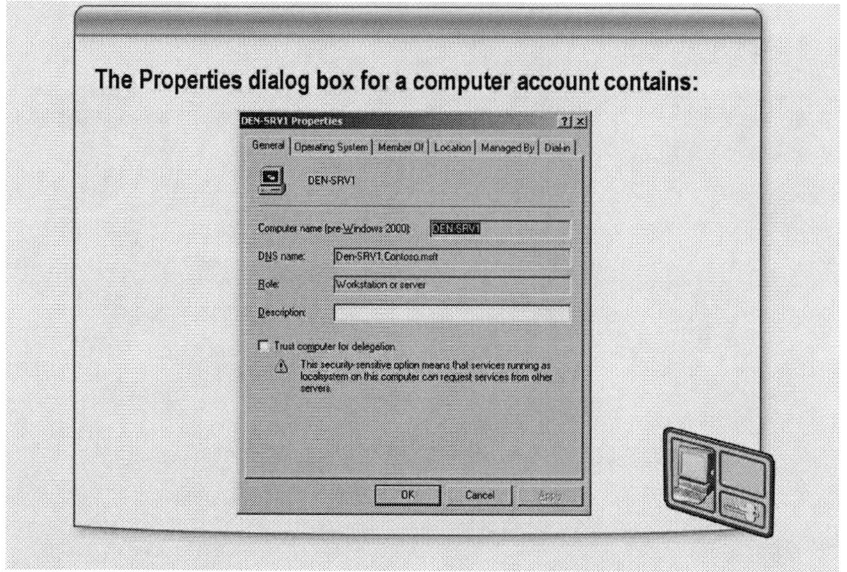

Introduction

The **Properties** dialog box for a computer account contains unique information about each computer account that is stored in Active Directory. The more complete the information in the **Properties** dialog box, the easier it is to search for computers in Active Directory.

Computer account properties

The following table lists the most commonly used properties for computer accounts.

Tab	Properties
General	Computer name, DNS name, description, and role
Operating System	Name and version of the operating system running on the computer and the latest service pack installed
Member Of	The groups in the local domain and any groups to which the computer belongs
Location	The location of the computer
Managed By	Name, office location, street, city, state or province, country or region, telephone number, and fax number of the person who manages the computer
Object	The canonical name of the object, object class, the date the computer account was created, the date it was last modified, and update sequence numbers (USNs)
Security	The users and groups who have permissions for the computer
Dial-in	Remote access permission, callback options, and routing options

Tools used to modify user or computer accounts

You can use Active Directory Users and Computers or the **dsmod** command to modify attributes of existing users or computers in Active Directory.

Note For the complete syntax of the **dsmod** command, at a command prompt, type **dsmod user /?** or **dsmod computer /?**.

Practice: Modifying User and Computer Account Properties

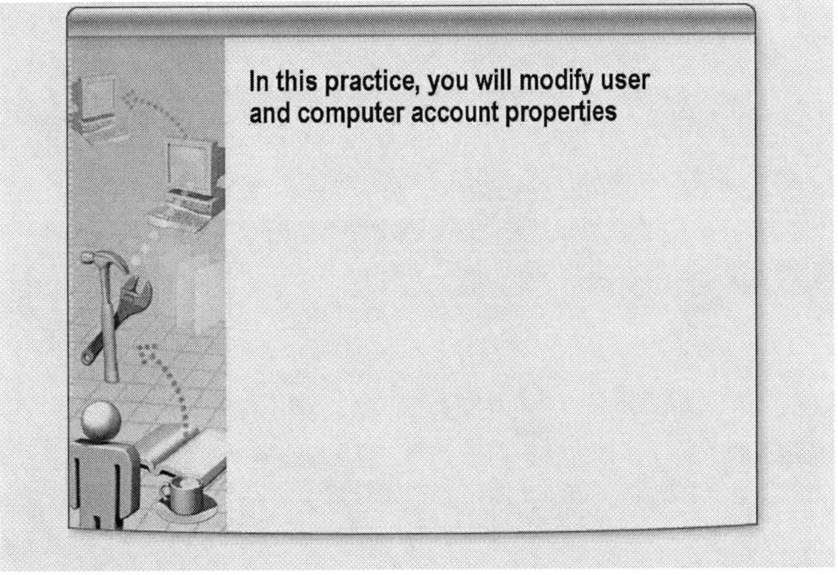
In this practice, you will modify user and computer account properties

Objective

In this practice, you will:

- Modify user and computer account properties.

Instructions

Ensure that the DEN-DC1 virtual machine is running.

Practice

► **Modify user and computer account properties**

1. Log on to DEN-DC1 as **Administrator**, with a password of **Pa$$w0rd**.
2. Open **Active Directory Users and Computers**.
3. In the **Sales** organizational unit, right-click **Jeff Hay**, and then click **Properties**. Modify the user properties as follows:
   a. On the **General** tab, set
      - **Telephone number: 204-555-0100**
      - **Office: Downtown**
      - **E-mail: Jeff@Contoso.msft**

   b. On the **Dial-in** tab, set **Remote Access Permission** to **Allow access**.

   c. On the **Account** tab, click **Logon Hours.** Configure logon hours to be permitted between 8:00 A.M. and 5:00 P.M and then click **OK.**
4. Close **Active Directory Users and Computers.**

5. Open a command prompt window, type the following command and then press ENTER:

   dsmod computer "cn=sales2,ou=sales,dc=contoso,dc=msft" -loc Downtown –desc Workstation

   You should get a "dsmod succeeded" message.

6. Close all windows and log off of DEN-DC1.

Important Do not shut down the virtual machines.

Lesson: Creating a User Account Template

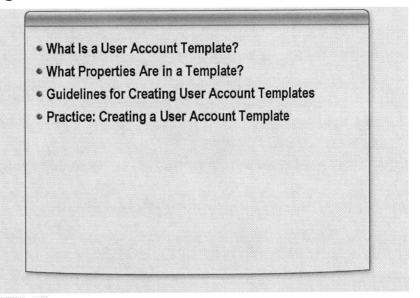

- What Is a User Account Template?
- What Properties Are in a Template?
- Guidelines for Creating User Account Templates
- Practice: Creating a User Account Template

Introduction

The information in this lesson presents the skills and knowledge that you need to create a user account template.

Lesson objectives

After completing this lesson, you will be able to:

- Explain the purpose of a user account template.
- Describe the properties of a user account template.
- Apply guidelines when creating user account templates.
- Create a user account template.

SAVE TIME BY CREATING A CLONE TEMPLATE

BEST PRACTICE: USE A PREFIX TO ID TEMPLATE AND DISABLE IT.

FOR HOME DIRECTORIES OR ROAMING USE %USERNAME%

What Is a User Account Template?

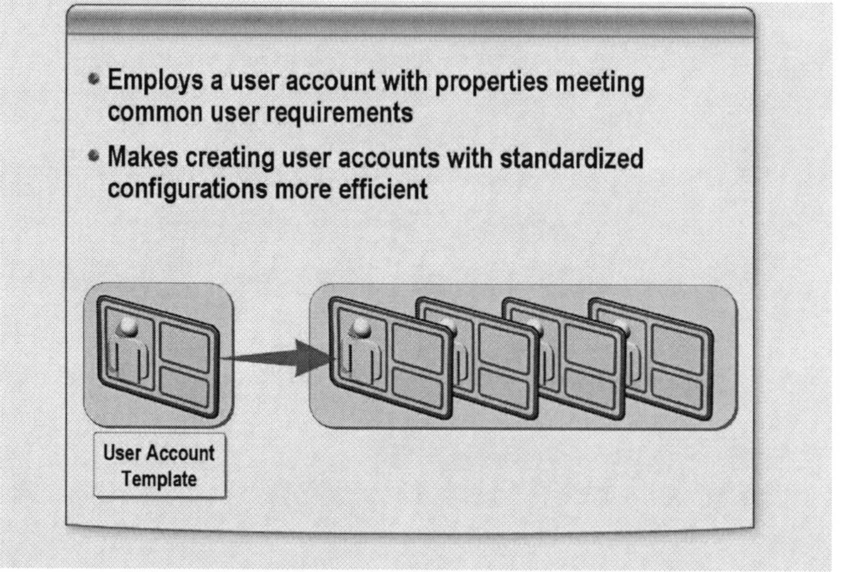

Employs a user account with properties meeting common user requirements
Makes creating user accounts with standardized configurations more efficient
User Account Template

Definition

You can simplify the process of creating domain user accounts by creating a user account template. A user account template is an account that has commonly used settings and properties already configured.

Using account templates

For each new user account, you need to add only the information that is unique to that user account. For example, if all sales personnel must be a member of 15 sales groups and have the same manager, you can create a template that includes membership to all the groups and the reporting manager. When the template is copied for a new salesperson, it retains the group memberships and manager that were in the template.

What Properties Are in a Template?

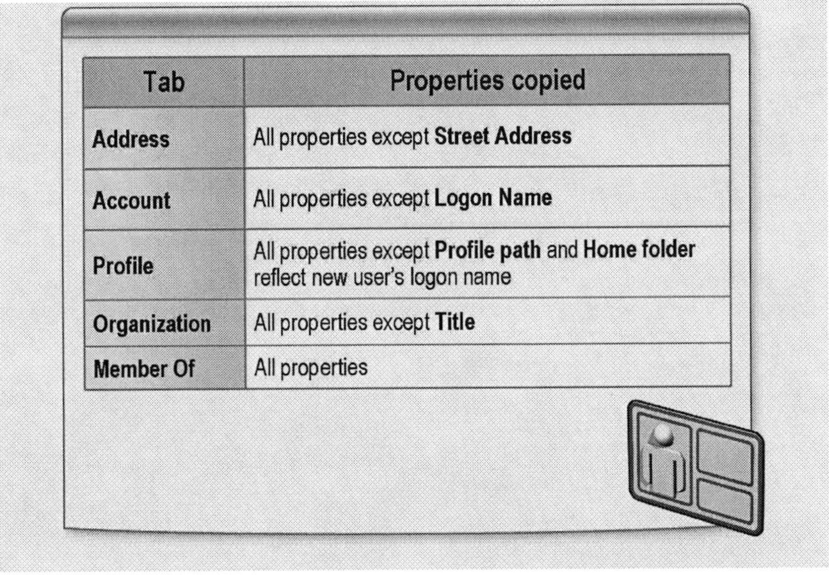
Tab
Properties copied
Address
All properties except Street Address
Account
All properties except Logon Name
Profile
All properties except Profile path and Home folder reflect new user's logon name
Organization
All properties except Title
Member Of
All properties

Properties

Numerous properties are associated with each account. However, only a limited number of properties can be copied in a template. The following table lists the user properties that can be copied from an existing domain user account to a new domain user account.

Properties tab	Properties copied to new domain user account
Address	All properties except **Street Address** are copied.
Account	All properties except **Logon Name**, which is copied from the **Copy Object – User** dialog box, are copied.
Profile	All properties except the **Profile path** and **Home folder** entries are modified to reflect the new user's logon name.
Organization	All properties except **Title** are copied.
Member Of	All properties are copied.

Additional reading

For more information about profiles, see article 324749, "HOW TO: Create a Roaming User Profile in Windows Server 2003," on the Microsoft Help and Support Web site.

Form more information about home folders, see article 325853, "HOW TO: Use Older Roaming User Profiles with Windows Server 2003," on the Microsoft Help and Support Web site.

Guidelines for Creating User Account Templates

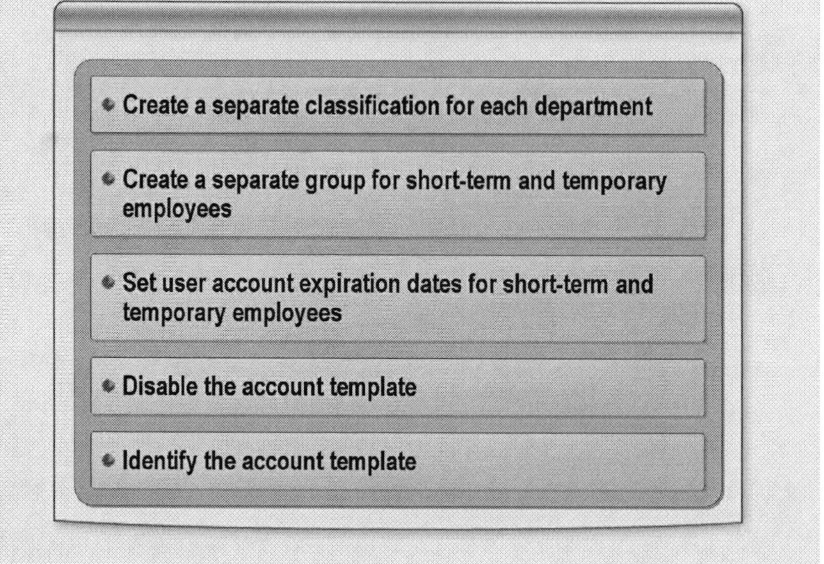

Guidelines

Consider the following best practices for creating user account templates:

- Create a separate classification for each department in your business group.
- Create a separate group for short-term and temporary employees with logon and workstation restrictions.
- Set user account expiration dates for short-term and temporary employees to prevent them from accessing the network when their contracts expire.
- Disable the account template.
- Identify the account template. For example, place a **T_** before the name of the account to identify the account as an account template or use an underscore at the beginning of the account name to ensure that the template always appears at the top of an alphabetized list.

Practice: Creating a User Account Template

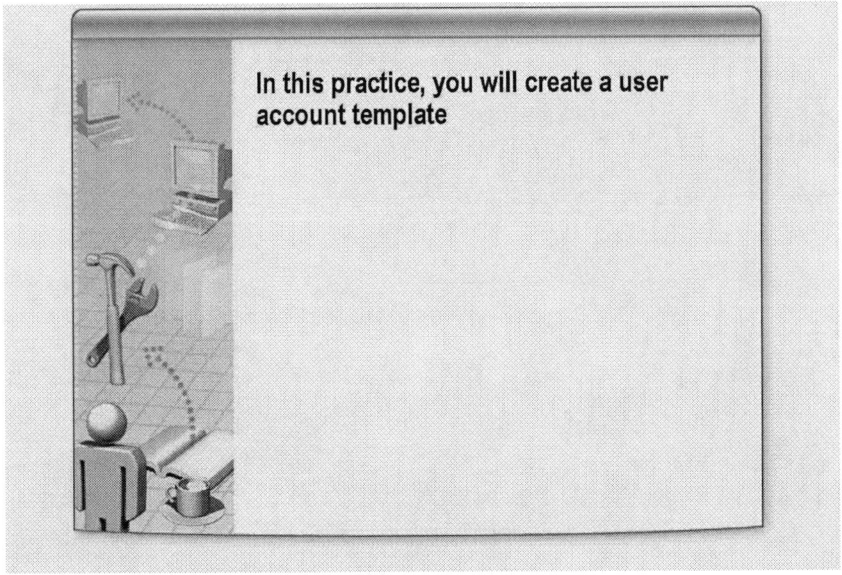
In this practice, you will create a user account template

Objective

In this practice, you will

- Create a user account template.

Practice

► **Create a user account template**

1. Log on to DEN-DC1 as **Administrator**, with a password of **Pa$$w0rd**.
2. Open **Active Directory Users and Computers**.
3. In the **Sales** organizational unit, create a user account with the following property settings:

Property	Value
First name	**Sales**
Last name	**Template**
Full name	**Sales Template**
User logon name	**_SalesTemplate**
Password	**Pa$$w0rd**
Description	**Salesperson**
Office	**Downtown**
Member Of	**G Sales**
Department	**Sales**
Profile path	**\\DEN-SRV1\profiles\%username%**
Logon Hours	**6:00 A.M – 6:00 P.M. Monday to Friday**
Disable the account	Enable

4. Click **OK** and then close **Active Directory Users and Computers**.
5. Log off of DEN-DC1.

Lesson: Managing User and Computer Accounts

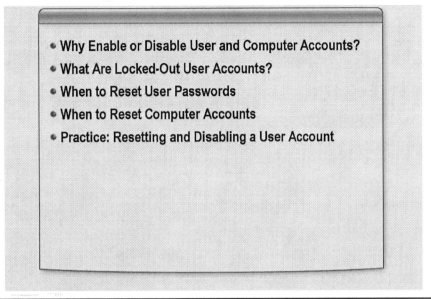

- Why Enable or Disable User and Computer Accounts?
- What Are Locked-Out User Accounts?
- When to Reset User Passwords
- When to Reset Computer Accounts
- Practice: Resetting and Disabling a User Account

Introduction

The information in this lesson presents the skills and knowledge that you need to enable and disable user and computer accounts.

Lesson objectives

After completing this lesson, you will be able to:

- Explain why you enable and disable user and computer accounts.
- Enable and disable user and computer accounts.
- Explain when to reset user passwords.
- Explain when to reset computer accounts.
- Reset and disable a user account.

Why Enable or Disable User and Computer Accounts?

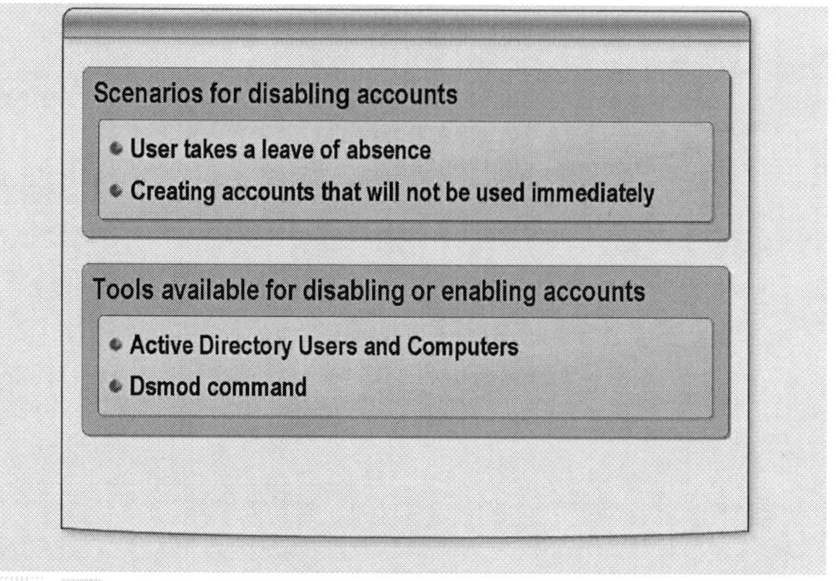

Introduction

After creating user accounts, you perform frequent administrative tasks to ensure that the network continues to meet the organization's needs. These administrative tasks include enabling and disabling user and computer accounts. When you enable or disable an account, you give or restrict access to the account.

Scenarios for enabling and disabling accounts

To provide a secure network environment, a systems administrator must disable user accounts when users do not need their accounts for an extended period but will need to use them later. The following are examples of when you need to enable or disable user accounts:

- If the user takes a two-month leave of absence from work, you disable the account when the user leaves and then enable the account when the user returns.
- When you add accounts in the network that will be used in the future or for security purposes, you disable the accounts until they are needed.

Tools for enabling and disabling accounts

You can use Active Directory Users and Computers to disable or enable an account. When an account is disabled, the user cannot log on. The account appears in the details pane with an **X** on the account icon.

Note To enable and disable user and computer accounts, you must be a member of the Account Operators group, the Domain Admins group, or the Enterprise Admins group in Active Directory, or you must be delegated the appropriate authority. As a security best practice, consider using **runas** to perform this procedure.

Using a command line

You can also enable or disable accounts by using the **dsmod** command. As a security best practice, consider using **runas** to perform this procedure.

To enable or disable accounts by using **dsmod**:

1. Open a command prompt window by using the **runas** command.
2. Type **dsmod user** *UserDN* **-disabled {yes|no}** at the command prompt.

Value	Description
UserDN	Specifies the distinguished name of the user object to be disabled or enabled
{**yes**|**no**}	Specifies whether the user account is disabled for log on (**yes**) or enabled (**no**)

What Are Locked-Out User Accounts?

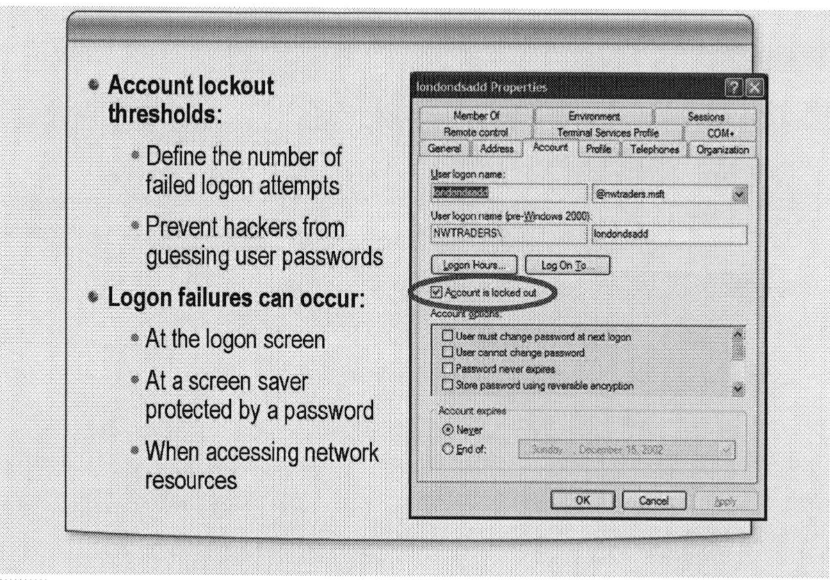

Introduction

A user account is locked out if the account has exceeded the account lockout threshold for a domain. This might happen if the user has attempted to access the account with an incorrect password too many times or if a computer hacker has attempted to guess users' passwords and invoked the lockout policy on the account.

Account lockout threshold

Authorized users can lock themselves out of an account by mistyping or by typing an incorrect password or by changing their password on a computer while they are logged on to another computer. The computer with the incorrect password continuously tries to authenticate the user. Because the password the computer is using to authenticate the user is incorrect, the user account is eventually locked out.

A security setting in Active Directory specifies the number of failed logon attempts that causes a user to be locked out. A user cannot use a locked-out account until an administrator resets the account or until the lockout duration for the account expires. When a user account is locked out, an error message appears, and the user is not allowed any further logon attempts.

What is a failed logon attempt?

A user can be locked out of an account if there are too many failed password attempts. Failed password attempts happen when:

- A user logs on at the logon screen and supplies a bad password.
- A user logs on with a local account and supplies a domain user account and a bad password while accessing network resources.
- A user logs on with a local account and supplies a domain user account and a bad password while accessing resources by using the **runas** command.

By default, domain account lockout attempts are not recorded when a user unlocks a workstation (by using a password-protected screen saver). You can change this behavior by modifying the **Interactive logon: Require Domain controller authentication to unlock workstation** Group Policy setting.

The built-in administrator cannot be locked out from the console of a domain controller or local machine.

When to Reset User Passwords

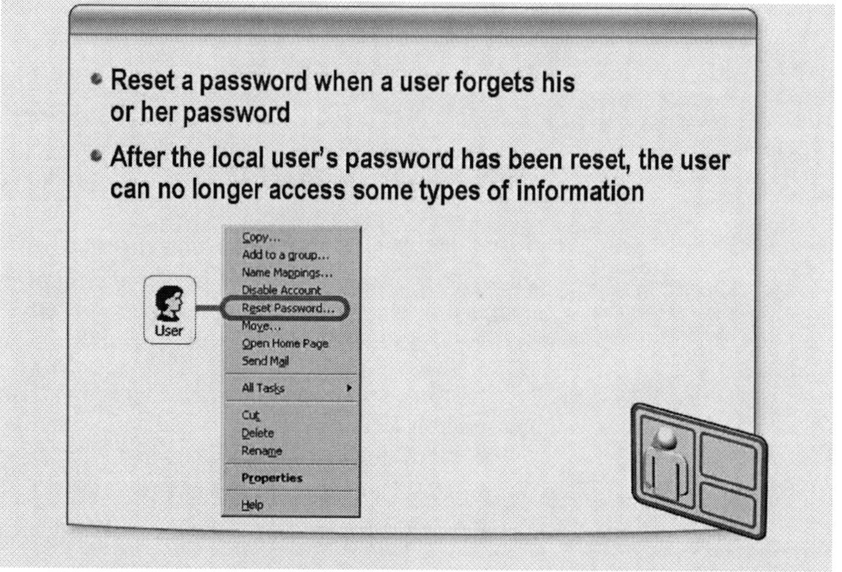

Introduction

People occasionally forget their passwords. Without their passwords, these people cannot access their user accounts. Administrators can reset users' passwords so that users can access their accounts again.

Who can reset user account passwords

When you need to reset a user password, you must remember that authorization to reset passwords is restricted.

- Only local administrators are authorized to reset local user passwords.
- Only domain administrators, enterprise administrators, account operators, and other users or groups that have the delegated authority to reset passwords are authorized to reset domain user passwords.

Consequences of resetting local user account passwords

After a local computer user's account password is reset, some types of encrypted information are no longer accessible. This is because the algorithm that generates a local user's encryption key incorporates the user's current password in the calculation. Some examples of information that might not be accessible are:

- E-mail that is encrypted by using the user's public key.
- Internet passwords that are saved on the computer.
- Files that the user has encrypted.

When to Reset Computer Accounts

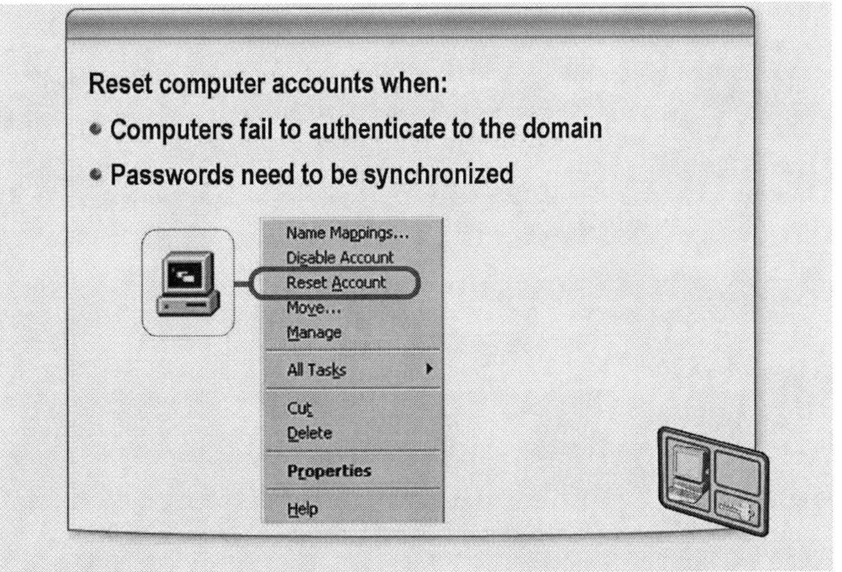
Reset computer accounts when:
Computers fail to authenticate to the domain
Passwords need to be synchronized
Name Mappings...
Disable Account
Reset Account
Move...
Manage
All Tasks
Cut
Delete
Properties
Help

Introduction

As a systems administrator, you occasionally need to reset computer accounts. For example, suppose that your network went through a full backup seven days ago. The computer relayed information to the domain controller that changed the password on the computer account. However, the computer's hard drive crashed, and the computer was restored from tape backup. The computer now has an outdated password, and the user cannot log on because the computer cannot authenticate to the domain. You now need to reset the computer account. Resetting a computer's account allows it to keep the same SID and GUID and the same group memberships.

Considerations

You must consider two issues before resetting the computer account:

- To perform this procedure, you must be a member of the Account Operators group, the Domain Admins group, or the Enterprise Admins group in Active Directory, or you must be delegated the appropriate authority. As a security best practice, consider using **runas** to perform this procedure.

- When you reset a computer account, you break the computer's connection to the domain, and you must rejoin the computer to the domain.

Additional reading

For more information about resetting a domain controller account and resetting a computer account with a script, see article 325850, "HOW TO: Use Netdom.exe to Reset Machine Account Passwords of a Windows Server 2003 Domain Controller," on the Microsoft Help and Support Web site.

For more information about how the data protection API in Windows handles stored passwords, see the article "Windows Data Protection," on the Microsoft MSDN Web site.

Practice: Resetting and Disabling a User Account

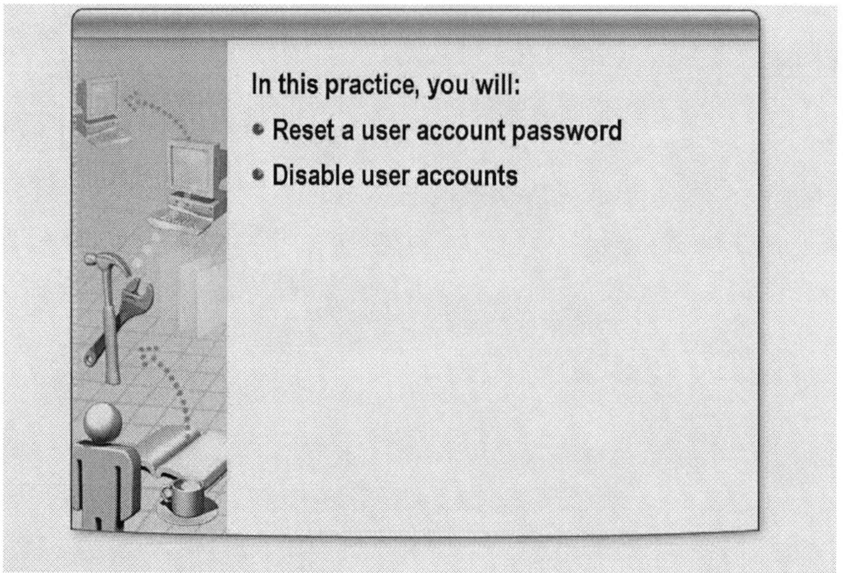
In this practice, you will:
Reset a user account password
Disable user accounts

Objective

In this practice, you will

- Reset a user account password.
- Disable user accounts.

Instructions

Ensure that the DEN-DC1 and DEN-CL1 virtual machines are running.

Practice

► **Reset a user account password**

1. Log on to DEN-DC1 as **Administrator**, with a password of **Pa$$w0rd**.
2. Open **Active Directory Users and Computers** and then click the **IT Admin** organizational unit.
3. Right-click the **Kerim Hanif** user account, and then click **Reset Password.**
4. In the **Reset Password** dialog box, type **Pa$$w0rd1** in the **New password** and **Confirm password** fields, and then select the **User must change password at next logon** check box.
5. Click **OK.**
6. Click **OK** to confirm that the password has been changed.
7. Switch to DEN-CL1, and then log on as **Kerim@contoso.msft**, with a password of **Pa$$w0rd1**.
8. When prompted to change the password, enter **Pa$$w0rd2** (where 0 is zero) in the **New Password** and **Confirm New Password** fields, and then click **OK.**
9. Click **OK** to confirm that the password has been changed. The logon should be successful.
10. Log off of DEN-CL1.

▶ **Disable user accounts**

1. On DEN-DC1, in **Active Directory Users and Computers**, click the **IT Admin** OU.
2. Right-click the **Luis Bonifaz** user account, and then click **Disable Account**.
3. Click **OK** to confirm that the account has been disabled.
4. Disable the **Kerim Hanif** user account.
5. Close **Active Directory Users and Computers** and then log off of DEN-DC1.
6. Attempt to log on to DEN-CL1 as **luis@contoso.msft**, with a password of **Pa$$w0rd**. The logon should fail, displaying a message that the account has been disabled.
7. Attempt to log on to DEN-CL1 as **Kerim@contoso.msft**, with a password of **Pa$$w0rd2**. The logon attempt will succeed, but any subsequent logon attempt will fail, displaying an account disabled message.

Important If a user has successfully logged on to the computer and the computer has not been rebooted, the first logon after disabling the account might succeed due to the fast logon features of Windows XP Professional. Subsequent logons will fail.

Lesson: Using Queries to Locate User and Computer Accounts in Active Directory

- Multimedia: Introduction to Locating User and Computer Accounts in Active Directory
- Search Types
- What Is a Saved Query?
- Importing and Exporting Saved Queries
- Practice: Using Saved Queries to Locate Users and Computers in Active Directory

Introduction

The information in this lesson presents the skills and knowledge that you need to use common and custom queries.

Lesson objectives

After completing this lesson, you will be able to:

- Explain the criteria for locating a user or computer account.
- Describe the types of common queries.
- Describe what a saved query is.
- Import and export queries.
- Locate user and computer accounts in Active Directory by using saved queries.

Multimedia: Introduction to Locating User and Computer Accounts in Active Directory

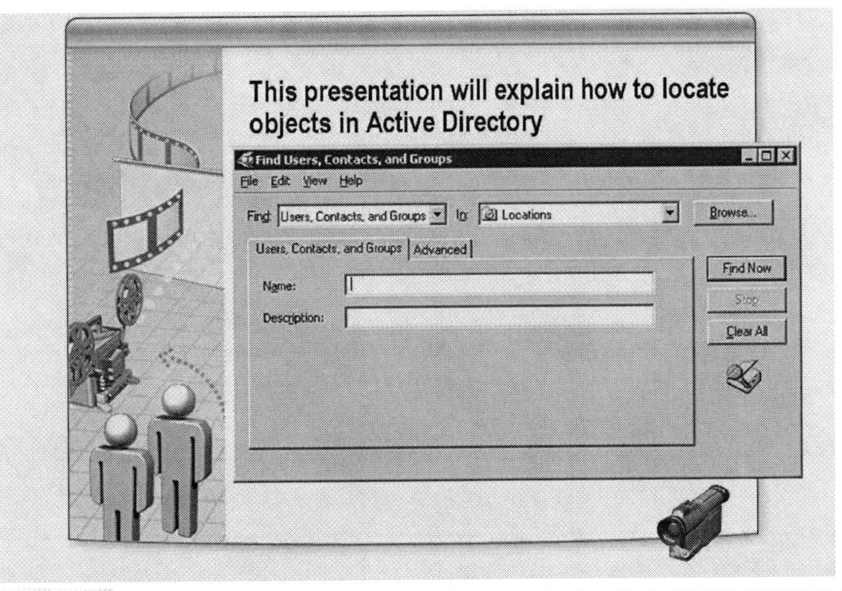

File location

To view the *Introduction to Locating User and Computer Accounts in Active Directory* presentation, open the Web page on the Student Materials compact disc, click **Multimedia**, and then click the title of the presentation. Do not open this presentation unless the instructor tells you to.

Search Types

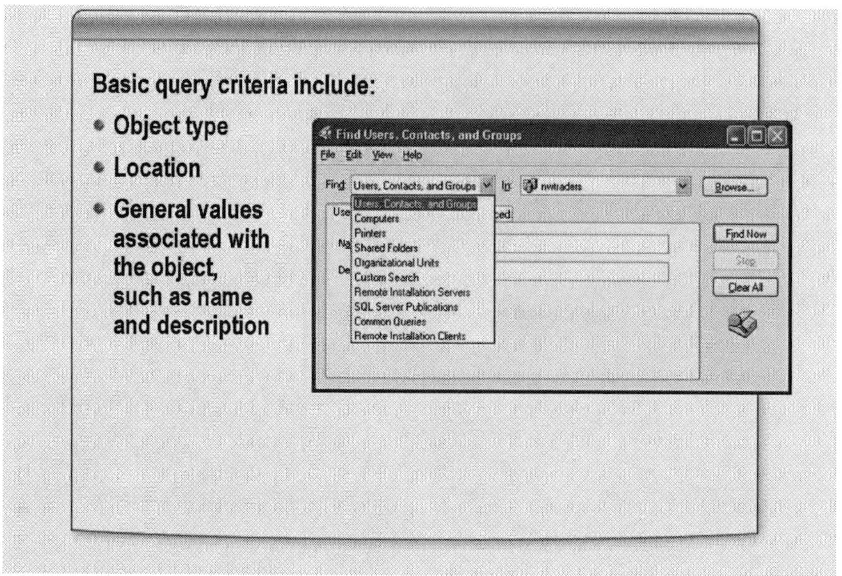

Introduction

Because all user accounts reside in Active Directory, administrators can search for the user accounts that they administer. By searching Active Directory for user accounts, you do not need to browse through hundreds or thousands of user accounts in Active Directory Users and Computers.

In addition to searching for user accounts, you can also search for other Active Directory objects, such as computers, printers, and shared folders. After locating these objects, you can administer them in the **Search Results** box.

Administering objects by using Search Results

After a successful search, the results are displayed, and you can then perform administrative functions on the found objects. The administrative functions that are available depend on the type of object you find. For example, if you search for user accounts, you can rename or delete the user account, disable the user account, reset the password, move the user account to another organizational unit, or modify the user account's properties.

To administer an object in the **Search Results** box, right-click the object, and then click an action on the menu.

Find Users, Contacts, and Groups

Active Directory provides information about all objects on a network, including people, groups, computers, printers, shared folders, and organizational units. It is easy to search for users, contacts, and groups by using the **Find Users, Contacts, and Groups** dialog box.

Find Computers

Use **Find Computers** to search for computers in Active Directory by using criteria such as the name assigned to the computer or the operating system on which the computer runs. After you find the computer you want, you can manage it by right-clicking the computer in the **Search Results** box and then clicking **Manage**.

Find Printers

When a shared printer is published in Active Directory, you can use **Find Printers** to search for the printer by using criteria such as its asset number, the printer language that it uses, or whether it supports double-sided printing. After you find the printer that you want, you can easily connect to it by right-clicking the printer name in the **Search Results** box and then clicking **Connect**, or by double-clicking the printer to connect to the printer.

Find Shared Folders

When a shared folder is published in Active Directory, you can use **Find Shared Folders** to search for the folder by using criteria such as keywords assigned to it, the name of the folder, or the name of the person managing the folder. After you find the folder that you want, open Windows Explorer and display the files located in the folder by right-clicking the folder in the **Search Results** box and then clicking **Explore**.

Find Custom Search

In Active Directory, you can search for familiar objects such as computers, printers, and users. You can also search for other objects, such as a specific organizational unit or certificate template. Use **Find Custom Search** to build custom search queries by using advanced search options or build advanced search queries by using LDAP, which is the primary access protocol for Active Directory.

Find Common Queries

You can use **Find Common Queries** to perform common administrative queries in Active Directory. For example, you can quickly search for user or computer accounts that have been disabled.

Advanced query options

For each search option except **Find Common Queries**, you can use the **Advanced** tab to define a more detailed search. For example, you can search for all users in a city or postal code on the **Advanced** tab.

Using a command line

You can use the **dsquery** command to find users and computers in Active Directory that match the specified search criteria.

For example, to display the user principal names of all users in the Sales organizational unit, at a command prompt, type the following:

dsquery user OU=Sales,DC=contoso,DC=msft -o upn

Note For the complete syntax of the **dsquery** command, at a command prompt, type **dsquery user /?** or **dsquery computer /?**.

Additional reading

For more information about searching Active Directory, see "Search Companion overview," on the Microsoft Windows Server 2003 Web Site.

What Is a Saved Query?

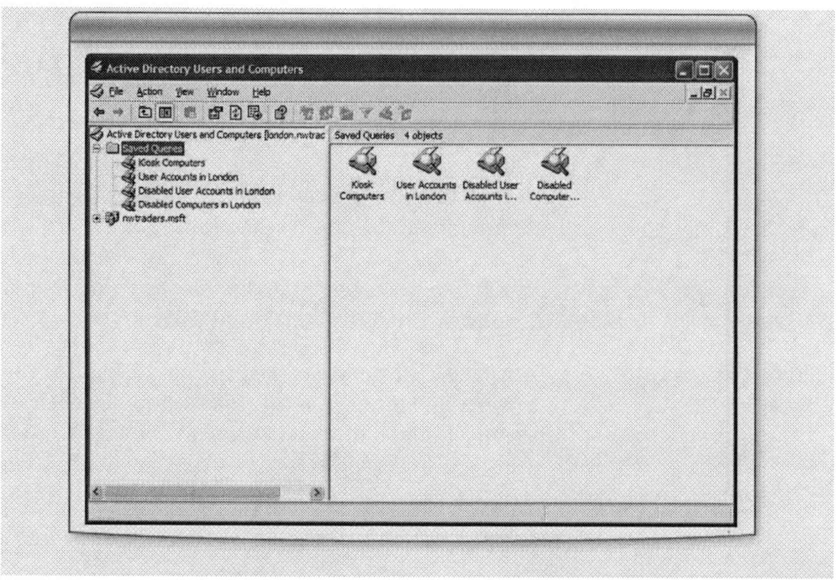

Introduction

Active Directory Users and Computers has a Saved Queries folder in which you can create, edit, save, and organize saved queries. Before saved queries, administrators were required to create custom Active Directory Services Interfaces (ADSI) scripts that performed a query on common objects. This was an often lengthy process that required knowledge of how ADSI uses LDAP search filters to resolve a query.

Definition

Saved queries use predefined LDAP strings to search only the specified domain partition. You can narrow searches to a single container object. You can also create a customized saved query that contains an LDAP search filter.

All queries are located in the Saved Queries folder named dsa.msc, which is stored in Active Directory Users and Computers. You can create subfolders in the Saved Queries folder to allow you to organize queries. Queries are specific to the domain controller that they were created on. After you successfully create your customized set of queries, you can copy the .msc file to other Windows Server 2003 domain controllers that are in the same domain and reuse the same set of saved queries. You can also export saved queries to an Extensible Markup Language (XML) file. You can then import the queries into other Active Directory Users and Computers consoles located on Windows Server 2003 domain controllers that are in the same domain.

Additional reading

For more information about saved queries, see the article "Using saved queries," on the Microsoft Windows Server 2003 Web site.

Importing and Exporting Saved Queries

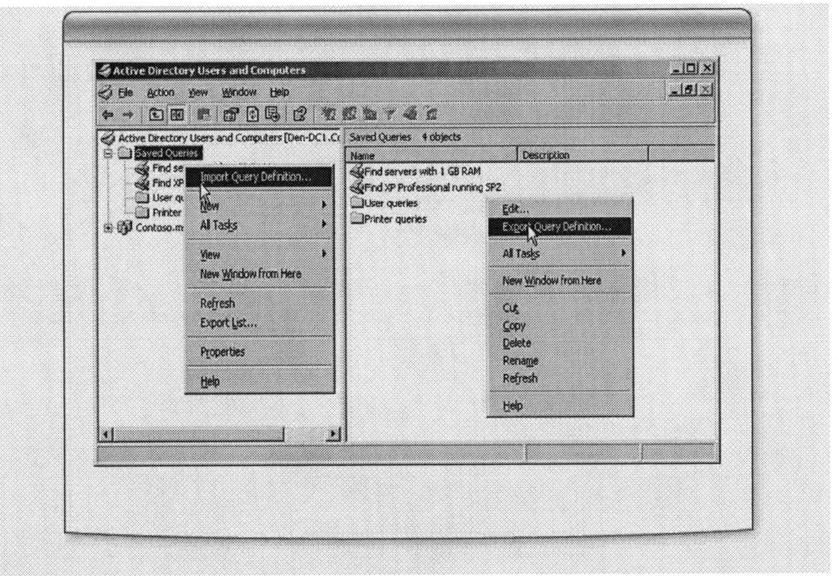

Introduction

Queries are valuable tools that assist in finding objects in Active Directory based on many different criteria. But queries are specific to the domain controller that they were created on. Queries can be shared throughout the domain by exporting them to XML files and then importing those files to other domain controllers. In that way, one administrator can write scripts for administrators in other locations to use.

Exporting queries

If you write a complex query that would be useful to other administrators, you can export that query by right-clicking on the query and then clicking **Export Query Definition**. You will be prompted to **Save As an .XML file**. Save the file to a shared folder on the network that only authorized administrators have access to.

Importing queries

You can import a query by right-clicking the Saved Queries folder and then clicking **Import Query Definition**. Navigate to the location of the XML file, and then select it.

Practice: Using Queries to Locate Users and Computers in Active Directory

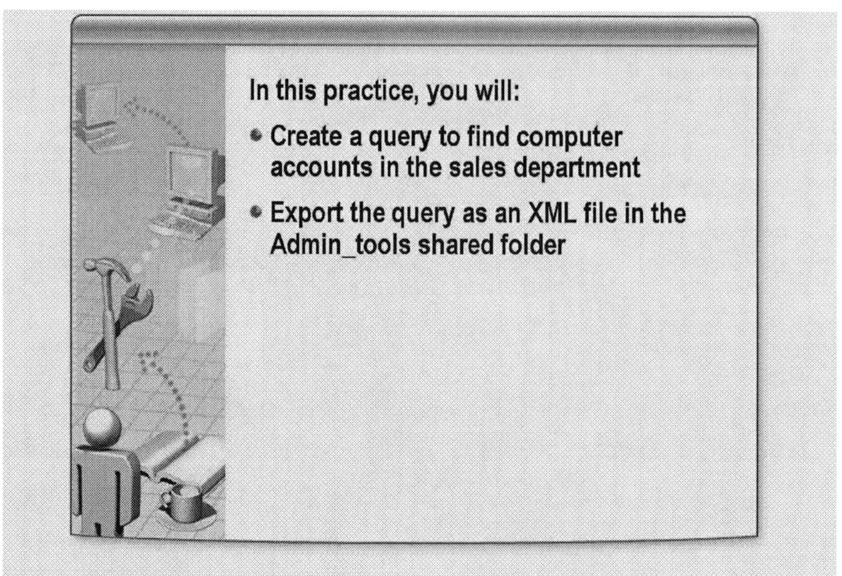

Objectives

In this practice, you will:

- Create a query to find computer accounts in the sales department.
- Export the query as an XML file in the Admin_tools shared folder.

Instructions

Ensure that the DEN-DC1 and the DEN-CL1 virtual machines are running.

Practice

► **Create a query to find computer accounts in the sales department.**

1. Log on to DEN-DC1 as **Administrator** using a password of **Pa$$w0rd.**
2. Open **Active Directory Users and Computers**, right-click the **Saved Queries** folder, point to **New** and then click **Query**.
3. In the **New Query** dialog box, type **Find Sales Department Computers** in the **Name** field.
4. Click **Define Query**.
5. In the **Find Common Queries** dialog box, click the **Computers** tab. In the **Name** field, click **Starts with.**
6. Type **Sales** in the **Starts with** field.
7. Click **OK** twice.
8. Click the **Find Sales Department Computers** query.
9. The query should find Sales1, Sales2, and Sales3.

► Export the query as an XML file in the Admin_tools shared folder

1. Right-click the **Find Sales Department Computers** query in the **Saved Queries** folder, and then click **Export Query Definition**.
2. In the **Save As** dialog box, navigate to the **D:\2274\Labfiles\Admin_tools** folder, name the query **Find_Sales_Computers.xml** and then click **Save**.
3. Close **Active Directory Users and Computers** and then Log off of DEN-DC1.

Important Do not shut down the virtual machines.

Lab: Managing User and Computer Accounts

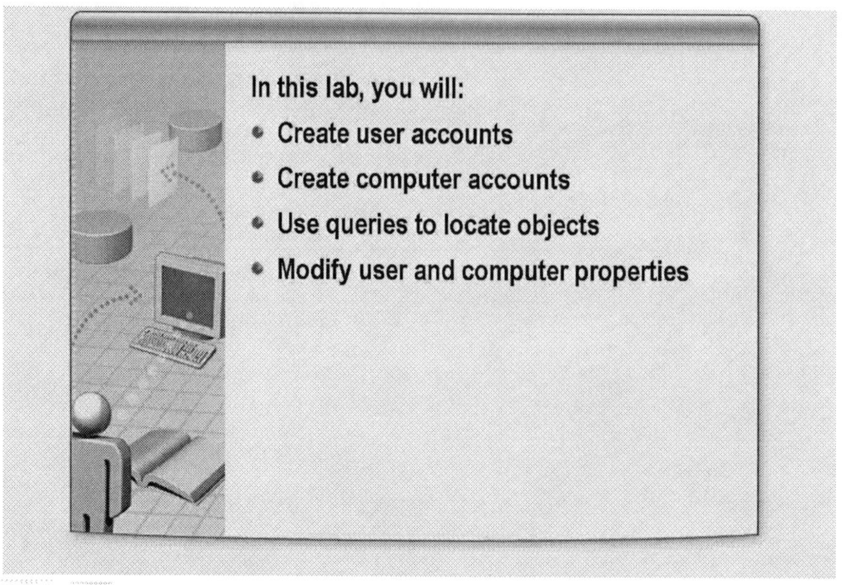
In this lab, you will:
Create user accounts
Create computer accounts
Use queries to locate objects
Modify user and computer properties

Objectives

After completing this lab, you will be able to:

- Create user accounts.
- Create computer accounts.
- Use queries to locate objects.
- Modify user and computer properties.

Prerequisites

To complete this lab, you must have the following virtual machines:

- DEN-DC1
- DEN-SRV1

Lab setup

Shut down the DEN-CL1 virtual machine without saving changes. Start the DEN-SRV1 virtual machine.

Estimated time to complete this lab: 20 minutes

Exercise 1
Creating User Accounts

In this exercise, you will use a custom MMC to create two new user accounts based on the sales template.

Scenario

Two new salespeople have been hired by Contoso Ltd. You need to create accounts for the new users in the Sales organizational unit in Active Directory.

Tasks	Specific Instructions
1. Create a custom MMC.	a. Log on to DEN-SRV1 as **Judy@contoso.msft** with the password of **Pa$$w0rd**. b. Create a custom MMC, and then add the **Active Directory Users and Computers** snap-in. c. Close the console, and save it as **AD_Admin** in the default location. d. Click **Start**, point to **All Programs**, point to **Administrative Tools**, and then launch **AD_Admin** by using the **Run as** command. Provide the domain administrator's credentials, **contoso\administrator**, with a password of **Pa$$w0rd**.
2. Create user accounts in the Sales organizational unit.	a. In **Active Directory Users and Computers**, click the **Sales** OU. b. Right-click the **Sales Template** user, and then click **Copy**. c. In the **Copy Object – User** dialog box, enter the following: • First Name: **Sunil** • Last Name: **Koduri** • User Logon Name: **Sunil** • Password: **Pa$$w0rd** d. Repeat the preceding steps to create another account with the following information: • First Name: **Jon** • Last Name: **Morris** • User Logon Name: **Jon** • Password: **Pa$$w0rd** e. Enable the accounts.
3. Verify that the template properties were transferred successfully.	a. Open the **Properties** dialog box for one of the accounts that you just created, and verify that the group membership, logon hours, and profile mappings are correct. Review the settings on the **General** tab and the **Organization** tab. b. What values did not transfer from the template?

Exercise 2
Creating Computer Accounts

In this exercise, you will create two new computer accounts.

Scenario

Two new network administrators have been hired by Contoso, Ltd. You added their user accounts earlier. Now you need to create accounts for their computers in the IT Admin organizational unit.

Task	Specific Instructions
1. Create two computer accounts for the new administrators.	a. On DEN-SRV1, in **Active Directory Users and Computers**, click the **IT Admin** organizational unit. b. Create a new computer account with the following parameters: • Name: **Admin2** • Give Kerim Hanif permissions to join the computer to the domain c. Create a second computer with the following parameters: • Name: **Admin3** • Give Luis Bonifaz permissions to join the computer to the domain

Exercise 3
Using Queries to Locate Objects

In this exercise, you will create a query to find users and import a query to find computer accounts.

Scenario

Because new salespeople are frequently hired, you need a query that will easily locate all the current users in the Sales department. You also need a query that will locate all the Sales department computers. Another administrator has built and shared that query. You will import it to you MMC.

Tasks	Specific Instructions
1. Create a saved query to find sales users.	a. Ensure that you are logged on to DEN-SRV1 as Judy Lew. Also make sure that the **AD_Admin** console is open. b. In **Active Directory Users and Computers**, create a new query in the **Saved Queries** folder named **Find Sales Users.** c. Configure the query to use **Find Users, Contacts and Groups.** d. In the **Find Users, Contacts and Groups** dialog box, click the **Advanced** tab. e. In the **Field** list, select **User – Department.** f. Ensure that **Starts with** is the condition, and type **Sales** in the **Value** field. The query should display all the users in the Sales department.
2. Import a query to locate the computer accounts in the Sales department.	a. Right-click the **Saved Queries** folder, and click **Import Query Definition.** b. Navigate to **\\DEN-DC1\admin_tools.** c. Select **Find_Sales_Computers.xml**, and click **Open.** d. Click **OK.** The query should display the three sales computers.

Exercise 4
Modifying User and Computer Properties

In this exercise, you will modify the properties of multiple users and computer accounts.

Scenario

The location of the Sales department has changed. You need to change the **Office** attribute for the users and the **Description** attribute for the computers in the Sales department.

Tasks	Specific Instructions
1. Use a saved query to locate all the Sales department users and update their **Office** attribute.	**a.** Ensure that you are logged on to DEN-SRV1 as Judy Lew. Also make sure that the **AD_Admin** console is open. **b.** In **Active Directory Users and Computers**, expand the **Saved Queries** folder, and then click the **Find Sales Users** query. *Select the first account, and then hold down the SHIFT key and select the last account in the list to select the entire list.* **c.** Right-click the selected accounts, and then click **Properties.** **d.** In the **Properties On Multiple Objects** dialog box, select the **Office** check box, and then type **Main Street** in the **Office** field.
2. Use the imported query to locate all the Sales computer accounts and modify their **Description** attribute.	**a.** In **Active Directory Users and Computers**, expand the **Saved Queries** folder, and then click the **Find Sales Department Computers** query. **b.** In the Details pane, select all of the computer accounts. **c.** Right-click the selected accounts, and then click **Properties.** **d.** On the **General** tab in the **Properties On Multiple Objects** dialog box, change the **Description** setting to **Sales Department.**
3. Complete the lab exercise.	**a.** Close all programs and shut down all computers. Do not save changes. **b.** To prepare for the next module, start the DEN-DC1 and DEN-SRV1 virtual computers.

Microsoft®

Module 3: Managing Groups

Contents

Overview

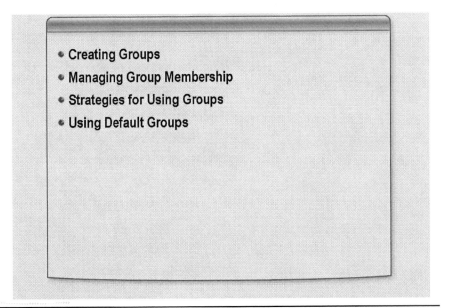

- Creating Groups
- Managing Group Membership
- Strategies for Using Groups
- Using Default Groups

Introduction

A *group* is a collection of user accounts. You use groups to efficiently manage access to domain resources, which helps simplify network maintenance and administration. You can use groups separately, or you can place one group within another to further simplify administration.

Before you can effectively use groups, you must understand the function of groups and the types of groups that you can create. The Active Directory® directory service supports different types of groups and also provides options to determine the group's scope, which is how the group can be used in multiple domains.

Objectives

After completing this module, you will be able to:

- Create groups.
- Manage group membership.
- Apply strategies for using groups.
- Manage default groups.

Lesson: Creating Groups

- What Are Groups?
- What Are Domain Functional Levels?
- What Are Global Groups?
- What Are Universal Groups?
- What Are Domain Local Groups?
- What Are Local Groups?
- Guidelines for Creating and Naming Groups
- Who Can Create Groups?
- Practice: Creating Groups

Introduction

The information in this lesson presents the skills and knowledge that you need to create groups.

Lesson objectives

After completing this lesson, you will be able to:

- Explain what groups are and the purpose of groups, group types, and group scopes.
- Identify the domain functional levels.
- Describe global groups.
- Describe universal groups.
- Describe domain local groups.
- Describe local groups.
- Apply best practices for creating and naming groups.
- Explain who can create groups.
- Create groups.

What Are Groups?

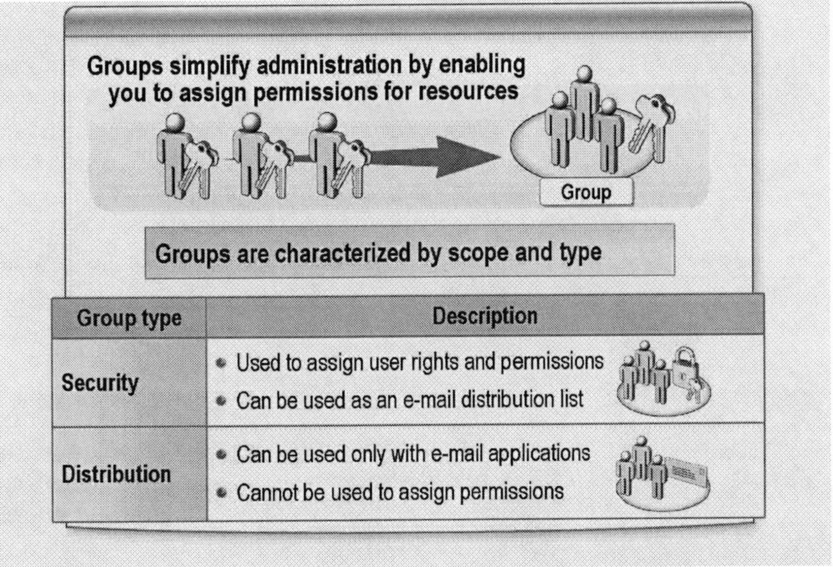

Definition

Groups are a collection of user and computer accounts that you can manage as a single unit. Groups:

- Simplify administration by enabling you to grant permissions for resources once to a group rather than to many user accounts individually.
- Can be located in Active Directory or local to an individual computer.
- Are characterized by scope and type.
- Can be nested, which means that you can add a group to another group.

Group scopes

The group scope defines whether the group spans multiple domains or is limited to a single domain. Group scopes enable you to use groups to grant permissions. The group scope defines:

- The domains from which you can add members to the group.
- The domains in which you can use the group to grant permissions.
- The domains in which you can nest the group within other groups.

The group scope also specifies who the members of the group are. Membership rules govern the members that a group can contain and the groups of which a group can be a member. Group members consist of user accounts, computer accounts, and other groups.

To assign the correct members to groups and to use nesting, you must understand the characteristics of the group scope. The group scopes in Active Directory are as follows:

- Global
- Domain local
- Universal

Group types

You use groups to organize user accounts, computer accounts, and other group accounts into manageable units. Working with groups instead of individual users helps simplify network maintenance and administration. The group types in Active Directory are:

- Security groups

  You use security groups to assign user rights and permissions to groups of users and computers. Rights specify what members of a security group can do in a domain or forest, and permissions specify what resources a member of a group can access on the network.

  You can also use security groups to send e-mail messages to multiple users. Sending an e-mail message to the group sends the message to all members of the group. Therefore, security groups have the capabilities of distribution groups.

- Distribution groups

  You use distribution groups with e-mail applications, such as Microsoft® Exchange Server, to send e-mail messages to collections of users. The primary purpose of this type of group is to gather related objects, not to grant permissions.

  Distribution groups are not security-enabled, meaning that they cannot be used to assign permissions. If you need a group for controlling access to shared resources, create a security group.

  Even though security groups have all the capabilities of distribution groups, distribution groups are still required, because some applications can use only distribution groups.

Both distribution and security groups support the three group scopes.

What Are Domain Functional Levels?

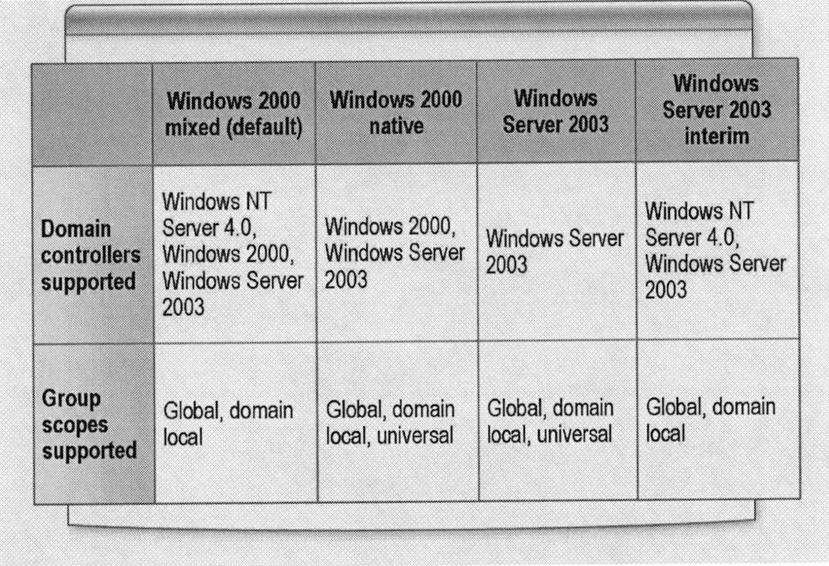

	Windows 2000 mixed (default)	Windows 2000 native	Windows Server 2003	Windows Server 2003 interim
Domain controllers supported	Windows NT Server 4.0, Windows 2000, Windows Server 2003	Windows 2000, Windows Server 2003	Windows Server 2003	Windows NT Server 4.0, Windows Server 2003
Group scopes supported	Global, domain local	Global, domain local, universal	Global, domain local, universal	Global, domain local

Group characteristics

The characteristics of groups in Active Directory depend on the domain functional level. Domain functionality enables features that will affect the entire domain and that domain only. Four domain functional levels are available: Microsoft Windows® 2000 mixed, Windows 2000 native, Windows Server™ 2003 interim, and Microsoft Windows Server 2003. By default, domains operate at the Windows 2000 mixed functional level. You can raise the domain functional level to either Windows 2000 native or Windows Server 2003.

The table in the preceding slide lists the domain functional levels and the domain controllers and group scopes that they support.

Note You can convert a group from a security group to a distribution group, and vice versa, at any time, but only if the domain functional level is set to Windows 2000 native or higher.

Additional reading

For more information about raising functional levels, see article 322692, "How to Raise Domain and Functional Levels in Windows Server 2003," on the Microsoft Help and Support Web site.

What Are Global Groups?

	Global group rules
Membership can include	• Mixed functional level: **User and computer accounts from same domain** • Native functional level: **User and computer accounts and global groups from same domain**
Can be a member of	• Mixed functional level: **Domain local groups** • Native functional level: **Universal and domain local groups in any trusting domain and global groups in the same domain**
Scope	**Visible in its own domain and all trusting domains**
Permissions	**All domains in the forest and trusting domains**

Definition

A global group is a security or distribution group that can contain users, groups, and computers that are from the same domain as the global group. You can use global security groups to assign user rights, delegate authority to Active Directory objects, or assign permissions to resources in any domain in the forest or any other trusting domain in another forest.

Characteristics of global groups

The following summarizes the characteristics of global groups:

- **Membership can include:**
  - In Windows 2000 mixed and Windows 2003 interim functional levels, global groups can contain user and computer accounts that are from the same domain as the global group.
  - In Windows 2000 native and Windows Server 2003 functional levels, global groups can contain user accounts, computer accounts, and global groups that are from the same domain as the global group.
- **Global groups can be a member of:**
  - In Windows 2000 mixed and Windows 2003 interim functional levels, a global group can be a member of only domain local or local groups.
  - In Windows 2000 native and Windows Server 2003 functional levels, a global group can be a member of universal, local, and domain local groups in any trusting domain and global groups that are from the same domain as the global group.
- **Scope:**

  A global group is visible within its domain and all trusting domains, which includes all of the domains in the forest.
- **Permissions:**

  You can grant permissions to a global group within its domain and all trusting domains.

When to use global groups

Because global groups have a forest-wide visibility, do not create them for domain-specific resource access. Use a global group to organize users who share the same job tasks and have similar network access requirements. A different group type might be more appropriate for controlling access to resources within a domain.

GLOBAL GROUPS = USED TO ORGANIZE USERS FROM THE DOMAIN WHERE THE GROUP ITSELF LIVES

G CONTOSE [illegible]

IN NATIVE MODE YOU CAN NEST OTHER GLOBAL GROUPS

What Are Universal Groups?

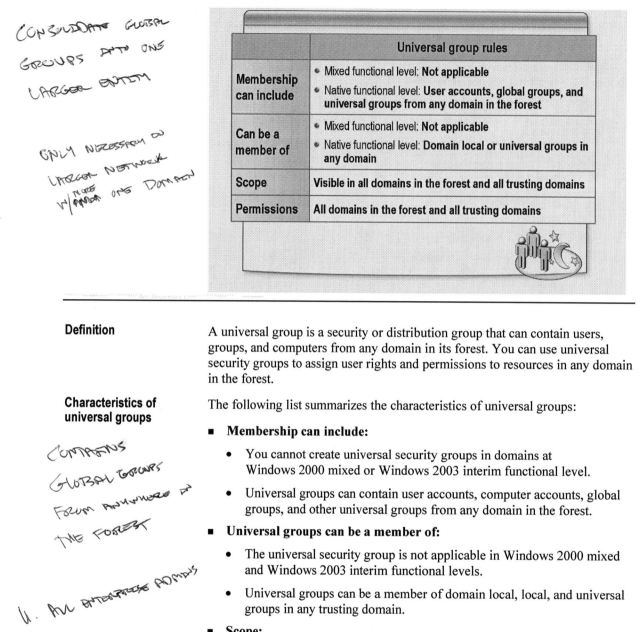

	Universal group rules
Membership can include	• Mixed functional level: **Not applicable** • Native functional level: **User accounts, global groups, and universal groups from any domain in the forest**
Can be a member of	• Mixed functional level: **Not applicable** • Native functional level: **Domain local or universal groups in any domain**
Scope	Visible in all domains in the forest and all trusting domains
Permissions	All domains in the forest and all trusting domains

Definition

A universal group is a security or distribution group that can contain users, groups, and computers from any domain in its forest. You can use universal security groups to assign user rights and permissions to resources in any domain in the forest.

Characteristics of universal groups

The following list summarizes the characteristics of universal groups:

- **Membership can include:**
  - You cannot create universal security groups in domains at Windows 2000 mixed or Windows 2003 interim functional level.
  - Universal groups can contain user accounts, computer accounts, global groups, and other universal groups from any domain in the forest.
- **Universal groups can be a member of:**
  - The universal security group is not applicable in Windows 2000 mixed and Windows 2003 interim functional levels.
  - Universal groups can be a member of domain local, local, and universal groups in any trusting domain.
- **Scope:**

  Universal groups are visible in all domains in the forest and all trusting domains.
- **Permissions:**

  You can grant permissions to universal groups for all domains in the forest and all trusting domains. The domain must be at the Windows 2000 native or high functional level.

When to use universal groups

Use universal groups to nest global groups so that you can assign permissions to related resources in multiple domains. You can use universal distribution groups to send mail to groups of users. Universal distribution groups can be created in any domain in a Windows 2003 forest in any functional level.

What Are Domain Local Groups?

	Domain local group rules
Membership can include	• Mixed functional level and Windows interim 2003: **User and computer accounts and global groups from any trusted domain** • Native functional level: **User and computer accounts, global and universal groups from any domain in the forest or trusted domains, plus domain local groups from the same domain**
Can be a member of	• Mixed functional level and Windows interim 2003: None • Native functional level: **Domain local groups in the same domain**
Scope	**Visible only in its own domain**
Permissions	**Domain to which the domain local group belongs**

Definition

A domain local group is a security or distribution group that can contain other domain local groups that are from its own domain. It can also contain universal groups, global groups, and accounts from any domain in the forest or any trusted domain. You can use domain local security groups to assign user rights and permissions to resources only in the same domain where the domain local group is located.

Characteristics of domain local groups

The following list summarizes the characteristics of domain local groups:

- **Membership can include:**
  - In Windows 2000 mixed and Windows 2003 interim functional levels, domain local groups can contain user accounts, computer accounts, and global groups from any trusted domain. Member servers cannot use domain local groups in Windows 2000 mixed and Windows 2003 interim functional levels.
  - In Windows 2000 native and Windows Server 2000 functional levels, domain local groups can contain user accounts, computer accounts, global groups, and universal groups from any domain in the forest or trusted domains and domain local groups that are from the same domain as the domain local group.
- **Domain local groups can be a member of:**
  - In Windows 2000 mixed and Windows 2003 interim functional levels, a domain local group cannot be a member of any group.
  - In Windows 2000 native and Windows Server 2000 functional levels, a domain local group can be a member of domain local groups that are from the same domain as the domain local group.

- **Scope:**

  A domain local group is visible only in the domain that the domain local group belongs to.

- **Permissions:**

  You can assign permissions to a domain local group for the domain that the domain local group belongs to.

When to use domain local groups

Use a domain local group to assign permissions to resources that are located in the same domain as the domain local group. You can place all global groups that need to share the same resources into the appropriate domain local group.

What Are Local Groups?

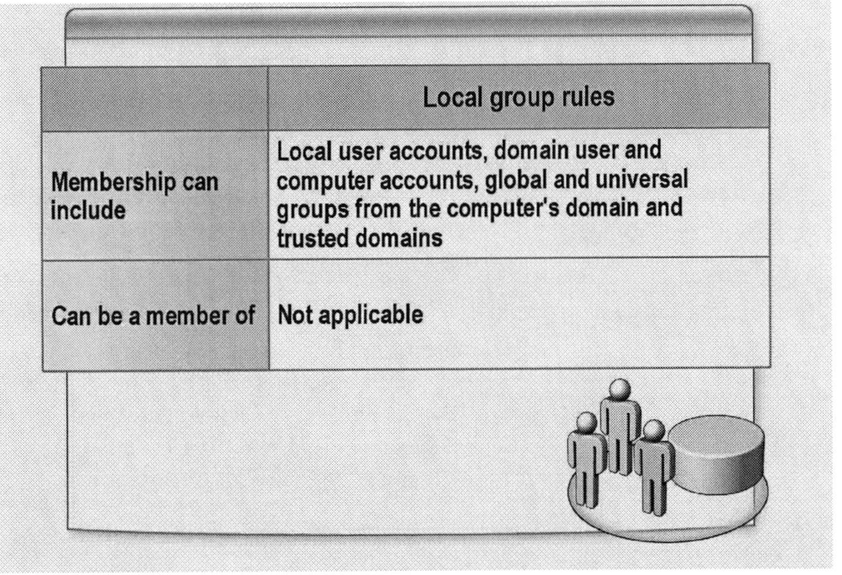

	Local group rules
Membership can include	Local user accounts, domain user and computer accounts, global and universal groups from the computer's domain and trusted domains
Can be a member of	Not applicable

Definition

A local group is a collection of user accounts or domain groups created on a member server or a stand-alone server. You can create local groups to grant permissions for resources residing on the local computer. Windows 2000 and Windows Server 2003 create local groups in the local security database. Local groups can contain users, computers, global groups, and universal groups.

Because groups with a domain local scope are sometimes referred to as local groups, it is important to distinguish between a local group and a group with domain local scope. Local groups are sometimes referred to as machine local groups to distinguish them from domain local groups.

Characteristics of local groups

The following list summarizes the characteristics of local groups:

- In a workgroup environment, local groups can contain only local user accounts from the computer where you create the local group. If the computer is a member of a domain, the local groups can contain domain user and computer accounts, global groups, and universal groups from the computer's domain and trusted domains. Local groups cannot be members of any other group.

When to use local groups

The following are guidelines for using local groups:

- You can use local groups only on the computer where you create the local groups. Local group permissions provide access to resources only on the computer where you created the local group.
- You can use local groups on computers running currently supported Microsoft client operating systems and member servers running Windows Server 2003. You cannot create local groups on domain controllers, because domain controllers cannot have a security database that is independent of the database in Active Directory.
- You can create local groups to limit the ability of local users and groups to access network resources when you do not want to create domain groups.
- Because local groups do not have any built-in redundancy, be sure that the registry of the computer where local groups are used is backed up along with the resources on the computer. In an environment where access to the data is essential, it is better to use domain local groups that are replicated to multiple domain controllers automatically.

Guidelines for Creating and Naming Groups

- Create groups in organizational units by using the following naming considerations:
  - Naming conventions for security groups
    - Incorporate the scope in the group name
    - Should reflect the group ownership
    - Use a descriptor to identify the assigned permissions
  - Naming conventions for distribution groups
    - Use short alias names
    - Do not include a user's alias name in the display name
    - Allow a maximum of five co-owners of a single distribution group

Introduction

In Active Directory, groups are created in domains. You use Active Directory Users and Computers to create groups in their appropriate containers based on the administrative model.

A standardized naming convention can help you locate and identify groups more easily in a large environment.

Choosing a domain or an organizational unit

Choose the particular domain or organizational unit where you create a group based on the administration requirements for the group.

For example, suppose that your directory has multiple organizational units based on departments. You could create a managers global group in each departmental organizational unit to house the managers accounts and then consolidate them by nesting all those global groups into a Domain_Managers global group.

Important Group Policy assigned to an organizational unit does not affect the members of a group if the user accounts of those members are not located in the same container as the group. For example, if Don Hall is a member of the global group named Domain_Managers, but his user account does not reside in the same container as Domain_Managers, any Group Policy object assigned to the container that contains that global group will not be applied to his user account.

In a multidomain environment, you can nest the groups into universal groups (or other groups with global scope) that can be used elsewhere in the forest. It might be more efficient to nest global groups if the domain functional level is set to Windows 2000 native or higher, the domain contains a hierarchy of organizational units, and administration is delegated to administrators at each organizational unit.

Naming guidelines

A large organization might have many security and distribution groups. The following naming conventions help you manage these groups. Organizations develop their own naming conventions for their security and distribution groups. A group name should identify the scope, the type, who the group was created for, and what permissions the group can have.

Security groups

Consider the following when defining a naming convention for security groups:

- **Scope of security groups:**

  Although the group type and scope are displayed as the group type in Active Directory Users and Computers, organizations can incorporate the scope in the naming convention of the group name.

  For example, Contoso, Ltd., identifies the scope of security groups by adding a first letter to the group name:

  - **G** IT Admins

    G for global groups

  - **U** Enterprise IT Admins

    U for universal groups

  - **DL** IT Resources Full Control

    DL for domain local groups

- **Ownership of the security group:**

  The name for any domain-level security group, whether universal, global, or domain local, should clearly identify function by including the name of the division or team that owns the group.

  The following is an example of a naming convention that Contoso, Ltd., might use to identify group ownership:

  - G **Marketing** Managers
  - DL **IT Admins** Full Control

- **Domain name:**

  In a multidomain environment, the domain name or abbreviation should be placed at the beginning of the group name. For example:

  - G **Contoso** Marketing

- **Purpose of the security group:**

  You can also include the business purpose of the group and maximum permissions the group should have on the network. This naming convention is more applicable to domain local or local groups.

  - DL IT Contoso **OU Admins**
  - DL IT Resources **Full Control**

Distribution groups

Because distribution groups are used only for e-mail purposes, the naming convention must be relevant to an end user.

When defining a naming convention for distribution groups, consider the following:

- **E-mail names:**
  - *Length.* Use a short alias name. To conform to current downstream data standards, the minimum length of this field is three characters and the maximum length is eight characters.
  - *Allowed characters.* You can use all ASCII characters. The only allowed special characters are the hyphen (-) and underscore (_).
  - *Special designations.* Do not use the following character combinations for distributions groups:
    - An underscore (_) as the beginning character of the group name of the alias name
    - A first name or combination of first name and last name that might easily be confused with a user account name
- **Display names:**
  - *User alias names.* For standardization purposes, do not include a user's alias name as part of a display name (for example, Jhay Direct Reports). Include the full name (for example, Jeff Hay's Direct Reports).
  - *Social discussions.* Distribution groups for social discussions should not be allowed, because public folders are a more efficient means of transmitting and storing high-volume communications associated with social discussions. Because a post is visible to multiple users, both network traffic and data storage are minimized if you use public folders instead of corporate distribution groups.
  - *Length.* The maximum length of this field is 40 characters. Abbreviations are acceptable as long as the meaning is clear.
  - *Top of the address book.* Do not use the word *A*, numbers, special characters (especially quotation marks), or a space to begin a description. This makes the name appear at the top of the address book. The address book should begin with individual user names starting with the letter *A*.
  - *Special characters.* Slashes (/) are acceptable in display names, but do not use them in front of server names. Do not use more than one apostrophe (') and do not use the following special characters: " * @ # $ % | [ ] ; < > =
- **Ownership:**

  There can be a maximum of five co-owners of a single distribution group.

Local groups

A local group name cannot be identical to any other group or user name on the local computer being administered. A local group name cannot consist solely of periods (.) or spaces. It can contain up to 256 uppercase or lowercase characters, except the following:
" / \ [ ] : ; | = , + * ? < >

Who Can Create Groups?

- In the domain:
  - Account Operators group
  - Domain Admins group
  - Enterprise Admins group
  - Or users with appropriate delegated authority
- On the local computer:
  - Power Users group
  - Administrators group on the local computer
  - Or users with appropriate delegated authority

Introduction

Groups provide administrators with the ability to assign permissions to multiple security principals at one time. The authority to create groups is limited in Active Directory and at the local computer level.

Who can create groups in the domain?

To create groups in Active Directory, you must be a member of the Account Operators group, the Domain Admins group, or the Enterprise Admins group, or you must be delegated the appropriate permissions. As a security best practice, consider logging on with a regular user account and using **Run as** when creating groups.

Who can create local groups?

To create local groups, you must be a member of the Power Users group or the Administrators group on the local computer, or you must be delegated the appropriate authority. If the computer is joined to a domain, members of the Domain Admins group are able to perform this procedure. As a security best practice, consider using **Run as** to perform this procedure.

Tools to create groups

You can use the following tools to create local and domain groups:

- *Local Users and Groups snap-in in Computer Management.* Allows you to create local groups.
- *Active Directory Users and Computers.* Allows you to create groups in any trusted domain where you have authority.
- *Command line.* Allows you to create global, domain local, or universal groups For example, you can use the **dsadd** command to create a global security group named Finance Users. At a command prompt, you would type the following:

  dsadd group "cn=Finance Users,ou=finance,dc=contoso,dc=msft" -samid FinanceUsers -secgrp yes -scope g 

The following table lists the most commonly used syntax for the **dsadd** group command.

Value	Description
groupDN	Specifies the distinguished name of the group object that you want to add
samid	Specifies the Security Accounts Manager (SAM) name as the unique SAM account name for this group (for example, operators)
secgrp yes | no	Specifies whether the group you want to add is a security group (**yes**) or a distribution group (**no**)
scope l | g | u	Specifies whether the scope of the group you want to add is domain local (**l**), global (**g**), or universal (**u**)

Note To view the complete syntax for this command, type **dsadd group /?** at a command prompt.

Practice: Creating Groups

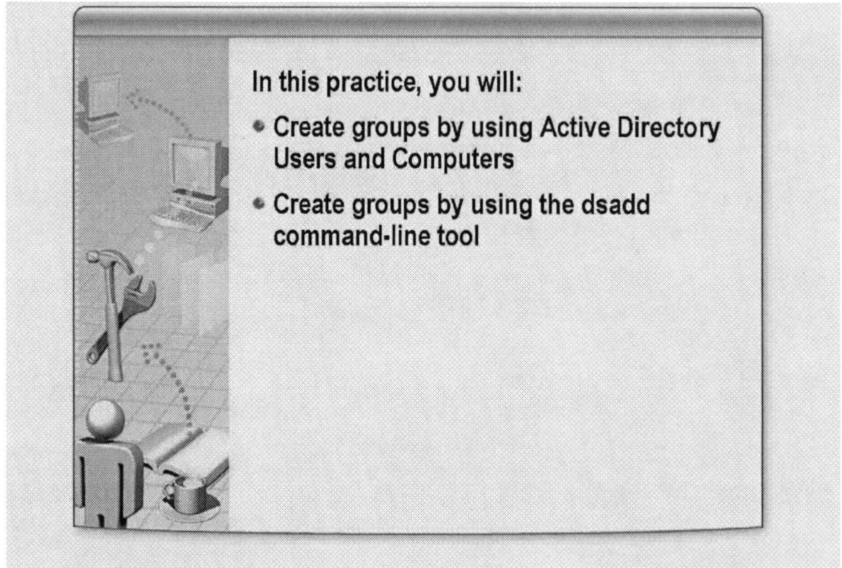

Objective

In this practice, you will:

- Create groups by using Active Directory Users and Computers.
- Create groups by using the **dsadd** command-line tool.

Instructions

Ensure that the DEN-DC1 virtual machine is running.

Practice

► **Create groups by using Active Directory Users and Computers**

1. Log on to DEN-DC1 as **Administrator**, with a password of **Pa$$w0rd**.
2. Open **Active Directory Users and Computers**, and select the **Graphics** organizational unit.
3. Right-click the **Graphics** organizational unit, point to **New**, and then click **Group**.
4. In the **New Object – Group** dialog box, ensure that **Global** is selected as the group scope and that **Security** is selected as the group type.
5. Type **G Graphics Managers** in the **Group Name** field.
6. Click **OK**.
7. Repeat steps 3 through 6 to create a second global group named **G Graphics Users**.
8. Create a new domain local group, and then type **DL Graphics Managers** in the **Group Name** field.
9. Change the **Group Scope** to **Domain local**.
10. Click **OK**.
11. Repeat steps 8 through 10 to create the final domain local group, named **DL Graphics Users**.

Practice: Using the command line

► **Create groups by using the dsadd command-line tool**

1. Open a command prompt window.
2. Enter the following command and then press ENTER:

   dsadd group "cn=IT Admin,ou=IT Admin,dc=contoso,dc=msft" –samid ITadmin –secgrp yes –scope g

3. Close all windows and log off of DEN-DC1.

Important Do not shut down the virtual machine.

Lesson: Managing Group Membership

- Determining Group Membership
- Adding and Removing Members from a Group
- Practice: Managing Group Membership

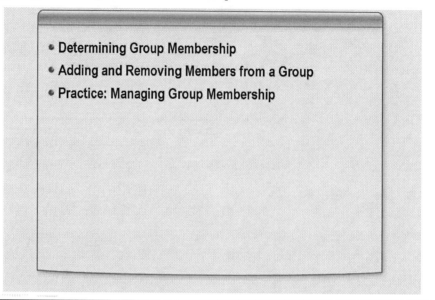

Introduction

Because many users often require access to different resources throughout an organization, administrators might have to grant membership to groups that reside in Active Directory or on local computers.

Lesson objectives

After completing this lesson, you will be able to:

- Determine the membership of a group.
- Add members to and remove members from a group.
- Manage group memberships.

Determining Group Membership

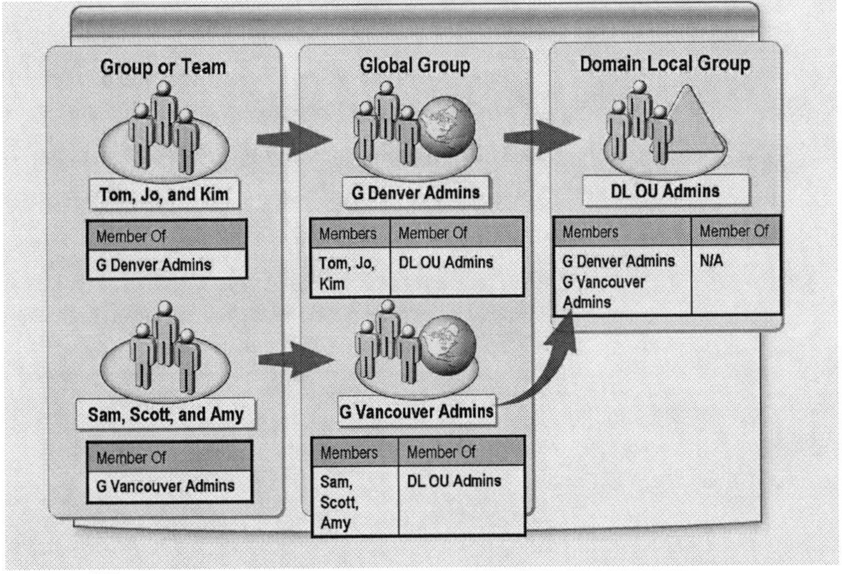

Introduction

All user accounts have a **Member Of** attribute that lists all of the groups that the user is a member of. All groups have a **Members** attribute and a **Member Of** attribute. The **Members** attribute lists all user accounts or other group accounts that are members of the group. The preceding illustration describes the **Members** and **Member Of** attributes.

Members and Member Of tabs

Tom, Jo, and Kim are *members of* the G Denver Admins global group. The global group G Denver Admins is a *member of* the domain local group DL OU Admins.

Sam, Scott, and Amy are *members of* the G Vancouver Admins global group. The global group G Vancouver Admins is a *member of* the domain local group DL OU Admins.

The following table summarizes the information in the slide.

User or group	Members	Member Of
Tom, Jo, Kim	N/A	G Denver Admins
G Denver Admins	Tom, Jo, Kim	DL OU Admins
Sam, Scott, Amy	N/A	G Vancouver Admins
G Vancouver Admins	Sam, Scott, Amy	DL OU Admins
DL OU Admins	G Denver Admins G Vancouver Admins	N/A

By viewing the **Members** and **Member Of** attributes, you can determine which groups a user belongs to or which groups a group belongs to.

Determining group membership

After you add users to groups, Active Directory updates the **Member Of** attribute of their user accounts.

To determine the groups that a user is a member of:

1. In **Active Directory Users and Computers**, in the domain node, click **Users** or click the container that holds the user account.
2. In the Details pane, right-click a user account, and then click **Properties**.
3. In the **Properties** dialog box, click the **Member Of** tab.

Note You do not need administrative credentials to perform this task. Therefore, as a security best practice, consider performing this task as a user without administrative credentials.

Using a command line

To determine the groups a user is a member of by using **dsget**:

1. Open a command prompt window.
2. Type **dsget user** *UserDN* **-memberof** at the command prompt.

Value	Description
UserDN	Specifies the distinguished name of the user object for which you want to display group membership

---

Note To view the complete syntax for this command, type **dsget user /?** at a command prompt.

Adding and Removing Members from a Group

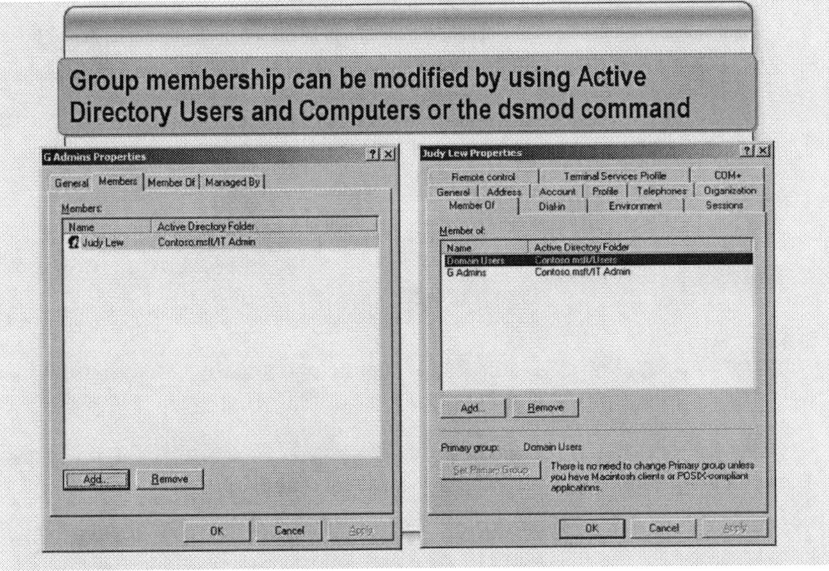
Group membership can be modified by using Active Directory Users and Computers or the dsmod command
G Admins Properties
Judy Lew Properties

Introduction

After creating a group, you can add members by using Active Directory Users and Computers. Members of groups can include user accounts, computers, or other groups. You can modify membership from the user account or the group account Properties dialog box.

Using Active Directory Users and Computers to modify group membership

To add members to or remove members from a group by configuring the group properties:

1. In Active Directory Users and Computers, in the console tree, click the folder that contains the group to which you want to add a member.
2. In the Details pane, right-click the group, and then click **Properties**.
3. In the **Properties** dialog box, on the **Members** tab, click **Add**.

   If you want to remove a member from the group, click the member, and then click **Remove**.
4. In the **Select Users, Contact, Computers, or Groups** dialog box, in the **Enter the object names to select** box, type the name of the user, group, or computer that you want to add to the group, and then click **OK**.

Tip You can also add a user account or group by using the **Member Of** tab in the **Properties** dialog box for that user account or group. Use this method to quickly add the same user or group to multiple groups.

To add a user to a group by using the shortcut menu:

1. In **Active Directory Users and Computers**, select the user that you want to add to a group.
2. Right-click the account, and then click **Add to a group**.
3. In the **Select Group** dialog box, in the **Enter the object names to select** box, type the name of the group that you want to add to the user to, and then click **OK**.

Tip You can also use the shortcut menu for a user that you have located by using the **find** command.

Using dsmod to modify group membership

To modify group membership by using **dsmod**, open a command prompt window, and use the following syntax:

Dsmod group *groupDN* [{**-addmbr** | **-rmmbr** | **-chmbr**} *memberDN*...]
{**-addmbr** | **-rmmbr** | **-chmbr**} **MemberDN** ...

Members specified by **MemberDN ...** are to be added to, removed from, or replaced in the group. Only one of these parameters can be specified in any single command invocation. **MemberDN ...** specifies the distinguished names of one or more members to be added to, deleted from, or replaced in the group specified by **GroupDN**. Each member must be listed using a distinguished name.

Practice: Managing Group Membership

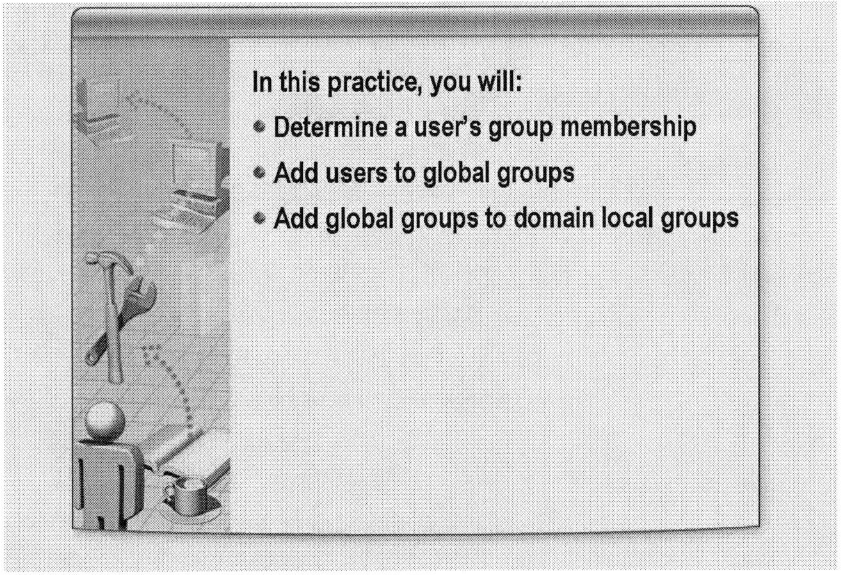

Objectives

In this practice, you will:

- Determine a user's group membership.
- Add users to global groups.
- Add global groups to domain local groups.

Instructions

Ensure that the DEN-DC1 virtual machine is running.

Practice

► **Determine a user's group membership**

1. Log on to DEN-DC1 using the **Administrator** account with the password of **Pa$$w0rd**.
2. Open **Active Directory Users and Computers**.
3. Click the **Sales** organizational unit.
4. Open the **Properties** dialog box for **Don Hall.** Click the **Member Of** tab. What groups is **Don Hall** a member of?

   ____

5. In the **Sales** organizational unit, open the **Properties** dialog box for the **G Sales** group.
   a. Click the **Members** tab. Who is in the G Sales group?

      ____

   b. Click the **Member Of** tab. What groups does **G Sales** belong to?

      ____

► **Add users to global groups**

1. In **Active Directory Users and Computers**, right-click the domain node, and then click **Find.**
2. In the **Find Users, Contacts, and Groups** dialog box, click the **Advanced** tab.
3. In the **Field** list, point to **User** and then click **Department.**
4. Select **Is (exactly)** in the **Condition** list, and then type **Graphics** in the value field.
5. Click **Add** to add the criteria to the condition list.
6. Click **Find Now.**

   The query should return two users, **Graphics User** and **Graphics Manager.**
7. Select both users. Right-click, and then click **Add to a group.**
8. In the **Select Group** dialog box, type **G** in the **Object Name** field, and then click **Check Names.**

   (A list of all global groups will be displayed because your naming convention uses the first letter *G* to distinguish global groups.)
9. Select **G Graphics Users** in the list.
10. Click **OK.**
11. Click **OK** again to add the accounts to the G Graphics Users group.
12. Click **OK** to confirm the group addition.
13. Select just the **Graphics Manager** user account, right-click, and then click **Add to a group.**
14. Repeat steps 8 through 12 to add **Graphics Manager** to the **G Graphics Managers** global group.
15. Close the **Find Users, Contacts, and Groups** dialog box.

► **Add global groups to domain local groups**

1. In Active Directory Users and Computers, click the **Graphics** organizational unit.
2. In the Details pane, double-click **DL Graphics Users.**
3. Click the **Members** tab.
4. Click **Add.**
5. In the **Select Users, Contacts, Computers, or Groups** dialog box, type **G Graphics Users** in the object name field, and then click **Check Names.**
6. Click **OK** twice.
7. Repeat steps 2 through 6 to add the **G Graphics Managers** global group to the **DL Graphics Managers** domain local group.
8. Close Active Directory Users and Computers.
9. Log off of DEN-DC1.

Important Do not shut down the virtual machines.

Lesson: Strategies for Using Groups

- Multimedia: Strategy for Using Groups in a Single Domain
- What Is Group Nesting?
- Group Strategies
- Class Discussion: Using Groups in a Single-Domain or Multiple-Domain Environment
- Practice: Nesting Groups and Creating Universal Groups
- Modifying the Scope or Type of a Group?
- Why Assign a Manager to a Group?
- Practice: Changing the Scope and Assigning a Manager to a Group

Introduction

To use groups effectively, you need strategies for applying different group scopes. This lesson covers the skills and knowledge that you need to use groups optimally by employing different strategies with groups.

Lesson objectives

After completing this lesson, you will be able to:

- Explain the A G DL P strategy for using groups in a single domain.
- Describe group nesting.
- Describe the following strategies for using groups:
  - A G P
  - A G DL P
  - A G U DL P
  - A G L P
- Implement strategies for using groups.
- Configure group nesting using universal groups.
- Explain what it means to modify the scope or type of a group.
- Explain why you assign a manager to a group.
- Change group scopes and assign group managers.

Multimedia: Strategy for Using Groups in a Single Domain

File location

To view the *Strategy for Using Groups in a Single Domain* presentation, open the Web page on the Student Materials compact disc, click **Multimedia**, and then click the title of the presentation. Do not open this presentation until the instructor tells you to.

Key points

The A G DL P model represents a group strategy where users are placed into global groups, global groups are placed into domain local groups and domain local groups are assigned permission to resources.

User accounts → Global groups → Domain local groups ← Permissions

(A) (G) (DL) (P)

What Is Group Nesting?

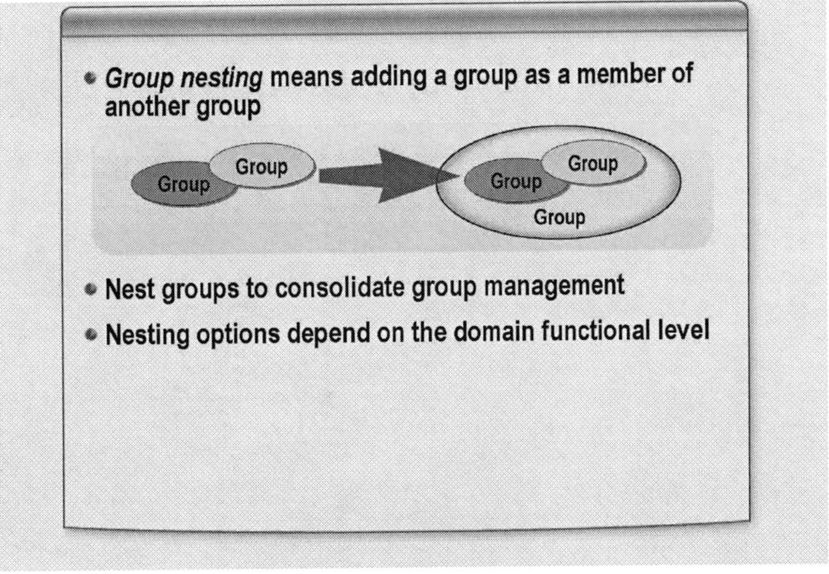

Introduction

By using nesting, you can add a group as a member of another group. You can nest groups to consolidate group management. Nesting increases the member accounts that are affected by a single action and reduces replication traffic caused by the replication of changes in group membership.

Nesting options

Your nesting options depend on the domain functional level of your Windows Server 2003 domain. In domains where the domain functional level is set to Windows 2000 native or Windows Server 2003, group membership is determined as follows:

- Universal groups can have as their members: user accounts, computer accounts, universal groups, and global groups from any trusted domain.
- Global groups can have as their members: user accounts, computer accounts, and global groups from the same domain.
- Domain local groups can have as their members: user accounts, computer accounts, universal groups, and global groups, all from any trusted domain. They can also have other domain local groups from within the same domain.

You cannot create security groups with universal scope in domains where the domain functional level is set to Windows 2000 mixed or Windows 2003 interim.

Note Minimize the levels of nesting. A single level of nesting is the most effective method, because tracking permissions is more complex with multiple levels.

Also, troubleshooting becomes difficult if you must trace permissions through multiple levels of nesting. Therefore, document group membership to keep track of permissions.

Group Strategies

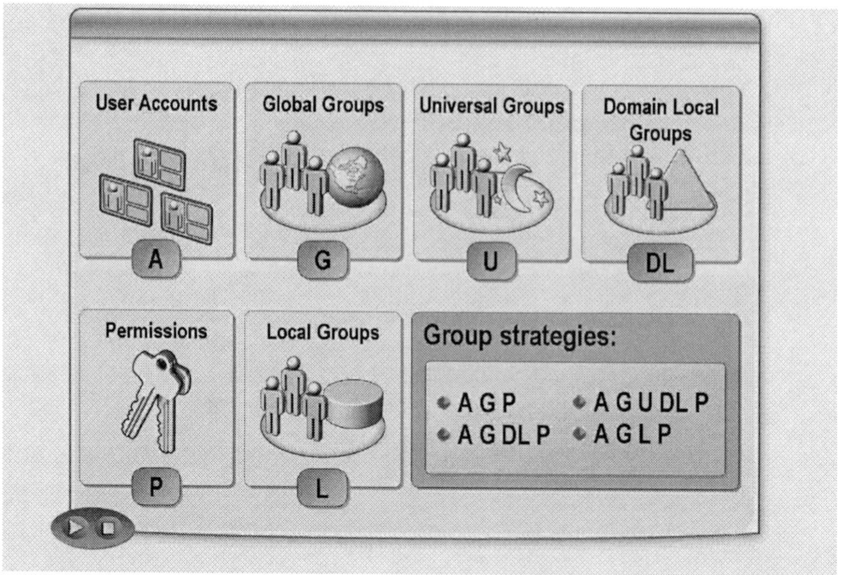

Introduction

To use groups effectively, you need strategies for applying the different group scopes. The strategy that you choose depends on the Windows network environment of your organization. In a single domain, the common practice is to use global and domain local groups to grant permissions for network resources. In a network with multiple domains, you can incorporate nested global or universal groups into your strategy.

A G P

With A G P, you place user accounts (A) in global groups (G), and you grant permissions (P) to the global groups. The limitation of this strategy is that it complicates administration when you use multiple domains. If global groups from multiple domains require the same permissions, you must grant permissions to each global group individually.

When to use the A G P strategy

Use A G P for forests with one domain and very few users and to which you will never add other domains.

A G P has the following advantages:

- Groups are not nested and therefore troubleshooting might be easier.
- Accounts belong to a single group scope.

A G P has the following disadvantages:

- Every time a user authenticates with a resource, the server must check the global group membership to determine whether the user is still a member of the group.
- Performance degrades, because a global group is not cached.

Note Another strategy might be to put users directly into domain local groups and not use global groups. The A DL P strategy has similar characteristics and could be suitable in the same circumstances.

A G DL P

With A G DL P, you place user accounts (A) in global groups (G), place the global groups in domain local groups (DL), and then grant permissions (P) to the domain local groups. This strategy creates flexibility for network growth and reduces the number of times you must set permissions.

When to use the A G DL P strategy

Use A G DL P for a forest consisting of one or more domains and to which you might have to add future domains.

A G DL P has the following advantages:

- Domains are flexible.
- Resource owners require less access to Active Directory to flexibly secure their resources.

A G DL P has the following disadvantage:

- A tiered management structure is more complex to set up initially, but easier to manage over time.

A G U DL P

With A G U DL P, you place user accounts (A) in global groups (G), place the global groups in universal groups (U), place the universal groups in domain local groups (DL), and then grant permissions (P) to the domain local groups.

When to use the A G U DL P strategy

Use A G U DL P for a forest with more than one domain so that administrators can consolidate global groups from multiple domains into one universal group. That universal group could then be placed into any domain local group in any trusting domain and thereby grant rights or permissions to many global groups across multiple domains with one action.

A G U DL P has the following advantages:

- There is flexibility across the forest.
- It enables centralized administration.

Note Domain local groups should not be used to assign permissions to Active Directory objects in a forest with more than one domain because domain local groups cannot be evaluated in other domains. For more information, see article 231273, "Group Type and Scope Usage in Windows," on the Microsoft Help and Support Web site.

A G U DL P has the following disadvantages:

- The membership of universal groups is stored in the global catalog.

  Note The global catalog is a domain controller that stores a copy of all Active Directory objects in a forest. The global catalog stores a full copy of all objects in Active Directory for its host domain and a partial copy of all objects for all other domains in the forest.

- It might be necessary to add more global catalog servers.
- There might be global catalog replication latency. When referring to the global catalog, *latency* is the time it takes to replicate a change to each global catalog server in the forest.

There is a disadvantage to using universal groups only if the universal groups have a very dynamic membership with a lot of global catalog replication traffic as the membership changes in a multidomain forest. With A G U DL P, this is less of an issue, because the membership of universal groups is relatively static (that is, the universal group has global groups, not individual users, as members).

Important Even if you do not use universal groups, in native functional level, a global catalog server must be available to determine whether a universal group membership exists in order for users to have a successful logon. If you are sure you will never use universal groups, you can disable this requirement. For more information, see article 241789, "How to disable the requirement that a global catalog server be available to validate user logons," on the Microsoft Help and Support Web site.

A G L P

Use the A G L P strategy to place user accounts in a global group and grant permissions to the local group. One limitation of this strategy is that you cannot grant permissions for resources outside the local computer.

Therefore, place user accounts in a global group, add the global group to the local group, and then grant permissions to the local group. With this strategy, you can use the same global group on multiple local computers.

Note Use domain local groups whenever possible. Use local groups only when a domain local group has not been created for this purpose.

When to use the A G L P strategy

Use the A G L P strategy when your domain has the following requirements:

- To upgrade from Microsoft Windows NT® 4.0 to Windows Server 2003
- To maintain a Windows NT 4.0 group strategy
- To maintain centralized user management with decentralized resource management

It is recommended that you use A G L P with Windows Server 2003 Active Directory and Windows NT 4.0 member servers.

A G L P has the following advantages:

- It maintains the Windows NT 4.0 group strategy.
- Resource owners own membership to every group that needs access.

A G L P has the following disadvantages:

- Active Directory does not control access.
- You must create redundant groups across member servers.
- It does not enable centralized administration of resources.
- Local group memberships are not replicated.

Class Discussion: Using Groups in a Single-Domain or Multiple-Domain Environment

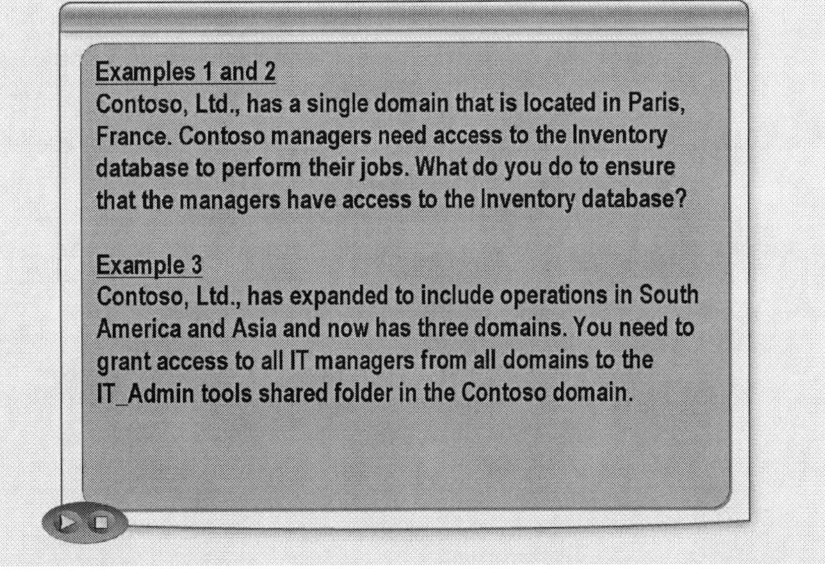
Examples 1 and 2
Contoso, Ltd., has a single domain that is located in Paris, France. Contoso managers need access to the Inventory database to perform their jobs. What do you do to ensure that the managers have access to the Inventory database?
Example 3
Contoso, Ltd., has expanded to include operations in South America and Asia and now has three domains. You need to grant access to all IT managers from all domains to the IT_Admin tools shared folder in the Contoso domain.

Example 1

Contoso, Ltd., has a single domain that is located in Paris, France. Contoso, Ltd., managers need access to the Inventory database to perform their jobs.

What do you do to ensure that the managers have access to the Inventory database?

____

____

____

____

____

____

____

Example 2

Contoso, Ltd., has determined that all Accounting division personnel must have full access to the accounting data. Also, Contoso, Ltd., executives must be able to view the data. Contoso, Ltd., wants to create the group structure for the entire Accounting division, which includes the Accounts Payable and Accounts Receivable departments.

What do you do to ensure that the managers have the required access and that there is a minimum of administration?

A GGDLP

____

____

____

____

____

____

Example 3

Contoso, Ltd., has expanded to include operations in South America and Asia and now contains three domains: the Contoso.msft domain, the Asia.contoso.msft domain, and the SA.contoso.msft domain. You need to grant access to all IT managers across all domains to the Admin_tools shared folder in the Contoso domain. You will also need to grant those users access to other resources in the future. How can you achieve the desired result with the least amount of administrative effort?

____

____

____

____

____

____

____

Practice: Nesting Groups and Creating Universal Groups

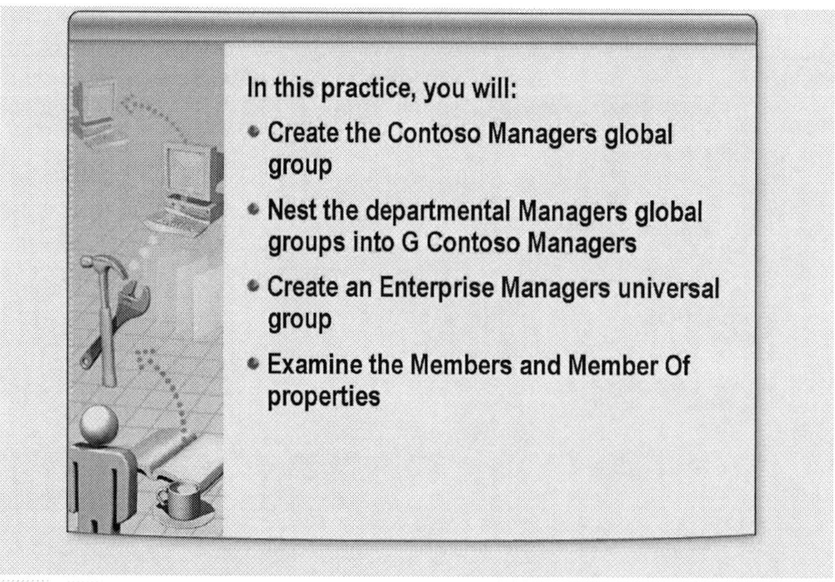
In this practice, you will:
Create the Contoso Managers global group
Nest the departmental Managers global groups into G Contoso Managers
Create an Enterprise Managers universal group
Examine the Members and Member Of properties

Objective

In this practice, you will:

- Create the Contoso Managers global group.
- Nest the departmental Managers global groups into G Contoso Managers.
- Create an Enterprise Managers universal group.
- Examine the Members and Member Of properties.

Instructions

Ensure that the DEN-DC1 virtual machine is running.

Practice

► **Create the Contoso Managers global group**

1. Log on to DEN-DC1 by using the **Administrator** account with the password of **Pa$$w0rd**.
2. Open **Active Directory Users and Computers**.
3. Right-click the **Users** container, point to **New**, and then click **Group**.
4. Name the new group **G Contoso Managers**.
5. Ensure that the group scope is set to **Global**, and then click **OK**.

► **Nest the departmental Managers global groups into G Contoso Managers**

1. Open the **Properties** dialog box for **G Contoso Managers.**
2. Click the **Members** tab, and then click **Add.**
3. Find the names of objects that start with *G.*
4. Add the **G Graphics Managers, G Legal Managers,** and **G Sales Managers** groups to **G Contoso Managers.**

Tip Hold down the CTRL key and click to select noncontiguous objects in the list.

5. Click **OK** three times.

► **Create an Enterprise Managers universal group**

1. In the Users container, create a new group, named **U Enterprise Managers.**
2. Change the Group scope setting to **Universal.**
3. Click **OK.**
4. Open the **Properties** dialog box for **U Enterprise Managers,** and then click the **Members** tab.
5. Click **Add,** and then type **G Contoso Managers.**
6. Click **OK** twice.

Note If there were multiple domains, you would add the global domain managers groups from all domains to the universal managers group.

▶ Examine the Members and Member Of properties

1. Open the **Properties** dialog box for the **G Graphics Managers** global group, and then click the **Members** tab. Who are the members?
2. Click the **Member Of** tab. What groups is **G Graphics Managers** a member of?

   ____

   ____

3. Open the **Properties** dialog box for the **G Contoso Managers** global group. Click the **Members** tab. What groups are members?

   ____

   ____

4. Now click the **Member Of** tab. What groups is **G Contoso Managers** a member of?

   ____

   ____

5. Close all windows and log off of DEN-DC1.

Important Do not shut down the virtual machines.

Modifying the Scope or Type of a Group?

- Changing group scope
  - Global to universal
  - Domain local to universal
  - Universal to global
  - Universal to domain local
- Changing group type
  - Security to distribution
  - Distribution to security

Introduction

When you create a new group, by default, the new group is configured as a security group with global scope, regardless of the current domain functional level.

Changing group scope

Although you cannot change group scope in domains with a domain functional level set to Windows 2000 mixed or Windows Server 2003 Interim, you can make the following scope changes in domains with the domain functional level set to Windows 2000 native or Windows Server 2003:

- *Global to universal.* This is allowed only if the group you want to change is not a member of another global group.

> **Note** You cannot change a group's scope from global to domain local directly. To do that, you must change the group's scope from global to universal and then from universal to domain local.

- *Domain local to universal.* This is allowed only if the group you want to change does not have another domain local group as a member.
- *Universal to global.* This is allowed only if the group you want to change does not have another universal group or a global group from outside of its domain as a member.
- *Universal to domain local.* There are no restrictions for this change.

Changing group type

You can convert a group from a security group to a distribution group, and vice versa, at any time, but only if the domain functional level is set to Windows 2000 native or higher. You cannot convert a group while the domain functional level is set to Windows 2000 mixed or Windows Server 2003 Interim.

You can convert groups from one type to the other in the following scenarios:

- *Security to distribution.* A company splits into two companies. Users migrate from one domain to another domain, but they keep their old e-mail addresses. You want to send them e-mail messages by using old security groups, but you want to remove security context from the group.
- *Distribution to security.* A distribution group gets very large, and the users want to use this group for security-related tasks. However, they still want to use the group for e-mail.

Note Although you can add a contact to a security group and to a distribution group, you cannot grant permissions to contacts. You can send contacts e-mail messages.

Why Assign a Manager to a Group?

Manager
Group
Enables you to:
Track who is responsible for groups
Delegate to the manager of the group the authority to add and remove users
Distribute the administrative responsibility to the people who request the group

Advantages of assigning a manager to a group

Active Directory in Windows Server 2003 allows you to assign a manager to a group as a property of the group. This enables you to:

- Track who is responsible for groups.
- Delegate to the manager of the group the authority to add users to and remove users from the group.

Because people in large organizations are added to and removed from groups so often, some organizations distribute the administrative responsibility of adding users to groups to the people who request the group.

If you document who the manager of the group is, the contact information for that user account is recorded. If the group ever needs to be migrated to another domain or needs to be deleted, the network administrator has a record of who owns the group and that person's contact information. The network administrator can then call or send an e-mail message to the manager to notify the manager about the change that must be made to the group.

Practice: Changing the Scope and Assigning a Manager to a Group

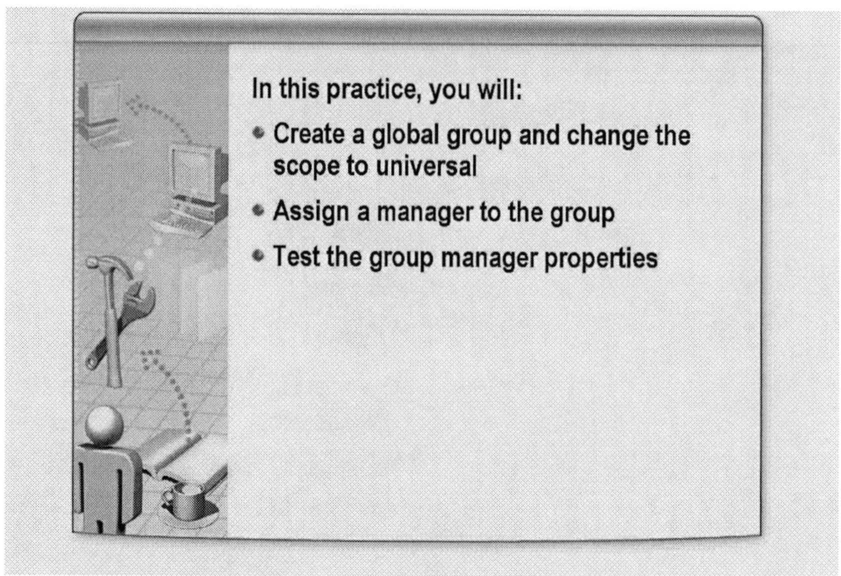

Objective

In this practice, you will:

- Create a global group and change the scope to universal.
- Assign a manager to the group.
- Test the group manager properties.

Instructions

Ensure that the DEN-DC1 and DEN-SRV1 virtual machines are running.

Practice

► **Create a global group and change the scope to universal**

1. Log on to DEN-DC1 as the **Administrator** account with the password of **Pa$$w0rd**.
2. Open **Active Directory Users and Computers**.
3. In the **Users** container, create a global group named **G Contoso Helpdesk**.
4. Open the **Properties** dialog box for the group, and then click the **Universal** option in the **Group scope** settings.
5. Click **OK**.

► **Assign a manager to the group**

1. Open the **Properties** dialog box for the **G Contoso Helpdesk** group.
2. Click the **Managed By** tab, and then click **Change**.
3. In the **Select User, Contact, or Group** dialog box, enter **Judy Lew**.
4. Click **OK**.
5. On the **Managed By** tab, select the **Manager can update membership list** check box.
6. Click **OK**.
7. Close all windows and log off of DEN-DC1.

► **Test the group manager properties**

1. Log on to DEN-SRV1 as **Judy** with the password of **Pa$$w0rd**.
2. Create a custom Microsoft Management Console (MMC), and then add the Active Directory Users and Computers snap-in.
3. Open **Active Directory Users and Computers**.
4. Click the **Users** container, and then open the **Properties** dialog box for the **G Contoso Managers** global group.
5. Click the **Members** tab, and then click **Add**.
6. Attempt to add **Anne Paper** to this group.

   You should not be able to add any users to this group.
7. Close the **G Contoso Managers Properties** dialog box.
8. Open the **Properties** dialog box for **G Contoso Helpdesk**.
9. Attempt to add **Jeff Hay** to this group.

   This should succeed because Judy Lew was given authority to add users to this group.
10. Close the custom MMC without saving changes.
11. Log off of DEN-SRV1.

Important Do not shut down the virtual machines.

Lesson: Using Default Groups

- Default Groups on Member Servers
- Default Groups in Active Directory
- When to Use Default Groups
- Security Considerations for Default Groups
- System Groups
- Class Discussion: Using Default Groups vs. Creating New Groups
- Best Practices for Managing Groups

Introduction

This lesson demonstrates how default groups are used.

Lesson objectives

After completing this lesson, you will be able to:

- Explain how default groups are used on member servers.
- Explain how default groups are used in Active Directory.
- Identify when to use default groups.
- Identify the security considerations for default groups.
- Explain how system groups are used.
- Plan a strategy for using default groups or creating new groups.
- Implement best practices for managing groups.

Default Groups on Member Servers

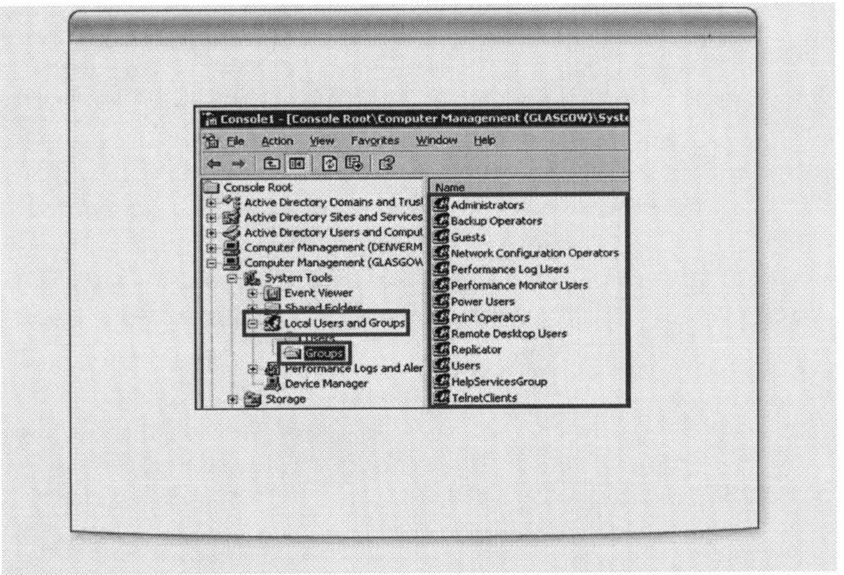

Definition

The Groups folder is located on a member server in the Local Users and Groups console, which displays all built-in default local groups and any local groups you create. The default local groups are created automatically when you install Windows Server 2003. The local groups can contain local user accounts, domain user accounts, computer accounts, global groups, and universal groups.

Default local groups on member servers

The following table describes some of the default local groups on a member or stand-alone server running Windows Server 2003.

Group	Description
Administrators	• Members have full control of the server and can assign user rights and access control permissions to users as necessary. • Administrator is a default member account and has full control of the server. • Users should be added with caution. • When joined to a domain, the Domain Admins group is automatically added to this group.
Guests	• A temporary profile is created for a member when the member logs on. • When the guest member logs off, the profile is deleted. • The Guest account is disabled by default.
Performance Log Users	• Members can manage performance counters, logs, and alerts on the server locally and from remote clients without being a member of the Administrators group.
Backup Operators	• Members can override security restrictions for the sole purpose of backing up and restoring files on the local machine.

(continued)

Group	Description
Performance Monitor Users	• Members can monitor performance counters on the server locally and from remote clients without being a member of the Administrators or Performance Log Users groups.
Power Users	• Members can create user accounts and then modify and delete the accounts that they have created. • Members can create local groups and then add or remove users from the local groups that they have created. • Members can add or remove users from the Power Users, Users, and Guests groups. • Members can create shared resources and administer the shared resources that they have created. • Members cannot take ownership of files, back up or restore directories, load or unload device drivers, or manage security and auditing logs.
Print Operators	• Members can manage printers and print queues.
Users	• Members can perform common tasks, such as running applications, using local and network printers, and locking the server. • Users cannot share directories or create local printers. • The Domain Users, Authenticated Users, and Interactive groups are members of this group. Therefore, any user account created in the domain becomes a member of this group.

Note Group memberships can be controlled by configuring restricted group policies in Group Policy. For more information, see Module 9, "Managing the User Environment by Using Group Policy," in Course 2274, *Managing a Microsoft Windows Server 2003 Environment*.

The following additional groups, also default groups on a member server, are not commonly used:

- Network Configuration Operators
- Remote Desktop Users
- Replicator
- HelpServicesGroup
- Terminal Server Users

Note For more information about default groups on member servers, search for "default local groups" in Windows Server 2003 Help.

Default groups used by network services

The following table describes the default groups used by network services and installed only with the Dynamic Host Configuration Protocol (DHCP) service or the Windows Internet Name Service (WINS).

Group	Membership
DHCP Administrators	• Members have administrative access to the DHCP service. • The DHCP Administrators group provides security to assign limited administrative access to the DHCP server only, while not providing full access to the server. • Members can administer DHCP on a server by using the DHCP console or the **Netsh** command, but they cannot perform other administrative actions on the server.
DHCP Users	• Members have read-only access to the DHCP service. • Members can view information and properties stored on a specified DHCP server. This information is useful to support staff when they need to obtain DHCP status reports.
WINS Users	• Members are permitted read-only access to WINS. • Members can view information and properties stored on a specified WINS server. This information is useful to support staff when they need to obtain WINS status reports.

Default Groups in Active Directory

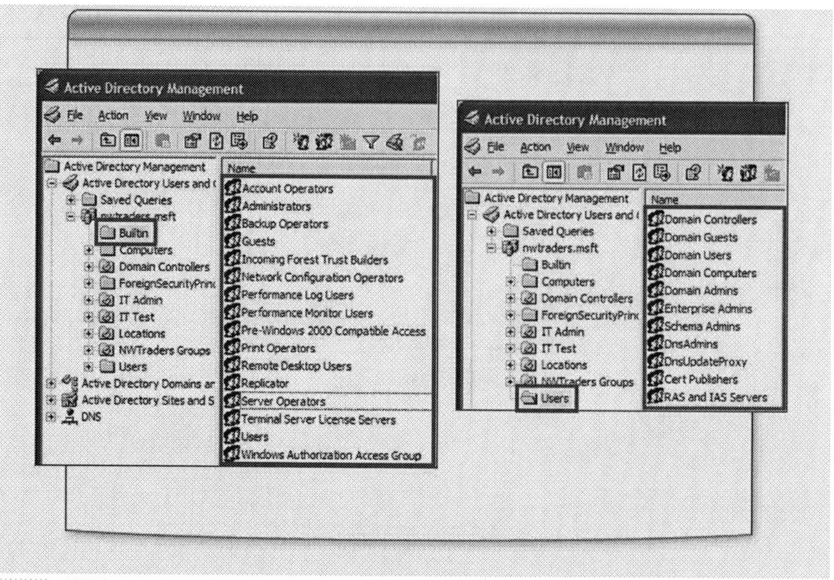

Definition

Default groups are security groups that are automatically created when you install an Active Directory domain. You can use these predefined groups to manage shared resources and delegate specific domain-wide administrative roles.

Default groups and user rights

Many default groups are automatically assigned a set of user rights that determine what each group and their members can do within the scope of a domain or forest. User rights authorize members of a group to perform specific actions, such as log on to a local system or back up files and folders. For example, a member of the Backup Operators group has the right to perform backup operations for all domain controllers in the domain.

Default groups and containers

Several default groups are available in the Users and Builtin containers of Active Directory. The Builtin container contains domain local groups. The Users container contains global groups and domain local groups. You can move groups in the Users and Builtin containers to other group or organizational unit folders in the domain, but you cannot move them to other domains.

Default groups in the Builtin container

The following table describes each default group in the Builtin container in Active Directory. When a member server or stand-alone server becomes a domain controller, all of these default groups are added, along with the user rights that are assigned to each group.

Group	Description
Account Operators	• Members can create, modify, and delete accounts for users, groups, and computers located in the Users or Computers container and organizational units in the domain, except the Domain Controllers organizational unit. • Members do not have permission to modify the Administrators or the Domain Admins group or accounts for members of those groups. • Members can log on locally to domain controllers in the domain and shut them down. • Because this group has significant power in the domain, add users with caution.
Incoming Forest Trust Builders	• Members can create one-way, incoming forest trusts to the forest root domain. • Has no default members.
Pre-Windows 2000 Compatible Access	• Members have read access on all users and groups in the domain. • Provided for backward compatibility for computers running Windows NT 4.0 and earlier. • Add users to this group only if they are using Remote Access Service (RAS) on a computer running Windows NT 4.0 or earlier.
Server Operators	• Members can log on interactively, create and delete shared resources, start and stop some services, back up and restore files, format the hard disk, and shut down the computer. • Has no default members. • Because this group has significant power on domain controllers, add users with caution.

Default groups in the Users container

The following table describes some of the default groups in the Users container and the user rights that are assigned to each group.

Group	Description
Domain Controllers	• Contains all domain controllers in the domain.
Domain Guests	• Contains all domain guests.
Domain Users	• Contains all domain users. • Any user account that is created in the domain is a member of this group automatically.
Domain Computers	• Contains all workstations and servers joined to the domain. • Any computer account that is created becomes a member of this group automatically.
Domain Admins	• Members have full control of the domain. • Is a member of the Administrators group on all domain controllers, all domain workstations, and all domain member servers at the time they are joined to the domain. • The Administrator account is a member of this group. Because the group has full power in the domain, add users with caution.
Enterprise Admins	• Members have full control of all domains in the forest. • Is a member of the Administrators group on all domain controllers in the forest. • The Administrator account is a member of this group. Because this group has full control of all domains in the forest, add users with caution.
Group Policy Creator Owners	• Members can modify Group Policy in the domain. • The Administrator account is a member of this group. Because this group has significant power in the domain, add users with caution.

The following list contains the additional default groups that have special purposes:

- Schema Admins
- DnsAdmins
- DnsUpdateProxy
- Cert Publishers
- RAS and IAS Servers

Note For more information about other groups in the Users container, search for "Active Directory default groups" in Windows Server 2003 Help.

When to Use Default Groups

- **Default groups are:**
  - Created during the installation of the operating system or when services are added
  - Automatically assigned a set of user rights
- **Use default groups to:**
  - Control access to shared resources
  - Delegate specific domain-wide administration

Using default groups

Predefined groups help you to control access to shared resources and delegate specific domain-wide administrative roles. Many default groups are automatically assigned a set of user rights that authorize members of the group to perform specific actions in a domain, such as logging on to a local system or backing up files and folders.

When you add a user to a group, the user receives all the user rights assigned to the group and all the permissions assigned to the group for any shared resources.

As a security best practice, it is recommended that members of default groups with broad administrative access use **Run as** to perform administrative tasks.

Security Considerations for Default Groups

- Place a user in a default group when you are sure that you want to give the user all the user rights and permissions assigned to that group in Active Directory; otherwise, create a new security group
- As a security best practice, members of default groups should use Run as

Security considerations for default groups

Only place a user in a default group when you are sure that you want to give the user:

- All the user rights assigned to that group in Active Directory.
- All of the permissions assigned to that group for any shared resources associated with that default group.

Otherwise, create a new security group and assign to the group only those user rights or permissions that the user absolutely requires.

As a security best practice, members of default groups that have broad administrative access should not perform an interactive logon by using administrative credentials. Instead, users with this level of access should use **Run as**.

Warning Only add members to default groups when members need all rights associated with the group. For example, if you need to add a service account to back up and restore files on a member server, you add the service account to the Backup Operators group. The Backup Operators group has the user rights to back up and restore files on the computer.

However, if your service account only needs to back up files and not restore them, it is better to create a new group. You can then grant the group the user right to back up files and not grant the group the right to restore files.

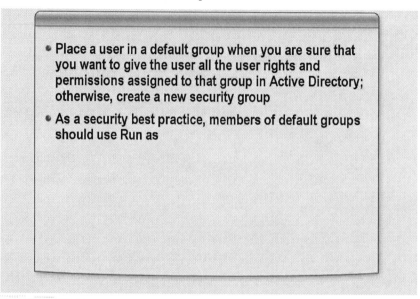

System Groups

- System groups represent different users at different times
- You can grant user rights and permissions to system groups, but you cannot modify or view the memberships
- Group scopes do not apply to system groups
- Users are automatically assigned to system groups whenever they log on or access a particular resource

Introduction

You cannot change the membership of system groups. The operating system creates them, and you cannot change or manage them. It is important to understand system groups, because you can use them for security purposes.

Definition

Servers running Windows Server 2003 include several special identities in addition to the groups in the Users and Builtin containers. For convenience, these identities are generally referred to as system groups.

System groups represent different users at different times, depending on the circumstances. Although you can grant user rights and permissions to the system groups, you cannot modify or view their memberships.

Group scopes do not apply to system groups. Users are automatically assigned to system groups whenever they log on or access a particular resource.

System groups are often referred to as "special identities."

System groups

The following table describes some of the system groups.

System group	Description
Anonymous Logon	• Represents users and services that access a computer and its resources through the network without using an account name, password, or domain name. • On computers running Windows NT and earlier, the Anonymous Logon group is a member of the Everyone group by default. • On computers running a member of the Windows Server 2003 family, the Anonymous Logon group is not a member of the Everyone group by default. If you want to create a file share for an anonymous user, you grant permissions to the Anonymous Logon group.
Everyone	• Represents all current network users, including guests and users from other domains. Whenever a user logs on to the network, the user is automatically added to the Everyone group. • If security is not a concern for a specific group in your domain, you can grant permissions to the Everyone group. However, because the Anonymous Logon group can become a member of the Everyone group, it is not recommended that you use this group for permissions above read-only.
Network	• Represents users currently accessing a given resource over the network, as opposed to users who access a resource by logging on locally at the computer where the resource is located. Whenever a user accesses a given resource over the network, the user is automatically added to the Network group.
Interactive locally logged on	• Represents all users currently logged on to a particular computer and accessing a given resource located on that computer, as opposed to users who access the resource over the network. Whenever a user accesses a resource on the computer to which they are currently logged on, the user is automatically added to the Interactive group.
Authenticated Users	• Represents all users within Active Directory. Always use the Authenticated Users group when granting permissions for a resource instead of using the Everyone group, to prevent guests from accessing resources.
Creator Owner	• Includes the user account for the user who created or took ownership of a resource. If a member of the Administrators group creates a resource, the Administrators group is the owner of the resource.

Note These groups have well known Security Identifiers (SIDs). A list of these, along with the well known SIDs of the built-in accounts, is available by searching for "Security Identifiers" on the Microsoft Help and Support Web site.

Class Discussion: Using Default Groups vs. Creating New Groups

Contoso, Ltd., has over 100 servers across the world. You must determine:

- The current tasks that administrators must perform and what minimum level of access users need to perform specific tasks
- Whether you can use default groups or must create groups and assign specific user rights or permissions to the groups

Scenario

Contoso, Ltd., has over 100 servers across the world. You must determine current tasks that administrators must perform and what minimum level of access those users need to perform specific tasks. You also must determine whether you can use default groups or whether you must create groups and assign specific user rights or permissions to the groups to perform the tasks.

Discussion

You must assign default groups or create new groups for the following tasks. List the name of the default group that has the most restrictive user rights for performing the following actions, or determine whether you must create a new group.

1. Backing up and restoring domain controllers

   BUILT IN - BACKUP OPERATORS

2. Backing up member servers

   CREATE

3. Creating groups in the Contoso, Ltd., Sales organizational unit

   CREATE

4. Logging on to the domain

   BUILT IN USERS

5. Providing read-only access to the DHCP servers

   DHCP USER BUILT IN

6. Help desk employees who need access to control the desktop remotely

   REMOTE DESKTOP USERS BUILT IN

7. Providing administrative access to all computers in the entire domain

   BUILT IN ADMINISTRATOR

8. Providing access to a shared folder named Data on a server named Den-SRV1

   CREATE

9. Managing the print queue of a specific printer on a print server

CREATE

10. Configuring network settings on a member server

BUILT IN NETWORK CONFIG OPERATOR

Best Practices for Managing Groups

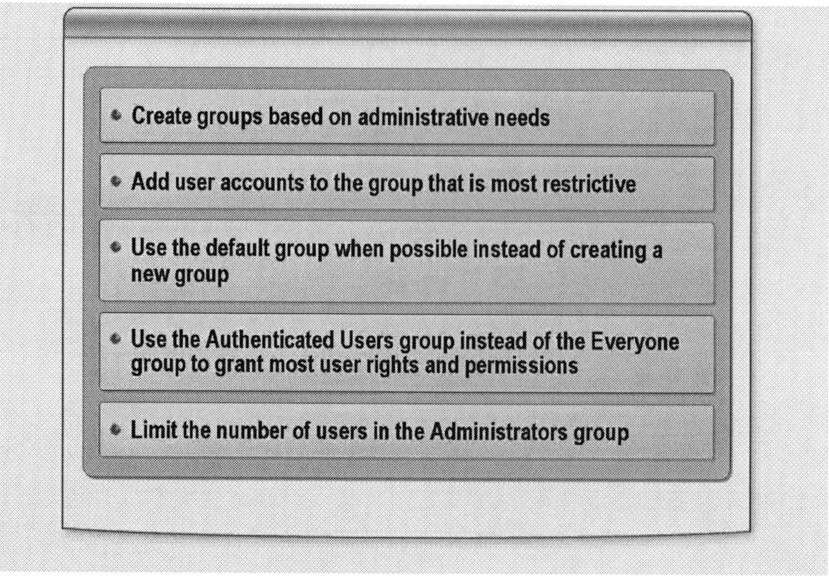

Best practices

Consider the following best practices for managing groups:

- Create groups based on administrative needs. When you create a group based on a job function and another person takes over that job, you need to change only the group membership. You do not need to change all permissions that are granted to the individual user account. Because of this, it is sometimes advantageous to create a group that has only one member.
- If you have multiple groups to which you can add user accounts, add user accounts to the group that is most restrictive. However, ensure that you grant the appropriate user rights and permissions so that users can accomplish any required task.
- Whenever a default group enables users to accomplish a task, use the default group instead of creating a new group. Create groups only when there are no default groups that provide the required user rights and permissions.
- Use the Authenticated Users group instead of the Everyone group to grant user rights and permissions to most users. Using this group minimizes the risk of unauthorized access, because Windows Server 2003 adds only valid user accounts to members of the Authenticated Users system group.
- Limit the number of users in the Administrators group. Members of the Administrators group on a local computer have Full Control permissions for that computer. Add a user to the Administrators group if the user will perform only administrative tasks.

Lab: Creating and Managing Groups

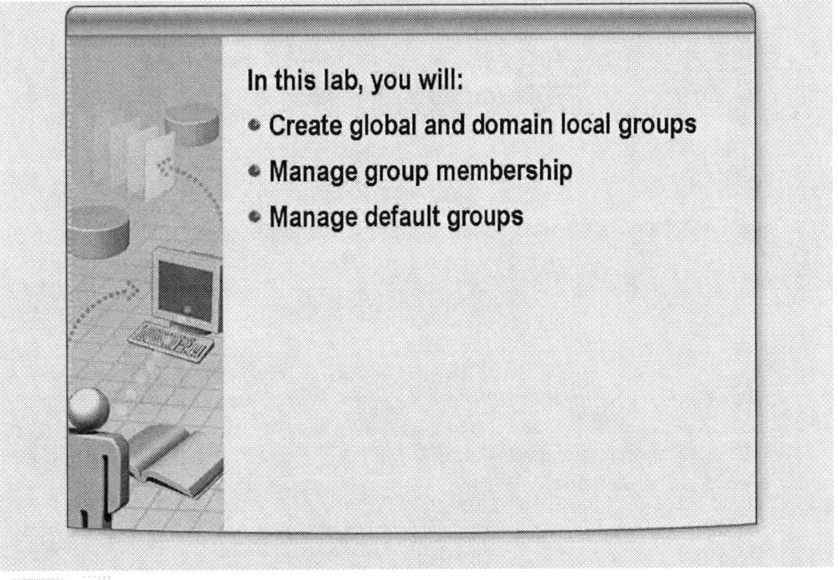

Objectives

After completing this lab, you will be able to:

- Create global and domain local groups.
- Manage group membership.
- Manage default groups.

Prerequisites

To complete this lab, you must have the following virtual machines:

- DEN-DC1
- DEN-SRV1

Estimated time to complete this lab: 30 minutes

Exercise 1
Creating Global and Domain Local Groups

In this exercise, you will create an organizational unit and create two users in that organizational unit. You will also create domain local and global groups.

Scenario

You have to create an organizational unit for the newly created Marketing department. Currently there are only two users. One of them is the marketing manager. You must create accounts and groups according to the approved naming strategy.

Tasks	Specific instructions
1. Create an organizational unit for the Marketing department.	a. Log on to DEN-DC1 as **Administrator** with the password of **Pa$$w0rd.** b. Open **Active Directory Users and Computers.** c. Select the domain node. d. Create a new organizational unit named **Marketing.**
2. Create two users accounts in the Marketing organizational unit.	a. Create a user account called **Marketing Manager** with a logon name of **Mktmgr** and a password of **Pa$$w0rd.** b. Create a user account called **Marketing User** with a logon name of **Mktuser** and a password of **Pa$$w0rd.**
3. Create two global groups, one for Marketing Managers and one for Marketing Users.	a. Create a global group named **G Marketing Managers.** b. Create a global group named **G Marketing Users.**
4. Create domain local groups that will be used to assign permissions to resources for the Marketing team.	a. Create a domain local group named **DL Marketing Full Control.** b. Create a domain local group named **DL Marketing Read-only.**

Exercise 2
Managing Group Membership

In this exercise, you will configure group membership.

Scenario

Now that the organizational unit and the user and group accounts have been created, you must place the proper users in their groups and put the global groups into their appropriate groups.

Tasks	Specific instructions
1. Add users to their global groups.	a. Add the **Marketing Manager** account and the **Marketing User** account to the **G Marketing Users** global group. b. Add the **Marketing Manager** account to the **G Marketing Managers** global group.
2. Nest the Marketing Managers global group into the G Contoso Managers global group.	a. In the Users container, open the **Properties** dialog box for the **G Contoso Managers** group. b. Click the **Members** tab, and then click **Add.** c. Find the **G Marketing Managers** group. d. Click **OK** twice.
3. Add the global groups to the domain local groups.	a. Add the **G Marketing Managers** group to the **DL Marketing Full Control** group. b. Add the **G Marketing Users** group to the **DL Marketing Read-only** group.

Exercise 3
Managing Default Groups

In this exercise, you will add users to the proper groups to allow them to perform their administrative tasks.

Scenario

As domain administrator, you must delegate some of the administrative responsibility to other users. You will give Judy Lew the right to back up and restore information on domain controllers. You will also give her the right to manage printers on domain controllers. You will give Don Hall the right to back up and restore data and configure the network settings on DEN-SRV1.

Tasks	Specific instructions
1. Add Judy Lew to the appropriate default built-in group.	**a.** In **Active Directory Users and Computers**, locate the user account for **Judy Lew**. **b.** Open the **Properties** dialog box for **Judy Lew**, and then click the **Member Of** tab. **c.** Click **Add**, and add the **Print Operators** group. **d.** Click **Add**, and add **Judy Lew** to the **Backup Operators** group. **e.** Close **Active Directory Users and Computers**.
2. Add Don Hall to the appropriate default built-in group.	**a.** Log on to DEN-SRV1 as **Administrator** with the password of **Pa$$w0rd**. **b.** Open **Computer Management**. **c.** In **Computer Management**, expand **Local Users and Groups**. **d.** Click the Groups container, and then open the **Properties** dialog box for the **Backup Operators** group. **e.** Click **Add**, and then add **Don Hall** to the group. Click **OK**. **f.** Open the **Properties** dialog box for the **Network Configuration Operators** group. **g.** Click **Add** and then add **Don Hall** to the group. Click **OK**. **h.** Close all windows.
3. Complete the lab exercise.	**a.** Close all programs and shut down all computers. Do not save changes. **b.** To prepare for the next module, start the DEN-DC1 virtual computer.

Module 4: Managing Access to Resources

Contents

Overview

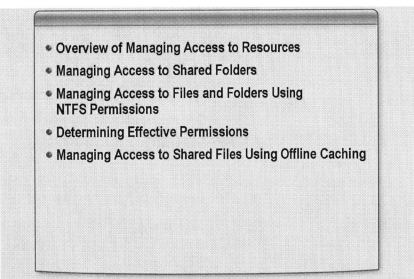

- Overview of Managing Access to Resources
- Managing Access to Shared Folders
- Managing Access to Files and Folders Using NTFS Permissions
- Determining Effective Permissions
- Managing Access to Shared Files Using Offline Caching

Introduction

This module introduces the job function of managing access to resources. Specifically, the module provides the skills and knowledge that you need to manage access to files and folders by using shared folder permissions, NTFS permissions, or effective permissions and to manage access to shared files by using offline caching.

Objectives

After completing this module, you will be able to:

- Manage access to resources.
- Manage access to shared folders.
- Manage access to files and folders by using NTFS permissions.
- Determine effective permissions.
- Managing access to shared files by using offline caching.

Lesson: Overview of Managing Access to Resources

- Multimedia: Access Control in Microsoft Windows Server 2003
- What Are Permissions?
- What Are Standard and Special Permissions?
- Practice: Examining NTFS Permissions
- Multimedia: Permission States

Introduction

The information in this lesson presents the knowledge that you need to manage access to resources.

Lesson objectives

After completing this lesson, you will be able to:

- Describe the components of access control in Microsoft® Windows Server™ 2003.
- Define permissions.
- Explain the differences between standard and special permissions.
- Determine permissions that are assigned to NTFS folders.
- Explain the characteristics of implicit and explicit permission states.

Multimedia: Access Control in Microsoft Windows Server 2003

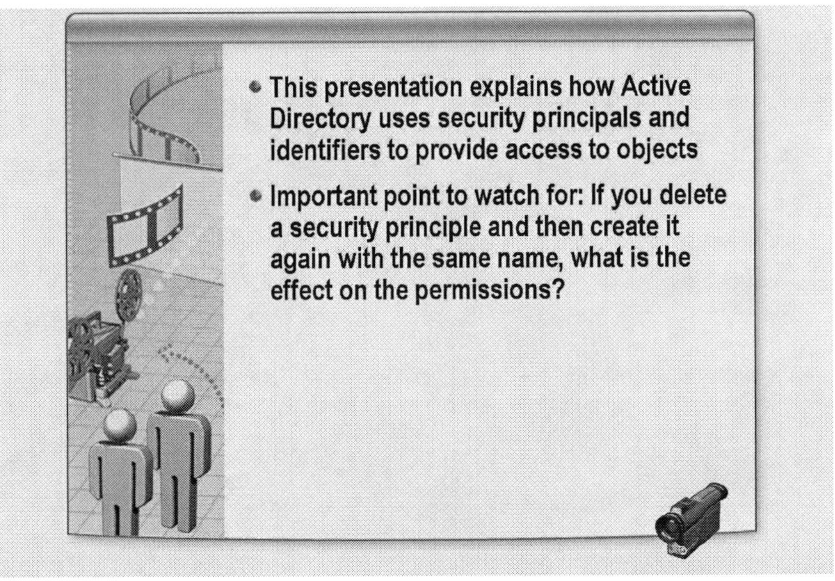

File location

To view the *Access Control in Microsoft Windows Server 2003* presentation, open the Web page on the Student Materials compact disc, click **Multimedia**, and then click the title of the presentation.

Key points

Key points from the presentation are summarized in the following list:

- Security principal

  A security principal is an account that can be authenticated.

- Security identifier (SID)

  An SID is an alphanumeric structure that is issued when an account is created and that uniquely identifies a security principal.

- Discretionary access control list (DACL)

  Each resource is associated with a DACL, which identifies the users and groups that are allowed or denied access to that resource.

- Access control entry (ACE)

  A DACL contains multiple ACEs. Each ACE specifies a SID, special permissions, inheritance information, and an Allow or a Deny permission.

Additional reading

For more information about access control, see "Access Control Components" on the MSDN Library Web site.

What Are Permissions?

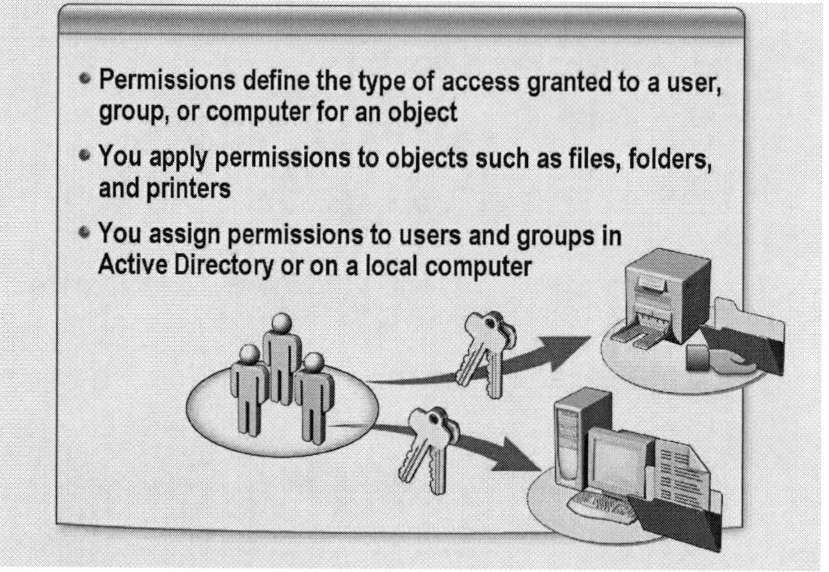

Definition

Permissions define the type of access that is granted to a user, group, or computer for an object. For example, you can let one user read the contents of a file, let another user make changes to the file, and prevent all other users from accessing the file. You can set similar permissions on printers so that certain users can configure the printer and other users can only print from it.

Permissions are also applied to any secured objects, such as files, objects in the Active Directory® directory service, and registry objects. Permissions can be granted to any user, group, or computer.

You can grant permissions for objects to:

- Groups, users, and computers and special identities in any trusted domains.
- Local groups and users on the computer where the object resides.

Permission types

There are two levels of permissions. Shared folder permissions allow security principals remote access to shared resources across the network. Shared folder permissions are only in effect when a resource is accessed from the network. NTFS permissions, on the other hand, are always in effect, whether connecting across the network or logged on to the local machine where the resource is located. NTFS permissions are built in to the NTFS file system and cannot be disabled on an NTFS volume.

Note This lesson discusses NTFS permissions. Additional information about NTFS permissions is covered later in this module. Shared folder permissions are discussed in the next lesson.

When you set permissions, you specify the level of access for groups and users. The permissions attached to an object depend on the type of object. For example, the permissions that are attached to a file are different from those that are attached to a registry key. Some permissions, however, are common to most types of objects.

The following permissions are common permissions:

- Read permissions
- Write permissions
- Delete permissions

What Are Standard and Special Permissions?

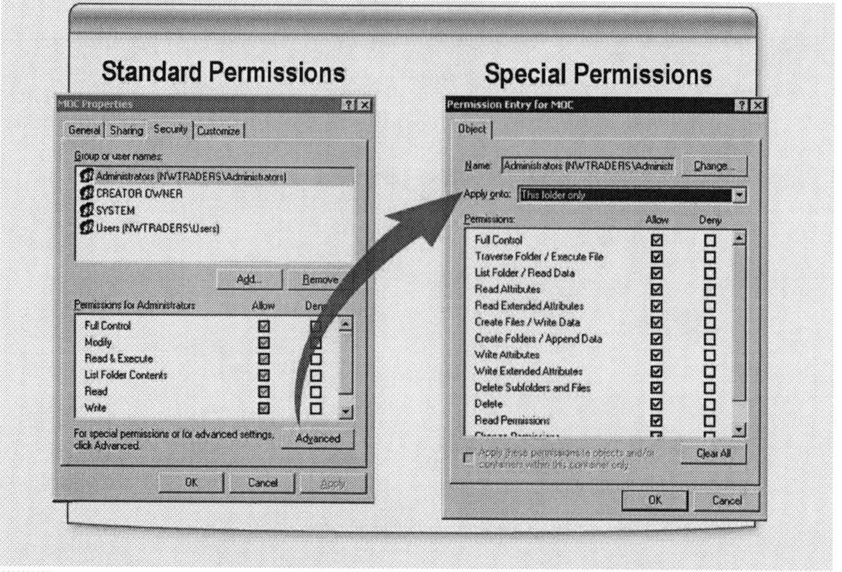

Introduction

You can grant standard and special permissions for objects. Standard permissions are the most frequently assigned permissions. Special permissions provide you with a finer degree of control for assigning access to objects.

Standard permissions

The system has a default level of security settings for a specific object. These are the most common set of permissions that a systems administrator uses on a daily basis. The list of standard permissions that are available varies depending on what type of object you are modifying the security for.

Special permissions

Special permissions are a more detailed list of permissions. A standard NFTS permission of Read is related to the following special permissions:

- List Folder/Read Data
- Read Attributes
- Read Extended Attributed
- Read Permissions

If the systems administrator removes a special permission that relates to a standard permission, the check box for the standard permission is no longer selected. The check box for the special permission in the standard permission list is selected.

Practice: Examining NTFS Permissions

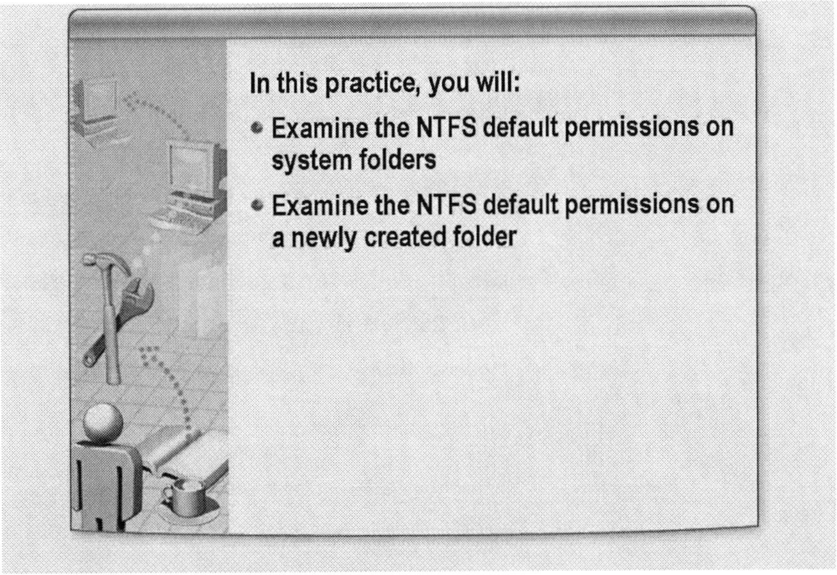

Objectives

In this practice, you will:

- Examine the NTFS default permissions on the system folders.
- Examine the NTFS default permissions on a newly created folder.

Instructions

Ensure that the DEN-DC1 virtual machine is running.

Practice

► **Examine the NTFS default permissions on the system folders**

1. Log on to DEN-DC1 as **Administrator** with a password of **Pa$$w0rd**.
2. Open **My Computer** (or Windows Explorer).
3. Expand the **C:**\ drive.
4. Right-click **Windows**, and then click **Sharing and Security**.
5. Click the **Security** tab.

   What are the default permissions of **Authenticated Users**?

   ____

   ____

   What are the default permissions of **Server Operators**?

   ____

   ____

What are the default permissions of **Creator Owner**?

____

____

6. Click **Cancel.**

► Examine the NTFS default permissions on a newly created folder

1. Create a new folder named **Test** at the root of the **C:** drive.
2. Right-click the **Test** folder and then click **Sharing and Security**.
3. Click the **Security** tab.

   How are these permissions different from those in the Windows folder?

   ____

   ____

   ____

   ____

4. Close all open windows and log off of DEN-DC1.

► To prepare for the next practice

1. Start the DEN-CL1 virtual machine.
2. Start the DEN-SRV1 virtual machine.

Multimedia: Permission States

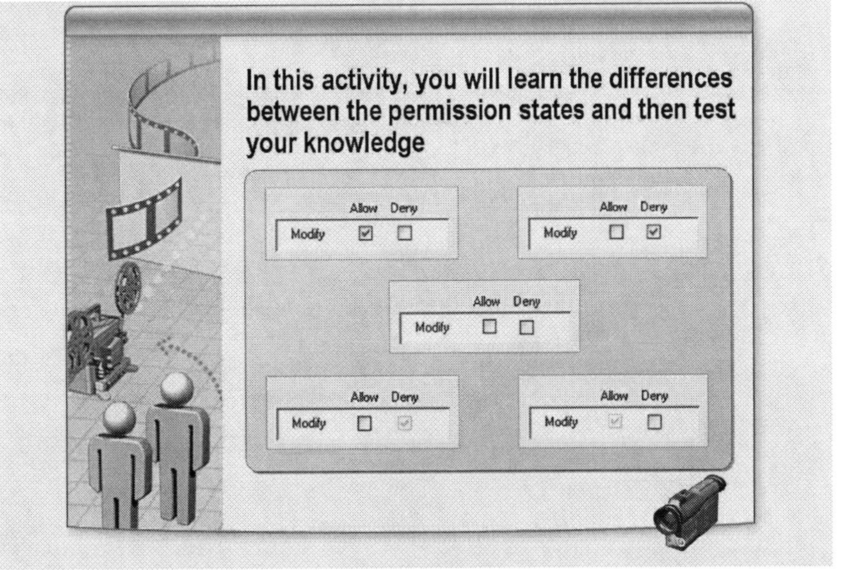

File location

To start the *Permission States* activity, open the Web page on the Student Materials compact disc, click **Multimedia**, and then click the title of the activity.

Lesson: Managing Access to Shared Folders

- What Are Shared Folders?
- What Are Administrative Shared Folders?
- Tools to Create and Manage Shared Folders
- Shared Folder Permissions
- Methods to Connect to Shared Folders
- What Are Published Shared Folders?
- How Published Shared Folders Are Used
- Best Practices For Using Shared Folders
- Practice: Managing Access to Shared Folders

Introduction

The Windows Server 2003 family organizes files into directories that are graphically represented as folders. These folders contain all types of files and can contain subfolders. Some of these folders are reserved for operating system files and program files. Users should never place any data into the operating system folders or program file folders.

Shared folders give users access to files and folders over a network. Users can connect to the shared folder over the network to access the folders and files that they contain. Shared folders can contain applications, public data, or a user's personal data. Using shared application folders centralizes administration by enabling you to install and maintain applications on a server instead of client computers. Using shared data folders provides a central location for users to access common files and makes it easier to back up data contained in those files.

Lesson objectives

After completing this lesson, you will be able to:

- Explain what shared folders are.
- Explain what administrative shared folders are.
- Use tools to create and manage shared folders.
- Explain what shared folder permissions are.
- Describe the various methods to connect to a shared folder.
- Explain what published shared folders are.
- Explain how published shared folders are used.
- Describe the best practices for using shared folders.
- Manage access to shared folders.

What Are Shared Folders?

- Shared folders show an icon of a hand holding the folder
- You can share only folders, not files
- Default permission on shared folders is Everyone, Read
- When you copy or move a shared folder, the folder is no longer shared
- To hide a shared folder, include a $ after the name of the shared folder
- Users access hidden shares by typing the UNC path

Introduction

When you share a folder, the folder is made accessible to multiple users simultaneously over the network. After a folder is shared, users can access all of the files and subfolders in the shared folder if they are granted permission.

You can place shared folders on a file server and also place them on any computer on the network. You can store files in shared folders according to categories or functions. For example, you can place shared data files in one shared folder and shared application files in another.

Characteristics of shared folders

Some of the most common characteristics of shared folders are as follows:

- A shared folder appears in Microsoft Windows® Explorer with an icon of a hand holding the folder.
- You can share only folders, not individual files. If multiple users need access to the same file, you must place the file in a folder and then share the folder.
- When a folder is shared, Read permission is granted to the Everyone group as the default permission. Remove the default permission and grant Change permission or Read permission to groups as needed.
- When users or groups are granted permissions to a shared folder, the default permission is Read.
- When you copy a shared folder, the original shared folder is still shared, but the copy is not shared. When a shared folder is moved to another location, the folder is no longer shared.
- You can hide a shared folder if you append a dollar sign ($) to the name of the shared folder. The user cannot see the shared folder in the user interface, but the user can access the shared folder by typing the Universal Naming Convention (UNC) name—for example, **\\server\secrets$**.

What Are Administrative Shared Folders?

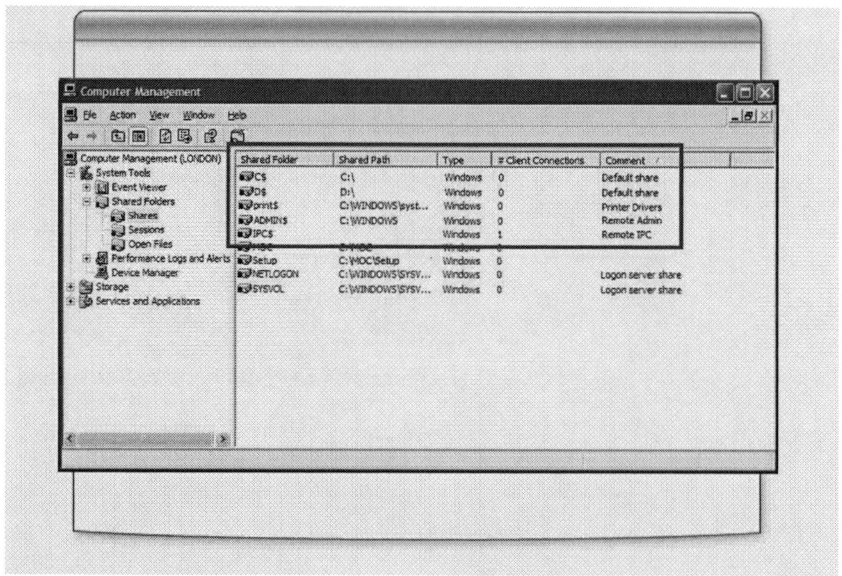

Introduction

Windows Server 2003 automatically shares folders that enable you to perform administrative tasks. These default administrative shares have a dollar sign ($) at the end of the share name. The dollar sign hides the shared folder from users who browse to the computer in My Network Places. Administrators can quickly administer files and folders on remote servers by using these hidden shared folders.

Types of administrative shared folders

By default, members of the Administrators group have the Full Control permission for administrative shared folders. You cannot modify the permissions for administrative shared folders. The following table describes the purpose of the default administrative shared folders in Windows Server 2003.

Shared folders	Purpose
C$, D$, E$	Use these shared folders to remotely connect to a computer and perform administrative tasks. The root of each partition (that has a drive letter assigned to it) on a hard disk is automatically shared. When you connect to this folder, you have access to the entire partition.
Admin$	This is the systemroot folder, which is C:\Windows by default. Administrators can access this shared folder to administer Windows Server 2003 without knowing the name of the actual folder in which the operating system is installed.
Print$	This folder provides access to printer driver files for client computers. When you install the first shared printer, the *systemroot*\system32\spool\drivers folder is shared as Print$. Only members of the Administrators, Server Operators, and Print Operators groups have Full Control permission for this folder. The Everyone group has Read permission for this folder.

(*continued*)

Shared folders	Purpose
IPC$	This interprocess communications share is used during remote administration of a computer and when viewing a computer's shared resources.
FAX$	This shared folder is used to temporarily cache files and access cover pages on the server.

Additional reading

For more information about IPC$, see article 101150, "Operating Characteristics and Restrictions of Named Pipes," on the Microsoft Help and Support Web site.

Tools to Create and Manage Shared Folders

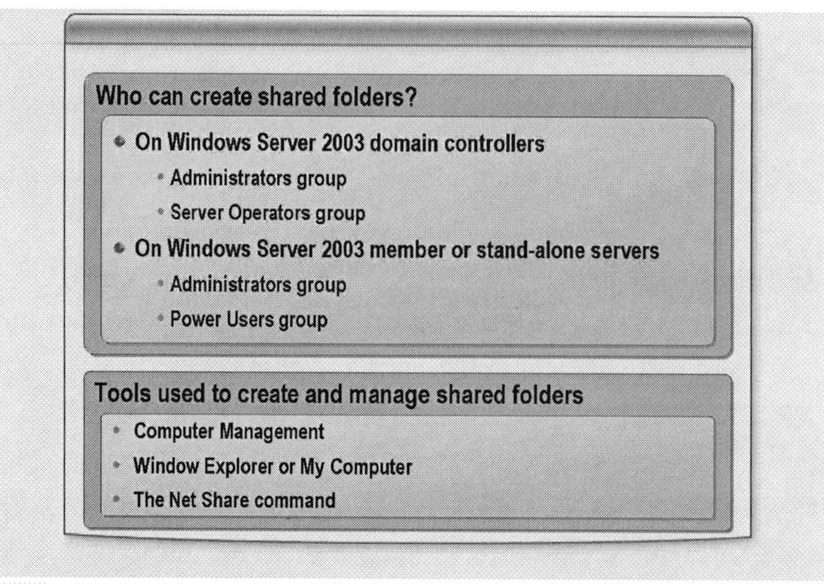

Who can create shared folders?
On Windows Server 2003 domain controllers
Administrators group
Server Operators group
On Windows Server 2003 member or stand-alone servers
Administrators group
Power Users group
Tools used to create and manage shared folders
Computer Management
Window Explorer or My Computer
The Net Share command

Introduction

In Windows Server 2003, the only groups that can create shared folders are the Administrators, Server Operators, and Power Users groups. These groups are built-in groups that are placed in the Groups folder in Computer Management or the Built-In container in Active Directory Users and Groups.

When you create a shared folder, you assign a shared folder name and can provide a comment that describes the folder and its contents. You can also limit the number of users who can access the folder, grant permissions, and share the same folder multiple times under different network share names.

Groups that can create shared folders

The following table describes who can share folders.

To share folders:	You must be a member of:
On a Windows Server 2003 domain controller	The Administrators or Server Operators group
On a stand-alone or member server running Windows Server 2003	The Administrators or Power Users group

Using Computer Management to create shared folders

You can use the Computer Management Microsoft Management Console (MMC) to create and manage shared folders. You can start the Computer Management MMC by using the **runas** command, which allows you, as an administrator, power user, or server operator to share folders without logging onto the system. Computer Management can also be used remotely. Computer Management has three subfolders:

- *The Shares folder*. Displays a listing of the share names of all the shared folders on the machine. This folder also displays the actual path in the file system to the shared folder. You can create new shared folders by using the shortcut menu for the Shares folder. You can also stop sharing existing shared folders.

- *The Sessions folder*. Displays information about the current remote sessions in place and allows you to forcefully disconnect users.
- *The Open Files folder*. Displays information about the files that are in use by the current sessions and allows you to forcefully close open files.

You can also send console messages to currently connected machines from Computer Management.

Using My Computer or Windows Explorer

Both My Computer and Windows Explorer provide views of the file system. By accessing the **Properties** dialog box for a folder, you can share, or stop sharing, folders.

Using the net share command

The **net share** command creates, deletes, or displays shared folders. For example, to share a folder named C:\data on the network with the share name Data, type:

net share data=C:\data

The **net share** command uses the following syntax:

net share *SharedFolderName=Drive*:*Path*

Value	Description
SharedFolderName=Drive:*Path*	This is the network name of the shared folder and the absolute path of its location.

For a complete listing of the **net share** syntax, type **net share /?** at a command prompt.

Shared Folder Permissions

Permission	Description
Read (Default, applied to the Everyone group)	• Allows you to view data in files and attributes • Allows you to view file names and subfolder names • Allows you to run program files
Change (Includes all Read permissions)	• Allows you to add files and subfolders • Allows you to change data in files • Allows you to delete subfolders and files
Full Control (Includes all Read and Change permissions)	• Allows you to change NTFS file and folder permissions

Introduction

Shared folder permissions apply only to users who connect to the folder over the network. They do not restrict access to users who access the folder at the computer where the folder is stored. You can grant shared folder permissions to user accounts, groups, and computer accounts.

Important By default, users will have the same level of access to subfolders under a shared folder as they have on the parent folder.

Permissions

Shared folder permissions include the following:

- **Read**

  Read is the default shared folder permission and is applied to the Everyone group. Read permission enables you to:

  - View file names and subfolder names.
  - View data in files and attributes.
  - Run program files.

- **Change**

  Change permission includes all Read permissions and also enables you to:

  - Add files and subfolders.
  - Change data in files.
  - Delete subfolders and files.

- **Full Control**

  Full Control includes all Read and Change permissions and also enables you to change permissions for NTFS files and folders.

Methods to Connect to Shared Folders

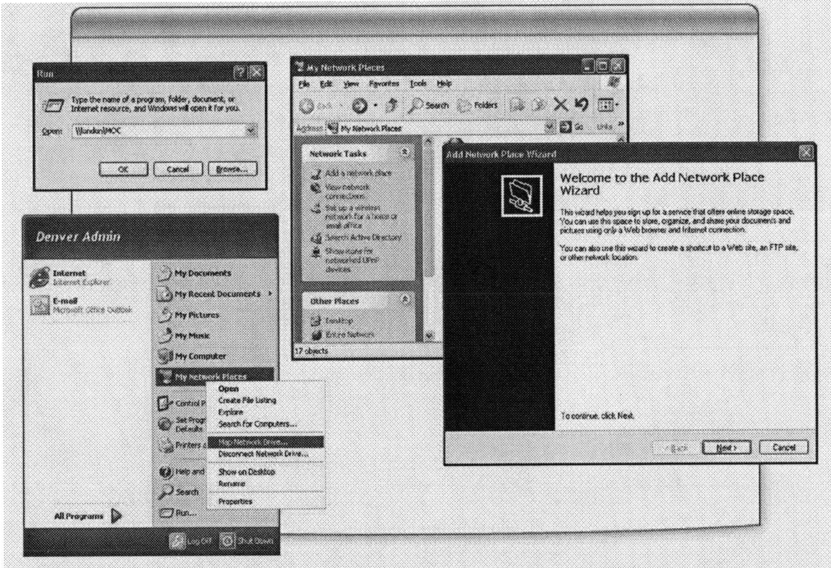

Introduction

After you create a shared folder, users can access the folder across the network by using multiple methods. Users can access a shared folder on another computer by using **My Network Places**, by using the Map Network Drive feature, by searching Active Directory, or by using the **Run** command on the **Start** menu.

Using My Network Places

The **My Network Places** dialog box can be launched from the **Network and Internet Connections** section of Control Panel. You can also configure the **Start** menu to display the **My Network Places** shortcut. From **My Network Places**, any user can launch the Add A Network Place wizard. The wizard allows a user to browse to, or type in the address of a network location, such as a UNC path or an FTP site, and provide a friendly name for the network location. For example, a user could use the wizard to map to the UNC path of *\\server\data*, but give it a friendly name of My Reports.

Note When you open a shared folder over the network, Windows Server 2003 automatically adds it to **My Network Places**.

Using Map Network Drive

When you want to associate a drive letter and icon with a specific shared folder, you must map to a network drive. This makes it easier to refer to the location of a file in a shared folder. You can also use drive letters to access shared folders for which you cannot use a UNC path, such as a folder for an older application. The **Map Network Drive** dialog box can be accessed on the shortcut menu of My Computer or on the **Tools** menu in Windows Explorer or My Computer. The **Map Network Drive** dialog box allows users to select a drive letter to assign to the mapping and either type in the UNC path or browse for the network path. It also allows users to connect using alternative credentials.

Using the Run command

When you use the **Run** command on the **Start** menu to connect to a network resource, a drive letter is not required. This enables you to connect to the shared folder an unlimited number of times, independent of available drive letters.

When you enter the server name in the format *servername*, a list of available shared folders appears. Windows Server 2003 gives you the option to choose one of the entries based on the shared folders that are available to you.

What Are Published Shared Folders?

- A published shared folder:
  - Is a shared folder object in Active Directory
  - Can maintain static friendly names
- Clients:
  - Can search Active Directory for published shared folders
  - Do not need to know the name of the server to connect to a shared folder
  - Can search by using keywords if they do not know the exact name of the share

Definition

Publishing resources and shared folders in Active Directory enables users to search Active Directory and locate resources on the network even if the physical location of the resources changes.

For example, if you move a shared folder to another computer, all shortcuts that users have on their desktops pointing to the Active Directory object that represents the published shared folder continue to work, as long as you update the reference to the physical location. Users do not have to update their shortcuts.

Publishing the folder

You can publish any shared folder in Active Directory that can be accessed by using a UNC name. You publish shared folders by creating a shared folder object in Active Directory that points to the UNC path of the shared folder. After a shared folder is published, a user at a computer running Microsoft Windows Server 2003 or a domain client running Microsoft Windows XP Professional can use Active Directory to locate the object representing the shared folder and then connect to the shared folder.

You can publish information about printers and shared folders by using Computer Management or Active Directory Users and Computers.

Viewing the published shared folder

When you publish the shared folder by using Computer Management, the shared folder becomes a child object of the computer account. To view shared folders as an object, in **Active Directory Users and Computers**, on the **View** menu, click **Users, Group, and Computers as containers**. Then, in the console tree, click the computer account. In the Details pane, you will see all the published shared folders that are associated with the computer account.

When a shared folder is published using Active Directory Users and Computers, it appears as an object in the container in which it was created.

Important You cannot use publishing to create new shared folders. You can only advertise existing shared folders by publishing them in the Active Directory.

Using keywords

Administrators who publish shared folders can create a list of keywords to assist users in searching for shared folders. For example, sales personnel might need to find a shared customer list but might not know the exact name of the share or the server where the shared folder is located. The administrator can configure a list of keywords such as customers, contacts, or clients and associate them with the share. This list of keywords should be developed in collaboration with the users who will be accessing the shared folders.

Static friendly names

The published name of a shared folder in Active Directory will remain static because it is merely a pointer to a UNC path. If a set of shared folders is moved to a new file server, the administrator need only change the properties of the shared folder object in Active Directory to reflect the new UNC path. End users' shortcuts to the published object will continue to function.

Important The permissions that you need to create or modify shared folder objects in the Active Directory have no direct correlation to the permissions that you need to access the contents of the shared folder. Administrators do not need any permission on the actual shared folder to create and modify its associated shared folder object in Active Directory.

How Published Shared Folders Are Used

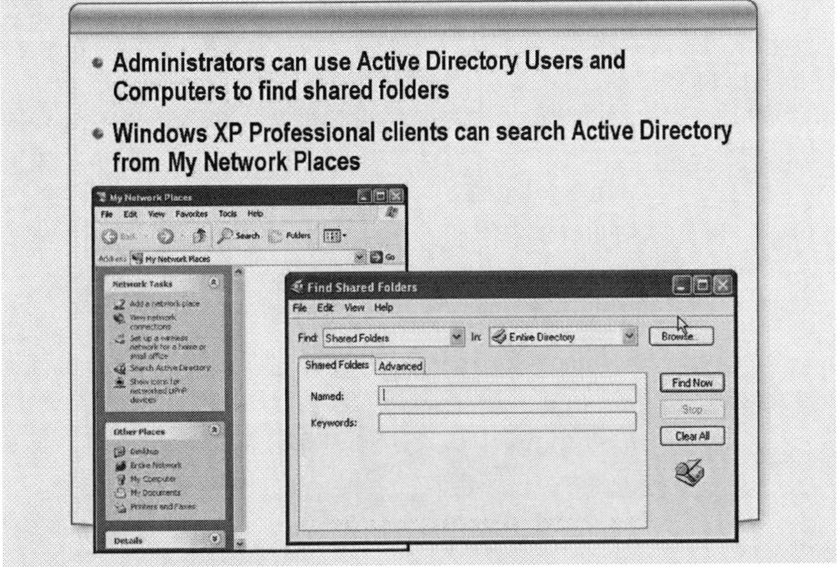

Introduction

In a large enterprise that has many shared folders available on many different network servers in multiple domains; users might have difficulty locating the shared folders they need to do their jobs. Clients can use **My Network Places** to search Active Directory for published shared folders.

Administrators might also have to locate shared folders to perform maintenance on them. For example, an administrator might have to change the root path when a set of folders is moved to a new server. Administrators can use the **Find** command in Active Directory Users and Computers to search for shared folders.

Using My Network Places

Client computers that have Windows XP Professional installed and have accounts in the domain can search Active Directory for shared folders by using the link in the **Network Tasks** section of **My Network Places.** To view the **Search Active Directory** link, the Windows XP client must have the **Show Common Tasks in Folders** feature turned on in **Folder Options.** This is the default setting. The link brings up the Active Directory search box. In the **Find** drop-down list, users can select **Shared Folders** as the type of object to search for. Users have the option to search in a particular domain or search all domains by selecting **Entire Directory** in the **Look In** box.

After users find the shared folders they are looking for, they can open the folders directly or map a drive letter to them from the search results list.

Important Any user can map a drive letter to connect to a shared folder. Shared folder permissions specify whether that user can open the folder and access the contents.

Best Practices for Using Shared Folders

- Use the Authenticated Users group instead of Everyone
- Share folders with the appropriate level of permission
- Use groups to grant access rather than individual users
- Publish shared folders in larger environments

Introduction

Shared folders provide access to network resources. Administrators must keep security and ease of management in mind when setting permissions on shared folders.

Using Authenticated Users instead of Everyone

Use the Authenticated Users group to grant permissions because on computers running Windows Server 2003, Everyone includes Authenticated Users and Guest. On computers running earlier versions of Windows, Everyone includes Authenticated Users and Guest plus Anonymous Logon.

The Authenticated Users group includes all users and computers whose identities have been authenticated, but it does not include Guest even if the Guest account has a password.

Sharing with appropriate permissions

Assign the least level of permissions to shared folders that users and groups need to perform their duties.

Granting access to groups rather than users

Groups simplify administration. Individual users might come and go from the organization, but groups can remain constant. It is easier to change group memberships than to reassign permissions for individual users as job functions change.

Publishing shared folders in larger environments

If many shared folders are spread across multiple servers, you can publish the shared folders in Active Directory to facilitate users locating and accessing the shares without having to know the exact location of the data.

Practice: Managing Access to Shared Folders

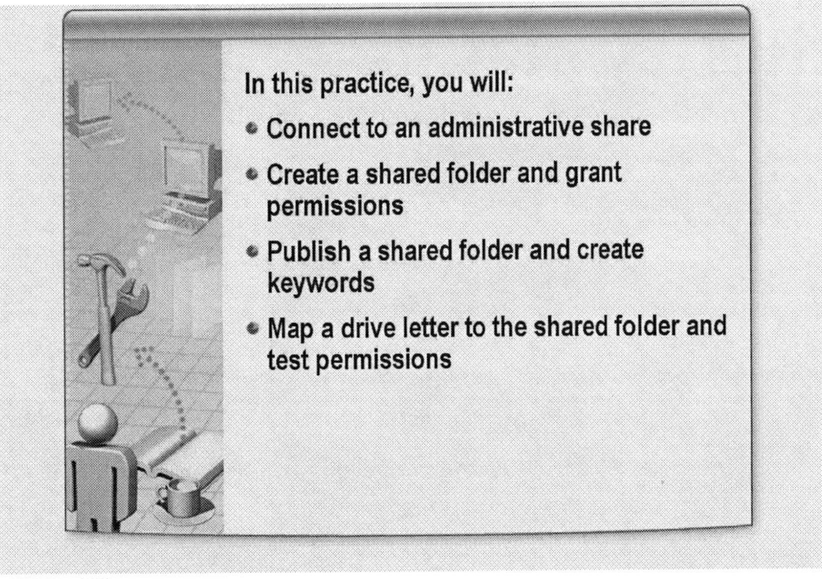

Objectives

In this practice, you will:

- Connect to an administrative share.
- Create a shared folder and grant permissions.
- Publish a shared folder and create keywords.
- Map a drive letter to the shared folder and test permissions.

Instructions

Ensure that the DEN-DC1 and DEN-CL1 virtual machines are started.

Practice

► **Connect to an administrative share**

1. Log on to DEN-CL1 as **Judy@contoso.msft** with the password of **Pa$$w0rd**.
2. Click **Start**, click **Run**, and then type **\\DEN-DC1\Admin$**. Click **OK**.
3. In the **Connect to den-dc1.contoso.msft** dialog box, enter the domain administrators credentials.

   The contents of the **Admin$** share will be displayed.
4. Open the **Properties** dialog box for any folder. Notice that you can use the Security tab to modify NTFS permissions but that you cannot create a new shared folder.
5. Close the **Admin$** share, and then log off DEN-CL1.

► Create a shared folder and grant permissions

1. Log on to DEN-DC1 as **Administrator** with the password of **Pa$$w0rd.**
2. Open Windows Explorer, and navigate to **C:\Sales.**
3. Right-click the **Sales** folder and then click **Sharing and Security.**
4. Click **Share this folder.**
5. Ensure that the **Share** name is **Sales.**
6. Click **Permissions.**
7. In the **Permissions for Sales** dialog box, remove the **Everyone** group.
8. Click **Add.**
9. In the **Select Users, Computers, or Groups** dialog box, type **DL Sales Read.**
10. Click **OK.**
11. Leave the default permission of **Read** for the **DL Sales Read** group.
12. Click **Add.**
13. In the **Select Users, Computers or Groups** dialog box, type **DL Sales Modify.**
14. Click **OK.**
15. Assign **Change** permission to the **DL Sales Modify** group.
16. Click **OK** twice.

► Publish a shared folder and create keywords

1. Open **Active Directory Users and Computers.**
2. Right-click the **Sales** organizational unit, point to **New**, and then click **Shared Folder.**
3. In the **New Object - Shared Folder** dialog box, type **Sales Data** in the **Name** field.
4. In the **Network Path** field, type **\\DEN-DC1\Sales.**
5. Click **OK.**
6. Right-click **Sales Data** and then click **Properties.**
7. Click the **Keywords** button.
8. In the **Keywords** dialog box, enter the following keywords, clicking **Add** after each one: **Contacts, Clients, Customers.**
9. Click **OK** twice.
10. Close all windows and then log off of DEN-DC1.

▶ Map a drive letter to the shared folder and test permissions

1. Log on to DEN-CL1 as **Don@contoso.msft** with a password of **Pa$$w0rd**.
2. Click **Start**, click **My Computer**, and then click **My Network Places** in **Other Places** on the taskbar.
3. In **My Network Places**, under **Network Tasks**, click **Search Active Directory**.
4. In the **Find** box, select **Shared Folders**.
5. In the **Keywords** field, type **clients**. (Keywords are not case-sensitive.)
6. Click **Find Now**.

   The **Sales Data** folder should appear in the list of results.
7. Right-click the **Sales Data** folder and then click **Map Network Drive**.
8. Click **Finish**.
9. Close the **Find Shared Folders** dialog box.
10. Close all open windows.
11. Open **My Computer**. In the **Network Drives** section, you should see an icon for **Sales on Den-dc1**.
12. Double-click the **Sales** drive. You should see the contents of the shared folder displayed.
13. Close **My Computer**, and log off.
14. Log on to DEN-CL1 as **Judy@contoso.msft** with a password of **Pa$$w0rd**.
15. Repeat steps 2 through 8 to map to the **Sales Data** folder.
16. Open **My Computer**, and attempt to access the Sales Data folder.

    You should see an "Access Denied" message. Although the user was able to map a drive letter to the shared folder, the user was not able to access the content of the share because the share permissions prevented it.
17. Log off.

Important Do not shut down the virtual machines.

Lesson: Managing Access to Files and Folders Using NTFS Permissions

- What Is NTFS?
- NTFS File and Folder Permissions
- What Is NTFS Permissions Inheritance?
- Effects on NTFS Permissions When Copying and Moving Files and Folders
- Best Practices for Managing Access to Files and Folders Using NTFS Permissions
- Practice: Managing Access to Files and Folders Using NTFS Permissions

Introduction

The information in this lesson presents the skills and knowledge that you need to manage access to files and folders by using NTFS permissions.

Lesson objectives

After completing this lesson, you will be able to:

- Explain what NTFS is.
- Explain what NTFS file and folder permissions are.
- Explain what NTFS permissions inheritance is.
- Explain the effects on NTFS permissions of copying and moving files and folders.
- Explain best practices for managing access to files and folders by using NTFS permissions.
- Manage access to files and folders using NTFS permissions.

What Is NTFS?

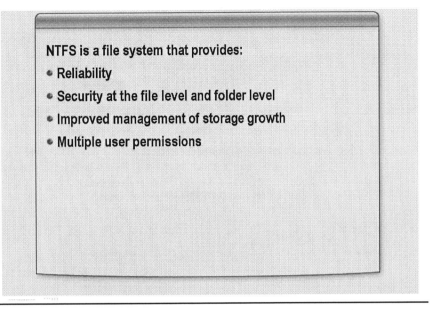

NTFS is a file system that provides:

- Reliability
- Security at the file level and folder level
- Improved management of storage growth
- Multiple user permissions

Introduction

NTFS is a file system that is available on Windows Server 2003. NTFS provides performance and features that are not found in either FAT (file allocation table) or FAT32.

Benefits of NTFS

NTFS provides the following benefits:

- *Reliability*. NTFS uses log file and checkpoint information to restore the integrity of the file system when the computer is restarted. If there is a bad-sector error, NTFS dynamically remaps the cluster containing the bad sector and allocates a new cluster for the data. NTFS also marks the cluster as unusable.
- *Greater security*. NTFS files use the Encrypting File System (EFS) to secure files and folders. If EFS is enabled, files and folders can be encrypted for use by single or multiple users. The benefits of encryption are data confidentiality and data integrity, which means that data is protected against malicious or accidental modification.

  NTFS also stores a DACL with every file and folder on an NTFS partition. The DACL contains a list of all user accounts, groups, and computers that are granted access for the file or folder and the type of access that they are granted. For a user to access a file or folder, the DACL must contain an entry, called an ACE, for the user account, group, or computer that the user is associated with. The ACE must specifically allow the type of access that the user is requesting for the user to access the file or folder. If no ACE exists in the DACL, Windows Server 2003 denies the user access to the resource.

- *Improved management of storage growth.* NTFS supports disk quotas, which enable you to specify the amount of disk space that is available to a user. By using disk quotas, you can track and control disk space usage and configure whether users are allowed to exceed a warning level or storage quota limit.

  NTFS supports larger files and a larger number of files per volume than FAT or FAT32. NTFS also manages disk space efficiently by using smaller cluster sizes. For example, a 30-gigabyte (GB) NTFS volume uses 4-kilobyte (KB) clusters. The same volume formatted with FAT32 uses 16-KB clusters. Using smaller clusters reduces wasted space on hard disks.

- *Multiple user permissions.* If you grant NTFS permissions to an individual user account and to a group to which the user belongs, you grant multiple permissions to the user. NTFS combines these multiple permissions to produce the user's effective permissions.

Additional reading

For more information about NTFS, see "NTFS" on the Microsoft TechNet Web site.

For more information about FAT and NTFS, see "Choosing Between FAT and NTFS" on the Microsoft Windows 2000 Advanced Server Documentation Web site.

NTFS File and Folder Permissions

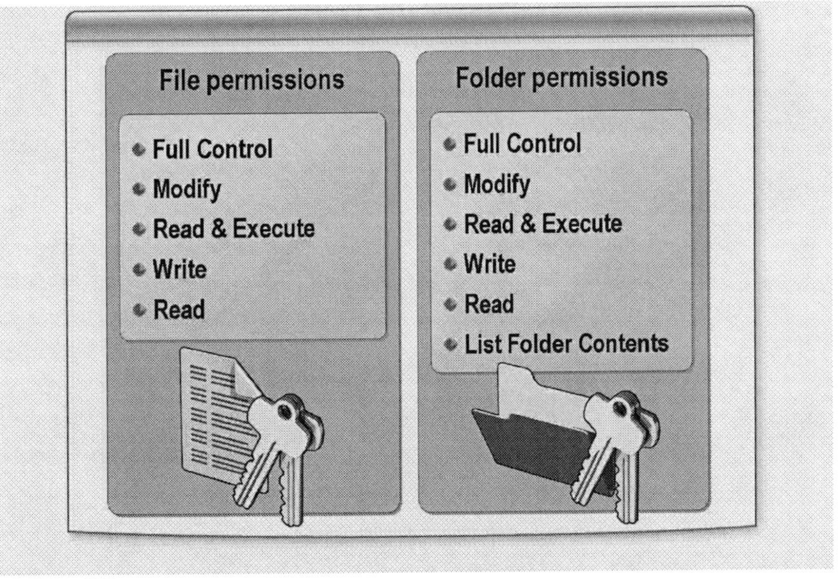

Introduction

NTFS permissions are used to specify which users, groups, and computers can access files and folders. NTFS permissions also dictate what users, groups, and computers can do with the contents of the file or folder.

NTFS file permissions

The following table lists the standard NTFS file permissions that you can grant and the type of access that each permission provides.

NTFS file permission	Allows the user to:
Full Control	Change permissions, take ownership, and perform the actions permitted by all other NTFS file permissions
Modify	Modify and delete the file and perform the actions permitted by Write permission and Read & Execute permission
Read & Execute	Run applications and perform the actions permitted by Read permission
Write	Overwrite the file, change file attributes, and view file ownership and permissions
Read	Read the file and view file attributes, ownership, and permissions

NTFS folder permissions

Permissions control access to folders and the files and subfolders that are contained in those folders. The following table lists the standard NTFS folder permissions that you can grant and the type of access that each permission provides.

NTFS folder permission	Allows the user to:
Full Control	Change permissions, take ownership, delete subfolders and files, and perform actions permitted by all other NTFS folder permissions
Modify	Delete the folder and perform actions permitted by Write permission and Read & Execute permission
Read & Execute	Traverse folders and perform actions permitted by Read permission and List Folder Contents permission
Write	Create new files and subfolders in the folder, change folder attributes, and view folder ownership and permissions
Read	View files and subfolders in the folder, folder attributes, ownership, and permissions
List Folder Contents	View the names of files and subfolders in the folder

Implicit and explicit Deny permission

Permissions can also be implicitly or explicitly denied. If a user does not have permissions assigned to his or her user account and does not belong to any groups that have been assigned permission, that user is implicitly denied access to the resource.

A user or a group can also be explicitly denied access to a resource. In that case, it does not matter what other permissions that user might have on the resource. An explicit Deny permission always overrides all other permissions. Explicit Deny permission should be used only in special cases. For example, suppose that all users in the Human Resources department have access to the employee records of all personnel but that only the Human Resources manager has access to the records of senior management. All other users are explicitly denied access.

Important An explicit Allow permission will override an inherited Deny permission.

What Is NTFS Permissions Inheritance?

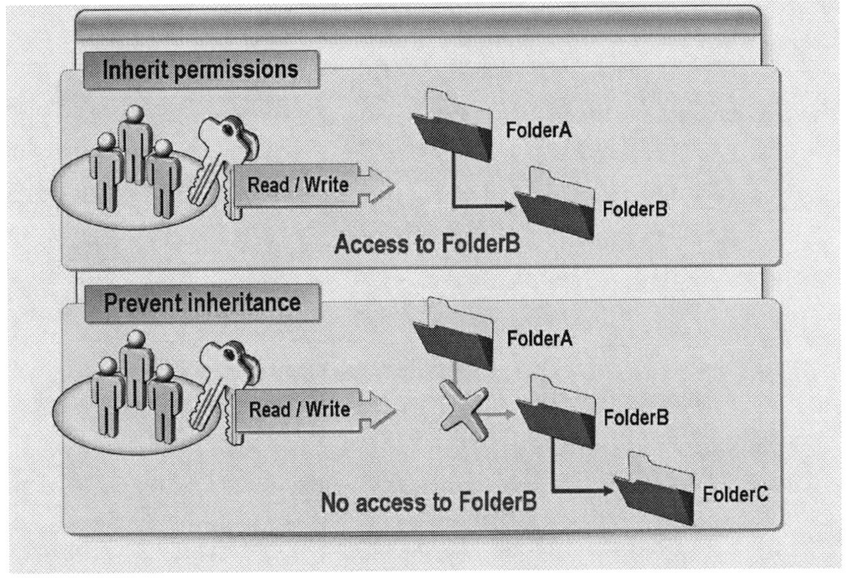

Definition

By default, permissions that you grant to a parent folder are inherited by the subfolders and files that are contained in the parent folder. When you create files and folders, and when you format a partition with NTFS, Windows Server 2003 automatically assigns default NTFS permissions. Inherited permissions are indicated by shaded permission check boxes on the **Security** tab.

Controlling permissions inheritance

A security principal that is inheriting permissions can have additional NTFS permissions assigned, but the inherited permissions cannot be removed until inheritance is blocked. You can prevent subfolders and files from inheriting permissions that are assigned to the parent folder. When you prevent permissions inheritance, you can either:

- Copy inherited permissions from the parent folder.

  \- or -

- Remove the inherited permissions and retain only the permissions that were explicitly assigned.

The folder on which you prevent permissions inheritance becomes the new parent folder, and the subfolders and files that are contained in it inherit the permissions assigned to it. Permissions can be inherited only from a direct parent.

Why prevent propagating permissions?

Permissions inheritance simplifies how permissions for parent folders, subfolders, and resources are assigned. However, you might want to prevent inheritance so that permissions do not propagate from a parent folder to subfolders and files.

For example, you might need to keep all Sales department files in one Sales folder for which everyone in the Sales department has Write permission. However, for a few files in the folder, you might need to limit the permissions to Read. To do so, prevent inheritance on each file so that the Write permission does not propagate to the files contained in the folder.

Effects on NTFS Permissions When Copying and Moving Files and Folders

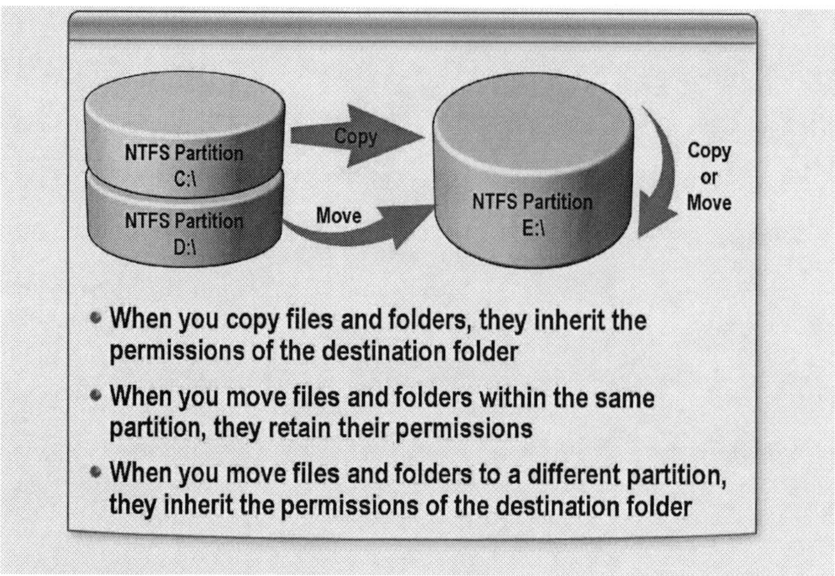

NTFS Partition
C:\
NTFS Partition
D:\
Copy
Move
NTFS Partition
E:\
Copy
or
Move
When you copy files and folders, they inherit the permissions of the destination folder
When you move files and folders within the same partition, they retain their permissions
When you move files and folders to a different partition, they inherit the permissions of the destination folder

Introduction

When you copy or move a file or folder, the permissions might change, depending on where you move the file or folder. It is important to understand the changes that the permissions undergo when being copied or moved.

Effects of copying files and folders

When you copy a file or folder from one folder to another folder, or from one partition to another partition, permissions for the files or folders might change. Copying a file or folder has the following effects on NTFS permissions:

- When you copy a file or folder within a single NTFS partition, the copy of the folder or file inherits the permissions of the destination folder.
- When you copy a file or folder to a different NTFS partition, the copy of the folder or file inherits the permissions of the destination folder.
- When you copy a file or folder to a non-NTFS partition, such as a FAT partition, the copy of the folder or file loses its NTFS permissions, because non-NTFS partitions do not support NTFS permissions.
- When you copy a file or folder within a single NTFS partition or between NTFS partitions, you must have Read permission for the source folder and Write permission for the destination folder.

Effects of moving files and folders

When you move a file or folder, permissions might change, depending on the permissions of the destination folder. Moving a file or folder has the following effects on NTFS permissions:

- When you move a file or folder within an NTFS partition, the folder or file retains its original permissions. If the permissions of the new parent folder are changed at a later time, the file or folder will inherit the new permissions. Permissions explicitly applied to the folder will be retained. Permissions previously inherited will be lost.
- When you move a file or folder to a different NTFS partition, the folder or file inherits the permissions of the destination folder. When you move a folder or file between partitions, Windows Server 2003 copies the folder or file to the new location and then deletes it from the old location.
- When you move a file or folder to a non-NTFS partition, the folder or file loses its NTFS permissions, because non-NTFS partitions do not support NTFS permissions.
- When you move a file or folder within an NTFS partition or between NTFS partitions, you must have both Write permission for the destination folder and Modify permission for the source file or folder. Modify permission is required to move a folder or file, because Windows Server 2003 removes the folder or file from the source folder after it copies it to the destination folder.

Effects of copying and moving within volumes

The following table lists the possible copy and move actions and describes how Windows Server 2003 handles the permission state of a file or folder.

Action	Result
Copy a file or folder within a volume	Inherits permission state of the destination folder
Move a file or folder within a volume	Retains original permission state of the source
Copy a file or folder between volumes	Inherits permission state of the destination folder
Move a file or folder between volumes	Inherits permission state of source file or folder

Best Practices for Managing Access to Files and Folders Using NTFS Permissions

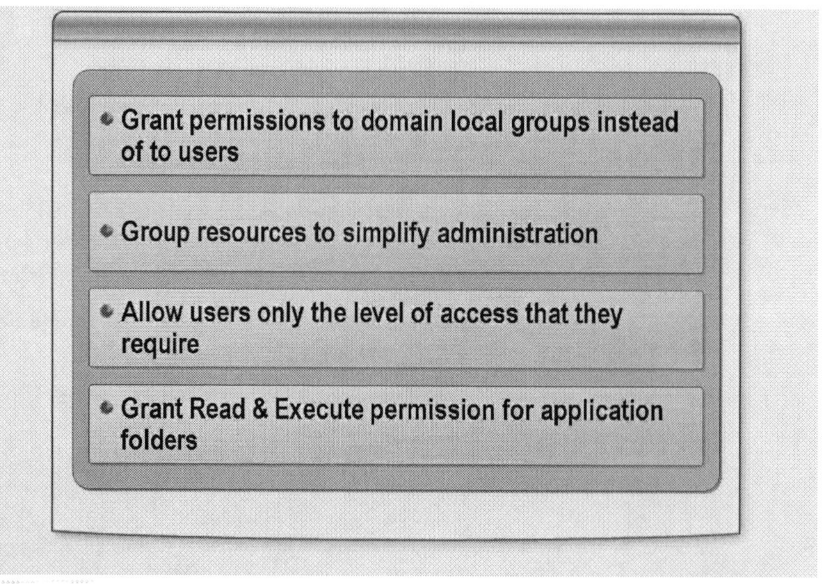

Best practices

When managing access to files and folders, consider the following best practices when granting NTFS permissions:

- Grant permissions to groups instead of users. Because it is inefficient to maintain user accounts directly, avoid granting permissions to individual users.
- Use Deny permissions in the following situations:
  - To exclude a subset of a group that has Allow permissions.
  - To exclude one permission when you have already granted Full Control permissions to a user or group.
- If possible, do not change the default permission entries for file system objects, particularly on system folders and root folders. Changing default permissions can cause unexpected access problems or reduce security.
- Never deny the Everyone group access to an object. If you deny everyone access to an object, you deny administrators access. Instead, it is recommended that you remove the Everyone group, as long as you grant permissions for the object to other users, groups, or computers.
- Grant permissions to an object that is as high on the tree as possible so that the security settings are propagated throughout the tree. You can quickly and effectively grant permissions to all children or a subtree of a parent object. By doing this, you affect the most objects with the least effort. Grant permissions that are adequate for the majority of users, groups, and computers.

- To simplify administration, group files according to function. For example:
  - Group program files into folders where commonly used applications are kept.
  - Group data folders containing home folders into one folder.
  - Group data files that are shared by multiple users into one folder.
- Grant Read & Execute permission to the Users and Administrators groups for application folders. This prevents users or viruses from accidentally deleting or damaging data and application files.
- Only allow users the level of access that they require. For example, if a user only needs to read a file, grant Read permission for the file to the user or group to which the user belongs.

Practice: Managing Access to Files and Folders Using NTFS Permissions

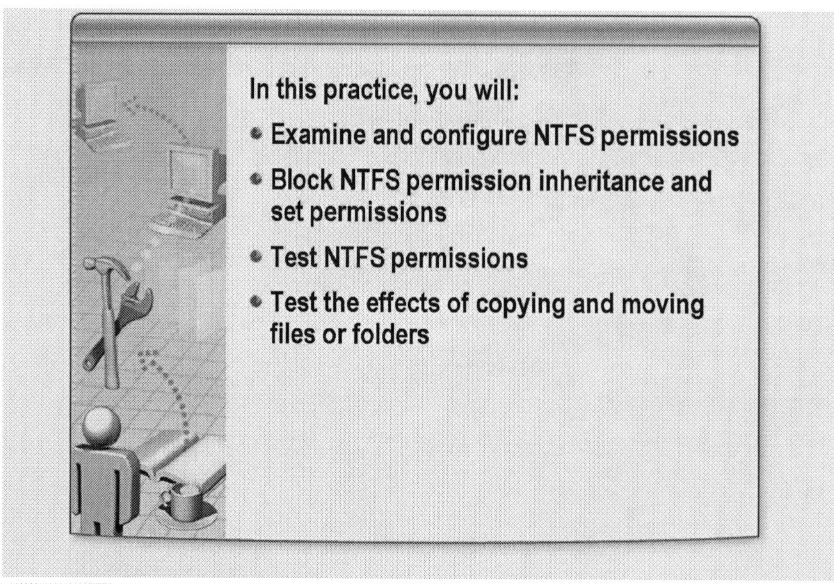

Objectives

In this practice, you will:

- Examine and configure NTFS permissions.
- Block NTFS permission inheritance and set permissions.
- Test NTFS permissions.
- Test the effects of copying and moving files or folders.

Instructions

Ensure that the DEN-DC1 and DEN-SRV1 virtual machines are started.

Practice

► **Examine and configure NTFS permissions**

1. Log on to DEN-SRV1 as **Administrator** with the password of **Pa$$w0rd.**
2. Open Windows Explorer, and then expand the **C:\Legal** folder.
3. Right-click the **Legal** folder, and then click **Sharing and Security**.
4. Click the **Security** tab, examine the default permissions.

   Notice that all the NTFS permissions that have been granted have shaded check boxes, indicating that they are inherited permissions. They are being inherited from the direct parent—in this case, C:\.
5. Select the **Users** group, and then click **Remove**. Read the message in the Security message box, and then click **OK**.

▶ Block NTFS permission inheritance and set permissions

1. Click the **Advanced** button.
2. Clear the check box **Allow inheritable permissions from the parent to propagate to this object and all child objects. Include these with entries explicitly defined here.**
3. Read the message in the **Security** message box, and then click **Remove.**
4. Click **OK.**
5. Click **Add.**
6. In the **Select Users, Computers, or Groups** dialog box, type **DL Legal Write** and then click **OK.**
7. Grant the **DL Legal Write** group **Read** and **Write** permissions.
8. Click **Add.**
9. Type **DL Legal Modify** and then click **OK.**
10. Assign the **DL Legal Modify** group **Modify** permission.
11. Click the **Administrators** account, and then assign it **Full Control.** Click **OK.**
12. Close Windows Explorer, and then log off.

▶ Test NTFS permissions

1. Log on to DEN-SRV1 as **LegalManager**, with a password of **Pa$$w0rd.**
2. Open Windows Explorer, and then click the **C:\Legal** folder.
3. Create a text file named **Legal.txt.**

   This should succeed, because the Legal Manager group is a member of G Legal Managers, which in turn is a member of DL Legal Modify.
4. Close Windows Explorer, and then log off.
5. Log on as **LegalUser**, with a password of **Pa$$w0rd.**
6. Open Windows Explorer.
7. Click the **Legal** folder, and then open **Legal.txt.**
8. Enter some text, and then save and close the file.

   This should succeed, because LegalUser is a member of G Legal, which in turn is a member of DL Legal Write.
9. Attempt to delete the **Legal.txt** file.

   You should receive an "Access Denied" error message because users must at least modify permission in order to delete files that they do not own.
10. Close all open windows, and then log off.

► Test the effects of copying and moving files or folders

1. Log on to DEN-SRV1 as **Administrator** with the password of **Pa$$w0rd**.
2. Open Windows Explorer and then click the **C:\Legal** folder.
3. Open the **Properties** dialog box for the **C:\Legal\Briefs** folder.
4. Click the **Security** tab. Note the current NTFS permissions. Click **Cancel**.
5. Connect to the administrative share **\\DEN-DC1\c$**.
6. Cut and paste the Briefs folder **C:\Legal\Briefs** to **\\den-dc1\c$**.
7. Open the **Properties** dialog box for the **C:\Briefs** folder on DEN-DC1, and examine the NTFS permissions.

   How are they different from the original location?

   ____

   ____

   ____

8. Close the administrative share window.
9. On DEN-SRV1, move the Documents folder **C:\Legal\Documents** to **C:**, and then examine the NTFS permissions.

   Have they changed from the original location?

   ____

   ____

10. Close all open windows and log off of DEN-SRV1.

Important Do not shut down the virtual machines.

Lesson: Determining Effective Permissions

- What Are Effective Permissions on NTFS Files and Folders?
- Class Discussion: Applying NTFS Permissions
- Effects of Combined Shared Folder and NTFS Permissions
- Class Discussion: Determining Effective NTFS and Shared Folder Permissions
- Practice: Determining Effective NTFS and Shared Folder Permissions

Introduction

If you grant NTFS permissions to an individual user account and a group to which the user belongs, you grant multiple permissions to the user. NTFS combines these multiple permissions to produce the user's effective permissions.

Lesson objectives

After completing this lesson, you will be able to:

- Explain what effective NTFS permissions are and how to determine them for files and folders.
- Explain the effects of combined shared folder and NTFS permissions.
- Determine the effective NTFS and shared folder permissions.

What Are Effective Permissions on NTFS Files and Folders?

- NTFS permissions are cumulative
- File permissions override folder permissions
- Deny overrides all permissions
- Creators of files and folders are their owners

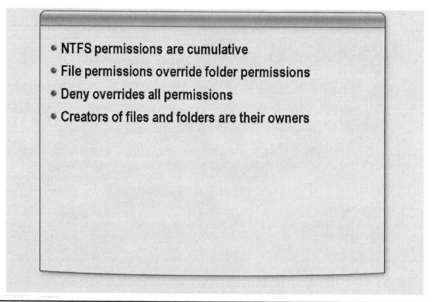

Introduction

Windows Server 2003 provides a tool that shows effective permissions, which are cumulative permissions based on group membership. The information is calculated from the existing permissions entries and is displayed in a read-only format.

Characteristics of effective permissions

Effective permissions have the following characteristics:

- *Cumulative permissions are the combination of the highest NTFS permissions granted to the user and all the groups that the user is a member of.* For example, if a user is a member of a group that has Read permission and a member of a group that has Modify permission, the user has Modify permission.
- *NTFS file permissions take priority over folder permissions.* For example, if a user has Modify permission to a folder but only has Read permission to certain files in that folder. The effective permission for those files will be Read.
- *Explicit Deny permissions override equivalent Allow permissions.* However, an explicit Allow permission can override an inherited deny permission. For example, if a user is explicitly denied write access to a folder but be explicitly allowed write access to a subfolder or a particular file, the explicit Allow would override the inherited Deny.
- *Every object is owned in an NTFS volume or in Active Directory.* The owner controls how permissions are set on the object and to whom permissions are granted. For example, a user can create a file in a folder where the user normally has Modify permission, but because that user created the file, the user will have the ability to change the permissions. The user could then grant himself or herself Full Control over the file.

Important An administrator who needs to repair or change permissions on a file but does not have Change Permission permission must take ownership of the file.

Ownership

By default, in the Windows Server 2003 family, the owner of an object is the user who creates the object. Objects created during installation and any object created by a member of the local Administrators group will be owned by the Administrators group. The owner can always change permissions on an object, even when the owner is denied all access to the object.

Ownership can be taken by the following individuals:

- An administrator. By default, the Administrators group is given the **Take ownership of files or other objects** user right.
- Anyone or any group that has **Take ownership** permission for the object in question.
- A user who has the **Restore files and directories** privilege.

Ownership can be transferred in the following ways:

- The current owner can grant **Take ownership** permission to another user. The user must actually take ownership to complete the transfer.
- An administrator can take ownership.
- A user who has the **Restore files and directories** privilege can double-click **Other users and groups** and specify any user or group to assign ownership to while performing a restore operation.

Important Permissions on a shared folder are not part of the effective permissions calculation. Access to shared folders can be denied through shared folder permissions even when access is allowed through NTFS permissions.

Class Discussion: Applying NTFS Permissions

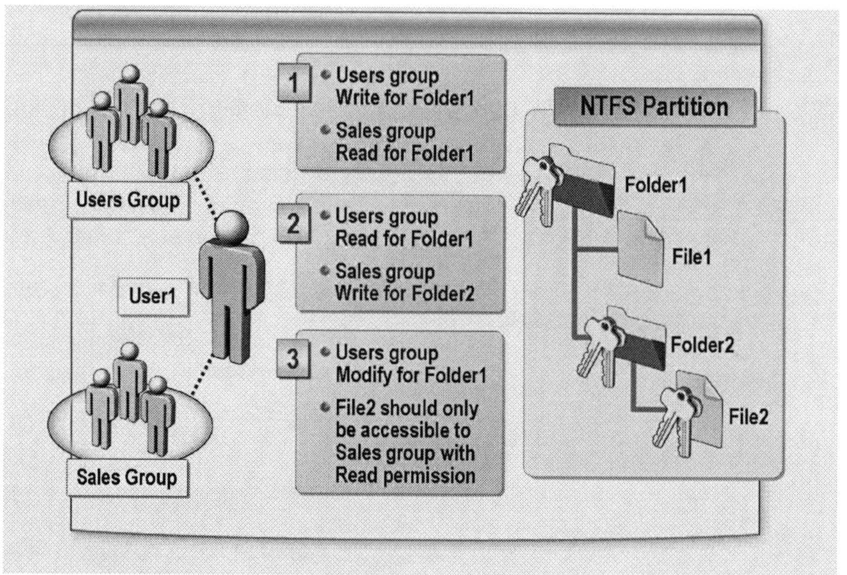

Introduction

In this exercise, you are presented with a scenario in which you are asked to apply NTFS permissions. You and your classmates will discuss possible solutions to the scenario.

Discussion

User1 is a member of the Users group and the Sales group.

1. The Users group has Write permission, and the Sales group has Read permission for Folder1. What permissions does User1 have for Folder1?

   Read & Write

2. The Users group has Read permission for Folder1. The Sales group has Write permission for Folder2. What permissions does User1 have for File2?

   Read & Write

3. The Users group has Modify permission for Folder1. File2 should be accessible only to the Sales group, and they should only be able to read File2. What do you do to ensure that the Sales group has only Read permission for File2?

____

____

____

____

Effects of Combined Shared Folder and NTFS Permissions

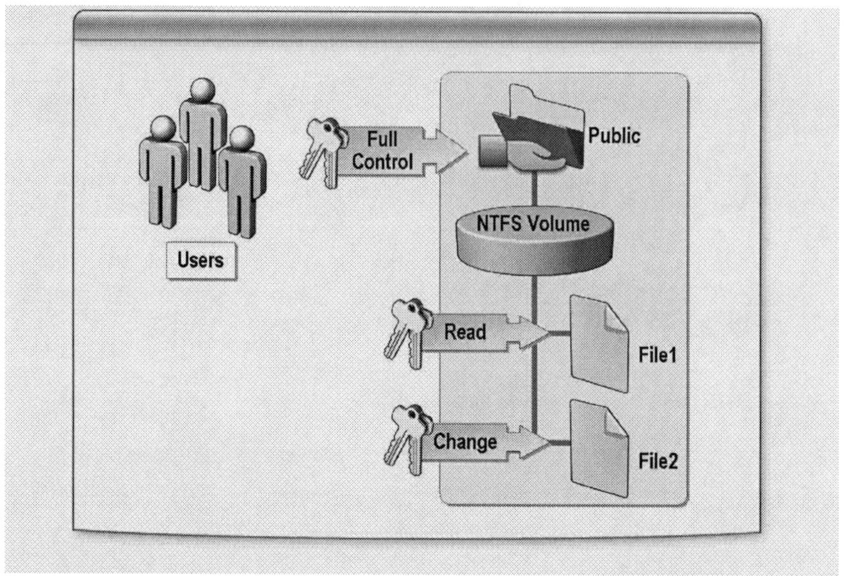

Introduction

When allowing access to network resources on an NTFS volume, it is recommended that you use the most restrictive NTFS permissions to control access to folders and files, combined with the most restrictive shared folder permissions that control network access.

What are combined permissions?

When you create a shared folder on a partition formatted with NTFS, both the shared folder permissions and the NTFS permissions combine to secure file resources. NTFS permissions apply whether the resource is accessed locally or over a network.

When you grant shared folder permissions on an NTFS volume, the following rules apply:

- By default, the Everyone group is granted the shared folder permission Read.
- Users must have the appropriate NTFS permissions for each file and subfolder in a shared folder, in addition to the appropriate shared folder permissions, to access those resources.
- When you combine NTFS permissions and shared folder permissions, the resulting permission is the most restrictive permission of the effective shared folder permissions or the effective NTFS permissions.

Class Discussion: Determining Effective NTFS and Shared Folder Permissions

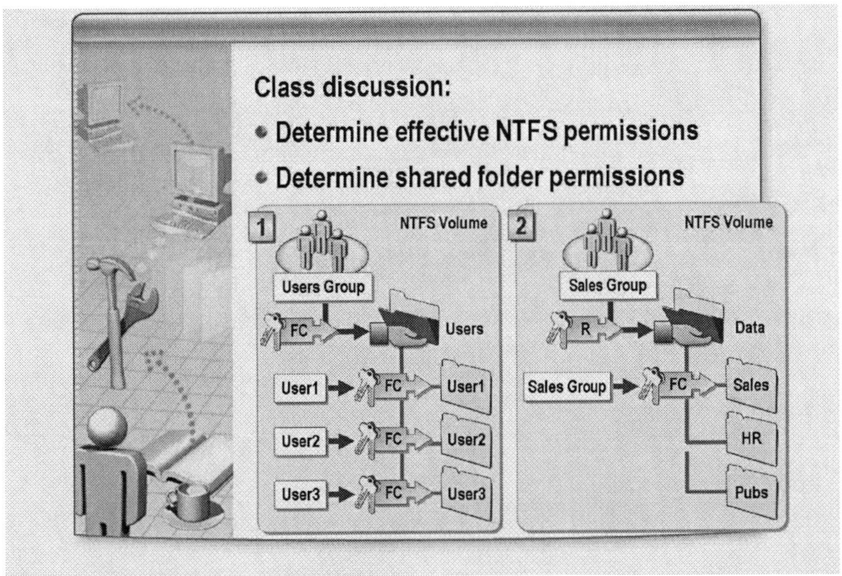

Objective

In this discussion, you will determine the effective NTFS and shared folder permissions.

Class discussion

The graphic on this page illustrates two shared folders that contain folders or files that have been assigned NTFS permissions. Look at each example and determine a user's *effective* permissions.

1. In the first example, the Users folder has been shared, and the Users group has the shared folder permission Full Control. User1, User2, and User3 have been granted the NTFS permission Full Control to *only* their folder. These users are all members of the Users group.

   Do members of the Users group have Full Control to *all* home folders in the Users folder once they connect to the Users shared folder?

   ____

   ____

   ____

2. In the second example, the Data folder has been shared. The Sales group has been granted the shared folder permission Read for the Data shared folder and the NTFS permission Full Control for the Sales folder.

   What are the Sales group's effective permissions when they access the Sales folder by connecting to the Data shared folder?

   ____

   ____

   ____

Practice: Determining Effective NTFS and Shared Folder Permissions

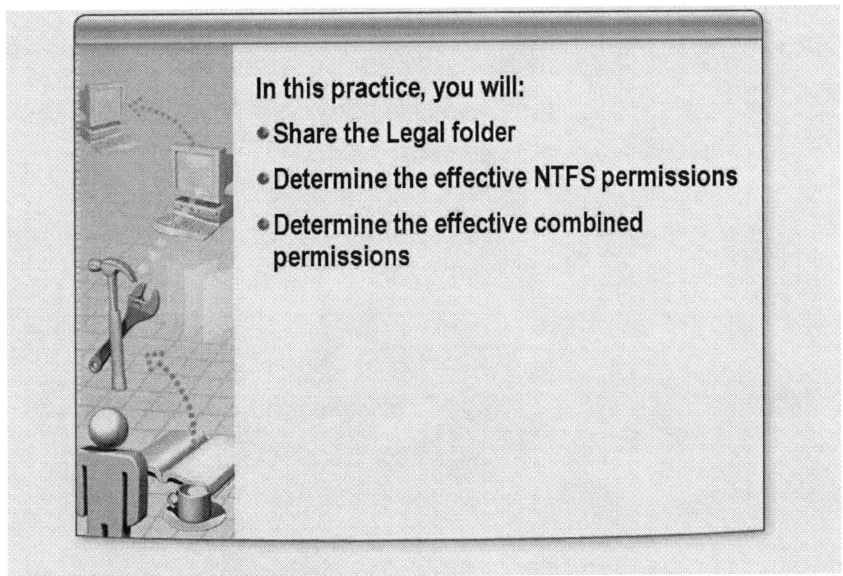

Objectives

In this practice, you will:

- Share the Legal folder.
- Determine the effective NTFS permissions.
- Determine the effective combined permissions.

Instructions

Ensure that the DEN-DC1, DEN-CL1 and DEN-SRV1 virtual machines are started.

Practice

► **Share the Legal folder**

1. Log on to DEN-SRV1 as **Administrator** with the password of **Pa$$w0rd**.
2. In Windows Explorer, locate the **C:\Legal** folder.
3. Right-click **C:\Legal** and then click **Sharing and Security**.
4. Click the **Sharing** tab and then share the folder using a share name of **Legal**.
5. Click **Permissions**. Remove the **Everyone** group, and then add the **Authenticated Users** group and assign **Read** permission.
6. Click **OK** twice. An icon of a hand should appear under the Legal folder to indicate that it is shared.

► **Determine the effective NTFS permissions**

1. Open the **Properties** dialog box for the Legal folder, and then click the **Security** tab.
2. Click **Advanced**.
3. Click the **Effective Permissions** tab.
4. Click **Select** to locate the user or group that you want to test.
5. Type **LegalManager**, and then click **OK**.

   What NTFS permissions does the LegalManager account have?

   Read/execute Write Read List

6. Test the LegalUser account.

   What NTFS permissions does the LegalUser account have?

   Read/execute Read Write List

7. Test the Authenticated Users group.

   What NTFS permissions does the Authenticated Users group have?

   None

8. Close all open windows and log off.

▶ Determine the effective combined permissions

1. Log on to DEN-CL1 as **Legalmanager**, with a password of **Pa$$w0rd**.
2. Click **Start**, click **Run**, and then type **\\DEN-SRV1\Legal**. Attempt to create a new text document in the Legal shared folder.

   Did it succeed? Why or why not?

   NO WRITE PERMISSIONS
   ____
   ____

3. Log off.
4. Log on as **Judy** with the password of **Pa$$w0rd**.
5. Click **Start**, click **Run**, and then type **\\DEN-SRV1\Legal** Attempt to create a new document in the Legal folder.

   What are the results?

   CANNOT CONNECT TO SHARE
   ____
   ____
   ____

6. Close all windows, and then log off.

Important Do not shut down the virtual machines.

Lesson: Managing Access to Shared Files Using Offline Caching

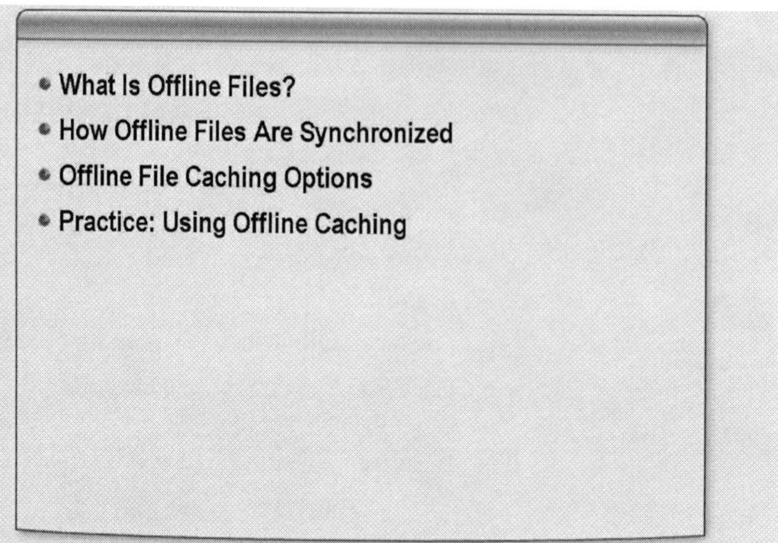
What Is Offline Files?
How Offline Files Are Synchronized
Offline File Caching Options
Practice: Using Offline Caching

Introduction

The information in this lesson presents the skills and knowledge that you need to manage access to shared files by using offline caching.

Lesson objectives

After completing this lesson, you will be able to:

- Explain what Offline Files is.
- Explain how offline files are synchronized.
- Explain the offline file caching modes.
- Configure offline caching.

What Is Offline Files?

- Offline Files is a document-management feature that provides the user with consistent online and offline access to files
- Advantages of using Offline Files:
  - Support for mobile users
  - Automatic synchronization
  - Performance advantages
  - Backup advantages

Definition

Offline Files is an important document-management feature that provides the user with consistent online and offline access to files. When the client disconnects from the network, anything that has been downloaded to the local cache remains available. Users can continue working as though they were still connected to the network. They can continue editing, copying, deleting, and so forth. The files are cached in a folder named CSC (Client Side Caching) in the %systemroot% directory.

From the user's perspective, the workspaces appear identical, whether they are on or off the network. Visual cues, such as icons, menus, and Active Directory, remain the same, including the view of the mapped network drives. Network files appear in the same network drive directory and can be accessed, copied, edited, printed, or deleted precisely as they are when they are online. When you reconnect to the network, client and server files are automatically resynchronized.

Advantages of using Offline Files

Using Offline Files has the following advantages:

- Support for mobile users

  When a mobile user views the shared folder while disconnected, the user can still browse, read, and edit files, because they have been cached on the client computer. When the user later connects to the server, the system reconciles the changes with the server.

- Automatic synchronization

  You can configure synchronization policy and behavior based on the time of day and network connection type by using Synchronization Manager. For example, you can configure synchronization so that it occurs automatically when the user logs on to a direct local area network (LAN) connection, but only at a user's request when he or she uses a dial-up connection.

- Performance advantages

  Offline Files provides performance advantages for networks. While connected to the network, clients can still read program files from the local cache, reducing the amount of data transferred over the network. Programs will generally start and run faster.

- Backup advantages

  Offline Files solves a dilemma facing most enterprise organizations today. Many organizations implement a backup policy that requires all user data to be stored on managed servers. The organization's IT department often does not back up data stored on local disks. This becomes a problem for mobile users of portable computers.

  If you want to access data when offline, a mechanism is needed to replicate data between the portable computer and the servers. Some organizations use the Briefcase tool. Others use batch files or replicate data manually. With clients running Windows Server 2003, Windows XP, or Windows 2000, replication between client and server is managed automatically. Files can be accessed while you are offline and are automatically synchronized with the managed server.

Additional reading

For more information about offline file security, see "Securing Offline Files" on the Microsoft TechNet Web site.

How Offline Files Are Synchronized

- Disconnected from the network
  - Files are synchronized at logoff. The user works with the locally cached copy
- Logged on to the network
  - Files are synchronized at logon. The user works with the network version of the files
- If a file has been modified in both locations
  - The user must choose which version of the file to keep or to rename one file and keep both versions

Introduction

A user can configure a file on a network to be available offline, provided that Offline Files is enabled for the folder in which the file resides and Offline Files are enabled on the client. By default, the Offline Files feature is disabled on all Microsoft servers and enabled on Windows 2000 Professional and Windows XP Professional. When users configure files to be available offline, the users work with the network version of the files while they are connected to the network and then with a locally cached version of the files when they are not connected to the network.

Synchronization events

When a user configures a file to be available offline, depending on the settings, the following synchronization events might occur when the user disconnects from the network:

- When the user logs off the network, the Windows client operating system synchronizes the network files with a locally cached copy of the file.
- While the computer is disconnected from the network, the user works with the locally cached copy of the file.
- When the user again logs on to the network, the Windows client operating system synchronizes any offline file that the user has modified with the network version of the file. If the file has been modified on both the network and the user's computer, the Windows client operating system prompts the user to choose which version of the file to keep, or the user can rename one file and keep both versions.

Important Using offline files is not a substitute for document version control. If two users work with the same offline file at the same time and then synchronize the file with the network version, one of the versions might be lost.

Additional reading

For more information about how clients synchronize offline files, see "Offline Files overview" on the Microsoft TechNet Web site.

Offline File Caching Options

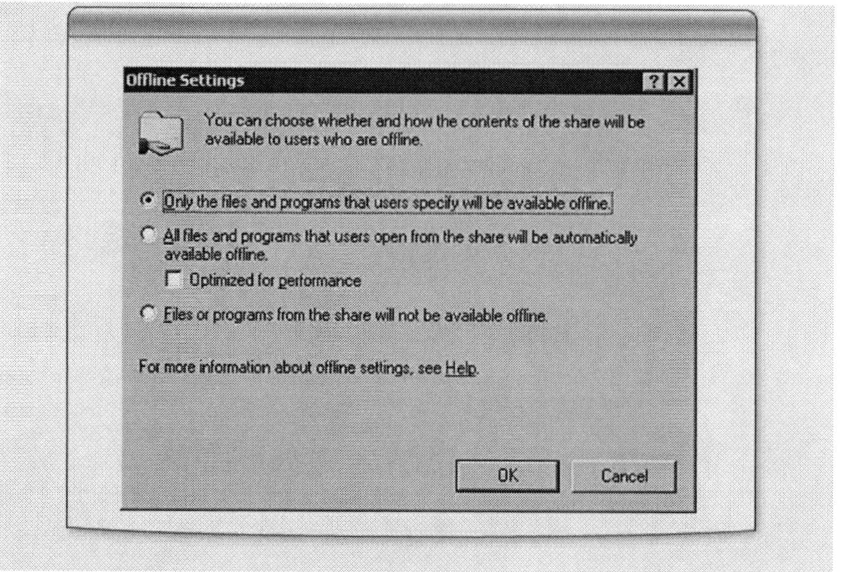

Introduction

When you create shared folders on the network, you can specify the caching option for the files and programs in that folder. There are three different caching options.

Manual caching of documents

Manual caching of documents provides offline access for only the files and programs that the user specifies will be available. This caching option is ideal for a shared network folder containing files that several people will access and modify. This is the default option when you configure a shared folder to be available offline.

Automatic caching of documents

With automatic caching of documents, all files and programs that users open from the shared folder are automatically available offline. Files that the user does not open are not available offline. Older copies are automatically overwritten by newer versions of files.

Automatic caching of programs

The **Optimized for performance** option provides automatic caching of programs, which provides offline access to shared folders containing files that are not to be changed. Automatic caching of programs reduces network traffic, because offline files are opened directly. The network versions are not accessed in any way, and the offline files start and run faster than the network versions.

When you use automatic caching of programs, be sure to restrict permissions for the files contained in the shared folders to Read access.

Practice: Using Offline Caching

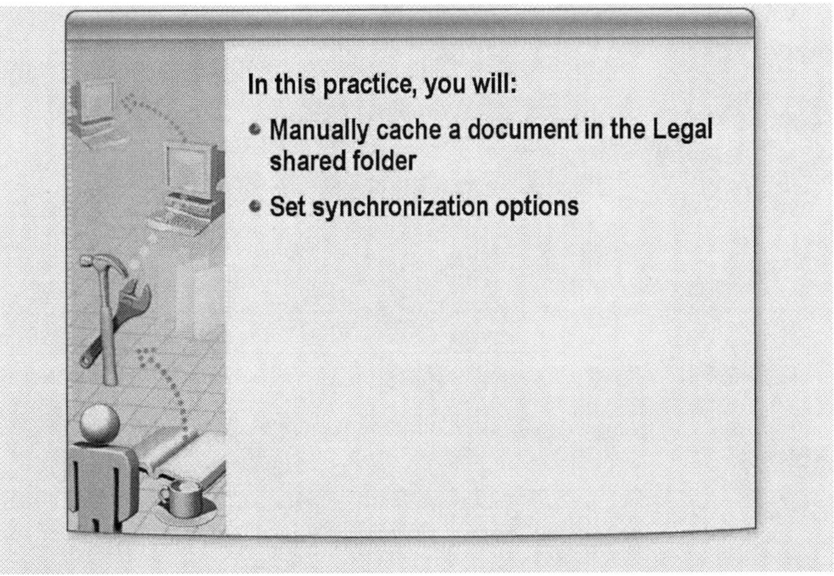

Objectives

In this practice, you will:

- Manually cache a document in the Legal shared folder.
- Set synchronization options.

Instructions

Ensure that the DEN-DC1, DEN-CL1 and DEN-SRV1 virtual machines are started.

Practice

► **Manually cache a document in the Legal shared folder**

1. Log on to DEN-SRV1 as **Administrator** with the password of **Pa$$w0rd.**
2. Open **Windows Explorer** and then click the **C:\Legal** folder.
3. Right-click **C:\Legal** and then click **Sharing and Security.**
4. On the **Sharing** tab, click **Permissions.**
5. Increase the permissions for the **Authenticated Users** group to **Change.** Click **OK** twice.

> **Important** This setting is configured for the purposes of the exercise and is not a recommended security best practice.

6. Create a text file named **cached.txt** and a file named **admin.txt** in the Legal folder.
7. Close all windows and log off of DEN-SRV1.
8. Log on to DEN-CL1 as **Legalmanager** with a password of **Pa$$w0rd.**
9. Click **Start**, click **Run**, and then type **\\DEN-SRV1**. Click **OK.**

10. In the DEN-SRV1 window, right-click the **Legal** shared folder, and then click **Map Network Drive**.
11. Click **Finish**, and then close all open windows.
12. Open **My Computer**, and then double-click the **Legal on den-srv1(Z)** drive.
13. Right-click the **Cached.txt** file, and then click **Make Available Offline**.
14. In the **Offline Files Wizard**, click **Next**.
15. Click the check box to accept synchronization at logon and logoff. Click **Next**.
16. Clear the **Enable Reminders** check box, and select the **Create a shortcut to the Offline Files folder on my desktop** check box.
17. Click **Finish**.
18. Close all open windows, and then log off.

► **Set synchronization options**

1. Log on to DEN-CL1 as **Administrator**.
2. Open **Control Panel**.
3. Click **Network Connections**, right-click **Local Area Connection**, and then click **Disable**.
4. Log off.
5. Log on to DEN-CL1 as **LegalManager**.
6. Open **My Computer** and then double-click the **Legal** mapped drive.
7. Only the **Cached.txt** file should appear in the list of files. It will have a double blue arrow to indicate that it is cached locally.
8. Open the **Cached.txt** file, enter some text, and then click **Save** and **Exit**.
9. Log off.
10. Log on as **Administrator**, and enable **Local Area Connection**.
11. Log off.
12. Log on to DEN-CL1 as **LegalManager**.

    Synchronization should occur.
13. Open the **Legal** mapped drive.

    You should see all files in the Legal folder now. The Cached.txt file should contain the changes you made while offline.

14. Close all open windows.
15. Click **Start**, point to **All Programs**, point to **Accessories**, and then click **Synchronize**.
16. In the **Items to Synchronize** dialog box, select the **\\den-srv1\Legal on Den-srv1** folder, and then click **Setup**.
17. In the **Synchronization Settings** dialog box, clear the **When I log on to my computer** check box.
18. Click **OK**.
19. Click **Close**.
20. Log off.

Important Do not shut down the virtual machines.

Lab: Managing Access to Resources

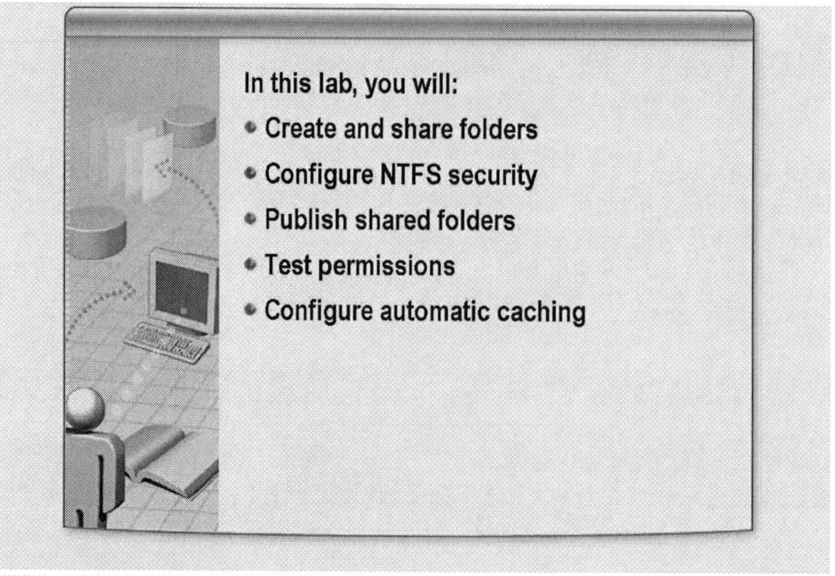

Objectives

After completing this lab, you will be able to:

- Create and share folders.
- Configure NTFS security.
- Publish shared folders.
- Test permissions.
- Configure automatic caching.

Prerequisites

To complete this lab, you must have the following virtual machines:

- DEN-DC1
- DEN-SRV1
- DEN-CL1

Estimated time to complete this lab: 30 minutes

Exercise 1
Creating and Sharing Folders

In this exercise, you will create and share two folders on DEN-SRV1.

Scenario

You are the Network Administrator for Contoso, Ltd. You have been asked to create two shared network folders to contain product information for Contoso, Ltd. The two folders will be named Research and Price List. The Administrators group should have Full Control permission for all folders. All Authenticated Users should have Read access. The Sales department managers should have Change permission for the Price List folder. The Legal department managers should have Change permission for the Research folder.

Tasks	Specific instructions
1. Create and share two folders.	**a.** Log on to DEN-SRV1 as **Administrator** with the password of **Pa$$w0rd**. **b.** Create two folders on C:\, one named **Research** and one named **Price List**.
2. Share the folders and set permissions.	**a.** Share the **Research** folder with the share name **Research**. **b.** Set the following share permissions for the **Research** folder: **Administrators:** **Full Control** **Authenticated Users:** **Read** **DL Research Change:** **Change** **c.** Share the **Price List** folder with the share name **Price List**. **d.** Set the following share permissions on the **Price List** folder: **Administrators:** **Full Control** **Authenticated Users:** **Read** **DL Sales Modify:** **Change**

Exercise 2
Configuring NTFS Security

In this exercise you will set the NTFS permissions on shared folders

Scenario

In this exercise, you will set the NTFS permissions on the shared folders to give the Administrators group Full Control permission for all folders. All Authenticated Users should have Read and Execute access. The Sales Managers group should have Modify permission for the Price List folder. The Legal Managers group should have Modify permission for the Research folder.

Task	Specific instructions
1. Configure NTFS permissions.	a. Right-click the **Research** folder and then click **Sharing and Security**. b. On the **Security** tab, click **Advanced**. c. Clear the check box to prevent permission inheritance, and then remove all permissions. Click **OK**. d. Configure the new NTFS permissions for the Research folder as follows: **Administrators:** **Full Control** **Authenticated Users:** **Read and Execute** **DL Research Change:** **Modify** e. Right-click the **Price List** folder and then click **Sharing and Security**. f. On the **Security** tab, click **Advanced**. g. Clear the check box to prevent permission inheritance, and then remove all permissions. Click **OK**. h. Configure the new NTFS permissions for the Price List folder as follows: **Administrators:** **Full Control** **Authenticated Users:** **Read and Execute** **DL Sales Modify:** **Modify**

Exercise 3
Publishing Shared Folders

In this exercise, you will publish the shared folders.

Scenario

Users in all domains must be able to find and access the Price List and Research folders. You will publish these folders in Active Directory with keywords to make it easy for users to find them.

Task	Specific instructions
1. Publish the folders in Active Directory by using Computer Management.	**a.** On DEN-SRV1, open **Computer Management.** **b.** Expand the **Shared Folders** node, and then click the **Shares** folder. **c.** Right-click the **Research** share, and then click **Properties.** **d.** On the **Publish** tab, select the **Publish this share in Active Directory** check box. **e.** Click the **Edit** box next to **Keywords**, and enter the keywords **Development** and **Products**, clicking **Add** after each one. **f.** Click **OK** twice. **g.** Publish the **Price List** shared folder with the keyword **Prices.** **h.** Close all open windows.

Exercise 4
Testing Permissions

In this exercise, you will test the network access by logging on as two different users and testing permissions.

Scenario

You must make sure that the right people have the right access. You will perform testing.

Task	Specific instructions
1. Test access as Don Hall and Judy Lew.	a. Log on to DEN-CL1 as the sales manager **Don** with the password of **Pa$$w0rd**. b. Connect to the **\\DEN-SRV1\Price List** shared folder. c. Create a new text document named **Prices.txt**. This will succeed because the domain local group DL Sales Managers has the proper access. d. Close all open windows, and then log off. e. Log on to DEN-CL1 as **Judy** with the password of **Pa$$w0rd**. f. Connect to the **\\DEN-SRV1\Price List** folder. g. Open the **Prices.txt** file. The file should open because the Authenticated Users group has Read access. h. Attempt to modify and save the file. This attempt should fail because the Authenticated Users group has Read access. i. Close all open windows, and then log off.

Exercise 5
Configuring Automatic Caching

In this exercise, you will configure a shared folder to provide automatic caching of documents.

Scenario

Many sales personnel use laptops and travel to client sites. You want to ensure that they automatically have the most recent versions of the price list on their laptops. You will configure the Price List folder to provide automatic caching.

Task	Specific instructions
1. Configure automatic caching for the Price List shared folder	**a.** Ensure that you are logged on to DEN-SRV1 as Administrator. **b.** Open **Windows Explorer** and then click the **Price List** folder. **c.** Right-click the **Price List** folder and then click **Sharing and Security**. **d.** On the **Sharing** tab, click **Caching**. **e.** Select **All files and programs that users open from the share will be automatically available offline.** **f.** Click **OK** twice. **g.** Close all open windows, and then log off.
2. Complete the lab exercise.	**a.** Close all programs and shut down all computers. Do not save changes. **b.** To prepare for the next module, start the DEN-DC1 and DEN-SRV1 virtual computers.

Microsoft®

Module 5: Implementing Printing

Contents

Overview

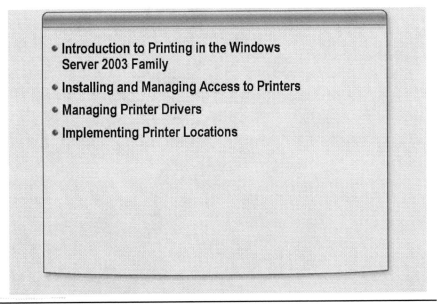

- Introduction to Printing in the Windows Server 2003 Family
- Installing and Managing Access to Printers
- Managing Printer Drivers
- Implementing Printer Locations

Introduction

Printers are common resources that are shared by multiple users on a network. As a systems administrator, you should set up a network-wide printing strategy that meets the needs of users. To set up an efficient network of printers, you must know how to install and share network printers and how to mange printer drivers and printer locations. The Microsoft® Windows Server™ 2003 family helps you to perform these tasks efficiently through an easy-to-use interface.

Objectives

After completing this module, you will be able to:

- Explain the printing process in the Windows Server 2003 family.
- Install and manage access to printers by using printer permissions.
- Manage printer drivers.
- Implement printer locations.

Lesson: Introduction to Printing in the Windows Server 2003 Family

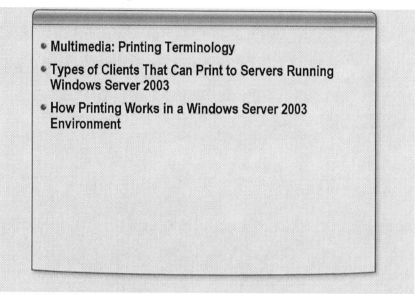

- Multimedia: Printing Terminology
- Types of Clients That Can Print to Servers Running Windows Server 2003
- How Printing Works in a Windows Server 2003 Environment

Introduction

The Windows Server 2003 family makes it easy for an administrator to set up network printing and configure the print resources from a central location. You can also configure your shared network printer to support client computers running Microsoft Windows® 95, Microsoft Windows 98, or Microsoft Windows NT®.

Before you set up printing in Windows Server 2003, you should be aware of the terms used and how printing works in a Windows Server 2003 environment.

Lesson objectives

After completing this lesson, you will be able to:

- Explain printing terminology.
- Describe the client computers that can print to servers running Windows Server 2003.
- Explain how printing works in a Windows Server 2003 environment.

Multimedia: Printing Terminology

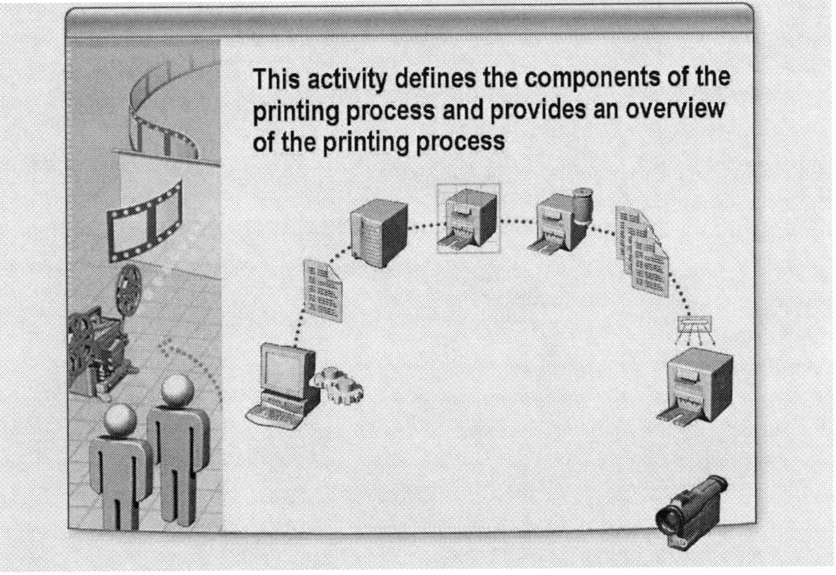

File location

To start the *Printing Terminology* activity, open the Web page on the Student Materials compact disc, click **Multimedia**, and then click the title of the activity.

Component definitions

In the first part of the activity, you drag labels to components of the printing process. When you drop a label on the correct component, the definition of that component is displayed. You can also click **Show me** to have all definitions displayed.

Printing process

After all component definitions are displayed, click **Play** to view an animation of the basic printing process.

Types of Clients That Can Print to Servers Running Windows Server 2003

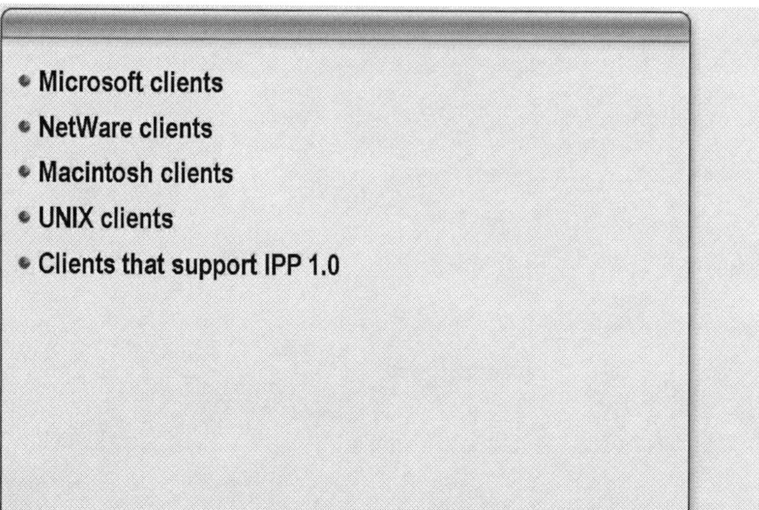

Introduction

Client computers can access a printer immediately after a systems administrator adds the printer to a print server running Windows Server 2003.

Client computers that can print to Windows Server 2003

A print server running Windows Server 2003 supports the following clients:

- Microsoft clients

  All 16-bit clients running Windows and clients running MS-DOS® require 16-bit printer drivers on each client. Necessary drivers are downloaded to 32-bit and 64-bit clients running Windows.

- NetWare clients

  NetWare clients require that Microsoft File and Print Services for NetWare is installed on the print server running Windows Server 2003. They also require that transport compatible with Internetwork Packet Exchange/ Sequenced Packed Exchange (IPX/SPX) is installed on the print server and on each client.

- Macintosh clients

  Macintosh clients require that Microsoft Print Services for Macintosh is installed on the print server running Windows Server 2003. They also require that the AppleTalk networking protocol transport is installed on the print server and on each client.

- UNIX clients

  UNIX clients require that Microsoft Print Services for UNIX is installed on the print server running Windows Server 2003. UNIX clients that support the Line Printer Remote (LPR) specification connect to a print server by using the Line Printer Daemon (LPD) service.

- Clients that support Internet Printing Protocol (IPP) 1.0

  Any client that supports IPP 1.0 can print to a print server running Windows Server 2003 by using Hypertext Transfer Protocol (HTTP). The clients that support IPP are clients running Windows 95, Windows 98, or Windows Server 2003. You must first install Internet Information Services (IIS) on the computer running Windows Server 2003.

Additional reading

For more information about IPP, see article 323428, "How To: Configure Internet Printing in Windows Server 2003," on the Microsoft Help and Support Web site.

How Printing Works in a Windows Server 2003 Environment

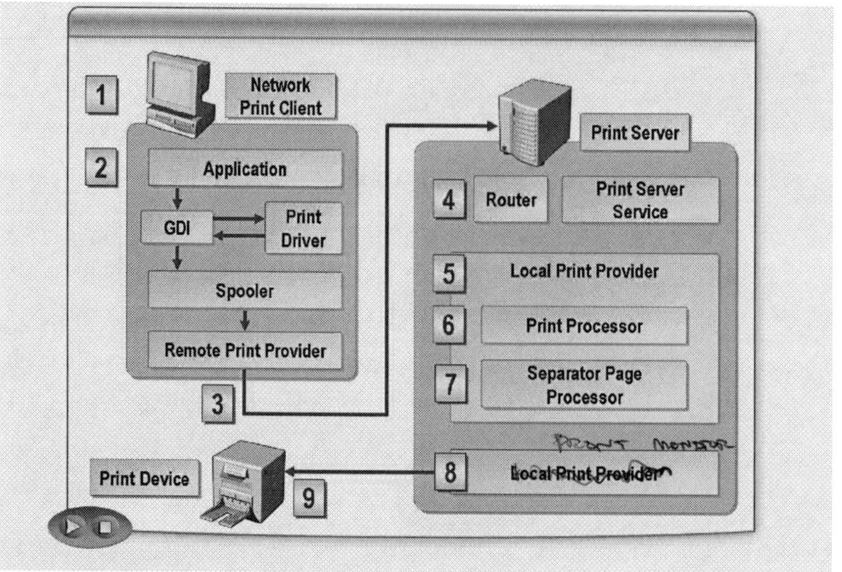

Introduction

When you add a printer that is connected to a network through a network adapter, you can implement printing in the following ways:

- Add a printer directly to each user's computer without using a print server computer.
- Add the printer once to a print server computer and then connect each user to the printer through the print server computer.

Printing without using a print server

Suppose that a small workgroup has only a few computers and a printer that is connected directly to the network. Each user on the network adds the printer to their Printers and Faxes folder without sharing the printer and sets their own driver setting.

Printing without a print server has the following disadvantages:

- Users do not know the actual state of the printer.
- Each computer has its own print queue that displays only those print jobs sent from that computer.
- You cannot determine where your print job is in relation to all the print jobs from other computers.
- Error messages, such as paper jams or empty paper trays, appear only on the print queue for the current print job.
- All the processes on a document submitted for printing are done on that one computer.

Printing by using a print server

A computer running Windows Server 2003 functions as a print server. The computer adds the printer and shares it with the other users. A computer running Microsoft Windows XP Professional can also function as a print server. However, it cannot support Macintosh or NetWare services, and it is limited to only 10 connections in the same local area network (LAN).

Printing with a print server has the following advantages:

- The print server manages the printer driver settings.
- A single print queue appears on every computer connected to the printer, enabling each user to see where their print job is in relation to others waiting to be printed.
- Because error messages appear on all computers, everyone knows the actual state of the printer.
- Some processing is passed from the client computer to the print server.
- You can have a single log for administrators who want to audit the printer events.

Note Typically, print servers are implemented on servers that also perform other functions.

Additional reading

For more information about the printing process, see:

- "Printing Overview" on the Microsoft TechNet Web site.
- "Printing and Print Servers" on the Microsoft TechNet Web site.

Lesson: Installing and Managing Access to Printers

- How to Manage Local and Network Printers
- Hardware Requirements for Configuring a Print Server
- What Are Printer Permissions?
- Why Modify Printer Permissions?
- Practice: Installing and Managing Access to Printers

Introduction

Users in a home environment mostly print to a local printer attached to their client computer. In a business environment, client computers print to a centralized print server that redistributes the print jobs to a print device. By using a print server, the network administrators can centrally manage all printers and print devices.

Lesson objectives

After completing this lesson, you will be able to:

- Manage a local printer and a network printer.
- Describe the hardware requirements for configuring a print server.
- Describe printer permissions.
- Describe when to modify printer permissions.
- Install, share, and manage permissions for local and network printers.

How to Manage Local and Network Printers

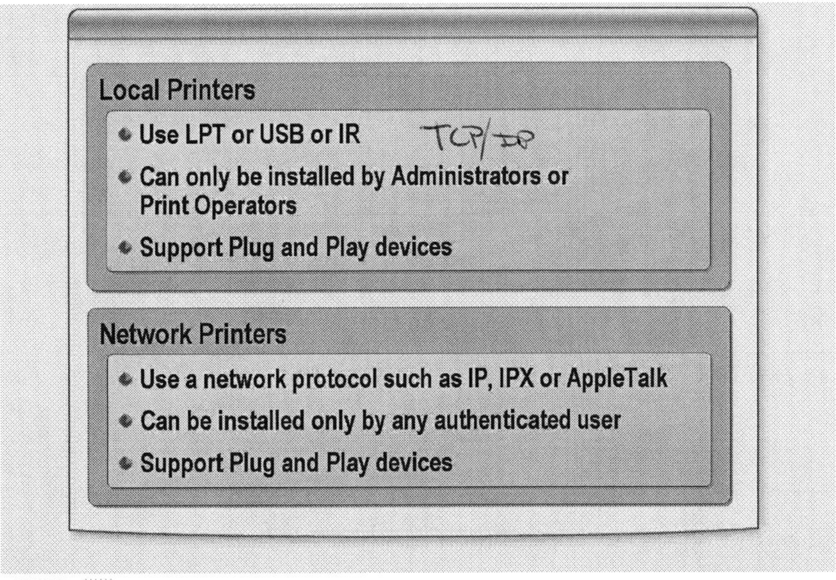

Local Printers
Use LPT or USB or IR
TCP/IP
Can only be installed by Administrators or Print Operators
Support Plug and Play devices
Network Printers
Use a network protocol such as IP, IPX or AppleTalk
Can be installed only by any authenticated user
Support Plug and Play devices

Introduction

As a systems administrator, you will be asked to create two types of printers: a local printer and a network printer. Both types of printers must be created before sharing them for others to use.

Definition

Local printers are created to print to a locally attached print device by using parallel (LPT), Universal Serial Bus (USB), or infrared (IR). Local printers also print to a network print device that uses Internet Protocol (IP) or IPX. They also support Plug and Play.

Network printers print to a shared network printer by using IP, IPX, or AppleTalk. The shared printer redirects the print job to a print device.

Installation

To install and share a local printer, you use the Add Printer Wizard, located in the Printers and Faxes folder. You can also add and configure printer ports in the Add Printer Wizard. The Add Printer Wizard prompts you to install a printer driver if one is needed or to replace the existing driver.

The Add Printer Wizard also enables you to connect to a remote shared printer and install its software interface on your computer, assuming that you have the correct permissions.

Who can install local and network printers?

On domain controllers, members of the Administrators and Print Operators groups can install local printers.

On member servers, members of the Administrators and the local Print Operators groups can install local printers.

On systems Windows XP Professional or Windows 2000 Professional, only Administrators can install local printers.

Any authenticated user can connect to and submit print jobs to a remote shared printer, assuming that they have the proper printer permissions.

Advantages and disadvantages

The following table lists the advantages and disadvantages of printing to a local printer or a network printer.

	Local printer	Network printer
Advantages	• The print device is in close proximity to the user's computer. • Plug and Play can detect local printers and automatically install drivers.	• Many users can access print devices. • Network printers support distributing updated printer drivers to multiple clients.
Disadvantages	• A print device is needed for every computer. • Drivers must be manually installed for every local printer. • A local printer takes more processor clock cycles to print.	• The print device might not be physically close to the user. • Physical security is limited on the print device.

Hardware Requirements for Configuring a Print Server

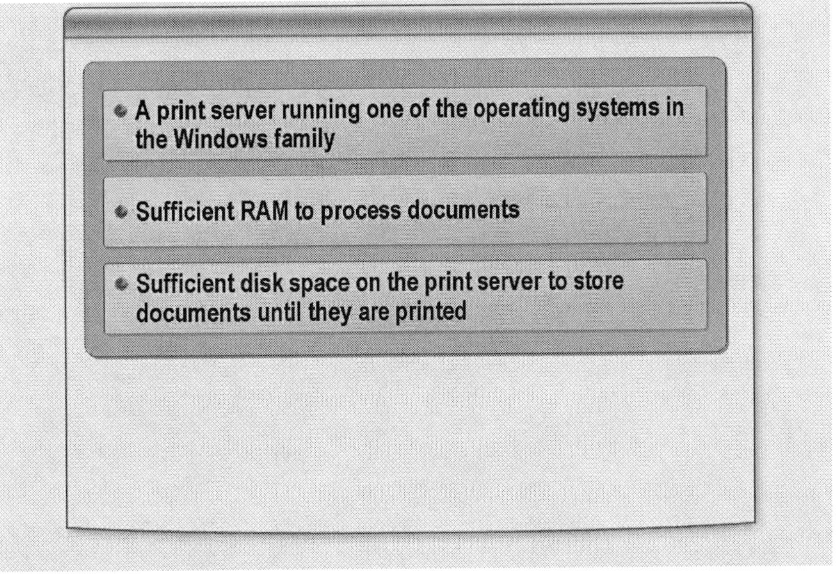

Introduction

There are certain hardware requirements for setting up an efficient printing environment. Whether you are using a local printer or a network printer, if the minimum hardware requirements are not met, network printing may be highly inefficient.

Hardware requirements

Setting up printing on a Windows Server 2003 network requires the following:

- At least one computer to function as the print server that is running one of the operating systems in the Windows family.

  Although any computer that is sharing a printer is acting as a print server, if the print server is expected to manage many print jobs, it is recommended that you dedicate a server for printing. The print server can run any operating system in the Windows Server family. Use one of the Windows Server products when you need to support a large number of connections in addition to Macintosh, UNIX, and NetWare clients.

- Sufficient RAM to process documents

  If a print server manages many printers or many large documents, the server might require additional RAM beyond what Windows Server 2003 requires for other tasks. If a print server does not have sufficient RAM for its workload, printing performance might decline.

- Sufficient disk space on the print server to store documents

  You must have enough disk space to ensure that Windows Server 2003 can store documents that are sent to the print server until the print server sends the documents to the print device. This is critical when documents are large or when documents accumulate. For example, if 10 users each send one large document to print at the same time, the print server must have enough disk space to hold all of the documents until the print server sends them to the print device.

What Are Printer Permissions?

Permission	Allows the user to:
Print	Connect to a printer and send documents to the printer
Manage Printers	Perform the tasks associated with Print permission. The user has complete administrative control of the printer
Manage Documents	Manage all aspects of documents that all users submit. The user cannot send documents to the printer or control the status of the printer

Printer permissions

Windows provides the following printer permissions:

- Print
- Manage Printers
- Manage Documents

When multiple permissions are granted to a group of users, those users get the cumulative effect of all those permissions. However, when a Deny permission is applied, it takes precedence over an equivalent Allow permission.

Tasks that can be performed at each permission level

The following is a brief explanation of the types of tasks that a user can perform at each permission level:

- Print

  The user can connect to a printer and send documents to the printer. By default, Print permission is granted to all members of the Everyone group.

- Manage Printers

  The user can perform the tasks that are associated with Print permission and has complete administrative control of the printer. The user can pause and restart the printer, change spooler settings, share a printer, adjust printer permissions, and change printer properties. By default, Manage Printers permission is granted to members of the Administrators and Power Users groups.

  By default, members of the Administrators and Power Users groups have full access, which means that the users are granted Print, Manage Documents, and Manage Printers permissions.

- Manage Documents

  The user can pause, resume, restart, cancel, and rearrange the order of documents submitted by all other users. The user cannot, however, send documents to the printer or control the status of the printer. By default, Manage Documents permission is granted to members of the Creator Owner group.

  When a user is granted Manage Documents permission, the user cannot access existing documents currently waiting to be printed. Users can access documents sent to the printer only after they are granted Manage Documents permission.

Printer permissions assigned to default groups

Windows assigns printer permissions to six groups of users: Administrators, Creator Owner, Everyone, Power Users, Print Operators, and Server Operators. By default, each group is granted a combination of Print, Manage Documents, and Manage Printers permissions, as shown in the following table.

Group	Print	Manage Documents	Manage Printers
Administrators	X	X	X
Creator Owner		X	
Everyone	X		
Power Users	X	X	X
Print Operators	X	X	X
Server Operators	X	X	X

Important Although Power Users and Server Operators have Manage Printers permissions, they cannot create new printers. They can only manage existing printers. Only Administrators and Print Operators can create new printers.

The combination of the Everyone group having Print permission and Creator Owner having Manage Documents permission means that any user can print and that all users can manage their own documents. For example, if user Sue and user Bob both print, Sue will be allowed to remove her own document from the print queue but cannot remove the document that is printed by Bob.

Caution Add a minimum number of trusted users to the Administrators, Power Users, Print Operators, and Server Operators groups.

Why Modify Printer Permissions?

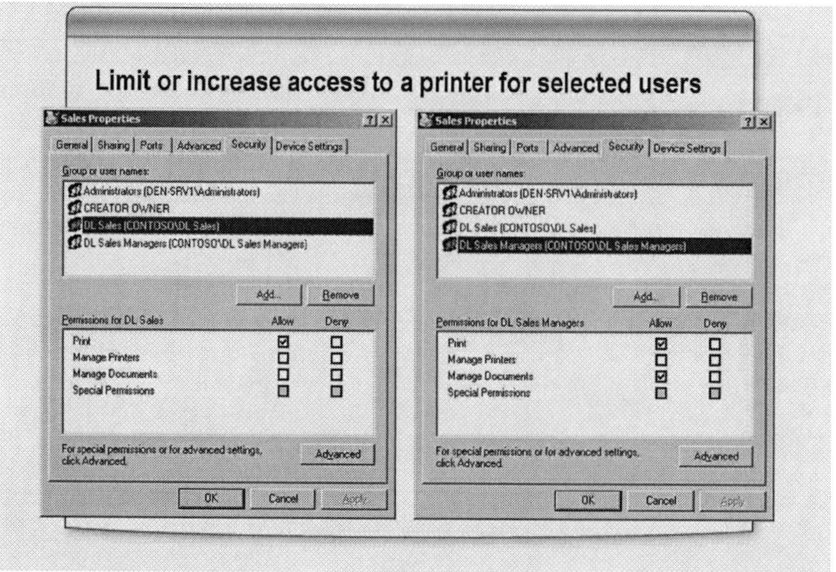
Limit or increase access to a printer for selected users
Sales Properties
Sales Properties

Introduction

When a shared printer is installed on a network, default printer permissions are assigned that enable all users to print. You can also enable selected groups to manage documents sent to the printer and enable selected groups to mange the printer. You can explicitly deny access to the printer through user or group membership.

Increase access to a printer for selected users

You might want to increase access for some users by granting specific printer permissions. For example, you can grant Print permission to all sales personnel in the Sales department and grant Print and Manage Documents permissions to all sales managers. As a result, all users and managers can print documents, but managers can also change the print status of any document sent to the printer.

Note The Creator Owner group is granted Manage Documents permission by default. If this permission is removed, users will be able to submit print jobs, but they will not be able to control their jobs in the queue.

Deny access to a printer for selected users

In some cases, you might need to give access to a printer to specific users. However, there might be some users whom you do not want to access the printer. In this case, you can grant permissions to the user or group that requires access and deny permission to other users. For example, a printer in the Finance department that is used to print checks should be used by only the finance managers; all other employees are denied access.

Practice: Installing and Managing Access to Printers

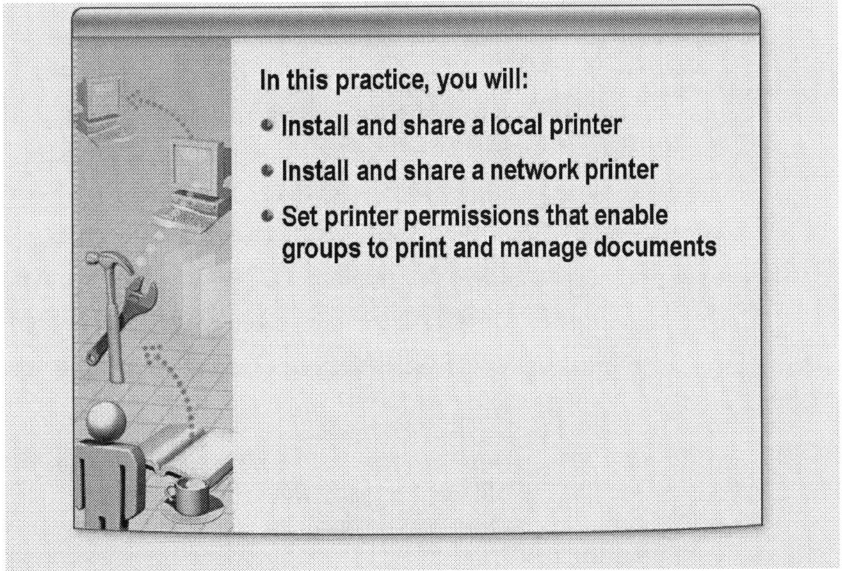
In this practice, you will:
Install and share a local printer
Install and share a network printer
Set printer permissions that enable groups to print and manage documents

Objectives

In this practice, you will:

- Install and share a local printer.
- Install and share a network printer.
- Set printer permissions that enable groups to print and manage documents.

Instructions

Ensure that the DEN-DC1 and the DEN-SRV1 virtual machines are running.

Practice

▶ **Install and share a local printer**

1. Log on to DEN-SRV1 as **Administrator** with the password of **Pa$$w0rd**.
2. Click **Start**, point to **Control Panel**, point to **Printers and Faxes** and then click **Add Printer**.
3. In the **Add Printer Wizard**, on the **Welcome** page, click **Next**.
4. On the **Local or Network Printer** page, click **Local printer attached to this computer**, clear the **Automatically detect and install my Plug and Play printer** check box, and then click **Next**.
5. On the **Select a Printer Port** page, leave the default **LPT1** selected, and then click **Next**.
6. On the **Install Printer Software** page, under **Manufacturer**, select **HP**. Under **Printers**, select **HP LaserJet 4**, and then click **Next**.
7. On the **Name Your Printer** page, type **Sales** in the **Name** field, and then click **Next**.
8. On the **Printer Sharing** page, leave the default share name of **Sales**, and then click **Next**.
9. On the **Location and Comment** page, click **Next**.
10. On the **Print Test Page** page, select **No**, and then click **Next**.
11. Click **Finish**.

► **Install and share a network printer**

1. Launch the **Add Printer Wizard** from the **Printer and Faxes** folder.
2. In the **Add Printer Wizard**, on the **Welcome** page, click **Next**.
3. On the **Local or Network Printer** page, click **Local printer attached to this computer**, clear the **Automatically detect and install my Plug and Play printer** check box, and then click **Next**.
4. On the **Select a Printer Port** page, select **Create a new port**.
5. In the **Type of port** list, select **Standard TCP/IP Port**, and then click **Next**.

   The **Add Standard TCP/IP Printer Port Wizard** will launch.
6. On the **Welcome** page, click **Next**.
7. On the **Add Port** page, type **127.0.0.1** in the **Printer Name or IP Address** field. Click **Next**.

Note Because there is no actual network device, you will use the loopback address. Normally, you would type the IP address of the network interface of the print device.

---

8. The **Additional Port Information Required** page will appear because no network device was detected. Leave the default **Generic Network Card** selected for the purposes of this practice, and then click **Next**.
9. Click **Finish**.
10. On the **Install Printer Software** page, under **Manufacturer**, select **HP**. Under **Printers**, select **HP LaserJet 5**, and then click **Next**.
11. On the **Name Your Printer** page, type **Finance** in the **Name** field, and then click **Next**.
12. On the **Printer Sharing** page, ensure that the default share name is **Finance**, and then click **Next**.
13. On the **Location and Comment** page, click **Next**.
14. On the **Print Test Page** page, select **No**, and then click **Next**.
15. Click **Finish**.

► **Set printer permissions that enable groups to print and manage documents**

1. Click **Start**, point to **Control Panel**, and then double-click **Printers and Faxes.**
2. Right-click the **Sales** printer and then click **Properties.**
3. Click the **Security** tab.
4. Remove the **Power Users** and **Everyone** groups.
5. Add the **G Sales** group, and then assign **Print** permission.
6. Add the **G Sales Managers** group, and then assign **Manage Documents** permission. Click **OK.**
7. Close all open windows and log off of DEN-SRV1.

Important Do not shut down the virtual machines.

Lesson: Managing Printer Drivers

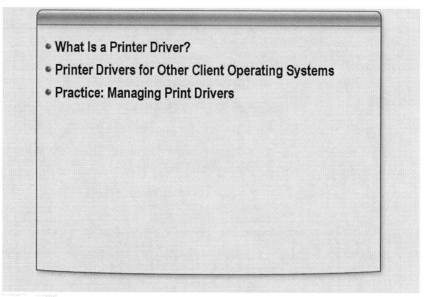

- What Is a Printer Driver?
- Printer Drivers for Other Client Operating Systems
- Practice: Managing Print Drivers

Introduction

This lesson introduces you to the skills and knowledge that you need to manage printer drivers.

Lesson objectives

After completing this lesson, you will be able to:

- Describe what a printer driver is.
- Describe how to enable drivers for other client systems.
- Manage printer drivers for other client operating systems.

What Is a Printer Driver?

- Software used to communicate with printers and plotters
- Translates the information sent from the computer into printer commands
- Consists of the following types of files:

Configuration or printer interface file	• Displays the Properties and Preferences dialog boxes when you configure a printer • Has a .dll extension
Data file	• Provides information about the capabilities of a specific printer • Can have a .dll, .pcd, .gpd, or .ppd extension
Printer graphics driver file	• Translates DDI commands into printer commands • Has a .dll extension

Definition

A printer driver is software that is used by computer programs to communicate with printers and plotters.

What is the purpose of printer drivers?

Printer drivers translate the information that you send from the computer into commands that the printer understands. Usually, printer drivers are not compatible across platforms, so various drivers must be installed on the print server to support different hardware and operating systems. For example, if your computer is running Windows XP and you share a printer with users with computers running Microsoft Windows NT®, you might need to install multiple printer drivers.

Printer driver files

Printer drivers consist of the following three types of files:

- Configuration or printer interface file
  - This file displays the **Properties** and **Preferences** dialog boxes when you configure a printer.
  - This file has a .dll extension.
- Data file
  - This file provides information about the capabilities of a specific printer, including its resolution capability, whether it can print on both sides of the page, and what size paper it can accept.
  - This file can have a .dll, .pcd, .gpd, or .ppd extension.
- Printer graphics driver file
  - This file translates device driver interface (DDI) commands into commands that a printer can understand. Each driver translates a different printer language. For example, the file Pscript.dll translates the PostScript printer language.
  - This file has a .dll extension.

Example of how printer driver files work

Printer driver files, which are usually accompanied by a Help file, work together to make printing possible. For example, when you install a new printer, the configuration file reads the data file and displays the available printer options. When you print, the printer graphics driver file queries the configuration file about your selections so that it can create the proper printer commands.

Signed print drivers

It is strongly recommended that you use only device drivers with the **Designed for Microsoft Windows XP** or **Designed for Microsoft Windows 2003 Server** logos. Installing device drivers that Microsoft has not digitally signed might disable the system, allow viruses on to your computer, or otherwise impair the correct operation of your computer either immediately or in the future.

Printer Drivers for Other Client Operating Systems

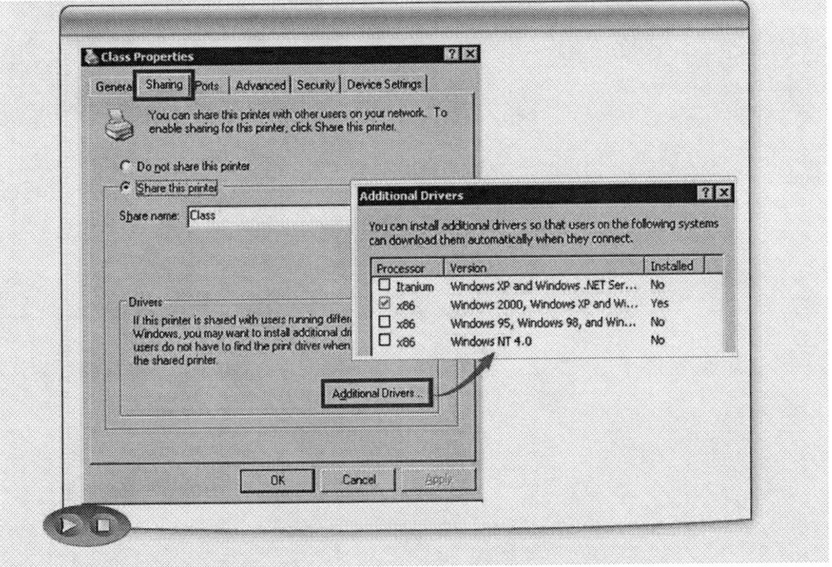

Introduction

If you share a printer with users running Windows 95, Windows 98, or Windows NT 4.0, you can install additional printer drivers on your computer so that those users can connect to your printer without being prompted to install the drivers that are missing from their systems. The drivers are located on the Windows Server 2003 CD. Printer drivers for Microsoft Windows NT version 3.1 and Microsoft Windows NT version 3.5 are not included but might be available from the print device manufacturer.

Note Printer drivers for operating systems such as Microsoft Windows 3.1, MS-DOS, UNIX, and Macintosh must be installed on each client computer. They cannot be downloaded from the print server.

Procedure

To add printer drivers for other versions of Windows:

1. In the Printers and Faxes folder, right-click the printer for which you want to install additional drivers, and then click **Properties**.
2. In the **Properties** dialog box, on the **Sharing** tab, click **Additional Drivers**.
3. In the **Additional Drivers** dialog box, select the check boxes for the additional environments and operating systems, and then click **OK**.

Additional reading

For more information about downloading print drivers to clients, see "Managing printer drivers" on the Microsoft Windows 2000 Advanced Server Documentation Web site.

Practice: Managing Printer Drivers

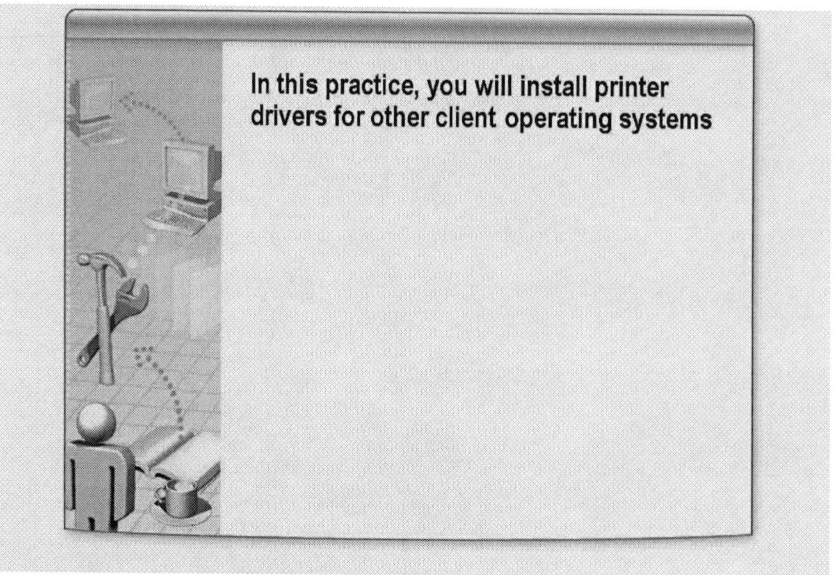
In this practice, you will install printer drivers for other client operating systems

Objective

In this practice, you will:

- Install printer drivers for other client operating systems.

Instructions

Ensure that the DEN-DC1 and the DEN-SRV1 virtual machines are running.

Practice

► **Install printer drivers for other client operating systems**

1. Log on to DEN-SRV1 as **Administrator** with the password of **Pa$$w0rd**.
2. Click **Start**, point to **Control Panel**, and then double-click **Printers and Faxes**.
3. In the **Printers and Faxes** folder, right-click the **Sales** printer, and then click **Properties**.
4. In the **Sales Properties** dialog box, on the **Sharing** tab, click **Additional Drivers**.
5. In the **Additional Drivers** dialog box, select the check box for **x86 – Windows NT 4.0**, and then click **OK**.

   If prompted for additional files, browse to **C:\Win2k3\I386**, and then click **OK**.
6. Close the **Sales Properties** dialog box.
7. Close all windows and log off of DEN-SRV1.

Important Do not shut down the virtual machines.

Lesson: Implementing Printer Locations

- What Are Printer Locations?
- Requirements for Implementing Printer Locations
- Naming Conventions for Printer Locations
- How Printer Locations Are Configured
- How to Locate Printers
- Practice: Implementing Printer Locations

Introduction

This lesson introduces you to the skills and knowledge that you need to implement printer locations.

Lesson objectives

After completing this lesson, you will be able to:

- Describe the purpose of printer locations.
- Describe the requirements for implementing printer locations.
- Describe the naming conventions for printer locations.
- Describe the tasks involved in configuring printer locations.
- Locate printers by using printer locations.
- Implement printer locations.

What Are Printer Locations?

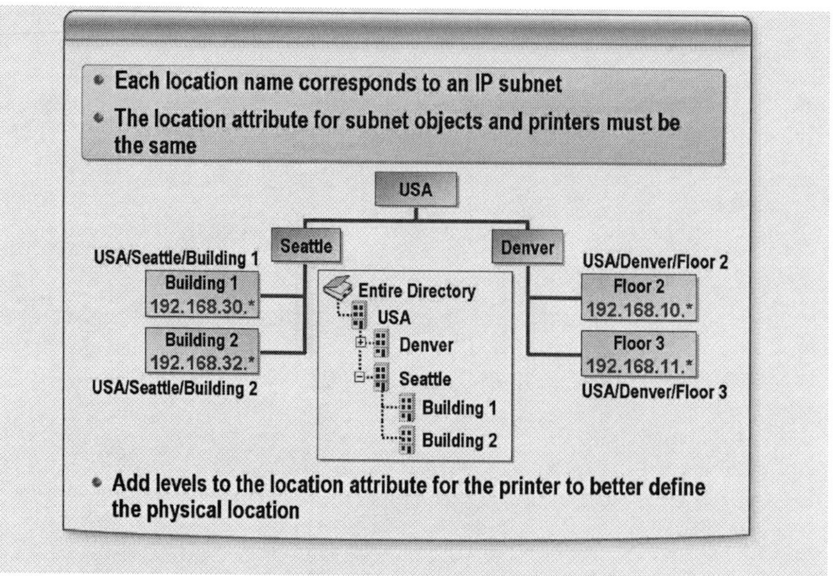

Definition

Printer locations enable users to search and connect to print devices that they are in close physical proximity to.

Why implement printer locations?

In a large company with multiple locations, mobile users need an easy method to locate printers in different offices, and users might occasionally have to send print jobs to remote printers. Printer locations can help them to easily find a particular printer in the following ways:

- When searching for printers, Group Policy can be used to prepopulate the location field in the **Printer Search** dialog box so that users do not have to know the exact naming conventions used.
- Users can run printer searches to find printers in other locations by browsing the hierarchy of locations.

Active Directory and printer locations

When you implement printer locations, a search for published printers in Active Directory returns a list of printers that are located in the same physical location (for example, in the same building or on the same floor) as the client computer that the user is using to perform the search.

This printer location tracking capability is based on the assumption that print devices that are physically located near a user reside on the same Internet IP subnet as the user's client computer. Subnets are subdivisions of an IP network. Each subnet possesses its own unique network address.

In Active Directory, an IP subnet is represented by a subnet object, which contains a **Location** attribute that is used during a search for printers. Active Directory uses the value of the **Location** attribute as the text string to display printer location. Therefore, when a user searches for a printer and a printer location is implemented, Active Directory:

- Finds the subnet object that corresponds to the subnet on which the user's computer is located.
- Uses the value in the **Location** attribute of the subnet object as the text string for a search for all published printers that have the same **Location** attribute value.
- Returns to the user a list of printers whose **Location** attribute value matches the one that is defined for the subnet object. The user can then connect to the nearest printer.

Additionally, users can search for printers in any location. This is useful if they need to find and connect to a printer in a physical location different from the one in which they normally work.

Requirements for Implementing Printer Locations

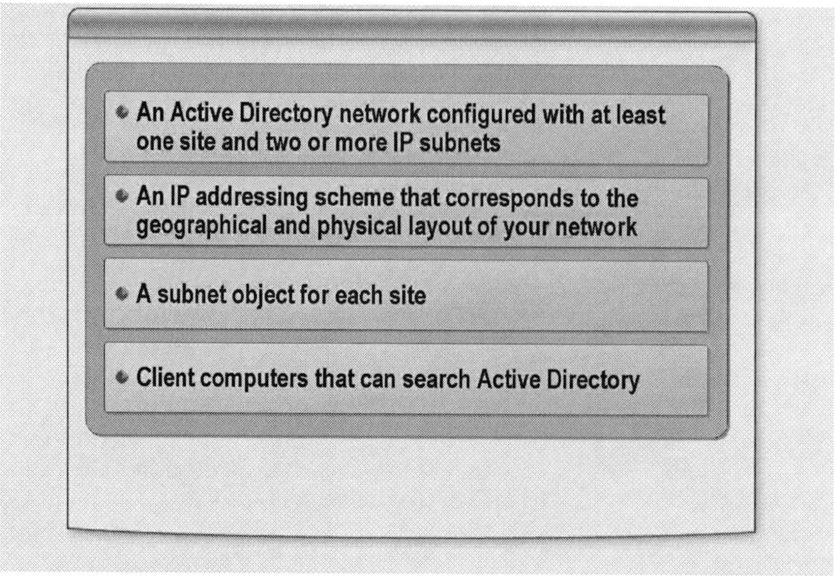

Requirements

Before you can implement printer locations, your Windows Server 2003 network must have the following:

- An Active Directory network configured with at least one site and two or more IP subnets

  Networks with one subnet do not need printer location tracking. Because IP subnets are used to identify the physical location of a printer, a network with only one subnet will generally have all printers in close proximity to users.

- An IP addressing scheme that corresponds to the geographical and physical layout of your network

  Computers and printers that reside on the same IP subnet must also reside in approximately the same physical location in order to be an effective strategy.

- A subnet object for each site

  The subnet object, which represents an IP subnet in Active Directory, contains a **Location** attribute that is used during a search for printers. The value of this **Location** attribute is used during a search in Active Directory to locate printers that reside near the physical location of the user's client computer.

- Client computers that can search Active Directory

  Users with client computers running Windows 2000 Professional or later, or clients running earlier versions of Windows on which Active Directory client software is installed, can use printer locations when searching for printers.

When printer location is disabled

You can add information to the **Location** box on the **General** tab of the printer's **Properties** dialog box even if printer location is disabled. However, this might make printers difficult for users to locate. When users search for printers on the tenth floor and printer location is disabled, they need to know exactly what to type in the **Find Printers** dialog box. When printer location is enabled, the **Location** box in the **Find Printers** dialog box is filled in automatically.

Naming Conventions for Printer Locations

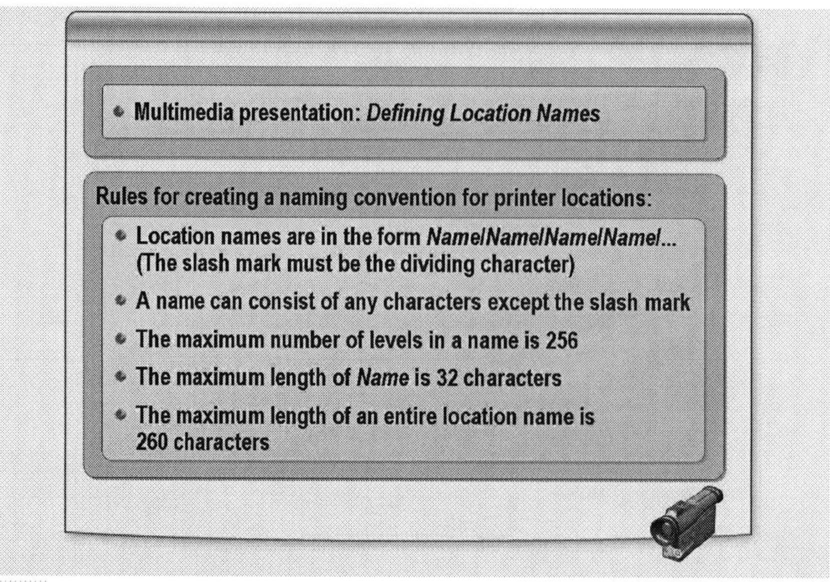

Introduction

The key to implementing printer locations is developing a naming convention for printer locations that corresponds to the physical layout of your network. Printer location names must correspond to an IP subnet. You use a naming convention to determine the values of the **Location** attributes for both the subnet object and the printer object.

Multimedia: Defining Location Names

The *Defining Location Names* presentation explains the relationship between the **Location** attributes of subnets and printers. To start the presentation, open the Web page on the Student Materials compact disc, click **Multimedia**, and then click **Defining Location Names**. Do not open the presentation until the instructor tells you to.

Rules for creating a naming convention for printer locations

To enable printer locations, create a naming convention for printer locations by using the following rules:

- Location names are in the form *Name/Name/Name/Name/...* (The slash mark must be the dividing character.)
- A name can consist of any characters except for the slash mark.
- The maximum number of levels in a name is 256.
- The maximum length of *Name* is 32 characters.
- The maximum length of an entire location name is 260 characters.

Because location names are used by end users, they should be simple and easy to recognize. Avoid using special names that only managers are familiar with. To make the name easier to read, avoid using special characters in a name, and keep names to a maximum of 32 characters so that the whole name string is visible in the user interface.

Example

Note that the naming tree can vary in depth depending on the complexity of the organization and the amount of detail required to find an exact printer location. For example, one large site might use a naming convention that needs a very detailed path such as *City/Building/Floor/Office#*, whereas another, smaller site might use a less detailed path such as *City/Department*.

How Printer Locations Are Configured

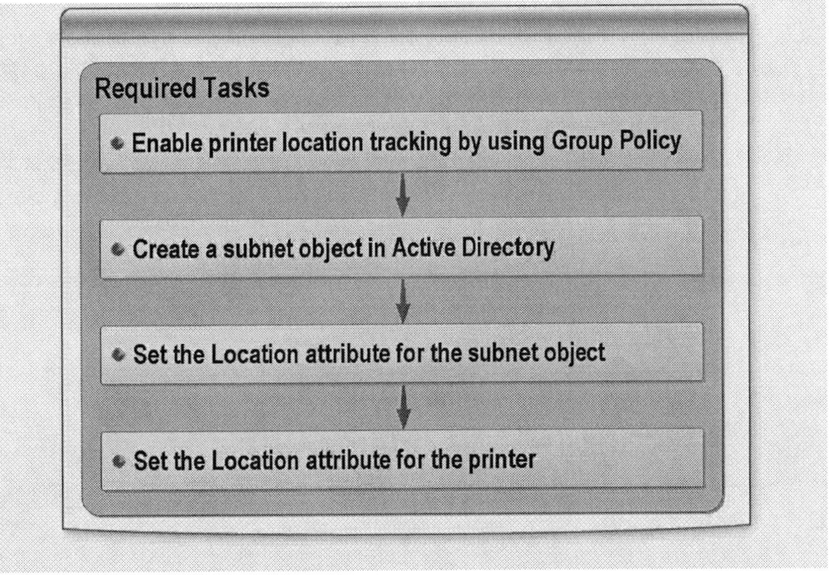
Required Tasks
Enable printer location tracking by using Group Policy
Create a subnet object in Active Directory
Set the Location attribute for the subnet object
Set the Location attribute for the printer

Introduction

To initially set up printer locations, you must have read/write access to Active Directory Sites and Subnet Objects so that you can create subnet objects, give the subnet object a location, and associate the subnet object with a site. When assigning locations to a printer, you must match the location for the printer with the location for the subnet object.

Required tasks

After a systems engineer ensures that the network meets the requirements for implementing printer locations and a naming convention is created, the systems engineer performs the following tasks to configure printer locations:

1. Enable printer location tracking by using Group Policy. Printer location tracking pre-populates the **Location** search field when a user searches for a printer in Active Directory. The value used to pre-populate the search field is the same value that is specified in the **Location** attribute of the subnet object that corresponds to the IP subnet in which the user's computer is located.
2. Create a subnet object in Active Directory. If a subnet object does not already exist, use Active Directory Sites and Services to create a subnet object.
3. Set the **Location** attribute of the subnet object. Use the naming convention that you developed for printer location names as the value of this attribute.

Note To set the **Location** attribute for the subnet object, in Active Directory Sites and Services, right-click the subnet object, and then click **Properties**. On the **Location** tab, type the location name that corresponds to the subnet object, and then click **OK**. These tasks are normally performed by the systems engineer.

4. Set the **Location** attribute of printers. For each printer, add the **Location** attribute of the IP subnet in which the printer resides to the printer's properties. You can use the same printer location name that you used for the location of the subnet object, or you can be more specific and extend the printer name to further identify the location. For example, the subnet location might be constructed as *City/Building/Floor* but the printer location could extend that to be *City/Building/Floor/Office#*. In that way, a search would return all the printers that correspond to the subnet location, but users would see the extended name to help them choose the closest printer.

How to Locate Printers

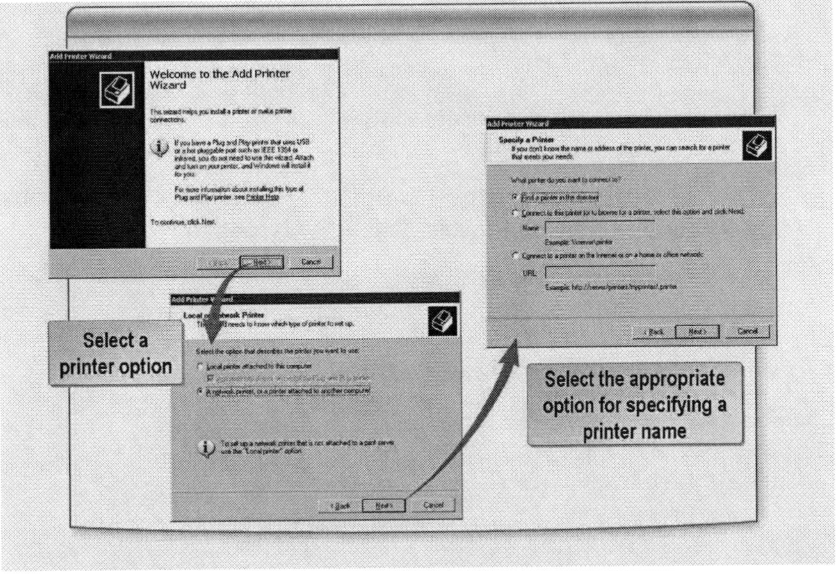

Introduction

Location tracking describes the ability of the printer location field in the **search** dialog box to be prepopulated by enabling a Group Policy setting. In this way, users do not need to know the naming conventions that the organization uses to describe printer locations.

Starting a query

To start a query, the user clicks **Start**, clicks **Search**, and then clicks **Find Printers**. Users can also click **Find a printer in the directory** in the Add Printer Wizard to open the **Find Printers** dialog box.

If location tracking is enabled, the system first determines where the client computer is physically located in the organization. This location will be based on the client's IP address. While this search is in progress, the **Location** box in the **Find Printers** dialog box displays **Checking**. After the location is determined, it is displayed in the **Location** box. If the location cannot be determined, the **Location** box is left blank.

When the user clicks **Find Now**, Active Directory lists all printers matching the user's query that have the same location attribute as the subnet of the user. Users can change the value in the **Location** box by clicking **Browse**.

For example, suppose that an organization is located in a building with several floors, and that each floor is configured as a subnet. If a user located on the first floor fails to locate a color printer on Floor 1, the user can change the location to **Organization 1/Floor 2** or even to **Organization 1** to increase the scope of the search.

Note The **Location** box is not automatically available for users running Windows 95, Windows 98, or Windows NT 4.0 without a directory service client.

Practice: Implementing Printer Locations

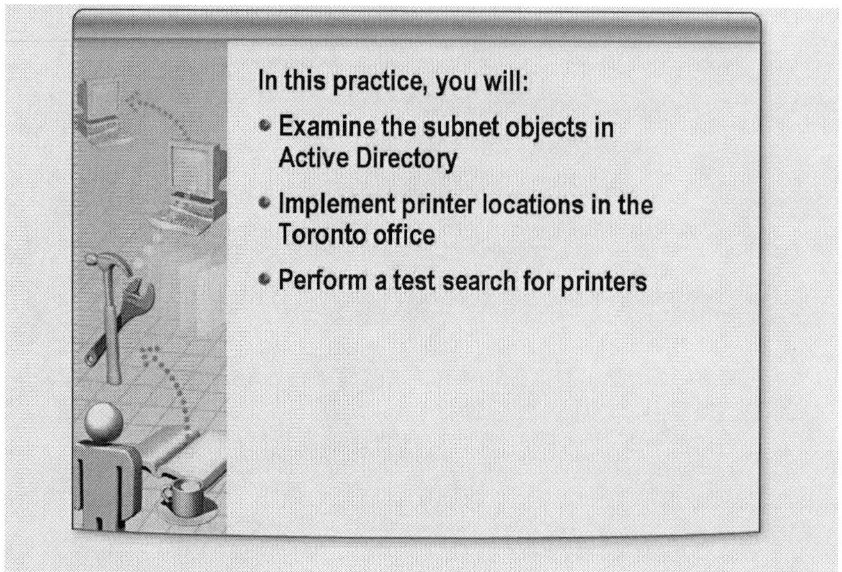

Objectives

In this practice, you will:

- Examine the subnet objects in Active Directory.
- Implement printer locations in the Toronto office.
- Perform a test search for printers.

Instructions

Ensure that the DEN-DC1 and the DEN-SRV1 virtual machines are running.

Practice

► **Examine the subnet objects in Active Directory**

1. Log on to DEN-DC1 as **Administrator** with the password of **Pa$$w0rd**.
2. Click **Start**, point to **Administrative Tools**, and then click **Active Directory Sites and Services**.
3. Expand the **Sites** container, and then expand the **Subnets** container.
4. Right-click the **10.10.0.0/16** subnet object, and then click **Properties**.
5. Click the **Location** tab.

   What location is associated with this subnet?

   DENVER / DOWNTOWN
   ____

6. Click **Cancel**.
7. Open the **Properties** dialog box for the **10.15.0.0/16** subnet, and then click the **Location** tab.

   What location is associated with this subnet?

   DENVER / WAREHOUSE
   ____

8. Click **Cancel** and then close **Active Directory Sites and Services**.

9. Click **Start**, point to **Administrative Tools**, and then click **Group Policy Management**.
10. Expand **Forest:contoso.msft/Domains/contoso.msft.**
11. Click the **Group Policy Objects** folder.
12. In the details pane, right-click the **Default Domain Policy** and then click **Edit**.
13. In the **Group Policy Object Editor** window, expand **Computer Configuration, Administrative Templates**, and then click **Printers**.
14. In the details pane, double-click **Pre-populate printer search location text.**
15. On the **Setting** tab, click **Enable** and then click **OK**.
16. Close all open windows.
17. Open a command prompt and refresh group policy by typing **Gpupdate /force**.
18. Close all windows and log off of DEN-DC1.

► **Implement printer locations in the Toronto office**

1. Log on to DEN-SRV1 as **Administrator** with the password of **Pa$$w0rd.**
2. Open a command prompt and refresh group policy by typing **Gpupdate /force**.
3. Click **Start**, and then click the **Printers and Faxes.**
4. Right-click the **Finance** printer and then select **Properties.**
5. In the **Location** field, type **Denver/Downtown**.
6. Click **OK.**
7. Repeat steps 4 through 6 to configure the **Sales** printer to the **Denver/Downtown** location.

► **Perform a test search for printers**

1. Double-click the **Add Printer** icon
2. On the **Welcome** page, click **Next.**
3. On the **Local or Network Printer** page, click **A network printer, or a printer attached to another computer** and then click **Next.**
4. On the **Specify a Printer** page, leave the default selection of **Find a printer in the directory**, and then click **Next.**
5. In the **Find Printers** dialog box, what is the value in the **Location** field?

6. Click **Find Now.**

   Both the **Sales** printer and the **Finance** printer should be returned in the results.

7. Close all windows and log off of DEN-SRV1.

► To prepare for the next lab

- Start the DEN-CL1 virtual machine.

Important Do not shut down the virtual machines.

Lab: Implementing Printing

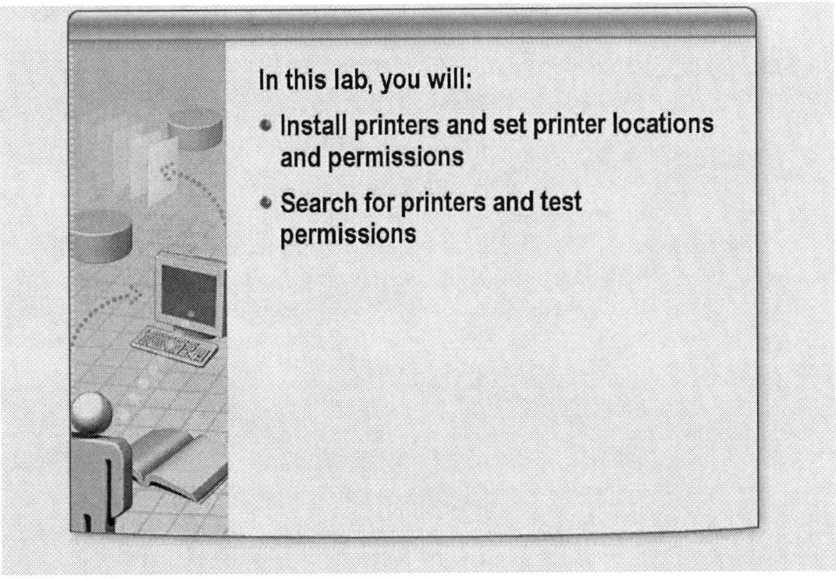

Objectives

After completing this lab, you will be able to:

- Install printers and set printer locations and permissions.
- Search for printers and test permissions.

Prerequisites

To complete this lab, you must have the following virtual machines:

- DEN-DC1
- DEN-SRV1
- DEN-CL1

Estimated time to complete this lab: 20 minutes

Exercise 1
Installing Printers and Setting Printer Locations and Permissions

In this exercise, you will install printers and set the location attribute.

Scenario

The Shipping department must install a printer on DEN-SRV1. The Sales department sends shipping orders to the printer. The Shipping printer is located at the Denver Warehouse location. Only the Sales department should be able to print documents to the printer. Sales managers and administrators should be able to control all aspects of the printer and the print queue. Install the printer, and then configure the location and the appropriate permissions.

Tasks	Specific Instructions
1. Add the Shipping printer and set the location.	a. Log on to DEN-SRV1 as **Administrator** with the password of **Pa$$w0rd**. b. Click **Start**, and then click **Printers and Faxes**. c. Double-click **Add Printer**. d. Use the **Add Printer Wizard** to install a local printer on **LPT1**. e. Install an **HP Laserjet 5Si**. f. Name the printer **Shipping**. g. Keep the share name **Shipping**. h. In the **Location** field, type **Denver/Warehouse**. Click **Next**. i. Click **Next**, and then click **Finish**.
2. Set permissions on the Shipping printer.	a. Right-click the **Shipping** printer, and then click **Properties**. b. On the **Security** tab, remove **Everyone** and **Power Users**. c. Add **G Sales**, and then assign **Print** permission. d. Add **G Sales Managers**, and then assign **Manage Documents** and **Manage Printers** permission. e. Click **OK** and then close the **Printers and Faxes** window.

Exercise 2
Searching for Printers and Testing Permissions

In this exercise, you will search Active Directory and test access to the Shipping printer.

Scenario

Now that the Shipping printer is installed and configured, you will test to make sure that it can be easily located and that only the proper users have access.

Tasks	Specific Instructions
1. Search Active Directory for the Shipping printer, and then connect as a Sales department user.	a. Log on to DEN-CL1 as **Jeff** with a password of **Pa$$w0rd**. b. Click **Start**, and then click **Printers and Faxes**. c. Click the **Add a printer** icon, and then click **Next**. d. On the **Local or Network Printer** page, notice that the option to create a local printer is disabled. Click **Next**. e. On the **Specify a Printer** page, click **Next**. f. In the **Find Printers** dialog box, click **Browse** to find the **Warehouse** location, click **OK**, and then click **Find Now**. g. The **Shipping** printer should appear in the results window. h. Right-click the **Shipping** printer and then click **Connect**. i. Click **OK**, and then click **Finish**. The **Shipping** printer should appear as a network printer in **Printers and Faxes**. j. Close all windows and log off of DEN-CL1.
2. Search Active Directory as a user without permissions to the Shipping printer.	a. Log on to DEN-CL1 as **Judy** with the password of **Pa$$w0rd**. b. Repeat the steps in task 1 to connect to the Shipping printer. When this user attempts to connect, a message box asking for credentials will appear because this user has no authority to connect to this printer. c. Click **Cancel** and then close all windows.
3. Complete the lab exercise.	a. Close all programs and shut down all computers. Do not save changes. b. To prepare for the next module, start the DEN-DC1 and DEN-SRV1 virtual computers.

This page intentionally left blank.

Microsoft®

Module 6: Managing Printing

Contents

Overview

- Changing the Location of the Print Spooler
- Setting Printer Priorities and Scheduling Printer Availability
- Configuring Printing Pools and Redirecting Print Queues

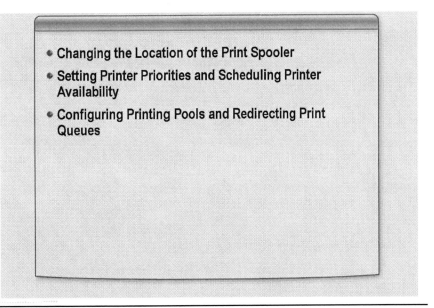

Introduction

As a systems administrator, you should set up a network-wide printing strategy that will meet the needs of users. To set up an efficient network of printers, you must know how to troubleshoot installation and configuration problems. Microsoft® Windows Server™ 2003 provides several configuration options to help you to perform these tasks efficiently.

Objectives

After completing this module, you will be able to:

- Change the location of the print spooler.
- Set printing priorities and schedule printer availability.
- Configure a printing pool and redirect print queues.

Additional reading

For more information about Windows Server 2003 printing, see "Print Services" on the Microsoft Windows Server 2003 Web site.

Lesson: Changing the Location of the Print Spooler

- What Is a Print Spooler?
- Why Change the Location of the Print Spooler?
- Practice: Changing the Location of the Print Spooler

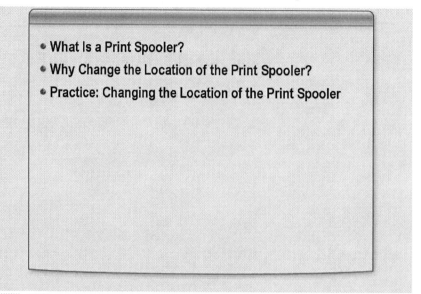

Introduction

This lesson introduces you to the skills and knowledge that you need to change the location of the print spooler.

Lesson objectives

After completing this lesson, you will be able to:

- Explain the purpose of the print spooler.
- Explain situations that require you to change the location of the print spooler.
- Change the location of the print spooler.

What Is a Print Spooler?

- A print spooler is executable file that manages the printing process
- The default location for the spool folder should be changed for high-volume print servers

Definition

The primary component of the printing interface is the print spooler. The print spooler is an executable file that manages the printing process. Management of the printing process involves:

- Retrieving the location of the correct printer driver.
- Loading that driver.
- Spooling high-level function calls into a print job.
- Scheduling the print job for printing.

The print spooler is loaded at system startup and continues to run until the operating system shuts down. The print spooler stores files that are to be printed on the hard disk and then sends them to the print device when the printer is ready. Additionally, you can log events during this process, or you can turn off logging during high-demand periods to minimize disk space and improve the performance of the print spooler service.

Location of the spool folder

Files that are waiting to be printed are collected in a spool folder that is located on the print server's hard drive. By default, the spool folder is located at *SystemRoot*\System32\Spool\Printers. However, this hard drive also holds the Microsoft Windows® system files. Because the operating system frequently accesses these files, performance of both Windows and the printing functions might be slowed.

When to relocate the spool folder

If your print server serves only one or two printers with low traffic volumes, the default location of the spool folder is sufficient. However, to support high traffic volumes, large numbers of printers, or large print jobs, you should relocate the spool folder. For best results, move the spool folder to a drive that has its own input/output (I/O) controller, which reduces the impact of printing on the rest of the operating system.

Why Change the Location of the Print Spooler?

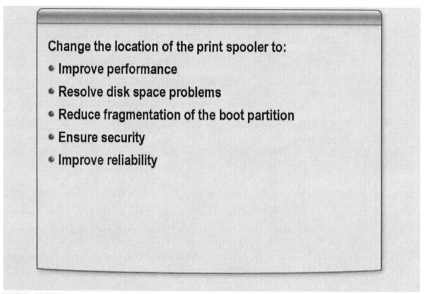

Change the location of the print spooler to:
- Improve performance
- Resolve disk space problems
- Reduce fragmentation of the boot partition
- Ensure security
- Improve reliability

Reasons to change the location of the print spooler

Change the location of the print spooler to do the following:

- *Improve performance* Print servers must have sufficient disk space and RAM to manage print jobs. Ideally, plan to have a minimum of two disks, each with its own I/O controller, where one disk holds the operating system, the startup files, and the paging file, and the other disk holds the spool folder. This isolates the spool folder from the operating system, which improves performance and stability. To improve efficiency, add one or more drives for the paging file.
- *Resolve disk space problems* Print servers create a print queue to manage print requests. Documents might be 20 MB in size if they include embedded graphics. As a result, you should use disk space on a drive other than the one being used for the operating system. This helps ensure that you do not use all the free disk space on the system or boot partitions, which can cause difficulties with the paging file. If you configure the print queue on the same disk as the operating system, Windows does not have sufficient disk space to write the paging file, which can lead to problems with the overall performance of the printer.
- *Reduce fragmentation of the boot partition* When a file prints to a network printer, a spool file is created and almost immediately deleted. This process alone is repeated hundreds or thousands of times during a normal working day. If the spool folder is on a volume that is shared with other data, the volume might become fragmented. You can eliminate fragmentation if you locate the spool folder on a volume that is dedicated to the printer. After all spool files are printed, they are deleted from the volume, and new print jobs can start on a clean disk.

- *Ensure security* If print jobs are configured to not be deleted after they are printed, it is advantageous to have the print jobs on a different disk or volume so that the spool folder does not inherit any changes in the security of any parent folders. It is also advantageous to move the spool folder for printers that print sensitive data, such as payroll checks or financial reports, so that you can audit all transactions on the disk that contains the spool folder.
- Improve reliability

  Typically, a boot partition is on a mirrored disk (RAID 1). For performance and recoverability, you might want to move the spool folder to a volume that has RAID 5 to decrease the odds of a single point of failure of a disk subsystem.

Note If you move the spool, the location of the folder will be changed immediately, and any documents waiting to be printed will not be printed. It is recommended that you wait for printing of all documents to be complete before changing the spool folder.

Practice: Changing the Location of the Print Spooler

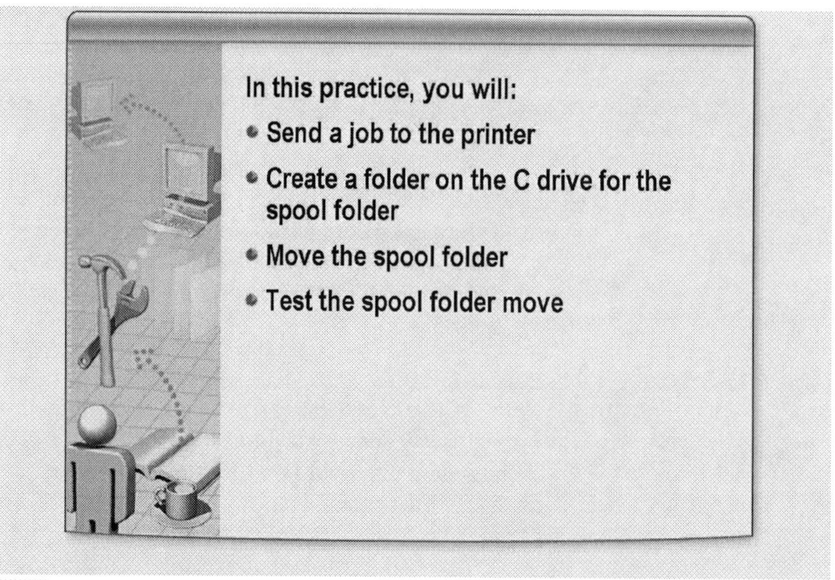
In this practice, you will:
Send a job to the printer
Create a folder on the C drive for the spool folder
Move the spool folder
Test the spool folder move

Objectives

In this practice, you will:

- Send a job to the printer.
- Create a folder on the C drive for the spool folder.
- Move the spool folder.
- Test the spool folder move.

Instructions

Ensure that the DEN-DC1 and the DEN-SRV1 virtual machines are running.

Practice

► **Send a job to the printer**

1. Log on to DEN-DC1 as **Administrator** with the password of **Pa$$w0rd**.
2. Click **Start** and then click **Printers and Faxes**.
3. Ensure that the **Graphics1** printer is paused. Right-click, and then click **Pause** to pause the printer if necessary.

Tip Position the mouse pointer over the printer icon. A message box will display the printer's status as either **Paused** or **Ready**.

4. Right-click **Graphics1** and then click **Properties**.
5. On the **General** tab, click **Print Test Page**.
6. Click **OK** twice.

► Create a folder on the C drive for the spool folder

- Create a folder on the C drive named **Spool** (C:\Spool).

Important Normally you would move the spool to a different partition or physical drive. You will use a folder on the C drive for the purposes of this practice.

► Move the spool folder

1. Open **Printers and Faxes**, click the **File** menu, and then click **Server Properties**.
2. In the **Print Server Properties** dialog box, click the **Advanced** tab.

   What is the current location of the spool folder?

   ____

3. Switch to **Windows Explorer**, and then browse to **C:\WINDOWS\System32\spool\PRINTERS**. The test job you sent should be in the folder.
4. Return to the **Print Server Properties Advanced** tab, and then change the location of the spool folder to **C:\Spool** and click **OK**.
5. Read the **Print Server Properties** warning message, and then click **Yes**.

► Test the spool folder move

1. Click **Start**, point to **Administrative Tools**, and then click **Services**.
2. Right-click the **Print Spooler** service, and then click **Restart**.
3. Open the **C:\Spool** folder. It should be empty. The print jobs did not move. They are still in the old location.
4. Print a test page, and then refresh the view of the **C:\Spool** folder. The job should now appear in the folder.
5. Close all open windows and log off of DEN-DC1.

Important Do not shut down the virtual machines!

Lesson: Setting Printer Priorities and Scheduling Printer Availability

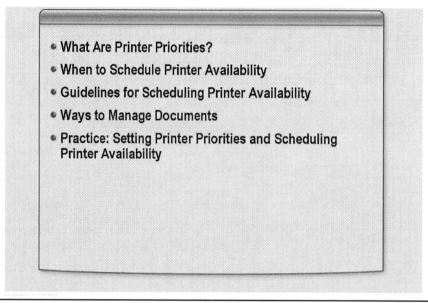

- What Are Printer Priorities?
- When to Schedule Printer Availability
- Guidelines for Scheduling Printer Availability
- Ways to Manage Documents
- Practice: Setting Printer Priorities and Scheduling Printer Availability

Introduction

You might want to configure printer priorities for two printers that print to the same print device. This configuration guarantees that the printer with the highest priority prints to the print device before the printer with the lower priority.

You might also want to schedule the availability of some printers so that they are available only during certain hours of the day for noncritical print jobs.

You can also manage individual print jobs in the queue. If a print job in the queue needs to be delayed or given a higher priority in the queue, you can do that on an individual print job basis.

The information in this lesson presents the skills and knowledge that you need to set printer priorities.

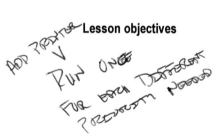

Lesson objectives

After completing this lesson, you will be able to:

- Explain the purpose of printer priorities.
- Explain when to schedule printer availability.
- Describe the guidelines for scheduling printer availability.
- Manage documents in the print queue.
- Set printer priorities and schedule printer availability.

What Are Printer Priorities?

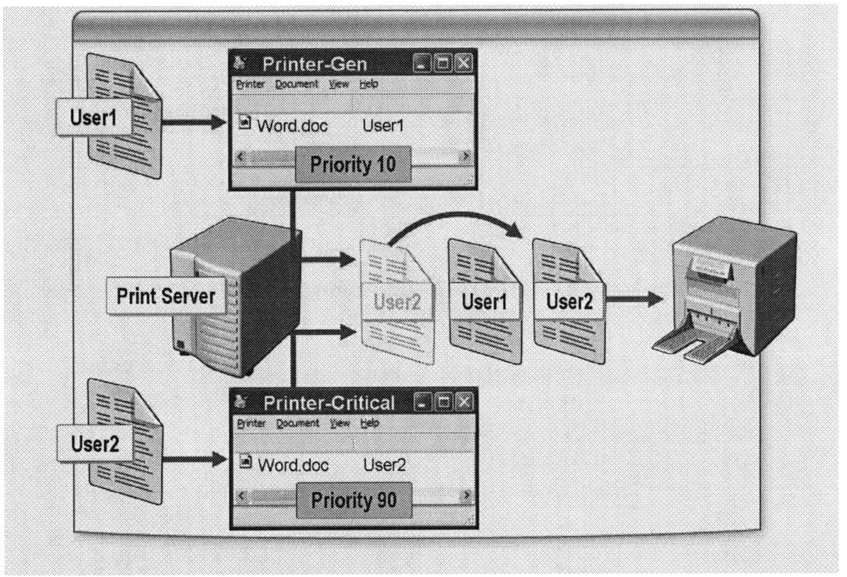

Introduction

Set priorities between printers to prioritize documents that print to the same print device. To do this, create multiple printers pointing to the same print device. Users can then send critical documents to a high-priority printer and documents that are not critical to a low-priority printer. The documents sent to the high-priority printer will be printed first. You can control access to the high priority printer by using printer permissions.

Key tasks

To set priorities between printers, perform the following tasks:

- Point two or more printers to the same print device (the same port). The port can be either a physical port on the print server or a port that points to a network-interface print device.
- Set a different priority for each printer that is connected to the print device, and then have different groups of users print to different printers. You can also have users send high-priority documents to the printer with higher priority and low-priority documents to the printer with lower priority.

How to use priorities

In the illustration on the slide, User1 sends documents to a printer with a low priority of 10, and User2 sends documents to a printer with a high priority of 90. In this example, User2's documents will be printed before User1's documents.

This is a good strategy if different groups of users have different printing requirements. High-priority users can select the printer with the higher print priority, and their print job will move to the top of the print queue. For example, a remote office might have only one print device but many users printing to it. Some users might require documents immediately and would send their job to the printer with the higher priority.

You can use printer priorities to expedite documents that must be printed immediately. Documents sent by users with high priority levels can bypass a queue of lower-priority documents waiting to be printed. If two logical printers are associated with the same print device, Windows Server 2003 routes documents with the highest priority level to the printer first.

When to Schedule Printer Availability

- Schedule printer availability to print long documents or certain types of documents
- Consider scheduling printer availability:
  - To postpone printing long documents during the day by routing them to a printer that prints only during off-hours
  - To set different printers for the same print device and configure each printer to be available at different times (For example, one printer is available from 6:00 P.M. to 6:00 A.M., and the other is available 24 hours a day)

Situations in which you schedule printer availability

One way to efficiently use printers is to schedule alternate printing times for long documents or certain types of documents. Consider scheduling printer availability in the following situations:

- Schedule printer availability if printer traffic is heavy during the day, and then postpone printing long documents by routing them to a printer that prints only during off-hours. The print spooler continues to accept documents, but it does not send them to the destination printer until the designated start time.
- Instead of dedicating an actual print device for only off-hours printing, which is not an efficient use of resources, you can set different logical printers for the same print device. You can then configure each with different times. One printer might be available from 6:00 P.M. to 6:00 A.M, and the other might be available 24 hours a day. You can then tell users to send long documents to the printer available only during off-hours and all other documents to the printer available all the time.
- Schedule printer availability if your company uses applications that automatically print reports that are not critical. For example, daily transaction reports are printed, but they are not critical print jobs. You can configure a printer that is available only during off-hours and configure the application to send the reports to that printer. The jobs will sit in the print queue until the printer is available.

Guidelines for Scheduling Printer Availability

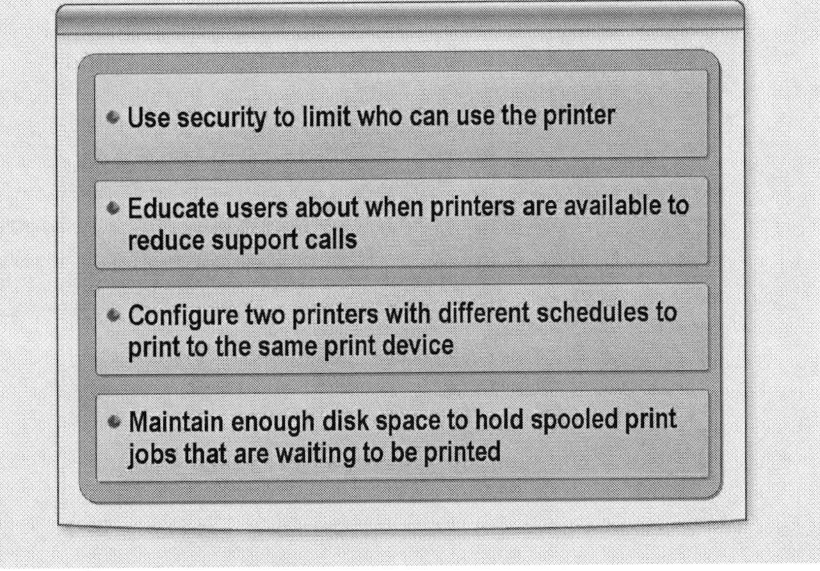

Introduction

If you schedule the availability of a printer, users and systems administrators must be aware of the security requirements and the additional support that the print server needs.

Guidelines

Consider the following guidelines when scheduling printer availability:

- *Use security to limit who can use the printer during available hours.* You might want to limit when one group can use a print device and give another group access to the same print device at all times. To do this, you must configure two printers to print to the same print device. You also must configure additional security to isolate the group that needs access to the printer at all times.
- *Educate users about when printers are available to reduce support calls when the printer is not available.* Many users are accustomed to having a printer available all the time. When they print to a printer that has a scheduling limitation, those users might try to reprint their job and then call the help desk to see why their print job was not printed. Educate these users that the print job is at the print server waiting to be delivered to the print device and that they should not try to reprint their job.
- *Configure two printers with different schedules to print to the same print device.* If a print device must be available to one group of people all the time and to other groups only during specific hours, configure two printers to print to the same print device.

Note If you have a printer scheduled to print only during off-hours, you should ensure that someone is available to physically take care of the print device. For example, if the print device runs out of paper or has a paper jam, someone must be available to fix the problem.

- *Maintain enough disk space to hold spooled print jobs that are waiting to be printed.* When you schedule a printer to be available only during certain hours, be aware that users can still print to the printer during off-hours and that the printer holds the print jobs until the available hours. Because the printer holds the print jobs during off-hours, you must have enough free disk space for the printer to hold the print jobs. If this becomes a problem and you cannot get more disk space, you can set quotas on the volume that holds the print queue.

Ways to Manage Documents

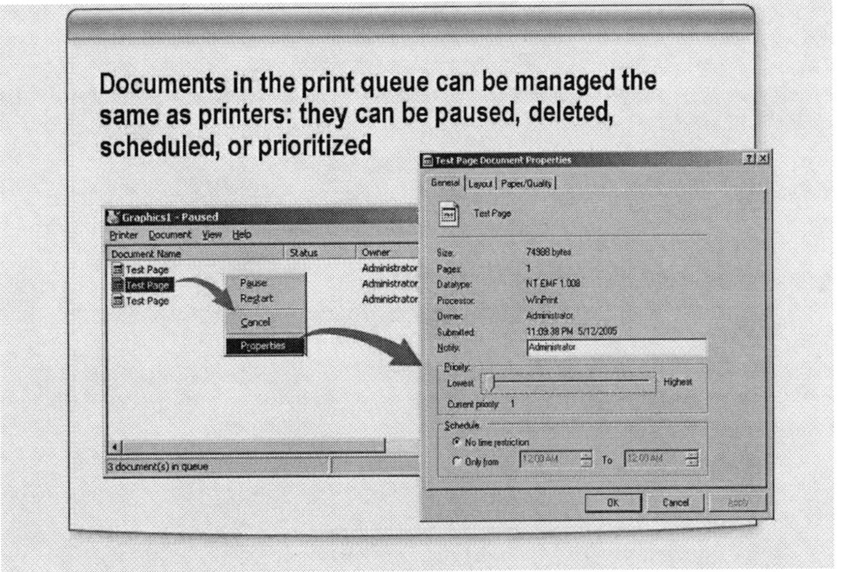
Documents in the print queue can be managed the same as printers: they can be paused, deleted, scheduled, or prioritized
Graphics1 - Paused
Test Page Document Properties
Pause
Restart
Cancel
Properties

Introduction

Documents in the print queue can be managed in the much the same ways that printers can be managed.

Managing documents

Documents can be paused and restarted or cancelled from the print queue. They can also be scheduled to be printed at a later time or given a higher priority to have them printed ahead of other documents in the queue. For example, in an office with only one heavily used printer, a user might have a critical job that must be printed quickly, but there might already be many jobs ahead of it in the queue. Anyone with Manage Documents permission could give the critical job a higher priority. The print job will not interrupt a job that is already being printed, but it will become the next job to be printed.

Where to manage documents

The shortcut menu of the document and the **Printer** menu provide a simple way to pause, restart, or cancel a job in the queue. Multiple jobs can be selected and paused or cancelled. The **Printer** menu also provides a way to cancel all documents in the print queue.

The **General** tab in the **Properties** dialog box for a document in the print queue allows scheduling and priorities to be set for individual print jobs. Print jobs will receive their schedule and priority settings from the settings that are on the printer, but these settings can be changed. For example, a print job sent to a printer with a priority of 90 could be changed to a priority of 95 to increase its priority over the other documents that are waiting in the print queue. Jobs that have been scheduled will sit in the queue until the appropriate time and then be printed. If an individual print job must be printed immediately, you can modify its schedule.

Notification field

The **General** tab also has a **Notification** field. This field specifies who will be notified when the document has been printed. By default, the owner of the document will be notified, but the owner or anyone with Manage Documents permission can change this setting. For example, suppose a user sends a large document to the printer near the end of a shift. That user could specify his or her replacement as the person to be notified when the job is complete.

Practice: Setting Printer Priorities and Scheduling Printer Availability

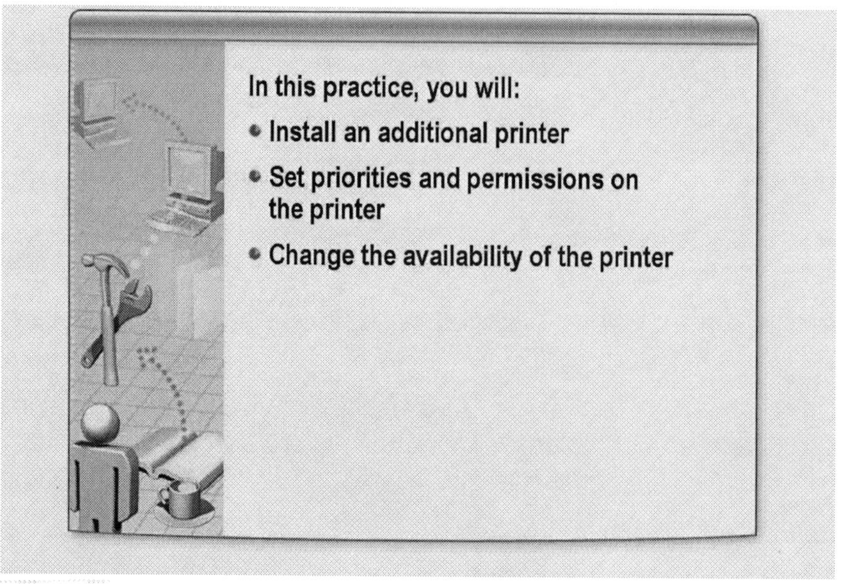
In this practice, you will:
Install an additional printer
Set priorities and permissions on the printer
Change the availability of the printer

Objectives

In this practice, you will:

- Install an additional printer.
- Set priorities and permissions on the printer.
- Change the availability of the printer.

Instructions

Ensure that the DEN-DC1 virtual machine is running.

Practice

► **Install an additional printer**

1. Log on to DEN-DC1 as **Administrator** with the password of **Pa$$w0rd.**
2. Click **Start**, and then click **Printers and Faxes.**
3. Click **Add a printer**. Click **Next.**
4. Select **Local printer attached to this computer.**
5. Use the **LPT1** port.
6. Select **HP LaserJet 4** in the list of printers.
7. On the **Use Existing Driver** page, ensure that **Keep existing driver** is selected.
8. Name the printer **Graphics_Manager.**
9. Specify the share name **Graphics_Manager.**
10. Finish the installation without printing a test page.

► **Set priorities and permissions on the printer**

1. Right-click **Graphics_Manager** and then click **Properties.**
2. Click the **Advanced** tab.
3. Set the **Priority** to **90.**
4. Click the **Security** tab.
5. Remove the **Everyone** group, and then add the **GraphicsManager** user account. Ensure that **Print** permission is assigned.
6. Click **OK.** Now any job sent to the **Graphics_Manager** printer will have priority over jobs sent to the **Graphics1** printer, and only the Graphics department manager has permission to print to the printer.

► **Change the availability of the printer**

1. Right-click **Graphics1** and then click **Properties.**
2. Click the **Advanced** tab.
3. Click **Available from,** and then make the printer available from **8:00 AM** to **10:00 PM.**
4. Click **OK.**
5. Close all open windows and log off of DEN-DC1.

Important Do not shut down the virtual machines!

Lesson: Configuring Printing Pools and Redirecting Print Queues

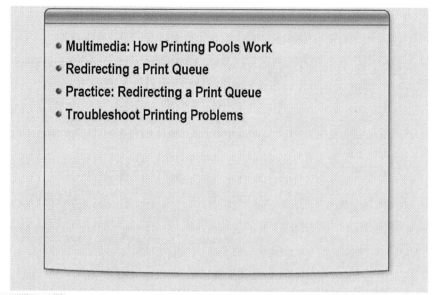

- Multimedia: How Printing Pools Work
- Redirecting a Print Queue
- Practice: Redirecting a Print Queue
- Troubleshoot Printing Problems

Introduction

The information in this lesson presents the skills and knowledge that you need to configure a printing pool.

Lesson objectives

After completing this lesson, you will be able to:

- Explain how printing pooling works.
- Explain the process for redirecting a print queue.
- Redirect a print queue.
- Troubleshoot printing problems.

RUN WIZARD ONCE

ENABLE PRINT POOLING

SPECIFY MULTIPLE PORTS

PRINTERS MUST BE DRIVER COMPATIBLE

SHOULD BE CLOSE TOGETHER

Multimedia: How Printing Pools Work

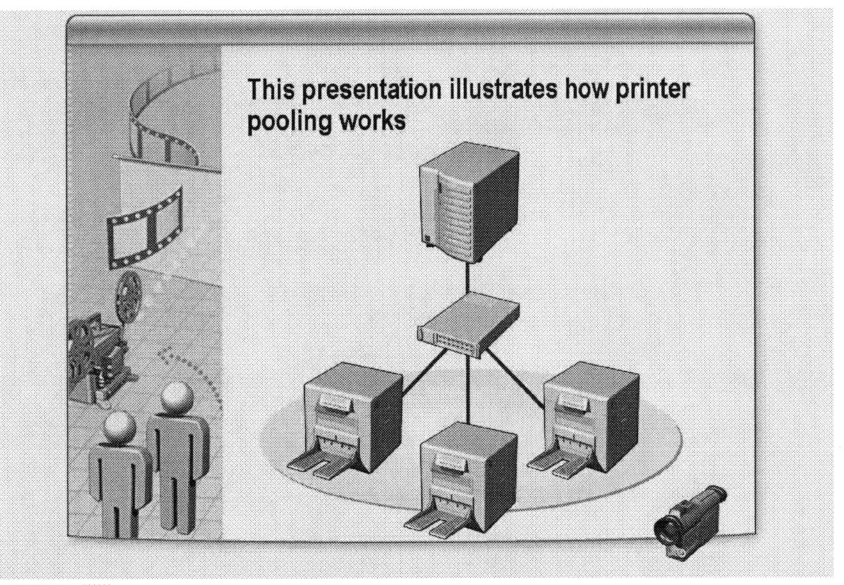

File location

To view the *How Printing Pools Work* presentation, open the Web page on the Student Materials compact disc, click **Multimedia**, and then click the title of the presentation. Do not open this presentation until the instructor tells you to.

PRINT POOLS ARE FAULT TOLERANT BECAUSE THERE ARE MULTIPLE PRINTERS EVEN THOUGH IT IS ONLY ONE ICON.

Redirecting a Print Queue

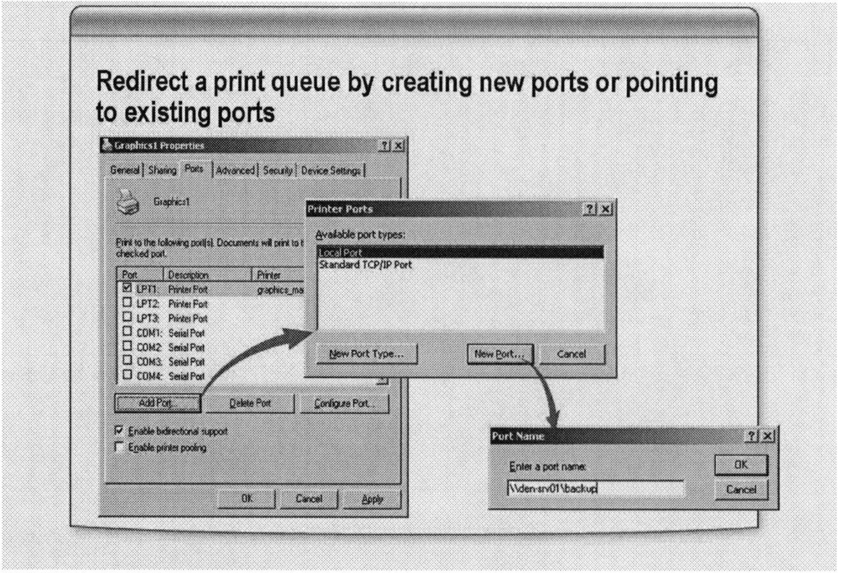

Introduction

If a print device fails, the jobs that are in the queue would normally be lost, and users would have to reprint to a different printer.

Printer redirection

With printer redirection, if the device fails, the jobs that are in that print queue can be redirected to another print queue as long as the printers use the same drivers. For example, if a department has multiple print devices and one of them fails, the jobs in that queue can be temporarily redirected to another print device in close proximity. In that way, user will not have to resubmit their current print jobs. The redirection can remain in place until the failed print device is replaced.

How to redirect the print queue

You can redirect documents to a printer on the same print server or on a different print server. However, both printers must use the same printer driver. To redirect the print queue to a different print server, you must create a new local port and configure it to use the UNC path pointing to the other print server. The printer will be automatically configured to use the new port. To redirect the print queue, you must have the Manage Printers permission on both printers.

Because the documents that are waiting in a printer's queue have been converted to that printer's language, you must redirect the documents to the same type of printer, such as a laser, ink-jet, or dot-matrix printer. The document currently being printed cannot be transferred to another printer.

CREATE NEW LOCAL PORT

SPECIFY UNC PATH TO WORKING PRINTER - SAME MAKE/MODEL

Practice: Redirecting a Print Queue

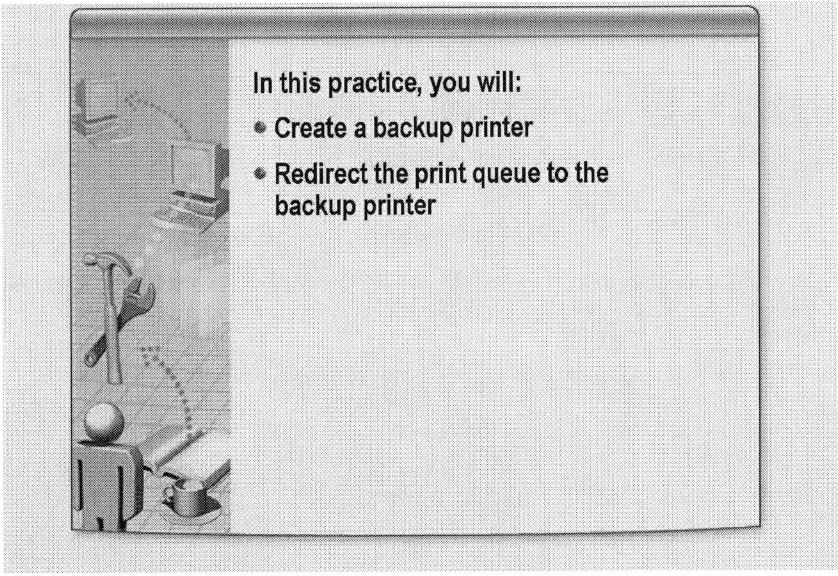

Objectives

In this practice, you will:

- Create a backup printer.
- Redirect the print queue to the backup printer.

Instructions

Ensure that the DEN-DC1 and DEN-SRV1 virtual machines are running.

Practice

► **Create a backup printer**

1. Log on to DEN-SRV1 as **Administrator** with the password of **Pa$$w0rd**.
2. Create a new local printer, based on the **HP LaserJet 4** driver. Name and share the printer as **Backup**.
3. Right-click the **Backup** printer.
4. Select **Pause Printing** from the shortcut menu.

Note If the printer is not paused, jobs might enter and leave the queue too quickly to be viewed.

5. Double-click the **Backup** printer to display the print queue.

► **Redirect the print queue to the backup printer**

1. Log on to DEN-DC1 as **Administrator** with the password of **Pa$$w0rd**.
2. Click **Start** and then click **Printers and Faxes**.
3. Double-click the **Graphics1** printer, and then examine the print queue. Cancel any existing test pages.
4. Ensure that the printer is paused, open the **Properties** dialog box and then print two test pages.
5. Click the **Ports** tab, and then click **Add Port**.
6. In the **Printer Ports** dialog box, ensure that **Local Port** is selected, and then click **New Port**.
7. In the **Port Name** dialog box, type **\\DEN-SRV1\Backup** in the **Enter a port name** field. Click **OK**.
8. Click **Close**.

   Notice that the UNC path has been created as a port and has already been selected.
9. Click **Close**.
10. While viewing the print queue, un-pause the **Graphics1** printer.
11. Switch to DEN-SRV1. Examine the print queue for the **Backup** printer. The print jobs from **DEN-DC1\Graphics1** have moved to **Backup**. The documents will all be named **Remote Downlevel Document**.
12. On the **Printer** menu, click **Cancel All Documents**.
13. Click **Yes**.
14. Delete the **Backup** printer.
15. Close all open windows.
16. Log off of both DEN-DC1 and DEN-SRV1.

Important Do not shut down the virtual machines.

Troubleshooting Printing Problems

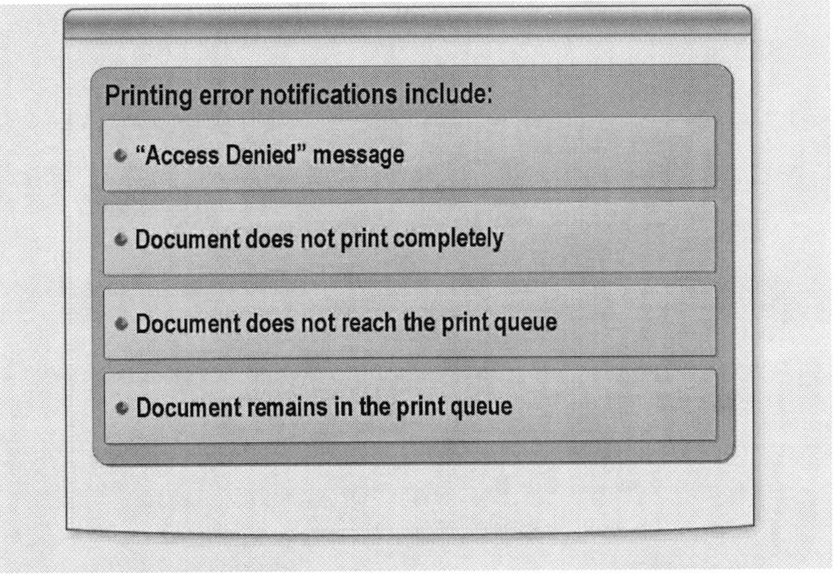

Printing error notifications include:
"Access Denied" message
Document does not print completely
Document does not reach the print queue
Document remains in the print queue

Introduction

Solving printing problems is one of the main help desk tasks. When you troubleshoot printing problems, use standard troubleshooting methods to determine and resolve the problem. For example, is it only one user who cannot print, or is the problem more widespread? Often the problem is a print driver issue that can be solved by deleting and reinstalling the printer on the client machine. Some other common problems are listed in the following table.

Printing problems, causes, and solutions

Problem	Possible cause	Solution
User receives an "Access Denied" message when trying to submit a job to a printer.	User does not have the appropriate permission to print to that printer.	Change the user's permissions, or refer the user to a printer that he or she has permission to use.
The document is not printed completely or comes out garbled.	Incorrect printer driver installed.	Change the current driver.
The hard disk experiences a high level of disk activity, and the document does not reach the print server.	Insufficient hard disk space for spooling.	Create more free space, or move the spooler location to another partition.
No one can print to the server. There are documents on the server that will not print and cannot be deleted.	Stalled print spooler.	Restart the Print Spooler service.

Lab: Managing Printing

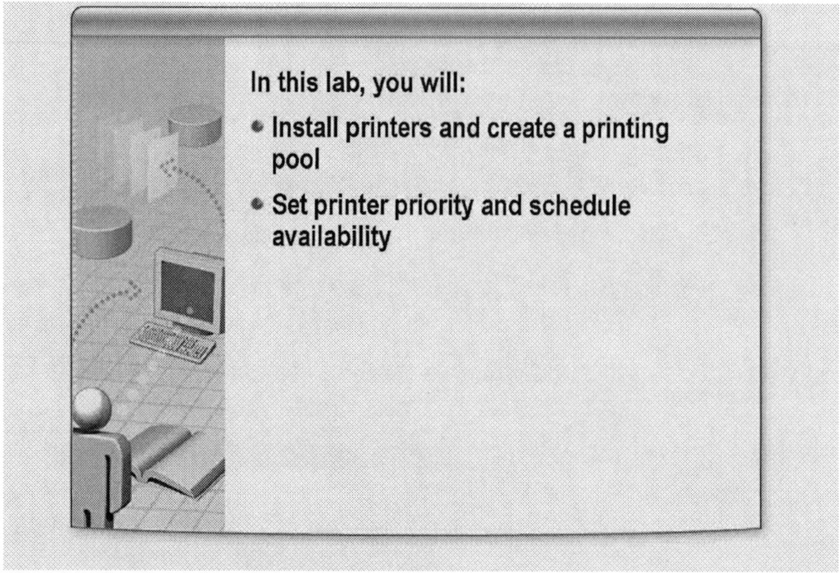

Objectives

After completing this lab, you will be able to:

- Install printers and create a printing pool.
- Set printer priority and schedule availability.

Prerequisites

To complete this lab, you must have the following virtual machines:

- DEN-DC1
- DEN-SRV1

Estimated time to complete this lab: 30 minutes

Exercise 1
Installing Printers and Creating a Printing Pool

In this exercise, you will install printers and create a printing pool.

Scenario

The Sales department has decided to implement printer pooling to provide redundancy for failed print devices. You will install a printer for the Sales department and configure it to send documents to a printing pool.

Tasks	Specific instructions
1. Create a new sales printer.	**a.** Log on to DEN-SRV1 as the **Administrator** with the password of **Pa$$w0rd**. **b.** Click **Start** and then click **Printers and Faxes.** **c.** Create a local **HP LaserJet 4 printer** named **SalesPool** that is configured to use a **Standard TCP/IP** port of **10.10.0.50**, and share it as **SalesPool.** **d.** Set the **Location** to **Denver/Downtown.**
2. Create a printing pool.	**a.** Right-click **SalesPool**, and then click **Properties.** **b.** Click the **Ports** tab. **c.** Add a new **Standard TCP/IP** port, pointing to **10.10.0.60.** **d.** On the **Ports** tab, select the **Enable printer pooling** check box. **e.** Select both the **10.10.0.50** port and the **10.10.0.60** port. **f.** Click **Close.**

Exercise 2
Setting Printer Priority and Scheduling Availability

In this exercise, you will set printer priorities and schedule printer availability.

Scenario

The Sales department manager has been experiencing long waits for documents that he submits for printing. The manager needs documents to be printed quickly. To provide the manager with faster printing, you will create another instance of the printer that has a higher priority than the normal sales printer and assign permission to the sales managers. You will also create a printer for large documents that are not high priority and schedule it to be available after hours.

Tasks	Specific instructions
1. Create a new sales printer.	a. On DEN-SRV1, ensure that the **Printers and Faxes** window is open. b. Create a local HP **LaserJet 4** printer configured to use **LPT1** and named **SalesManager**, and then share it as **SalesManager**.
2. Set the priority to high.	a. Open the **Properties** dialog box for the **SalesManager** printer. b. Click the **Advanced** tab. c. Set the **Priority** to **90**.
3. Set permissions on the SalesManager printer.	a. Click the **Security** tab. b. Remove **Everyone**. c. Add the **G Sales Managers** global group, and then assign **Print** permission.
4. Create a printer to be available after hours.	a. Create a local **HP LaserJet 4** printer configured to use **LPT1** and named **Overnight**, and then share it as **Overnight**. b. Open the **Properties** dialog box for the **Overnight** printer. c. Click the **Advanced** tab. d. Schedule the printer to be available from **12:00AM** to **6:00AM**. e. Click **OK**.
5. Complete the lab exercise.	a. Close all programs and shut down all computers. Do not save changes. b. To prepare for the next module, start the DEN-DC1 and DEN-CL1 virtual computers.

Module 7: Managing Access to Objects in Organizational Units

Contents

Overview

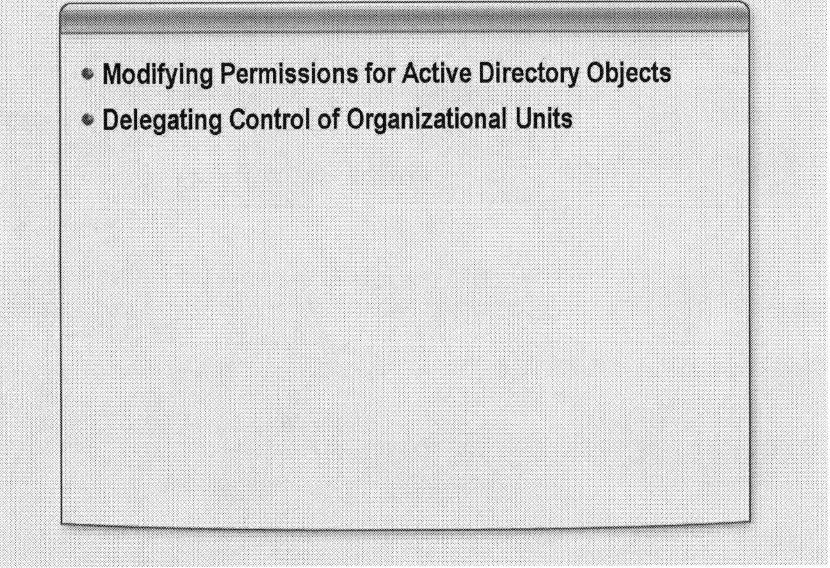
Modifying Permissions for Active Directory Objects
Delegating Control of Organizational Units

Introduction

The information in this module introduces the job function of managing access to objects in organizational units. Specifically, the module provides the skills and knowledge that you need to explain the permissions available for managing access to objects in the Active Directory® directory service and delegate control of an organizational unit.

Objectives

After completing this module, you will be able to:

- Modify permissions for Active Directory objects.
- Delegate control of organizational units.

Lesson: Modifying Permissions for Active Directory Objects

- What Are Active Directory Object Permissions?
- Characteristics of Active Directory Object Permissions
- Permissions Inheritance for Active Directory Object Permissions
- Effects of Moving Objects on Permissions Inheritance
- What Are Effective Permissions for Active Directory Objects?
- Practice: Modifying Permissions for Active Directory Objects

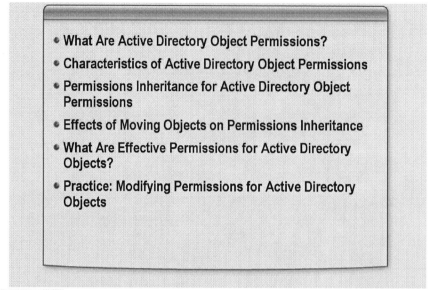

Introduction

Every object in Active Directory has a security descriptor that defines which accounts have permission to access the object and what type of access is allowed. The Microsoft® Windows Server™ 2003 family uses these security descriptors to control access to objects.

Lesson objectives

After completing this lesson, you will be able to:

- Explain what Active Directory object permissions are.
- Describe the characteristics of Active Directory object permissions.
- Describe permissions inheritance for Active Directory object permissions.
- Describe the effects of moving objects on permission inheritance.
- Explain what effective permissions are for Active Directory objects.
- Modify permissions for Active Directory objects.

What Are Active Directory Object Permissions?

Permission	Allows the user to:
Full Control	Change permissions, take ownership, and perform the tasks that are allowed by all other standard permissions
Write	Change object attributes
Read	View objects, object attributes, the object owner, and Active Directory permissions
Create All Child Objects	Add any type of object to an organizational unit
Delete All Child Objects	Remove any type of child object from an organizational unit

Introduction

Active Directory object permissions secure resources by enabling you to control which administrators or users can access individual objects or object attributes and the type of access allowed. You use permissions to assign administrative privileges for an organizational unit or a hierarchy of organizational units to manage Active Directory objects. You can also use permissions to assign administrative privileges for a single object class to a specific user or group.

Standard and special permissions

Standard permissions are the most frequently granted permissions and consist of a collection of special permissions. Special permissions give you a higher degree of control over the type of access that you can grant for objects. The standard permissions are as follows:

- Full Control
- Write
- Read
- Create All Child Objects
- Delete All Child Objects

Access authorized by permissions

An administrator or the owner of the object must grant permissions for the object before users can access it. The Windows Server 2003 family stores a list of user access permissions, called the discretionary access control list (DACL), for every object in Active Directory. The DACL for an object lists who can access the object and the specific actions that each user can perform on the object.

Additional reading

For more information about Active Directory permissions, see "Best practices for assigning permissions on Active Directory objects" on the Microsoft Web site.

Characteristics of Active Directory Object Permissions

Active Directory object permissions can be:

- Allowed or denied
- Implicitly or explicitly denied
- Set as standard or special permissions
  - Standard permissions are the most frequently assigned permissions
  - Special permissions provide a finer degree of control for assigning access to objects
- Set at the object level or inherited from its parent object

Introduction

NTFS permissions and Active Directory object permissions are similar. Active Directory object permissions can be allowed or denied, implicitly or explicitly denied, set as standard or special permissions, and set at the object level or inherited from the parent object.

Note To view the **Security** tab in the properties dialog box for Active Directory objects, you must enable **Advanced Features** on the **View** menu in the Active Directory administration tool.

Allowing and denying permissions

You can allow or deny permissions. Denied permissions take precedence over any permission that you otherwise allow to user accounts and groups. You should use Deny permissions only when it is necessary to remove a permission that a user is granted by being a member of a group.

Implicit or explicit permissions

You can implicitly or explicitly deny permissions as follows:

- *When permission to perform an operation is not allowed, it is implicitly denied.* For example, if the Marketing group is granted Read permission for a user object, and no other security principal is listed in the DACL for that object, users who are not members of the Marketing group are implicitly denied access. The operating system does not allow users who are not members of the Marketing group to read the properties of the user object.
- *You explicitly deny a permission when you want to exclude a subset within a larger group from performing a task that the larger group has permissions to perform.* For example, it might be necessary to prevent a user named Don from viewing the properties of a user object. However, Don is a member of the Marketing group, which has permissions to view the properties of the user object. You can prevent Don from viewing the properties of the user object by explicitly denying Read permission to him.

Standard and special permissions

You can configure most Active Directory object permissions tasks by using standard permissions. Standard permissions are the most commonly used; however, if you need to grant a finer level of permissions, you will use special permissions. Special permissions allow you to set permissions on a particular class of object or individual attributes of a class of object. For example, you could grant a user Full Control over the group object class in a container or just grant the user the ability to modify group memberships in a container. Or you can grant users just the permissions needed to change a single attribute, such as the phone number, on all user accounts.

Inherited permissions

In general, when permissions are set on a parent object, new objects inherit the permissions of the parent. You can remove inherited permissions, but you can also reenable them if needed.

The way that you assign permissions on the parent object affects permission inheritance. If you manually assign a standard permission on an organizational unit, the permission applies only to the organizational unit, not to the objects in the organizational unit. The two exceptions to this rule are the Create All Child Objects and Delete All Child Objects permissions, which will allow you to perform those actions in the organizational unit.

The reason for these exceptions is that permissions are applied to **This Object Only** by default when you assign permissions manually. For example, if a user named Greg has been manually assigned Full Control on an organizational unit, Greg can create an object, such as a user account, in that organizational unit because he has the Create All Child Objects permission. However, Greg will not be able to set the password or any other attributes for the new user account because he does not have permission on the **User** object class.

To modify this, use the **Advanced Security** settings at the organizational unit level to modify the permissions granted to **This object and all child objects**. The default selection is **This object and all child objects** when you assign permission by using the Delegation of Control Wizard.

Note The Delegation of Control Wizard will be discussed in the next lesson.

ALL AD. OBJECTS HAVE A DACL

TO VIEW YOU *MUST* TURN ON ADVANCED FEATURES FIRST

PERMISSIONS DO NOT INHERIT DOWN BY DEFAULT.

DELEGATION IS EASIEST WHEN USING WIZARD TO DELEGATE.

TO REVOKE PERMISSIONS YOU MUST OPEN DACL AND DO SO MANUALLY

Permissions Inheritance for Active Directory Object Permissions

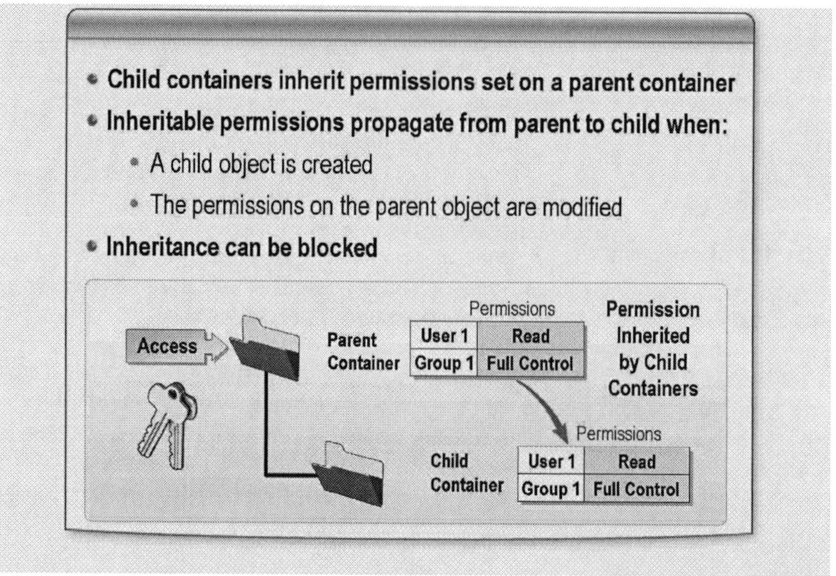

Benefits of permissions inheritance

A parent object passes permissions down to an object, called a child, through inheritance. A child object can inherit permissions only from its parent object. Permissions inheritance in Active Directory minimizes the number of times that you need to grant permissions for objects.

Permissions inheritance in Windows Server 2003 simplifies the task of managing permissions in the following ways:

- You do not need to apply permissions manually to child objects when they are created.
- The permissions that are applied to a parent object are applied consistently to all child objects.
- To modify permissions for all objects in a container, you need to modify only the permissions for the parent object. The child objects automatically inherit those changes.

Preventing permissions inheritance

You can prevent permissions inheritance so that a child object does not inherit permissions from its parent object. When you prevent inheritance, only the permissions that you set explicitly apply.

When you prevent permissions inheritance, the Windows Server 2003 family enables you to:

- *Copy inherited permissions to the object.* The new permissions are explicit permissions for the object. They are a copy of the permissions that the object previously inherited from its parent object. After the inherited permissions are copied, you can make any necessary changes to the permissions.
- *Remove inherited permissions from the object.* By removing these permissions, you eliminate all inherited permissions for the object. You can then grant any new permission that you want for the object.

Effects of Moving Objects on Permissions Inheritance

- Explicit permissions set on an object remain the same if an object is moved
- Moved objects inherit permissions from the new parent organizational unit
- Moved objects no longer inherit permissions from the previous parent organizational unit

Introduction

Modifying Active Directory objects affects permissions inheritance. As a systems administrator, you will be asked to move objects between organizational units in Active Directory when organizational or administrative functions change. When you do this, the inherited permissions will change. It is imperative that you are aware of these consequences prior to modifying Active Directory objects.

Effects of moving objects

When you move objects between organizational units, the following conditions apply:

- Permissions that are set explicitly remain the same.
- An object inherits permissions from the organizational unit that it is moved to.
- An object no longer inherits permissions from the organizational unit that it is moved from.

Note When modifying Active Directory objects, you can move multiple objects at the same time.

The following types of items can be moved within the Active Directory structure:

- User account
- Contact account
- Printer
- Group
- Shared folder
- Computer
- Domain controller
- Organizational unit

Tip You can use the click and drag method to move objects in Active Directory if you enable Users, Computers and Groups as Containers view.

What Are Effective Permissions for Active Directory Objects?

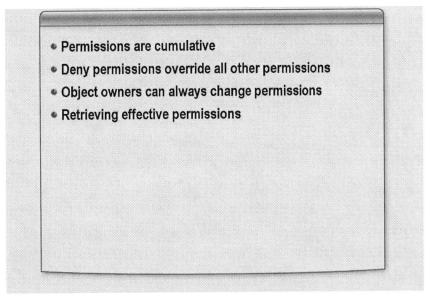

- Permissions are cumulative
- Deny permissions override all other permissions
- Object owners can always change permissions
- Retrieving effective permissions

Introduction

You can use the Effective Permissions tool to determine what the permissions for an Active Directory object are. This tool calculates the permissions that are granted to the specified user or group and takes into account the permissions that are in effect from group memberships and any permissions inherited from parent objects.

Characteristics

Effective permissions for Active Directory objects have the following characteristics:

- Cumulative permissions are the combination of Active Directory permissions that are granted to the user and group accounts.
- Deny permissions override the same level of inherited permissions. Permissions explicitly assigned take priority.

  Important An explicit Allow permission set on an object class or attribute will override an inherited Deny permission.

- Every object has an owner, whether in an NTFS volume or Active Directory. The owner controls how permissions are set on the object and to whom permissions are granted.

  The person who creates an Active Directory object is its owner. Objects that are created during Active Directory installation or by any member of the built-in Administrators group are owned by the Administrators group. The owner can always change permissions for an object, even when the owner is denied all access to the object.

  The current owner can grant **Take Ownership** permission to another user, which enables that user to take ownership of that object at any time. The user must actually take ownership to complete the transfer of ownership.

Retrieving effective permissions

To retrieve information about effective permissions in Active Directory, you must have permission to read membership information. If the specified user or group is a domain object, you must have permission to read the object's membership information on the domain. The following users have these default domain permissions:

- Domain administrators have permission to read membership information on all objects.
- Local accounts, including local administrators, on a workstation or stand-alone server do not have read membership permission and cannot read membership information for a domain user.
- Authenticated domain users can read membership information only when the domain is in pre-Windows 2000 functional level.

Practice: Modifying Permissions for Active Directory Objects

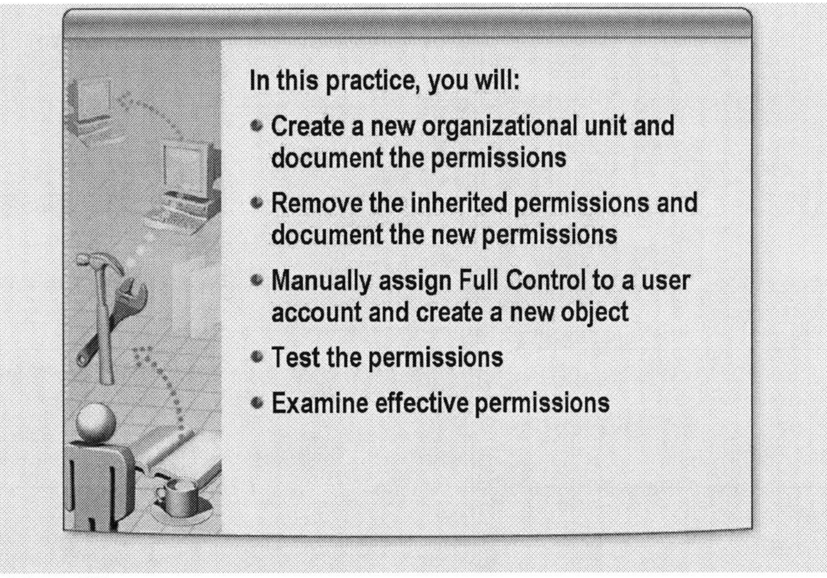
In this practice, you will:
Create a new organizational unit and document the permissions
Remove the inherited permissions and document the new permissions
Manually assign Full Control to a user account and create a new object
Test the permissions
Examine effective permissions

Objectives

In this practice, you will:

- Create a new organizational unit and document the permissions.
- Remove the inherited permissions and document the new permissions.
- Manually assign Full Control to a user account and create a new object.
- Test the permissions.
- Examine effective permissions.

Instructions

Ensure that the DEN-DC1 and the DEN-CL1 virtual machines are running.

Practice

► **Create a new organizational unit and document the permissions**

1. Log on to DEN-DC1 as **Administrator** with the password of **Pa$$w0rd**.
2. Open **Active Directory Users and Computers**.
3. At the domain level, create a new organizational unit named **Test**.
4. On the **View** menu of **Active Directory Users and Computers**, click **Advanced Features**.
5. Right-click the **Test** OU and then click **Properties**.

6. Click the **Security** tab. Examine the list of security entries. An explicit permission has a selected check box under **Allow** or **Deny**. Special and inherited permissions have a shaded selected check box under **Allow** or **Deny**. Document the following default permissions:

Group or user names	Inherited	Explicit
Account Operators		X
Administrators	X	
Authenticated Users		X
Domain Admins		X
Enterprise Admins	X	
Enterprise Domain Controllers	X	X
Pre-Windows 2000 Compatible Access	X	
Print Operators		X
System		X

Tip To determine whether a permission is explicit or inherited, look in the **Inherited From** column on the **Permissions** tab in the **Advanced Security Settings** dialog box.

► **Remove the inherited permissions and document the new permissions**

1. On the **Security** tab of the **Test Properties** dialog box, click **Advanced.**
2. In the **Advanced Security Settings for Test** dialog box, on the **Permissions** tab, clear the **Allow inheritable permissions from the parent to propagate to this object and all child objects. Include these with entries explicitly defined here** check box.
3. In the **Security** dialog box, click **Remove.**
4. In the **Advanced Security Settings for Test** dialog box, click **OK.**
5. Examine the new security settings for the **Test** organizational unit.

6. Document the new security settings.

Group or user names	Inherited	Explicit
Account Operators		X
Administrators		
Authenticated Users		X
Domain Admins		X
Enterprise Admins		
Enterprise Domain Controllers		X
Pre-Windows 2000 Compatible Access		
Print Operators		X
System		X

What groups are no longer on the list?

____

____

► Manually assign Full Control to a user account and create a new object

1. On the **Security** tab, click **Add**, and then type **Judy Lew**. Click **OK**.
2. Grant the Judy Lew account **Full Control**, and then click **Apply**.
3. Click **Advanced**, select **Judy Lew** in the **Permission entries** list, and then click **Edit**. Notice that Full Control permission applies to **This object only**. Click **Cancel**.
4. Click **OK** twice.
5. Create another organizational unit inside **Test** named **Test1**.
6. Examine the security properties of **Test1**. Notice that **Judy Lew** does not appear in the security list.
7. Click **Cancel**.
8. Close **Active Directory Users and Computers**.

► Test the permissions

1. Log on to DEN-CL1 as **Administrator** with the password of **Pa$$w0rd**.
2. Connect to **\\DEN-DC1\Admin_Tools**, and install the **adminpak** administrative tools.
3. Log off, and then log on to DEN-CL1 as **Judy** with the password of **Pa$$w0rd**.
4. At the **Run** command prompt, type **dsa.msc** to launch Active Directory Users and Computers, and then attempt to create a new user called **Test User** in the **Test** organizational unit. When you click **Finish**, you should receive an error message. Read the message, and then click **OK**.

5. Attempt to modify any of the properties of the user that you just created. You will not be able to.
6. Attempt to create an object in the **Test1** organizational unit. You will not be able to.
7. Attempt to modify the properties of the **Test1** organizational unit. You will not be able to.

► **Examine effective permissions**

1. On DEN-DC1, open **Active Directory Users and Computers**" click the **Test** organizational unit.

   Notice that the user account that Judy Lew created is disabled. Why?

   ____

   ____

   ____

   ____

2. Right-click the **Test** OU and then click **Properties.**
3. Click the **Security** tab, and then click **Advanced** to open the **Advanced Security Settings for Test** dialog box.
4. Click the **Effective Permissions** tab, and then click **Select.**
5. Enter **Judy Lew** and then click **OK.**

   What are her effective permissions?

   ____

   What are her effective permissions on the user account she created?

   ____

   What are her effective permissions on the Test1 organizational unit? Why does she have these permissions?

   ____

6. Close all open windows and log off of DEN-DC1 and DEN-CL1.

Important Do not shut down the virtual machines.

Lesson: Delegating Control of Organizational Units

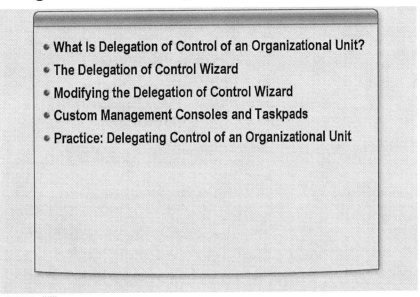

- What Is Delegation of Control of an Organizational Unit?
- The Delegation of Control Wizard
- Modifying the Delegation of Control Wizard
- Custom Management Consoles and Taskpads
- Practice: Delegating Control of an Organizational Unit

Introduction

Active Directory enables you to efficiently manage objects by delegating administrative control of the objects. You can use the Delegation of Control Wizard and customized consoles in Microsoft Management Console (MMC) to grant specific users the permissions to perform various administrative and management tasks.

Lesson objectives

After completing this lesson, you will be able to:

- Describe what it means to delegate control of an organizational unit.
- Describe the purpose and function of the Delegation of Control Wizard.
- Modify the Delegation of Control Wizard.
- Create custom management consoles and taskpads.
- Delegate control of an organizational unit by using the Delegation of Control Wizard.

What Is Delegation of Control of an Organizational Unit?

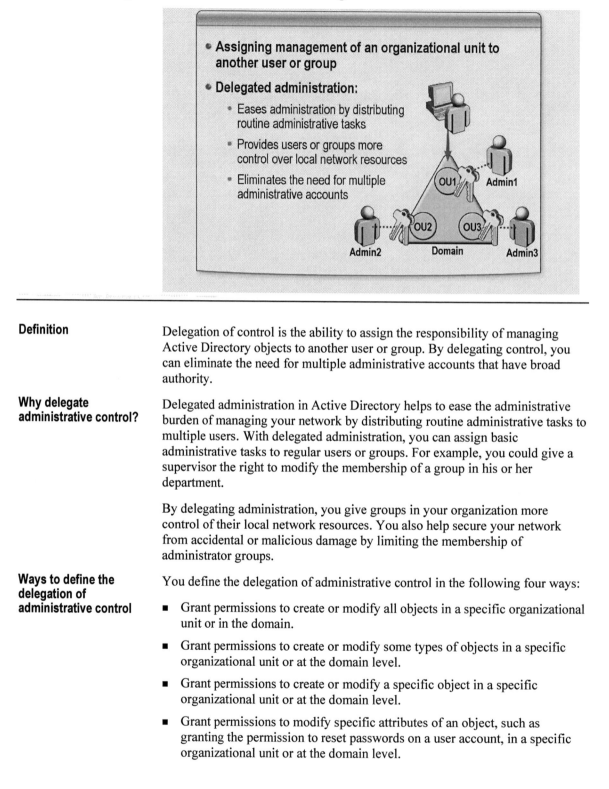

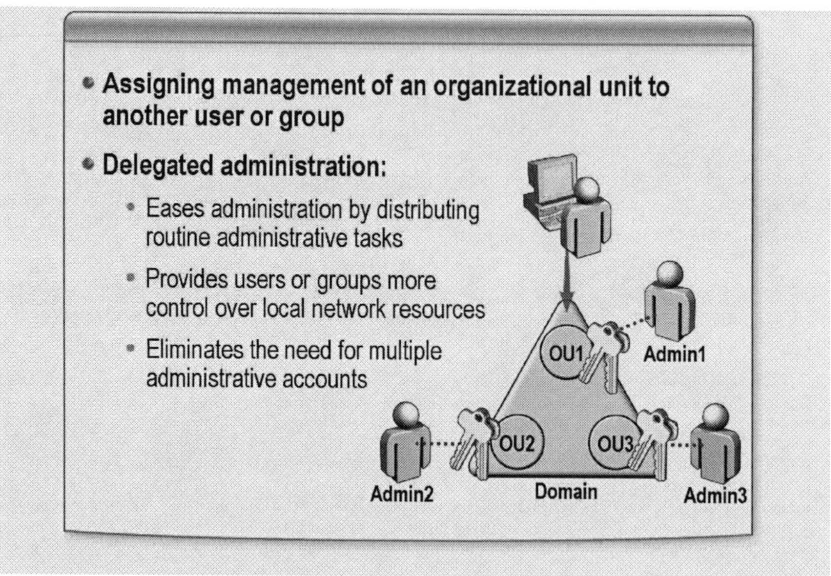

Definition

Delegation of control is the ability to assign the responsibility of managing Active Directory objects to another user or group. By delegating control, you can eliminate the need for multiple administrative accounts that have broad authority.

Why delegate administrative control?

Delegated administration in Active Directory helps to ease the administrative burden of managing your network by distributing routine administrative tasks to multiple users. With delegated administration, you can assign basic administrative tasks to regular users or groups. For example, you could give a supervisor the right to modify the membership of a group in his or her department.

By delegating administration, you give groups in your organization more control of their local network resources. You also help secure your network from accidental or malicious damage by limiting the membership of administrator groups.

Ways to define the delegation of administrative control

You define the delegation of administrative control in the following four ways:

- Grant permissions to create or modify all objects in a specific organizational unit or in the domain.
- Grant permissions to create or modify some types of objects in a specific organizational unit or at the domain level.
- Grant permissions to create or modify a specific object in a specific organizational unit or at the domain level.
- Grant permissions to modify specific attributes of an object, such as granting the permission to reset passwords on a user account, in a specific organizational unit or at the domain level.

The Delegation of Control Wizard

- **Use the Delegation of Control Wizard to specify:**
  - The user or group to which you want to delegate control
  - The organizational units and objects that you want to grant the user or group the permission to control
  - The tasks that you want the user or group to be able to perform
- **The Delegation of Control Wizard automatically assigns to users the appropriate permissions**

Introduction

You use the Delegation of Control Wizard to select the user or group to which you want to delegate control. You also use the wizard to grant users permissions to control organizational units and objects and to access and modify objects.

Delegating permissions

You can use the Delegation of Control Wizard to grant permissions at the organizational unit level. You must manually grant additional specialized permissions at the object level.

In **Active Directory Users and Computers**, right-click the organizational units that you want to delegate control for, and then click **Delegate control** to start the wizard. You can also select the organizational unit and then click **Delegate control** on the **Action** menu.

Options

The following table describes the options in the Delegation of Control Wizard.

Option	Description
Users or Groups	The user accounts or groups to which you want to delegate control.
Tasks to Delegate	A list of common tasks, or the option to customize a task. When you select a common task, the wizard summarizes your selections to complete the delegation process. When you choose to customize a task, the wizard presents Active Directory object types and permissions for you to choose from.
Active Directory Object Type	Either all objects or only specific types of objects in the specified organizational unit.
Permissions	The permissions to grant for the object or objects.

Note The Delegation of Control Wizard can append permissions to an organizational unit if the wizard is run more than once. However, you cannot use the wizard to remove permissions.

Modifying the Delegation of Control Wizard

- The list of common tasks in the Delegation Wizard is controlled by templates in the delegwiz.ini file
- You can modify the list of common tasks by modifying the delegwiz.ini file to include other templates

Introduction

The Delegation of Control Wizard provides a quick way to assign the permissions that are required to perform many common tasks. To suit their needs, some organizations might want to modify the list of common tasks that the wizard provides. You can modify the list of common tasks by creating templates and configuring the delegwiz.ini file to include the template in the common tasks list.

The delegwiz.ini file

The delegwiz.ini file is a text file that resides in the %systemroot%\inf folder—usually C:\Windows\Inf. The file consists of three sections. The first section contains the version signature. The next section lists the templates in the order in which they appear in the file. The last section contains the templates.

Modifying the delegwiz.ini file

You can modify the delegwiz.ini file by using any text editor. You can write your own templates, or you can use one of the templates available through the Microsoft Web site.

Note The Active_Directory_Delegation_Appendices.doc contains 70 templates that you can use to modify the delegwiz.ini file. The Active_Directory_Delegation_Appendices.doc is on the Student CD and can be downloaded from the Microsoft Web site.

To modify the delegwiz.ini file, create or copy a template into the delegwiz.ini file, and then modify the Templates line of the file to include your custom template in the correct position. You will need to copy the delegwiz.ini file into the %systemroot%\inf folder on all domain controllers on which you want the file to be available. You should make a backup copy of your custom delegwiz.ini file because the installation of service packs could overwrite the custom delegwiz.ini file with a default version.

Note For more information about Active Directory delegation, download the "Best Practices for Delegating Active Directory Administration" document from the Microsoft Download Center Web site.

Custom Management Consoles and Taskpads

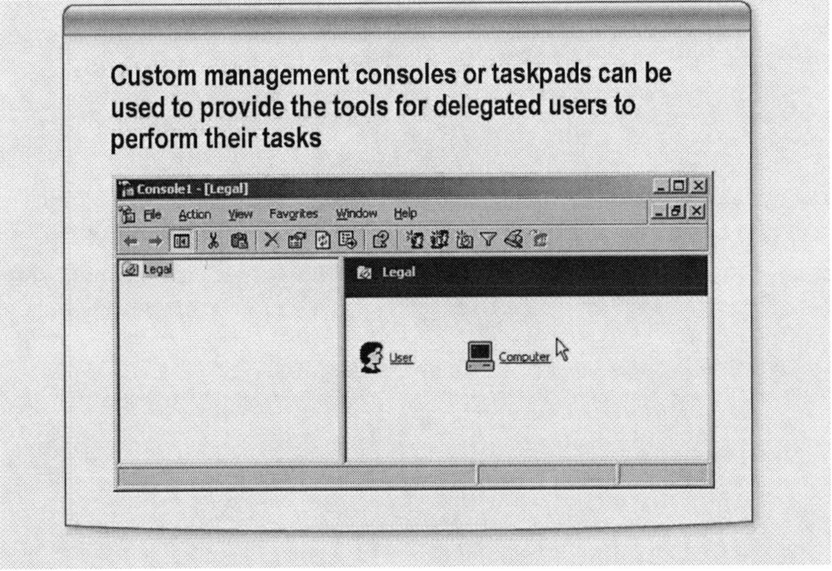

Introduction

After users have been delegated administrative tasks, they will need tools to perform the tasks that they have been authorized to do.

Custom management consoles

You can customize management consoles to display only the sections of Active Directory that you want the user to see. The view can be restricted such that users see only the portion of the directory where they have permissions. In that way, you can hide the complexities of the directory service. For example, if a user is responsible for managing user accounts in only one organizational unit, you can customize the view in Active Directory Users and Computers so that the user can view only the required organizational unit.

Taskpads

Taskpads can further simplify management tasks by providing a task-based management console that allows a user to perform a task by clicking a button in the management console. If you have users who need to perform simple Active Directory tasks such as reset passwords for all users in a specific organizational unit, you can create a taskpad that provides a very simple interface for performing that task.

The domain administrator can create a custom management console for Active Directory administration by launching a new MMC and adding the Active Directory Users and Computers snap-in. To restrict the view, right-click the section of the domain tree that you want to expose, and then click **New window from here**.

You can create taskpads by right-clicking an organizational unit and then selecting the option to create a **New taskpad view**. The New Taskpad Wizard will launch, allowing you to create the taskpad view. The administrator can then run the New Task Wizard to create icons that the user can click to perform tasks.

Important The Active Directory administrative tools must be installed on the workstation of the delegated user for custom consoles or taskpads to function.

Practice: Delegating Control of an Organizational Unit

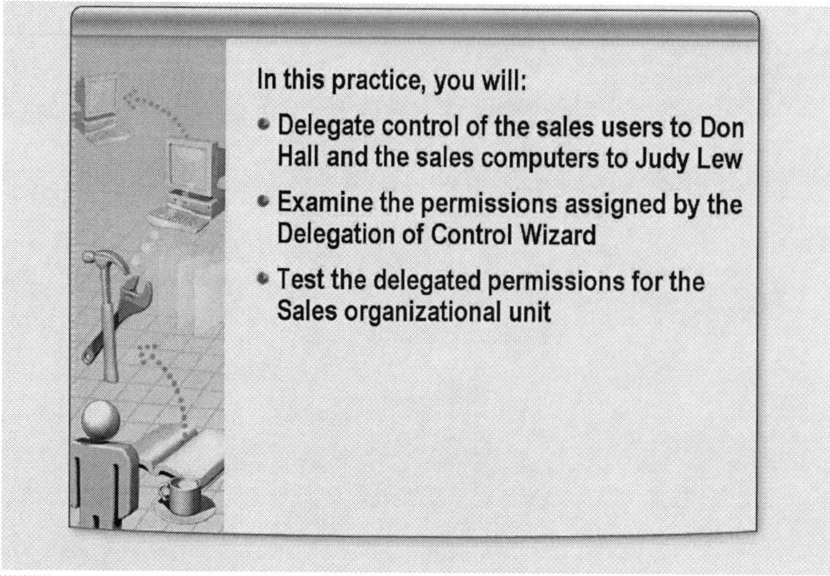

Objectives

In this practice, you will:

- Delegate control of the Sales users to Don Hall and the Sales computers to Judy Lew.
- Examine the permissions assigned by the Delegation of Control Wizard.
- Test the delegated permissions for the Sales organizational unit.

Instructions

Ensure that the DEN-DC1 and the DEN-CL1 virtual machines are running.

Practice

► **Delegate control of the sales users to Don Hall and the sales computers to Judy Lew**

1. Log on to DEN-DC1 as **Administrator** with the password of **Pa$$w0rd.**
2. Open **Active Directory Users and Computers**, right-click **Sales**, and then click **Delegate Control.**
3. In the **Delegation of Control Wizard**, on the **Welcome** page, click **Next.**
4. On the **Users or Groups** page, add **Don Hall**, and then click **Next.**
5. In the **Tasks to Delegate** page select the **Create, delete and manage user accounts** check box.
6. Click **Next**, click **Finish.**
7. Run the **Delegation of Control Wizard** again.
8. On the **Users or Groups** page, add **Judy Lew**, and then click **Next.**
9. On the **Tasks to Delegate** page, click **Create a custom task to delegate**, and then click **Next.**
10. On the **Active Directory Object Type** page, click **Only the following objects in the folder**, and then select the **Computer objects** check box.
11. Select the **Create selected objects in this folder** and **Delete selected objects in this folder** check boxes, and then click **Next.**

12. On the **Permissions** page, select the **General** check box.
13. Under **Permissions**, select the **Read** and **Write** check boxes, and then click **Next**.
14. On the **Completing the Delegation of Control Wizard** page, click **Finish**.

► Examine the permissions assigned by the Delegation of Control Wizard

1. Right-click the **Sales** OU and then click **Properties**.
2. Click the **Security** tab.
3. Click **Advanced**, and view **Don Hall** in the **Permission entries** list.

   What permissions are assigned to Don Hall?

   F/C USER OBJECTS CREATE/DELETE

   USER OBJS

4. Locate **Judy Lew**.

   What permissions are assigned to Judy Lew?

   CREATE/DELETE & SPECIAL FOR PC OBJECTS

5. Close all open windows.

► Test the delegated permissions for the Sales organizational unit

1. Log on to DEN-CL1 as **Don** with the password of **Pa$$w0rd**.
2. Open the **Run** command, and then type **dsa.msc** to launch **Active Directory Users and Computers**.
3. Right-click the **Sales** organizational unit, and then create a new user with the following:

   a. First name: **Test**

   b. Last name: **2**

   c. User name: **Test2**

   d. Password: **Pa$$w0rd**

   This task will succeed because Don Hall was delegated the authority to perform that task.

4. Right-click the **Legal** organizational unit.

   What permission does Don Hall have on the Legal organizational unit?

   READ ONLY

5. Log off.
6. Log on to DEN-CL1 as **Judy** with the password of **Pa$$w0rd**.
7. Click **Start**, **Run**, and then type **Dsa.msc** in the text box.
8. Create a new computer account named **Computer1** in the **Sales** organizational unit.

   This will succeed because Judy Lew was granted authority to perform that custom task.

9. Try to perform tasks on user objects.

   What other permission does Judy Lew have in the Sales organizational unit?

   READ ONLY

10. Close all windows and then log off of DEN-CL1 and DEN-DC1.

DSA.MSC = ADUC

Important Do not shut down the virtual machines.

Lab: Managing Access to Objects in Organizational Units

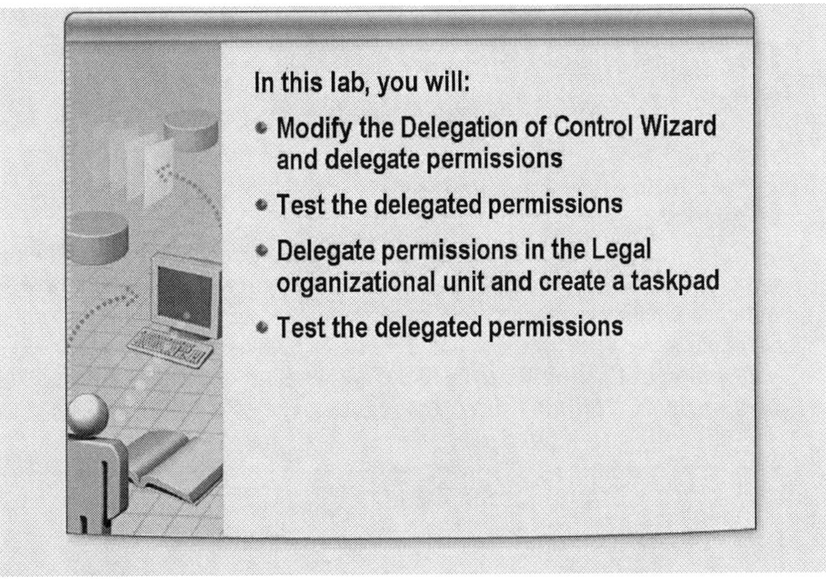

Objectives

After completing this lab, you will be able to:

- Modify the Delegation of Control Wizard and delegate permissions.
- Test the delegated permissions.
- Delegate permissions in the Legal organizational unit and create a taskpad.
- Test the delegated permissions.

Prerequisites

To complete this lab, you must have the following virtual machines:

- DEN-DC1
- DEN-CL1

Estimated time to complete this lab: 30 minutes

Exercise 1
Modifying the Delegation of Control Wizard and Delegating Permissions

In this exercise, you will delegate administrative control of objects in an organizational unit.

Scenario

Contoso, Ltd., has a password policy that allows three failed logon attempts before a user is locked out of their account. Since Contoso, Ltd. has enforced strong passwords, the occurrence of locked-out accounts has increased. You will delegate to the local department managers the authority to unlock a locked-out user account. To ease administration of this task, you will modify the Delegation of Control Wizard's list of common tasks to include the authority to unlock locked-out user accounts. You will use a preconfigured delegwiz.ini file to replace the default file.

Tasks	Specific instructions
1. Examine the default delegwiz.ini file.	**a.** Log on to DEN-DC1 as **Administrator.** **b.** Open the **C:\Windows\Inf\delegwiz.ini** file in Notepad. **c.** Examine the current **delgwiz.ini** file. **d.** Close Notepad. **e.** Open **Active Directory Users and Computers**, and run the **Delegation of Control Wizard** for the **Legal** organizational unit. **f.** Add the **Legalmanager** user account, and then click **Next.** **g.** On the **Tasks to Delegate** page, notice how the list of common tasks relates to the delegwiz.ini file. What is the first common task in the list? **h.** Cancel the Delegation of Control Wizard. **i.** Open the **D:\2274\Labfiles\Admin_Tools \delegwiz.ini** file in Notepad. **j.** Compare the modified file with the original. What new task has been added to the list of templates? What permission is being granted by the template? **k.** Close Notepad without saving the files.
2. Replace the delegwiz.ini file with the delegwiz.ini file located in the **D:\2274\ Labfiles\Admin_Tools** folder.	**a.** Copy the **delegwiz.ini** file from the **D:\2274\Labfiles\Admin_Tools** folder to the **C:\Windows\Inf** folder. **b.** Click **Yes** in the **Confirm File Replace** dialog box.

(continued)

Tasks	Specific instructions
3. Grant the Legal department manager the authority to unlock locked-out user accounts.	**a.** Switch to **Active Directory Users and Computers**, and run the **Delegation of Control Wizard** on the **Legal** organizational unit. **b.** Add the **Legalmanager** user account, and then click **Next**. **c.** On the **Tasks to Delegate** page, what is the last common task in the list now? **d.** Select the **Unlock locked User accounts** check box. Click **Next**. **e.** Click **Finish**.

Exercise 2
Testing the Delegated Permissions

In this exercise, you will unlock a locked-out user account as the Legal department manager.

Scenario

Now that the Legal department manager has been granted the authority to unlock locked-out user accounts, you need to ensure that the delegation is working properly.

Task	Specific instructions
1. Lock out the **Legaluser** account by attempting to log on with an incorrect password.	a. Attempt to log on to DEN-CL1 as **Legaluser** four times with the wrong password. On the fourth attempt, you will receive a message informing you that the account has been locked out.
	b. Log on to DEN-CL1 as **legalmanager** with a password of **Pa$$w0rd.**
	c. At the **Run** command prompt, type **dsa.msc**.
	d. In **Active Directory Users and Computers**, click the **Legal** organizational unit, and then open the **Properties** dialog box for the **Legal User** account.
	e. Click the **Account** tab, and then clear the **Account is locked out** check box. Can the Legal department manager modify any other properties of the user account?
	f. Close all windows and log off of DEN-CL1.

Exercise 3
Granting Permissions in the Legal Organizational Unit and Creating a Taskpad

In this exercise, you will delegate to Judy Lew the authority to create, delete, and manage user and computer accounts in the Legal organizational unit and then create a taskpad to allow her to perform those tasks.

Scenario

Judy Lew will be in control of creating new user and computer accounts for the Legal organizational unit. Delegate that authority, and then create a taskpad to facilitate those tasks.

Tasks	Specific instructions
1. Delegate control to Judy Lew.	a. Switch to DEN-DC1. b. Run the Delegation of Control Wizard for the **Legal** organizational unit. c. Add **Judy Lew**, and then delegate to her the authority to **Create, delete, and manage user accounts**. d. Run the **Delegation of Control Wizard** for the **Legal** organizational unit a second time. e. Add **Judy Lew**, and then delegate to her the authority to have **Full Control** over computer objects.
2. Create a taskpad for Judy Lew.	a. On DEN-DC1, at the **Run** command prompt, type **MMC**, and then add the **Active Directory Users and Computers** snap-in. a. Right-click the **Legal** organizational unit and then click **New Window from here.** b. On the **Window** menu of **Console 1 [Legal]**, switch to **Console Root** to display the entire forest again. c. Close **Console Root** view by clicking the X in the top-right corner of the window. d. Right-click the **Legal** organizational unit, and then select **New Taskpad View.** e. In the **New Taskpad View Wizard**, click **Next** on the **Welcome** page. f. On the **Taskpad Display** page, click **Next** to accept the defaults. g. On the **Taskpad Target** page, click **Next** to accept the defaults. h. Click **Next** to accept the name and description. i. Ensure that the **Start New Task Wizard** check box is selected, and then click **Finish.** j. On the **Welcome to the New Task Wizard** page, click **Next.** k. On the **Command Type** page, click **Next** to accept the default **Menu Command** selection. l. On the **Shortcut Menu Command** page, select **Tree Item Task** in the **Command Source** drop-down list.

(continued)

Tasks	Specific instructions
2. *(continued)*	**m.** In the **Available commands** list, select **New->Computer**, and then click **Next.** **n.** On the **Name and Description** page, type **Create a Computer Account** in the **Task name** field, and then click **Next.** **o.** On the **Task Icon** page, click a computer icon and then click **Next.** **p.** On the **Completing the New Task Wizard** page, select the **Run this wizard again** check box, and then click **Finish.** **q.** Repeat the steps to create the shortcut menu command **New->User.** **r.** Click **Finish.** **s.** On the console **File** menu, click **Options.** **t.** In the **Options** dialog box, in the **Console mode** drop-down list, select **User mode, limited access, single window.** **u.** Clear the **Allow the user to customize views** check box. Click **OK.** **v.** Save the custom taskpad in the **D:\2274\Labfiles\Admin_Tools** folder as **Legal.msc.**

Exercise 4
Testing the Delegated Permissions

In this exercise, you will log on as Judy Lew and use the taskpad to perform administrative tasks.

Scenario

Judy Lew will copy the taskpad to the client running Microsoft Windows® XP Professional and then use the taskpad to perform administrative tasks.

Tasks	Specific instructions
1. Copy the taskpad from Den-DC1 to DEN-CL1.	**a.** Log on to DEN-CL1 as **Judy** with the password of **Pa$$w0rd**. **b.** Connect to **\\DEN-DC1\admin_tools**. **c.** Copy the **Legal.msc** taskpad to the desktop of DEN-CL1.
2. Test the permissions.	**a.** Double-click **Legal.msc**. **b.** Click the **Create a User Account** icon. **c.** The **New Object – User** dialog box will appear. **d.** Create a test user account called **Test User 3**. It will succeed. Can you add a snap-in to the management console from the **File** menu?
3. Complete the lab exercise.	**a.** Close all programs and shut down all computers. Do not save changes. **b.** To prepare for the next module, start the DEN-DC1 and DEN-CL1 virtual computers.

Module 8: Implementing Group Policy

Contents

Overview

- Implementing Group Policy Objects
- Implementing GPOs in a Domain
- Managing the Deployment of Group Policy

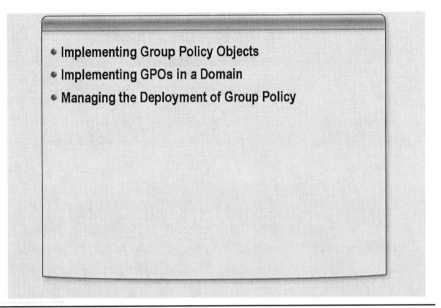

Introduction

The information in this module introduces the job function of implementing Group Policy. Specifically, the module provides the skills and knowledge that you need to explain the purpose and function of Group Policy in a Microsoft® Windows Server™ 2003 environment, implement Group Policy objects (GPOs), and manage GPOs.

Objectives

After completing this module, you will be able to:

- Implement GPOs.
- Implement GPOs in a domain.
- Manage the deployment of Group Policy.

Feature of Win2k/XP/2003 that
allows control of
- User environments
- Software deployment
- Desktop restrictions
- Security policies and more.

Lesson: Implementing Group Policy Objects

- What Is Group Policy?
- Processing Group Policy Objects
- What Are User and Computer Configuration Settings?
- Local Computer Group Policy
- Practice: Set Local Computer Group Policy

Introduction

Group Policy gives administrators the ability to control the user and computer environment. This lesson describes how to implement Group Policy.

Lesson objectives

After completing this lesson, you will be able to:

- Explain what Group Policy is.
- Describe how Group Policies are processed.
- Describe user and computer configuration settings.
- Describe local computer policies.
- Set local computer policy settings.

GP OBJECT EDITOR CAN BE USED WITH OR WITHOUT AD ON LOCAL PC.
(GPEDIT.MSC OR SNAP-IN)

WITH A.D. GROUP POLICY CAN ALSO BE IMPLEMENTED ON A SITE, DOMAIN OR OU

What Is Group Policy?

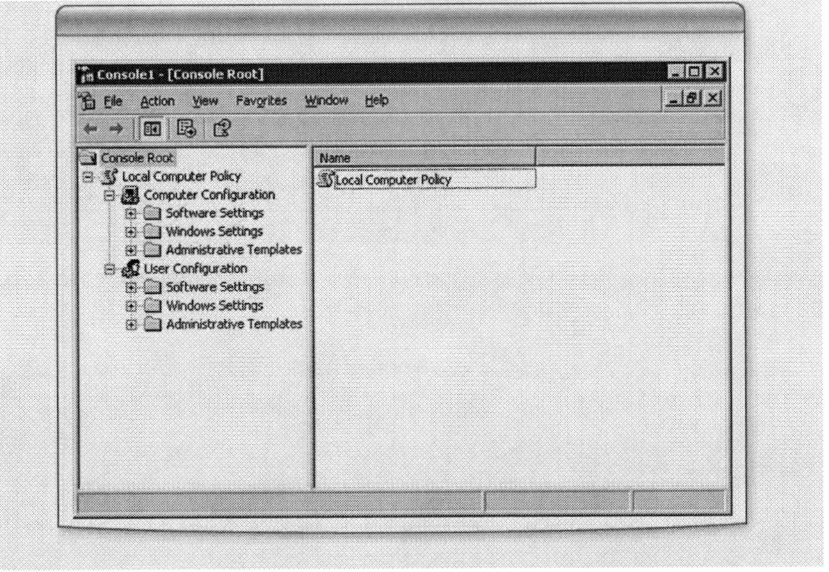

Definition

All computers with Microsoft Windows® 2000, Windows XP, or Windows Server 2003 operating systems are capable of accepting Group Policy settings. The local Group Policy settings can be used to manage the local computer in a standalone or domain environment. The Active Directory® directory service can use Group Policy to manage users and computers in a domain. For example, you can define Group Policy settings that affect the entire domain or define settings that affect specific organizational units (OUs) or use local Group Policy settings to affect a single computer.

When using Group Policy, you can define the state of a user's work environment, and then rely on the local operating system or Active Directory to enforce these Group Policy settings. You can apply Group Policy settings across an entire organization, or you can apply Group Policy settings to specific groups of users and computers.

Note You cannot apply Group Policy settings to computers that have legacy operating systems, such as Windows NT 4.0 or Windows 98.

Active Directory Group Policy settings are stored in GPOs. GPOs are stored in Sysvol in Active Directory. Local computer Group Policy settings are stored on the local hard drive in the %windir%/system32/GroupPolicy hidden folder.

GROUP POLICY MANAGEMENT CONSOLE
(DOWNLOAD)

CAN BE INSTALLED ON XP BUT MUST HAVE
.NET FRAMEWORK

Administrative Templates

There are several template files with an .adm extension that are included with Windows. These files, called Administrative Templates, provide policy information for the items that are under the Administrative Templates folder in the console tree of Group Policy Object Editor. Administrative Templates include registry-based settings, which are available under Computer Configuration and User Configuration in the Group Policy Object Editor.

An .adm file consists of a hierarchy of categories and subcategories that define how the policy settings appear. It also contains the following information:

- Registry locations that correspond to each policy setting
- Options or restrictions in values that are associated with each policy setting
- For many policy settings, a default value
- Explanation of each policy setting's function
- The versions of Windows that support each setting

Additional reading

For more information about Group Policy, see:

- "Introduction to IntelliMirror® Configuration Management Technologies" on the Microsoft Web site.
- "Group Policy settings overview" on the Microsoft Web site.

Processing Group Policy Objects

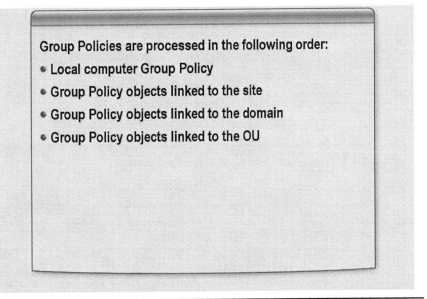

Group Policies are processed in the following order:

- Local computer Group Policy
- Group Policy objects linked to the site
- Group Policy objects linked to the domain
- Group Policy objects linked to the OU

Introduction

GPOs are processed in a particular order. Because the last policy applied determines the user and computer environment, the order of processing is an important consideration when designing a Group Policy strategy.

Local computer Group Policy

The Group Policy of the local computer is always applied first. Local policies are stored on the hard drive of the local computer and are applied to all users who log on to the local machine. Local policies are usually implemented in a workgroup or standalone environment.

Site Group Policy

If the computer is a member of an Active Directory forest, then any GPOs linked to the site will be applied after the local computer policy. Sites and domains do not have a physical relationship. One site may contain multiple domains or one domain may span multiple sites. Because a GPO resides in the Sysvol folder of a domain controller, a GPO linked to a site may force a GPO to be applied across domain boundaries if there are multiple domains in the site. This may result in Group Policy not being applied consistently across a single domain that spans multiple sites. Careful consideration should be given to linking a GPO to a site.

Domain Group Policy

After site GPOs have been applied, any GPOs linked to the domain will be applied. The domain GPO is unique because this is the only container where domain account policies can be applied.

Organizational Unit Group Policy

GPOs can be linked to any parent or child organizational unit. All GPOs that are linked to parent OUs and child OUs are applied to user and computer accounts. The GPOs linked to the parent OU are applied first, followed by GPOs linked to the child OUs. The GPOs linked to the immediate container object are applied last.

Additional reading

For more information about how clients apply Group Policy, see "Order of processing settings" on the Microsoft Web site.

What Are User and Computer Configuration Settings?

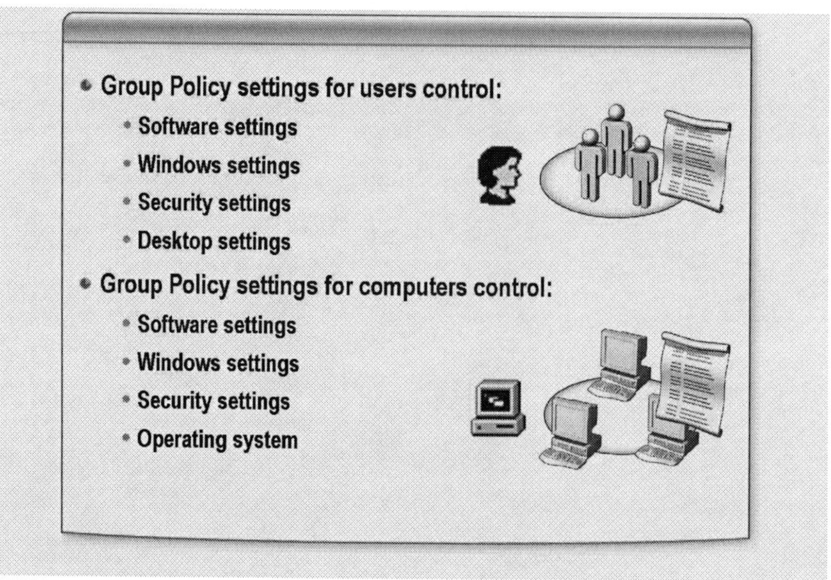

Introduction

You can enforce Group Policy settings for computers and users by using the Computer Configuration and User Configuration settings in Group Policy.

User configuration

The User Configuration setting modifies the HKEY_CURRENT_USER hive of the registry. Group Policy settings for users include software settings, Windows settings, desktop settings, security settings, application settings, folder redirection options, and user logon and logoff scripts. User-related Group Policy settings are requested when users log on to the computer and settings that have changed are applied during the periodic refresh cycle. Security settings are refreshed at least every 16 hours, whether they have changed or not.

Group Policy settings that customize the user's desktop environment or enforce lockdown policies on users are contained under User Configuration in Group Policy Object Editor.

Software settings for user configuration

The Software Settings folder under User Configuration contains software settings that apply to users regardless of which computer they log on to. This folder also contains software installation settings.

Windows settings for user configuration

The Windows Settings folder under User Configuration contains Windows settings that apply to users regardless of which computer they log on to. The Windows Settings folder also contains the following folders:

- Folder Redirection
- Security Settings
- Scripts

Desktop Settings

The Administrative Templates folder contains the following folders:

- Windows Components
- Start Menu and Taskbar
- Desktop
- Control Panel
- Shared Folders
- Network
- System

These Administrative Templates folders contain the Group Policy settings that control the user's environment. You can create your own .adm files or add existing ones to allow any aspect of the user environment to be controlled by Group Policy. For example, you can add the Microsoft Office 2003 templates from the Office 2003 resource kit and use Group Policy to control application settings.

Computer configuration

The computer configuration modifies the HKEY_LOCAL_MACHINE hive of the registry. Group Policy settings for computers control how the operating system behaves, security settings, computer startup and shutdown scripts, configuration of Windows components, computer-assigned application options, and application settings. Computer-related Group Policy settings are requested by the client computer when the operating system initializes, and only settings that have changed are applied during the periodic refresh cycle. Security settings are refreshed at least every 16 hours whether they have changed or not. In general, computer-related Group Policy settings take precedence over conflicting user-related Group Policy settings. However, this is not consistent, so we recommended that you read the information supplied with each policy setting.

Group Policy settings that customize the desktop environment for all users of a computer or enforce security policies on a network's computers are contained under Computer Configuration in the Group Policy Object Editor.

Software settings for computer configuration

The Software Settings folder under Computer Configuration contains software settings. Software assigned to a computer will be installed the next time the computer reboots and will be available to all users who log on to the computer. This folder also contains software installation settings.

Windows settings for computer configuration

The Windows Settings folder under Computer Configuration contains Windows settings that apply to all users who log on to the computer. This folder also contains the following items:

- Security Settings
- Security settings for computer configuration
- Scripts

Security settings are available in the Windows Settings folder under Computer Configuration and User Configuration in Group Policy Object Editor. Security settings are rules that you configure on a computer or multiple computers that protect resources on a computer or network. With security settings, you can define the security policy of an organizational unit, domain, or site.

Administrative Templates

The Administrative Templates folder contains the following folders:

- Windows Components
- System
- Network
- Printer

These folders contain settings to allow you to control operating system behavior for all computers affected by the policy. For example, you can configure how Terminal Services will function or pre-populate printer search locations.

Additional reading

For more information about extending Group Policy, see "Advanced methods of extending Group Policy" on the Microsoft Web site.

Local Computer Group Policy

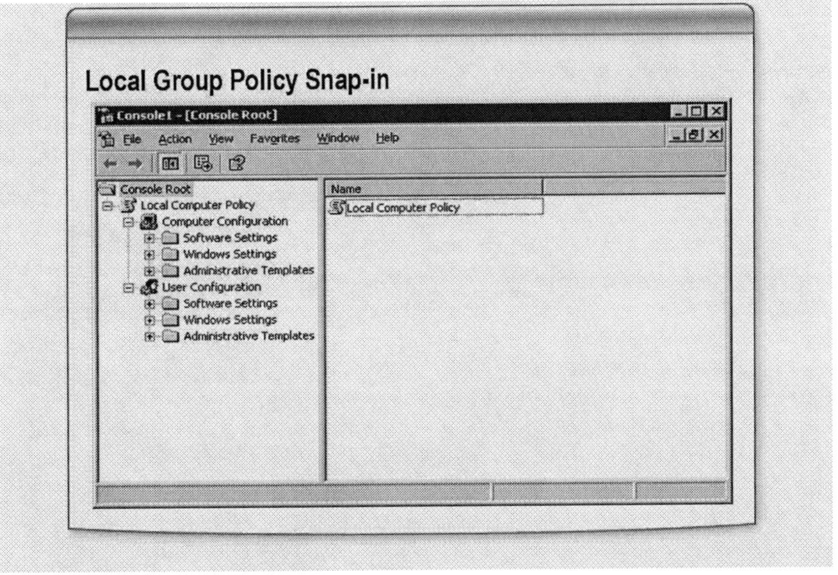

Introduction

All computers with Windows 2000, Windows XP, or Windows Server 2003 operating systems can have local Group Policy settings applied to the local computer's registry. The local Group Policy snap-in is similar, but it is not identical to the Group Policy Object Editor in Active Directory. Settings that deal with domain configurations are not included in the local Group Policy snap-in.

When to use local Group Policy

In a workgroup or a standalone situation, the only method available to control the user and computer environment so that users cannot modify the settings is by using local Group Policy settings or by directly accessing the registry. Direct modification of the registry is not recommended.

Local policies can also be used in the domain environment but are usually not used because it is more efficient to centralize the configuration of Group Policy through Active Directory rather than configure each individual computer.

How to set local Group Policy

To set local Group Policy, you must create a custom MMC and add the Group Policy snap-in and configure the snap-in to modify the local computer settings. Only administrators can set local Group Policy.

How to modify local Group Policy behavior

Any settings you configure in the local Group Policy will apply to all local or domain users who log on the computer. You can change this behavior by modifying NTFS permissions on the %systemroot%\system32\GroupPolicy hidden folder. You can deny permission to the Group Policy folder to users and groups that you do not want to be affected by local policy. For example, you may have a restrictive policy that you want to affect all users of the computer except administrators. You would deny access to administrators to the Group Policy folder to accomplish this. If an administrator needs to modify the policy later, the administrator would have to give permission back to the administrator account to allow the modification.

Local Security Policy snap-in

The Administration Tools folder includes a shortcut to the Local Security Policy snap-in. This snap-in is a link to the Security Settings folder of the local Group Policy. This snap-in allows Administrators quick access to the security settings of the local machine without having to create a custom MMC.

Practice: Set Local Computer Group Policy

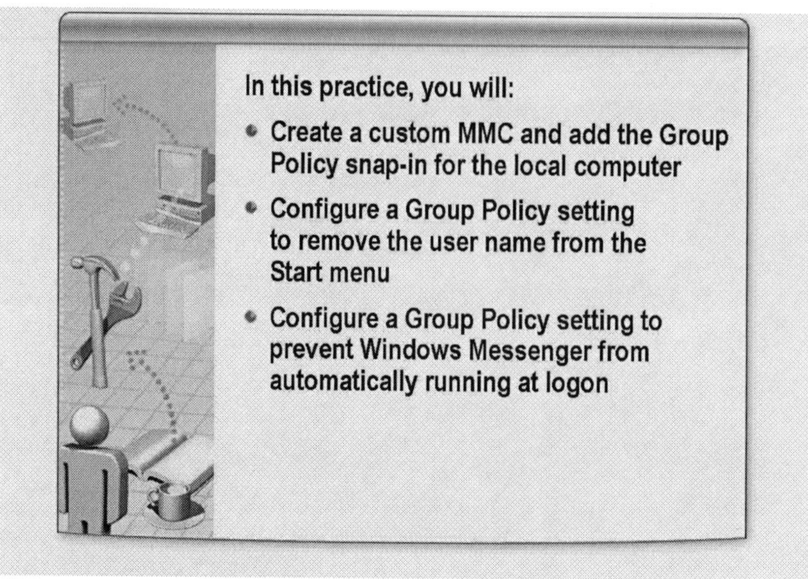

Objective

In this practice, you will:

- Create a custom MMC and add the Group Policy snap-in for the local computer.
- Configure a Group Policy setting to remove the user name from the Start menu.
- Configure a Group Policy setting to prevent Windows Messenger from automatically running at logon.

Instructions

Ensure that the DEN-DC1 and DEN-CL1 virtual machines are running.

Practice

► **Create a custom MMC and add the Group Policy snap-in for the local computer**

1. Log on to DEN-CL1 as **Administrator** with the password of **Pa$$w0rd.**
2. Click **Start**, click **Run** and type **MMC**. Click **OK.**
3. In the Console1 window, click the **File** menu, and then click **Add/Remove Snap-in.**
4. From the **Add/Remove Snap-in** dialog box, click **Add.**
5. Add the **Group Policy** snap-in.
6. On the **Select Group Policy Object** dialog box, ensure that **Local Computer** is entered in the field, and click **Finish.**
7. Click **Close**, and click **OK**.

► **Configure a Group Policy setting to remove the user name from the Start menu**

1. Expand **Local Computer Policy**, **User Configuration**, **Administrative Templates**, and then click the **Start Menu and Taskbar** folder.
2. Double-click the **Remove user name from start menu** setting.

Tip The **Remove user name from start menu** setting is the fourth setting from the bottom of the list.

---

3. Select **Enabled**, and click **OK**.
4. Open a command prompt and type **gpupdate /force** to force the refresh of Group Policy.
5. Click the **Start** menu. The name of the logged-on user should no longer be displayed.
6. Switch back to the custom MMC and double-click **Remove user name from start menu.**
7. Select **Not Configured**, and click **OK.**
8. Refresh the Group Policy application by using **gpupdate /force**.
9. Close the command prompt window.
10. Click the **Start** menu. The name of the logged-on user should be displayed again.

► **Configure a Group Policy setting to prevent Windows Messenger from automatically running at logon**

1. Switch back to the custom MMC and expand **Computer Configuration, Administrative Templates, Windows Components,** and then click **Windows Messenger**.
2. Select the **Do not automatically start Windows Messenger initially** setting and read the information associated with it.
3. Double-click the **Do not automatically start Windows Messenger initially** setting, click **Enabled**, and click **OK.**
4. Close the custom MMC without saving it.
5. Log off of DEN-CL1.

Lesson: Implementing GPOs in a Domain

- Tools Used to Manage GPOs
- What Is a GPO Link?
- How Group Policy Settings Are Inherited in Active Directory
- Backup, Restore, and Import GPOs
- Practice: Implementing GPOs in a Domain

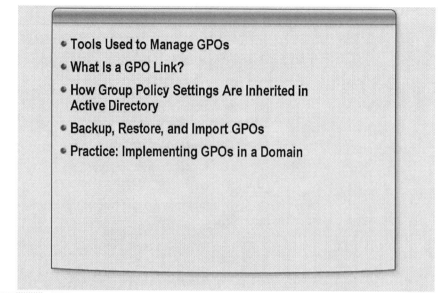

Introduction

Implementing Group Policy in a domain provides the network administrator with greater control over computer configurations throughout the network. Also, by using Group Policy in Windows Server 2003, you can create a managed desktop environment that is tailored to the user's job responsibilities and experience level, which can decrease demand for network support.

Lesson objectives

After completing this lesson, you will be able to:

- Understand the tools used to create GPOs.
- Explain what a GPO link is.
- Explain how Group Policy permission is inherited in Active Directory.
- Implement GPOs in a domain.

Tools Used to Manage GPOs

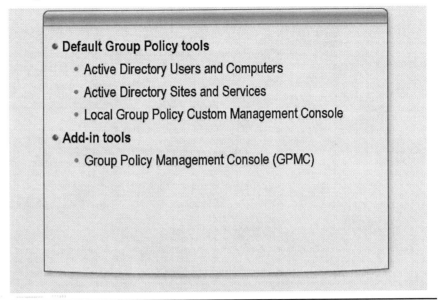

- **Default Group Policy tools**
  - Active Directory Users and Computers
  - Active Directory Sites and Services
  - Local Group Policy Custom Management Console
- **Add-in tools**
  - Group Policy Management Console (GPMC)

Introduction

The Group Policy Object Editor can be opened through various management consoles.

Active Directory Users and Computers

You can open the Group Policy Object Editor from Active Directory Users and Computers to manage GPOs for domains and organizational units. In the **Properties** dialog box for a domain or an organizational unit, there is a **Group Policy** tab. On this tab, you can manage GPOs for the domain or organizational units.

Active Directory Sites and Services

You can open Group Policy Object Editor from Active Directory Sites and Services to manage GPOs for sites. In the **Properties** dialog box for a site, there is a **Group Policy** tab. On this tab, you can manage GPOs for the site.

Note If the Group Policy Management Console (GPMC) is installed, the Active Directory Users and Computers and Active Directory Sites and Services Group Policy controls are replaced by a button to launch the Group Policy Management console.

Local Group Policy Custom Management Console

You can edit the local computer settings on all computers with Windows 2000, Windows XP, or Windows Server 2003 operating systems installed by creating a custom management console and adding the Group Policy snap-in.

Group Policy Management Console

The Group Policy Management Console is an add-on tool for managing Group Policy. The GPMC consolidates the management of Group Policy across the enterprise.

The Group Policy Management Console combines the functionality of multiple components in a single user interface (UI). The UI is structured to match the way you use and manage Group Policy. It incorporates functionality related to Group Policy from the following tools into a single MMC snap-in:

- Active Directory Users and Computers
- Active Directory Sites and Services
- Resultant Set of Policy (RSoP)

The GPMC also provides the following extended capabilities that were not available in previous Group Policy tools. With the GPMC, you can:

- Back up and restore GPOs.
- Copy and import GPOs.
- Use Windows Management Instrumentation (WMI) filters.
- Report GPO and Resultant Set of Polices (RSoP) data.
- Search for GPOs.

Group Policy Management vs. default Group Policy tools

Prior to Group Policy Management, you managed Group Policy by using a variety of Windows-based tools, including Active Directory Users and Computers, Active Directory Sites and Services, and RSoP. Group Policy Management consolidates management of all core Group Policy tasks into a single tool. Because of this consolidated management, Group Policy functionality is no longer required in these other tools.

After installing the GPMC, you still use each of the Active Directory tools for its intended directory management purpose, such as creating user, computer, and group objects. However, you must use the GPMC to perform all tasks related to Group Policy. Group Policy functionality is no longer available through the Active Directory tools when the GPMC is installed.

The GPMC does not replace Group Policy Object Editor. You still must edit GPOs by using Group Policy Object Editor. The GPMC integrates editing functionality by providing direct access to Group Policy Object Editor.

Note The Group Policy Management Console does not come with Windows Server 2003. It is a free download from the Microsoft Web site.

The GPMC can be used to manage Group Policy in a Windows 2000 domain, but it cannot be installed on a Windows 2000 server or Windows 2000 Professional operating system. It can be installed on a computer with the Windows XP Professional operating system if the .NET Framework 1.1 has been installed.

Note The dotnetfx.exe can be downloaded from the Microsoft Web site to install the .NET Framework 1.1.

What Is a GPO Link?

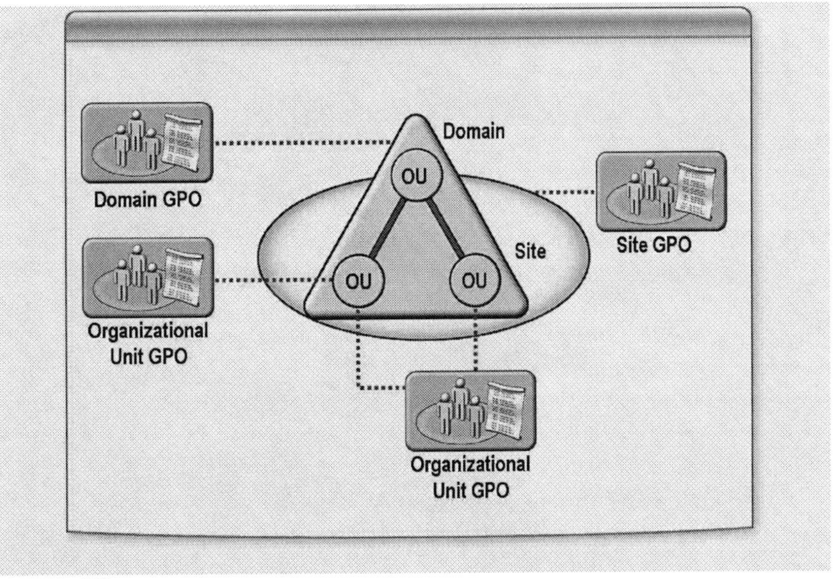

Introduction

All GPOs are stored in a container in Active Directory called Group Policy Objects. When a GPO is linked to a site, domain, or organizational unit, the GPO is also listed in the Group Policy Objects container. As a result, you can centrally administer and deploy the GPOs to many domains or organizational units.

Creating an unlinked GPO

When you create a GPO in the Group Policy Objects container, the GPO is not deployed to any users or computers until a GPO link is created. You can create an unlinked GPO by using the Group Policy Management Console. You might create unlinked GPOs in a large organization where one group creates GPOs and another group links the GPOs to the required site, domain, or organizational unit. Members of the Group Policy Creator Owners group can create GPOs, but they cannot link them.

Creating a linked GPO

When you create a GPO linked to a site, domain, or organizational unit, you actually perform two separate operations: creating the new GPO, and then linking it to the site, domain, or organizational unit. When delegating permissions to link a GPO to a domain, organizational unit, or site, you must have Modify permission for the domain, organizational unit, or site that you want to delegate.

By default, only members of the Domain Admins and Enterprise Admins groups have the necessary permissions to link GPOs to domains and organizational units. Only members of the Enterprise Admins group have the permissions to link GPOs to sites.

Important You cannot link a GPO to default containers in Active Directory. For example, the Users or Computers containers cannot be directly linked to GPOs. However, any GPO linked to the domain applies to users and computers in these containers.

How Group Policy Settings Are Inherited in Active Directory

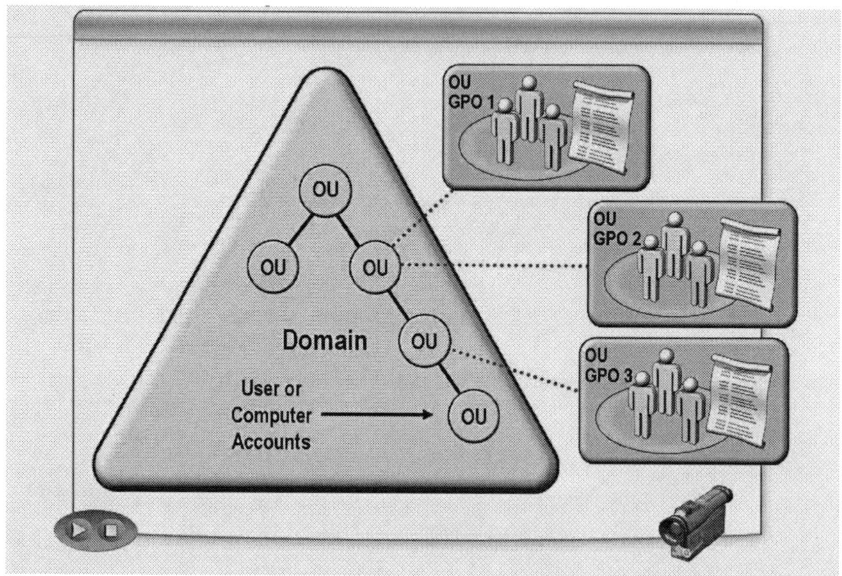

Introduction

The order in which Windows Server 2003 applies GPOs depends on the Active Directory container to which the GPOs are linked. The GPOs are applied first to the site, then to domains, and then to organizational units in the domains.

Flow of inheritance

A child container inherits GPOs from the parent container. This means that the child container can have many Group Policy settings applied to its users and computers without having a GPO directly linked to it. However, there is no inheritance of policies between parent and child domains like there is between parent and child organizational units.

Order of inheritance

GPOs are cumulative, meaning that they are inherited. Group Policy inheritance is the order in which Windows Server 2003 applies GPOs. The order in which GPOs are applied and how GPOs are inherited determines which settings affect users and computers. If there are multiple GPOs that have conflicting values, the GPO applied last takes precedence.

You can also have multiple GPOs linked to the same containers. For example, you can have three GPOs linked to a single domain. Because the order in which the GPOs are applied may affect the resultant Group Policy settings, there is a priority of Group Policy settings for each container.

To view the GPOs that will be applied to members of a site, domain or OU, view the inheritance tab in GPMC. The items listed with the lowest priority number are applied last and, therefore, take precedence.

Multimedia activity

The "Implementing Group Policy" activity includes multiple choice and drag-and-drop exercises that test your knowledge. To start the activity, open the Web page on the Student Materials CD, click **Multimedia**, and then click **Implementing Group Policy**. Read the instructions, and then click the **Effects of Group Policy Settings** tab to begin the activity.

Back Up, Restore, and Import GPOs

The GPMC allows you to

- Back up GPOs
- Restore GPOs
- Import settings from backed-up GPOs

Introduction

The GPMC supports backing up and restoring GPOs. This allows you to recover GPOs in case of loss or corruption. Once GPOs have been backed up, it is possible to import the settings into a new GPO to simplify the creation of policies that need similar, but not identical, settings.

Backing up GPOs

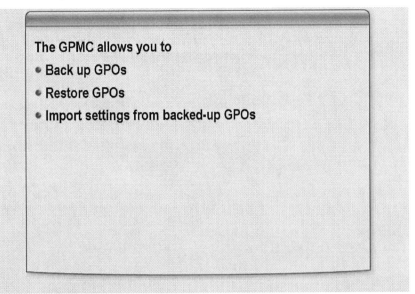

The GPMC allows you to back up individual GPOs or to back up all GPOs in a single operation. You only need to provide a storage location for the backup. Any local or network folder can be used as the backup location. To back up an individual GPO, right-click and select **Backup** and provide a location. To back up all policies, right-click the **Group Policy Objects** folder, select **Back Up All**, and provide a location.

Important WMI filters and IPSec policies are external to the GPO and will not be backed up by a backup operation of GPOs.

Restoring GPOs

Backed-up GPOs can be restored from the backup location in case of disaster recovery or a corrupted GPO. To restore a GPO, right-click the **Group Policy Objects** container and select **Manage Backups**. Then select the GPO you need and restore it. You can edit the view to see only the most recent version of the backups, and you can view the settings prior to restoring the GPO.

Importing GPOs

If you have a backup of a GPO, you can import those settings into a new or existing GPO. This can be a useful feature if you have organizational units with similar requirements. For example, one GPO could be created to hold both the user and computer settings that are common to all containers. Those settings could be imported into many other GPOs and then customized as required. The **Import Settings Wizard** will scan the settings during the import operation to check for references such as UNC paths or Windows security groups that may need to be adjusted in the destination GPO. If the wizard finds such references, it will prompt the user to create or locate a Migration Table. A Migration Table allows you to adjust any references that need to be changed in the GPO.

Important Importing settings into an existing GPO will overwrite all current settings.

Practice: Implementing GPOs in a Domain

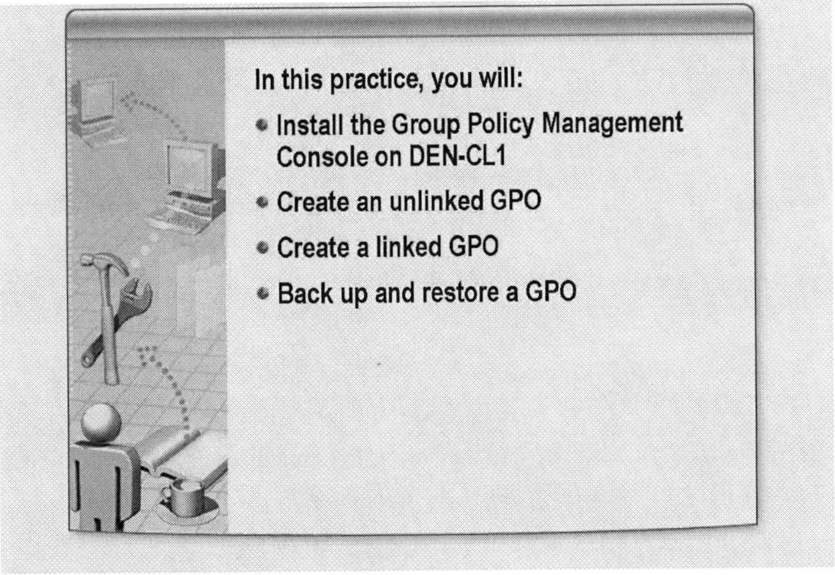

Objective

In this practice, you will:

- Install the Group Policy Management Console on DEN-CL1.
- Create an unlinked GPO.
- Create a linked GPO.
- Back up and restore a GPO.

Instructions

Ensure that the DEN-DC1 and DEN-CL1 virtual machines are running.

Practice

► **Install the Group Policy Management Console on DEN-CL1**

1. Log on to DEN-CL1 as **Administrator**.
2. Connect to **\\DEN-DC1\Admin_tools**, double-click the **dotnetfx.exe** file and click **Yes** to install the Microsoft .NET Framework 1.1.
3. Accept the license agreement, and click **Install.**
4. Click **OK** when the installation completes.
5. Double-click the **gpmc.msi** in the **Admin_Tools** folder to install the Group Policy Management Console.
6. On the Welcome screen, click **Next.**
7. Accept the license agreement, and click **Next.**
8. When installation completes, click **Finish.**
9. Close the Admin_Tools window.

► **Create an unlinked GPO**

1. Right-click the **Start menu**, and then click **Open All Users.**
2. Double-click the **Programs** folder.
3. Double-click **Administrative Tools,**
4. Double-click **Group Policy Management.**
5. Expand Forest:contoso.msft, expand Domains, expand the Contoso.msft, and expand the **Group Policy Objects** container.

   What GPOs are in the container?

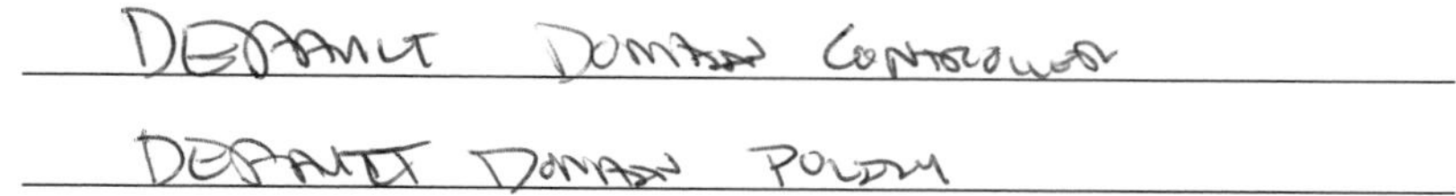

6. Right-click the **Group Policy Objects** container, and click **New.**
7. In the **New GPO** dialog box, type **Remove Search** and click **OK.**

► **Create a linked GPO**

1. Right-click the **Graphics** OU, and click **Create and Link a GPO Here.**
2. In the **New GPO** dialog box, type **Graphics Lockdown** and click **OK.**
3. Expand the **Graphics** OU. Notice an icon with a black arrow appears for the Graphics Lockdown GPO indicating that it is linked to the Graphics OU.
4. Expand the **Group Policy Objects** container. Notice that the Graphics Lockdown GPO resides in this container.

► **Back up and restore a GPO**

1. Right-click the **Graphics Lockdown** GPO, and click **Back up.**
2. In the **Backup Group Policy Object** dialog box, Browse to **C:** drive and create a **New Folder** called **GPO Backup**. Click **OK.**
3. Click **Back Up** and click **OK.**
4. Delete the **Graphics Lockdown** GPO from the Group Policy Objects folder.
5. Right-click the **Group Policy Objects** folder, and click **Manage Backups.**
6. Select the **Graphics Lockdown** GPO, and click **Restore.**
7. Click **OK** twice and click **Close**. Notice that the **Graphics Lockdown** GPO has been restored.
8. Close all open windows and log off.

Important Do not shut down the virtual machines.

Lesson: Managing the Deployment of Group Policy

- Attributes of a GPO Link
- Blocking the Inheritance of a GPO
- What Happens When GPOs Conflict
- Filtering the Deployment of a GPO
- Discussion: Modifying Group Policy Inheritance
- Practice: Managing the Deployment of Group Policy

Introduction

The deployment of Group Policy can be managed through a number of different methods. The effects of Group Policy can be modified by using the techniques described in this lesson.

Lesson objectives

After completing this lesson, you will be able to:

- Describe attributes of a GPO link.
- Block the inheritance of a GPO.
- Explain what happens when GPOs conflict.
- Explain what it means to filter the deployment of a GPO.
- Modify Group Policy inheritance.
- Manage the deployment of Group Policy.

CONTOSO.MSFT
- OU = TRAINEES
  - OU = EMPLOYEES
    - DAVE
    - KEITH
  - OU = CONTRACTORS
    - SANDI
    - BILL

Attributes of a GPO Link

- **Enforced**
  - Take precedence over other GPO settings
- **Link Enabled or Disabled**
  - Links can be disabled for troubleshooting
- **Deleted**
  - Links can be deleted without deleting the GPO
- **Multiple Links**
  - When there are multiple GPOs linked to a container there is an order of precedence

Introduction

You can enable, disable, enforce, and group GPO links. These options significantly affect the user and computer accounts in the organizational unit that the GPO is linked to.

The Enforced option

The **Enforced** option is an attribute of the GPO link, *not* the GPO itself. If you have a GPO that is linked to multiple containers, you configure the **Enforced** option on each individual container. Furthermore, if the same GPO is linked elsewhere, the **Enforced** option does not apply to that link unless you also modify that link.

All Group Policy settings contained in the GPO whose link is configured with **Enforced** apply, even if they conflict with Group Policy settings processed after them or if inheritance is blocked lower in the Active Directory tree. You should enable the **Enforced** option only for the links to the GPO that represents critical organization-wide rules. Link the GPO high in the Active Directory tree so that it affects multiple organizational units. For example, you will want to link a GPO with network security settings to a domain or site.

Important Before Group Policy Management is installed, the **Enforced** option is called **No Override** in Active Directory Users and Computers.

Enabling and disabling a link

Link Enabled is another attribute that you may use when you are troubleshooting a GPO. You can disable the GPO link by clearing the **Link Enabled** option, instead of deleting the GPO link. By disabling the link, you only change the effect on the user and computer accounts in the organizational unit and all child organizational units. You do not affect other links to the GPO. For example, you can temporarily disable a link to test if it was causing a conflict for one OU while still having the settings apply to other OUs.

Deleted

When a GPO link is deleted, the policy is not physically deleted. Just the link is deleted. In order to delete the GPO from the domain, you must delete it from the Group Policy Object container.

Multiple links

When multiple GPOs are linked to an organizational unit, GPOs are applied in priority. The policy with the lowest order number in the Group Policy list is applied last. Conflicting settings will be overwritten by policies with a higher priority (a lower number). If Group Policy settings in the GPO conflict, the last one applied takes precedence.

INHERITANCE & POLICY APPLICATION OVERRIDES

1. BLOCK INHERITANCE (GLOBAL SETTING - BLOCKS EVERYTHING)
   - SET AT A CONTAINER (OU) USUALLY LOWER IN THE AD STRUCTURE
   - DEFLECTS INHERITED POLICIES
   - DOES NOT AFFECT POLICY LINKED DIRECTLY
2. NO OVERRIDE (ENFORCED)
   - SET AT A GPO LINK (NOT AT A CONTAINER)
   - USUALLY SET HIGHER UP IN A.D. TO ENFORCE SETTINGS THAT YOU CANNOT HAVE BLOCKED WITH BLOCK INHERITANCE
3. FILTERING
   - ALLOWS YOU TO APPLY A POLICY TO JUST A SUBSET OF USERS OR COMPUTERS IN A CONTAINER
   - MODIFY DACL ON THE GPO

Blocking the Inheritance of a GPO

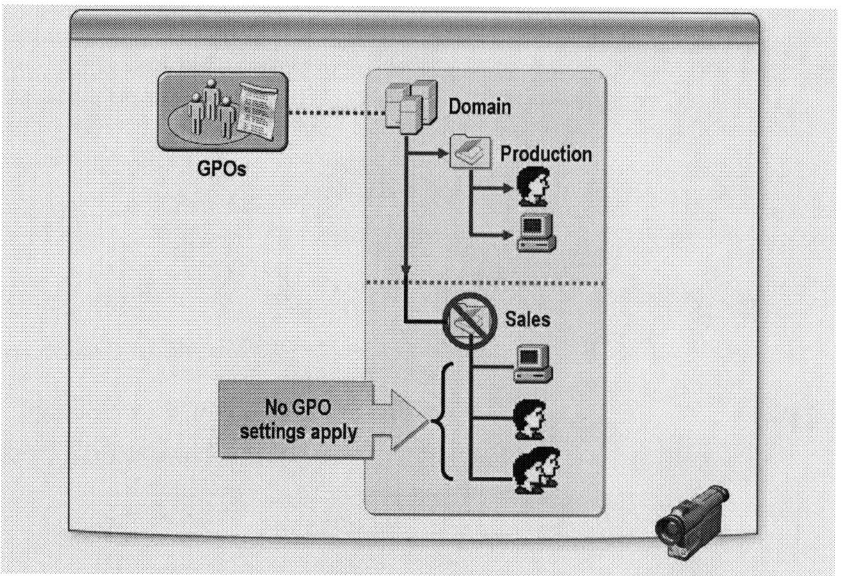

Introduction

You can prevent a child container from inheriting any GPOs from parent containers by enabling **Block Policy inheritance** on the child container.

Why use Block Policy inheritance?

Enabling **Block Policy inheritance** on a child container prevents the container from inheriting all Group Policy settings from all GPOs. This is useful when an Active Directory container requires unique Group Policy settings and you want to ensure that Group Policy settings are not inherited. For example, you can use **Block Policy inheritance** when the administrator of an organizational unit must control all GPOs for that container.

Considerations

Consider the following when using **Block Policy inheritance**:

- You cannot selectively choose which GPOs are blocked. **Block Policy inheritance** affects all GPOs from all parent containers, except GPOs configured with the **Enforced** option.
- **Block Policy inheritance** does not block the inheritance of a GPO linked to a parent container if the link is configured with the **Enforced** option.

Multimedia activity

The "Implementing Group Policy" activity includes multiple choice and drag-and-drop exercises that test your knowledge. To access the activity, open the Web page on the Student Materials CD, click **Multimedia**, and then click **Implementing Group Policy**. Read the instructions, and then click the **Managing the Deployment of Group Policy** tab to begin the activity.

What Happens When GPOs Conflict

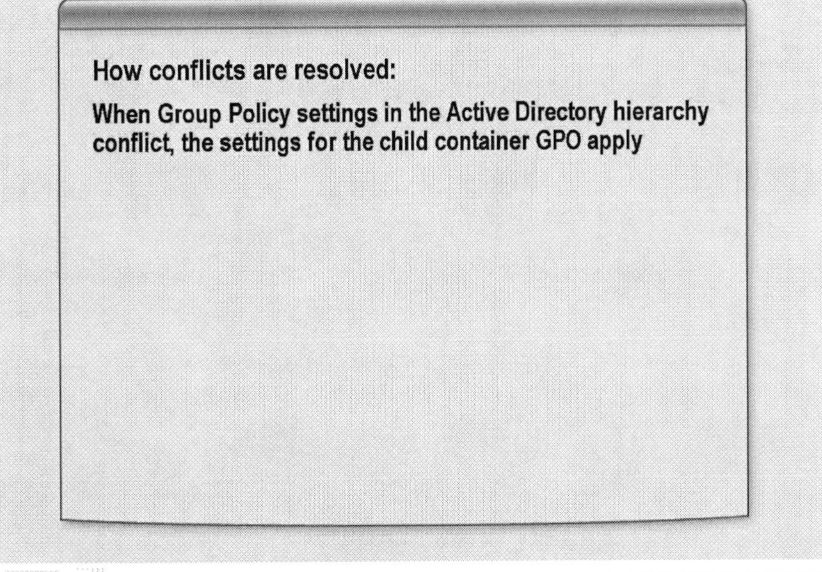

How conflicts are resolved:
When Group Policy settings in the Active Directory hierarchy conflict, the settings for the child container GPO apply

Introduction

Complex combinations of GPOs sometimes create conflicts; these conflicts could require modification to default inheritance behavior. When a Group Policy setting is configured for a parent organizational unit, and the same Group Policy setting is not configured for a child organizational unit, the objects in the child organizational unit inherit the Group Policy setting from the parent organizational unit.

How conflicts are resolved

When Group Policy settings are configured for both the parent organizational unit and the child organizational units, the settings for both organizational units apply. If the Group Policy settings conflict, the child organizational unit's settings will have priority. For example, a Group Policy setting for a parent organizational unit prohibits access to the Control Panel while a Group Policy setting applied to its child organizational unit specifically allows access to the Control Panel. Users in the child organizational unit will have access to the Control Panel because the policy linked to the child organizational unit was applied last.

Filtering the Deployment of a GPO

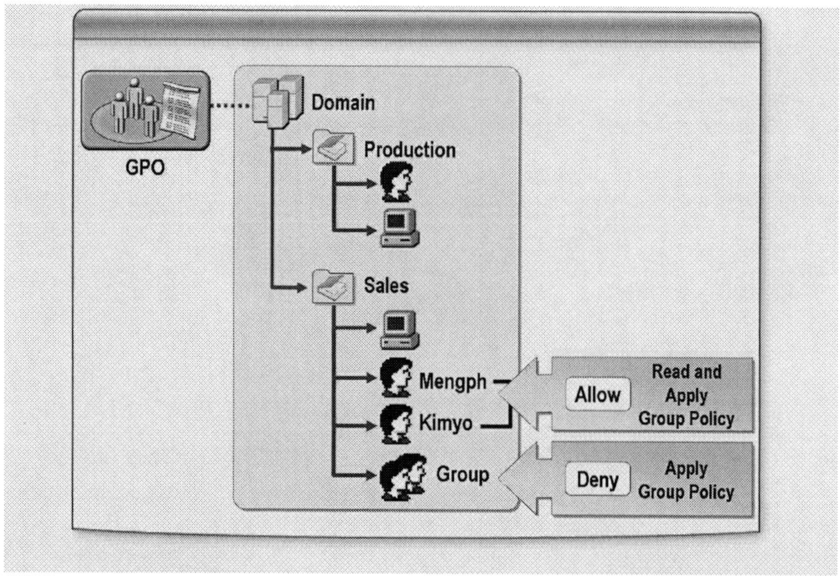

Introduction

By default, all Group Policy settings in GPOs that affect the container are applied to all users and computers in that container, which may not produce the results that you desire. By using the filtering feature, you can determine which settings are applied to the users and computers in the specific container.

Permissions for GPOs

You can filter the deployment of a GPO by setting permissions on the GPO link to determine the access of the read or deny permission on the GPO. Before Group Policy settings can apply to a user or computer account, an account must have both Read and Apply Group Policy permissions for the GPO. The default permissions for a new GPO have the following access control entries (ACEs):

- Authenticated Users—Allow Read and Allow Apply Group Policy
- Domain Admins, Enterprise Admins and SYSTEM—Allow Read, Allow Write, Allow Create All Child objects, Allow Delete All Child objects
- Creator Owner—Special permission to create and edit, but not apply, child objects
- Enterprise Domain Controllers—Allow Read

Filtering methods

Use the following methods to filter access:

- Explicitly deny

  Use this method to deny access to the Group Policy. For example, you could explicitly deny permission to the Administrators security group, which would prevent administrators in the organizational unit from receiving the GPO settings.

- Remove Authenticated Users

  You can remove the Authenticated Users group and add the specific users, groups, or computers to whom the GPO settings will be applied.

Discussion: Modifying Group Policy Inheritance

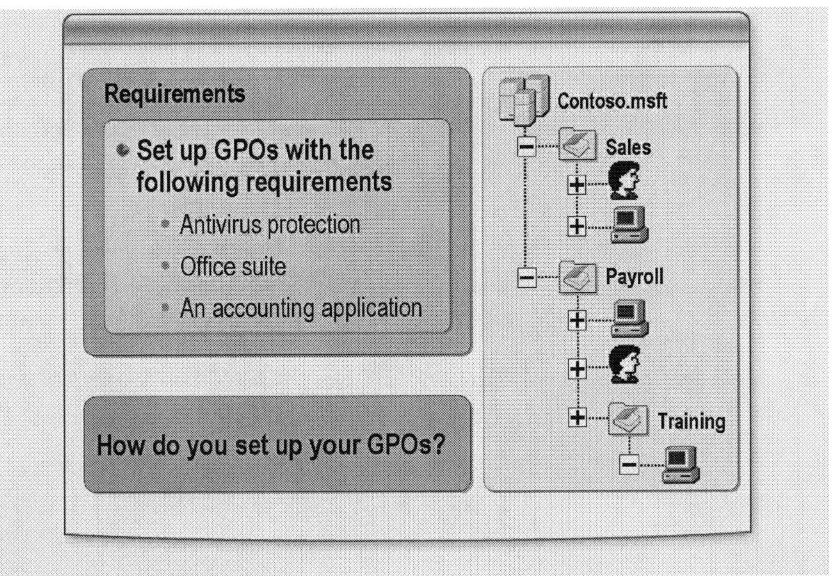

Class discussion

You have determined that the following conditions must exist in your network:

- An antivirus application must be installed on all computers in the domain.
- The Microsoft Office suite must be installed on computers in the domain, except those in the Payroll department.
- A line-of-business accounting application must be installed on all computers in the Payroll department, except those that are used by administrators of the Payroll organizational unit.

How do you set up GPOs so that the above conditions are met?

____

____

____

____

____

Practice: Managing the Deployment of Group Policy

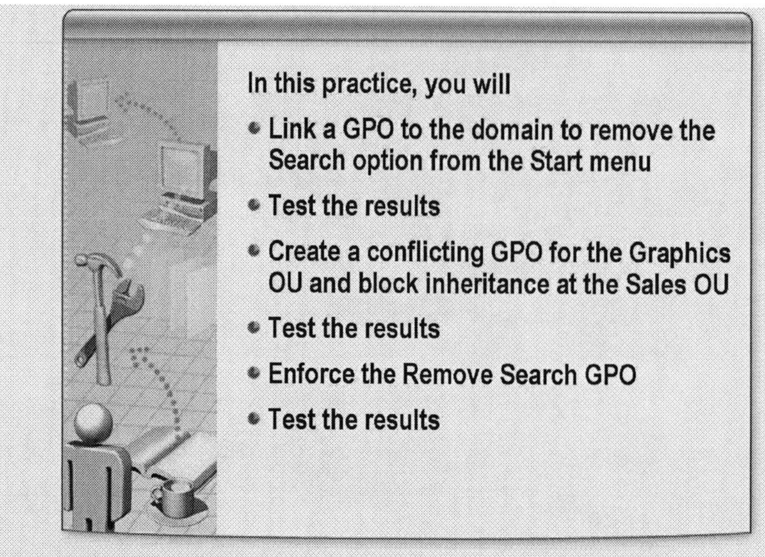

Objective

In this practice, you will:

- Link a GPO to the domain to remove the Search option from the Start menu.
- Test the results.
- Create a conflicting GPO for the Graphics OU and block inheritance at the Sales OU.
- Test the results.
- Enforce the Remove Search GPO.
- Test the results.

Instructions

Ensure that the DEN-DC1 and DEN-CL1 virtual machines are running.

Practice

► **Link a GPO to the domain to remove the Search option from the Start menu**

1. Log on to DEN-CL1 as **Administrator.**
2. Right-click the **Start** menu, and then click **Open All Users.**
3. Double-click the **Programs** folder.
4. Double-click **Administrative** Tools.
5. Create a shortcut on the desktop linked to **Group Policy Management.**
6. Double-click **Group Policy Management.**
7. Right-click the **Contoso.msft** domain. Click **Link an Existing GPO.**
8. In the **Select GPO** dialog box, click **Remove Search**, and click **OK.**
9. Right-click the **Remove Search** GPO, and click **Edit**
10. In the **Group Policy** dialog box, expand **User Configuration.**

11. Expand **Administrative Templates** and then click **Start Menu and Taskbar. Enable** the **Remove Search menu from Start Menu** setting.
12. Click **OK.**
13. Close all open windows and log off.

► Test the results

1. Log on to DEN-CL1 as **Don** with a password of **Pa$$w0rd.**
2. Click the **Start** menu. Ensure there is no Search folder.
3. Log off.
4. Log on as **GraphicsUser** with a password of **Pa$$w0rd.**
5. Click the **Start** menu. Ensure there is no Search folder. The Search folder has been removed for all users because the GPO was linked to the domain.
6. Log off.

► Create a conflicting GPO for the Graphics OU and block inheritance at the Sales OU

1. Log on to DEN-CL1 as **Administrator.** Notice there is no Search folder on the **Start** menu for Administrator.
2. Open the **GPMC** and create and link a GPO called **Enable Search** to the **Graphics** OU.
3. Edit the **Enable Search** policy and locate the **Remove Search menu from Start Menu,** set it to be **Disabled,** and click **OK.**
4. In the **GPMC,** right-click the **Sales** OU, and click **Block Inheritance.**
5. Close all windows and log off.

► Test the results

1. Log on to DEN-CL1 as **Don.**
2. Click the **Start** menu. Ensure that the Search folder is back on the **Start** menu.
3. Log off and log on as **GraphicsUser.**
4. Click the **Start** menu. Ensure that the Search folder is on the **Start** menu.
5. Log off and log on as **Administrator.**

   Does Administrator have a Search folder on the **Start** menu?

   No
   ____

   ____

▶ Enforce the Remove Search GPO

1. Open the GPMC and expand the domain.
2. Right-click the **Remove Search** GPO linked to the domain, and click **Enforced**.
3. Click **Run**, and type **GPupdate /force** to force **Group Policy** to refresh.
4. Log off of DEN-CL1.

▶ Test the results

1. Log on to DEN-CL1 as **Don** and then as **GraphicsUser**.

   Is the Search folder available on the Start menu for either user? Why or why not?

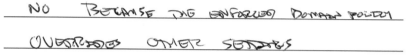

   NO BECAUSE THE ENFORCED DOMAIN POLICY

   OVERRIDES OTHER SETTINGS

2. Close all open windows and log off.

Important Do not shut down the virtual machines.

Lab: Implementing Group Policy

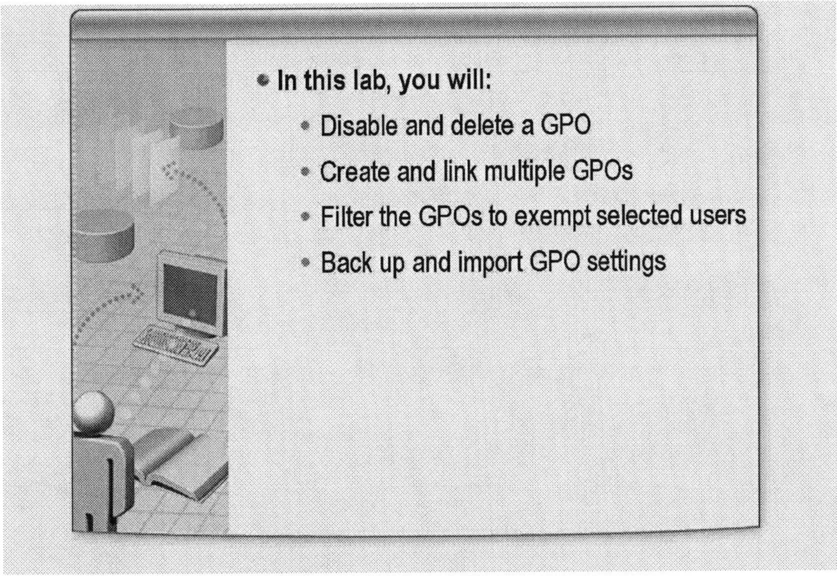

Objectives

After completing this lab, you will be able to:

- Disable and delete a GPO.
- Create and link multiple GPOs.
- Filter the GPOs to exempt selected users.
- Back up and import GPO settings.

Prerequisites

To complete this lab, you must have the following virtual machines:

- DEN-DC1
- DEN-CL1

Estimated time to complete this lab: 30 minutes

Exercise 1
Disabling and Deleting a GPO

In this exercise, you disable and delete a GPO link.

Scenario

Contoso Ltd. has determined that users need access to the Search utility to perform their jobs. You will disable the GPO and then delete the link.

Tasks	Detailed Steps
1. Disable the GPO link.	**a.** Log on to DEN-CL1 as **Administrator**. **b.** Open the **Group Policy Management** console and expand the domain. **c.** Right-click the **Remove Search** GPO and click **Link Enabled** to remove the checkmark. Notice the arrow on the link icon becomes dimmed.
2. Delete the GPO link.	**a.** Right-click the **Remove Search** GPO and click **Delete**. **b.** Read the warning message in the **Group Policy Management** dialog box and click **OK**. **c.** Open **Run** and type **GPupdate /force** to refresh the policy. **d.** Open the **Group Policy Objects** container. Has the Remove Search policy been deleted?

Exercise 2
Creating and Linking Multiple GPOs

Scenario

To limit the number of calls to the help desk, Contoso, Ltd., has decided to remove the Run command from the Start menu for all domain users and to remove access to Control Panel to users in the Sales OU and the Graphics OU. You will create and link the GPOs to accomplish this.

Tasks	Detailed Steps
1. Create and link a GPO to the domain.	a. In Group Policy Management, right-click the domain. b. Create and link a GPO called **Remove Run Command.** c. **Edit** the policy. d. Expand **User Configuration, Administrative Templates, Start Menu and Taskbar** folder, **Enable** the **Remove Run menu from the Start Menu** setting. e. Close the Group Policy window.
2. Create and link a GPO to the Sales OU and the Graphics OU that prohibits access to Control Panel.	a. Right click the **Sales** OU. b. Click **Block Inheritance** to remove the check mark. This will disable inheritance blocking for the **Sales** OU. c. Create and link a GPO to the **Sales** OU called **Remove Control Panel.** d. **Edit** the policy. e. Expand **User Configuration, Administrative Templates, Control Panel** folder, locate and **Enable** the **Prohibit access to the Control Panel** setting. f. Right-click the **Graphics** OU and click **Link an Existing GPO.** g. In the **Select GPO** dialog box, click the **Remove Control Panel** GPO and click **OK.**
3. Determine which OUs the Remove Control Panel GPO is linked to.	a. Expand the **Group Policy Objects** folder and click the **Remove Control Panel** GPO. b. In the right pane, on the **Scope** tab, look under the **Location** heading. c. What containers are listed under the **Location** heading? d. If necessary, log off of DEN-CL1.
4. Test the setting as the sales manager.	a. Log on to DEN-CL1 as **Don** with the password **of Pa$$w0rd.** b. Click the **Start** menu. Ensure that the **Run** command has been removed from the **Start** menu. Ensure that **Control Panel** does not appear on the **Start** menu. c. Log off.

Exercise 3
Filtering the GPOs to Exempt Selected Users

In this exercise, you will filter the GPO permissions to exempt selected users.

Scenario

It has been determined that the domain administrators need access to the Run command. You will filter permissions to exempt the domain administrators from the Remove Run Command GPO. It has also been determined that the sales managers need access to Control Panel. You will filter permissions to exempt the sales managers from the Remove Control Panel GPO.

Tasks	Detailed Steps
1. Filter permissions on the Remove Run Command GPO to exempt domain administrators.	a. Log on to DEN-CL1 as **Administrator**. b. Open **Group Policy Management** and expand the domain. c. Click the **Remove Run Command** GPO. d. In the right pane, click the **Delegation** tab. e. Click **Advanced**. f. In the **Remove Run Command Security Settings** dialog box, select **Domain Admins** and check the box to **Deny** the **Apply Group Policy** permission. g. Click **OK** and click **Yes** after reading the **Security** warning message. h. Log off and then log on again to DEN-CL1 as **Administrator**. i. Click the **Start** menu. The **Run** command should be on the **Start** menu.
2. Filter permissions on the Remove Control Panel GPO to exempt the sales managers.	a. Switch to the **Group Policy Management** console and expand the **Sales** OU. b. Click the **Remove Control Panel** GPO. c. In the right pane, click the **Delegation** tab. d. Click **Advanced.** e. In the **Remove Control Panel Security Settings** dialog box, click **Add.** f. Type **G Sales Managers** and click **OK.** g. **Deny** the **Apply Group Policy** permission to **G Sales Managers.** Click **OK** and click **Yes** at the security message. h. Close all windows and log off. i. Log on as **Don** with the password of **Pa$$w0rd.** j. Click the **Start** menu. Ensure that **Control Panel** appears and that the **Run** command does not appear on the Start menu. k. Close all windows and log off.

Exercise 4
Backing Up and Importing GPO Settings

In this exercise, you will back up and import GPO settings.

Scenario

Another organizational unit needs a similar GPO configuration as the Remove Control Panel GPO. You will back up the Remove Control Panel GPO and then import the settings into a new GPO.

Tasks	Detailed Steps
1. Back up the Remove Control Panel GPO.	**a.** Log on to DEN-CL1 as **Administrator**. **b.** Open the **Group Policy Management** console and expand the domain. **c.** Click the **Group Policy Objects** folder. **d.** Right-click the **Remove Control Panel** GPO and click **Backup.** **e.** In the **Backup Group Policy Object** dialog box, ensure that **C:\GPO Backup** is the location. **f.** Click **Back Up** and then click **OK.**
2. Import the settings into a new GPO named **Imported**.	**a.** Right-click the **Group Policy Objects** container, create a new policy called **Imported** and click **OK.** **b.** Right-click the **Imported** GPO and click **Import Settings.** **c.** In the **Import Settings Wizard**, click **Next.** **d.** On the **Backup GPO** page, click **Next.** **e.** On the **Backup Location** page, ensure that the location is set to **C:\GPO backup** and click **Next.** **f.** On the **Source GPO** page, select the **Remove Control Panel** GPO and click **Next.** **g.** On the **Scanning Backup** page, click **Next.** **h.** Read the summary and click **Finish.** Click **OK** after the import is complete. **i.** **Edit** the **Imported** GPO to see that the settings were imported correctly.
3. Complete the lab exercise.	**a.** Close all programs and shut down all computers. Do not save changes. **b.** To prepare for the next module, start the DEN-DC1 and DEN-CL1 virtual computers.

Course Evaluation

Your evaluation of this course will help Microsoft understand the quality of your learning experience.

At a convenient time before the end of the course, please complete a course evaluation, which is available on the Metrics That Matter page of the Knowledge Advisors Web site at http://www.metricsthatmatter.com/MTMStudent/ClassListPage.aspx?&orig=6&VendorAlias=survey.

Microsoft will keep your evaluation strictly confidential and will use your responses to improve your future learning experience.

Microsoft®

Module 9: Managing the User Environment by Using Group Policy

Contents

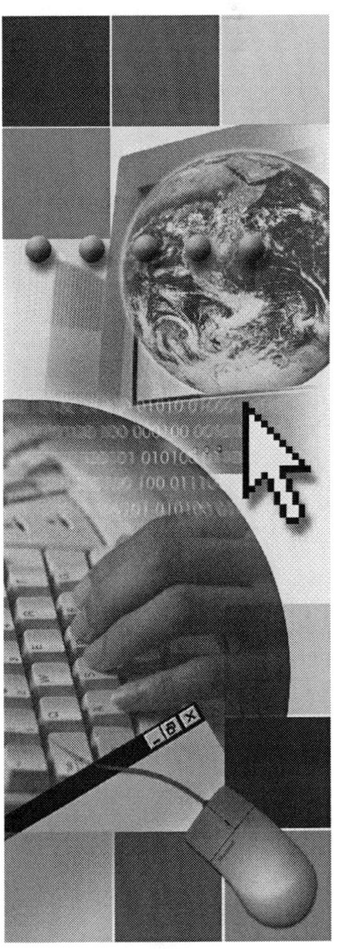

ADMINISTRATIVE TEMPLATES

SCRIPTS

SOFTWARE RESTRICTIONS

RESTRICTED GROUP MEMBERSHIP

FOLDER REDIRECTION

Overview

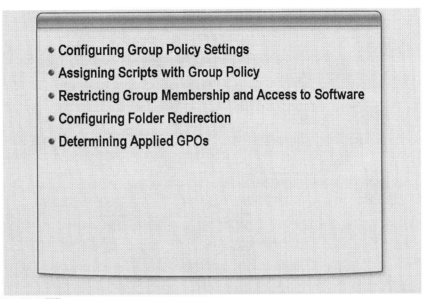

- Configuring Group Policy Settings
- Assigning Scripts with Group Policy
- Restricting Group Membership and Access to Software
- Configuring Folder Redirection
- Determining Applied GPOs

Introduction

This module introduces the job function of managing the user environment by using Group Policy. Specifically, the module provides the skills and knowledge that you need to configure Group Policy to assign scripts, restrict group membership, and restrict access to software and to configure Folder Redirection.

Objectives

After completing this module, you will be able to:

- Configure Group Policy settings.
- Assign scripts with Group Policy.
- Restrict group membership and access to software.
- Configure Folder Redirection.
- Determine Applied Group Policy objects (GPOs).

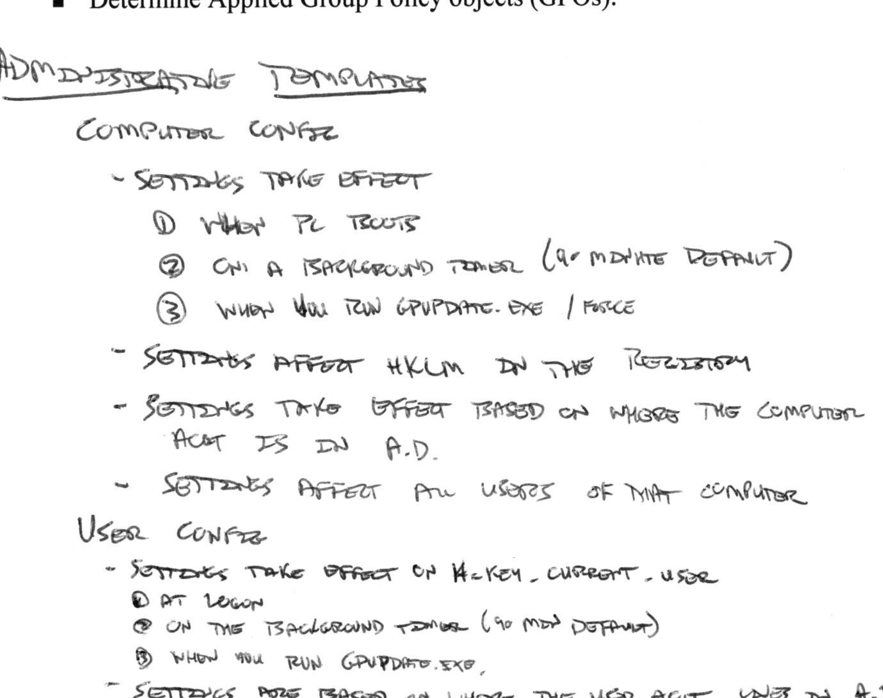

ADMINISTRATIVE TEMPLATES
COMPUTER CONFIG
- SETTINGS TAKE EFFECT
① WHEN PC BOOTS
② ON A BACKGROUND TIMER (90 MINUTE DEFAULT)
③ WHEN YOU RUN GPUPDATE.EXE /FORCE
- SETTINGS AFFECT HKLM IN THE REGISTRY
- SETTINGS TAKE EFFECT BASED ON WHERE THE COMPUTER ACCT IS IN A.D.
- SETTINGS AFFECT ALL USERS OF THAT COMPUTER
USER CONFIG
- SETTINGS TAKE EFFECT ON H-KEY_CURRENT_USER
① AT LOGON
② ON THE BACKGROUND TIMER (90 MIN DEFAULT)
③ WHEN YOU RUN GPUPDATE.EXE,
- SETTINGS ARE BASED ON WHERE THE USER ACCT LIVES IN A.D. REGARDLESS OF WHICH COMPUTER IS USED

Lesson: Configuring Group Policy Settings

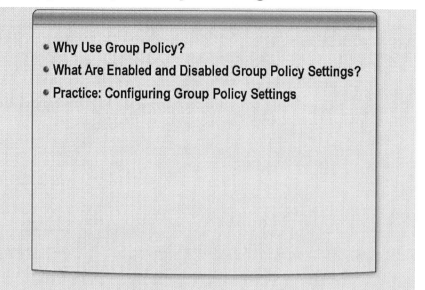

- Why Use Group Policy?
- What Are Enabled and Disabled Group Policy Settings?
- Practice: Configuring Group Policy Settings

Introduction

After completing this lesson, you will be able to configure Group Policy settings.

Lesson objectives

After completing this lesson, you will be able to:

- Explain why you use Group Policy.
- Explain disabled and enabled Group Policy settings.
- Configure Group Policy settings.

Why Use Group Policy?

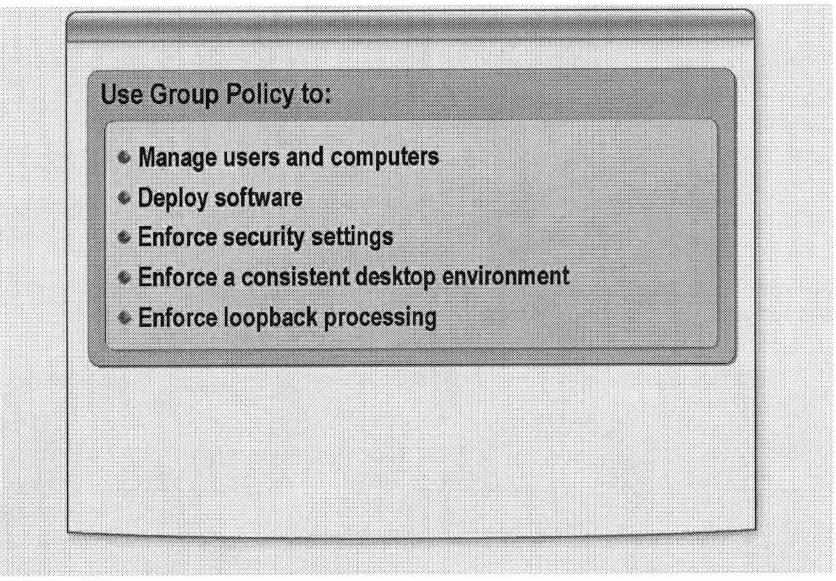
Use Group Policy to:
Manage users and computers
Deploy software
Enforce security settings
Enforce a consistent desktop environment
Enforce loopback processing

Introduction

Managing user environments means controlling what users can do when logged on to the network. You can control their desktops, network connections, and interface through Group Policy. You manage user environments to ensure that users have only enough access to the operating system and applications to perform their jobs. This can help reduce the number of support calls to the help desk.

Tasks you can perform with Group Policy

When you centrally configure and manage user environments, you can perform the following tasks:

- Manage users and computers

  By managing user desktop settings with registry-based policies, you ensure that users have the same computing environments even if they log on from different computers. You can control how Microsoft® Windows Server™ 2003 manages user profiles, which includes how a user's personal data is made available. You can control Windows® group memberships and restrict access to software. By redirecting user folders from the user's local hard disks to a central location on a server, you can ensure that the user's data is available to the user regardless of the computer he or she logs on to.

- Deploy software

  Software is deployed to computers or users through the Active Directory® directory service. With software deployment, you can ensure that users have their required programs, service packs, and hotfixes.

- Enforce security settings

  By using Group Policy in Active Directory, the systems administrator can centrally apply the security settings required to protect the user environment. In Windows Server 2003, you can use the Security Settings extension in Group Policy to define the security settings for local and domain security policies.

- Enforce a consistent desktop environment

  Group Policy settings provide an efficient way to enforce standards, such as logon scripts and password settings. For example, you can prevent users from making changes to their desktops.

- Enforce loopback processing

  In some situations, you may want the user configuration to be consistent for any user who logs on to the computer. For example, your company may provide access to a computer in a public space that allows access to the Internet. You want all users who log on to have the same user environment, regardless of whom the user is. By enabling the loopback setting in the computer configuration, you can configure a user environment that will be enforced for all users who log on to the computer.

Additional reading

For more information about desktop management, see:

- "Customizing the Desktop" at the Windows XP Resource Kit page on the Microsoft Web site.

What Are Enabled and Disabled Group Policy Settings?

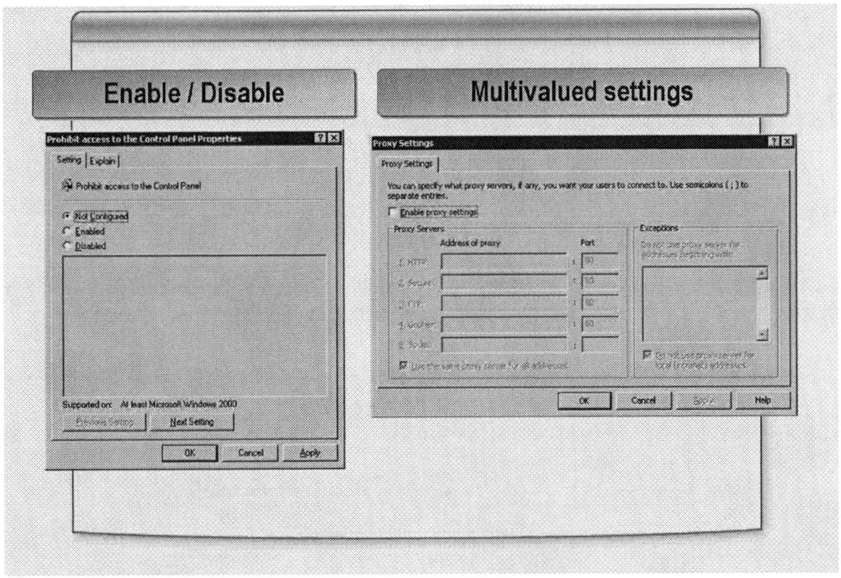

Enable a policy setting

If you enable a policy setting, you are enabling the action of the policy setting. For example, to revoke someone's access to Control Panel, you enable the policy setting **Prohibit access to the Control Panel.**

Disable a policy setting

If you disable a policy setting, you are reversing the action of the policy setting. For example, if a policy setting has enabled the **Prohibit access to the Control Panel** setting on a parent container and you need to reverse that setting for a child container, then you would use a specific policy that disables the **Prohibit access to the Control Panel at the child container level.**

This is helpful when you have one GPO that delivers many settings, and you want one group to be exempt from some, but not all, of the settings. You can apply a GPO that enables many policy settings on the parent organizational unit and another GPO that disables certain settings on a child organizational unit.

Not Configured

By default, a Group Policy has no enabled settings. When you enable settings, you are configuring the Group Policy setting. If you want to remove all enabled settings, you would click **Not Configured**.

For example, if a GPO setting is enabled in order to restrict access to a function and it is later determined that access to that function is required, then selecting the **Not Configured** option reverts the setting back to the default.

Multivalued policy settings

Some GPOs require you to provide additional information after you enable an object. Sometimes you may need to select a group or computer if the policy setting needs to redirect the user to information. Other times, as the slide shows, to enable proxy settings, you must provide the name or Internet Protocol (IP) address of the proxy server and the port number.

Note The **Settings** tab in the Administrative Templates folder indicates the operating systems that support the policy setting. The **Explain** tab has information about the effects of the **Enabled** and **Disabled** options on a user and computer account.

Practice: Configuring Group Policy Settings

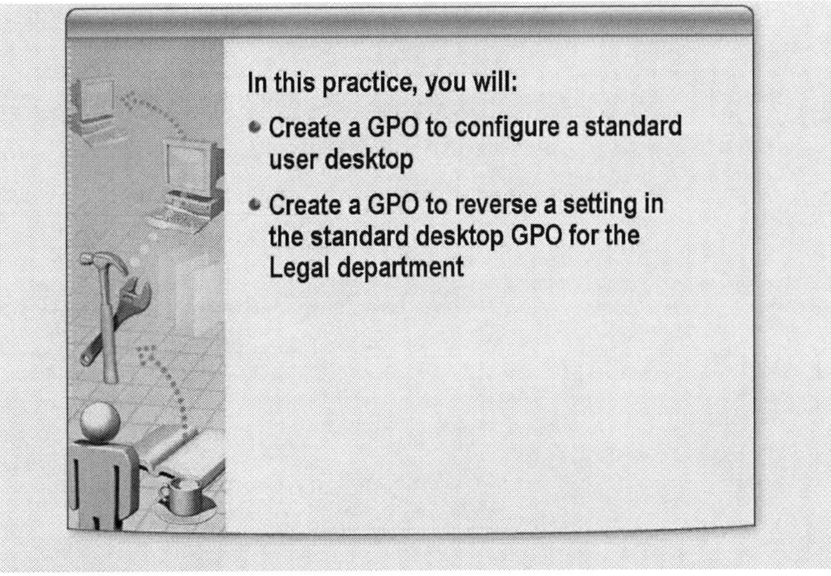

Objective

In this practice, you will:

- Create a GPO to configure a standard user desktop that:
  - Prohibits user configuration of Offline Files.
  - Hides the screen saver tab in display properties.
  - Prevents users from adding printers.
  - Configure Web proxy settings.
- Create a GPO to reverse a setting in the standard desktop GPO for the legal department.

Instructions

Ensure that the DEN-CL1 and the DEN-DC1 virtual machines are running.

Practice

► **Create a GPO to configure a standard user desktop**

1. Log on to DEN-DC1 as **Administrator** with the password of **Pa$$w0rd**.
2. Click **Start**, point to **Administrative Tools**, and then click **Group Policy Management**.
3. Expand **Forest: contoso.msft/ Domains**.
4. Right-click **contoso.msft** and then click **Create and Link a GPO Here**.
5. In the **New GPO** dialog box, type **Standard Desktop**. Click **OK**.
6. Right-click the **Standard Desktop** GPO and then click **Edit**.
7. Expand **User Configuration**, **Administrative Templates**, **Network**, and click **Offline Files**.
8. Double-click **Prohibit user configuration of Offline Files**, and then click **Enabled**.
9. Click **OK**.

10. Expand **User Configuration, Administrative Templates, Control Panel,** and then click **Display**.
11. Double-click **Hide Screen Saver tab**, and then click **Enabled**.
12. Click **OK**.
13. Click the **Printers** folder, double-click **Prevent addition of printers**, and then click **Enabled**.
14. Click **OK**.
15. Expand **Windows Settings, Internet Explorer Maintenance**, and click **Connection**.
16. Double-click **Proxy Settings**, and then click **Enable proxy settings**.
17. In the **HTTP** field, type **10.10.0.2**. In the **Port** field, type **8080**.
18. Click **OK** and then close the **Group Policy Object Editor**.
19. Click **Start**, click **Run**, and then type **gpupdate /force**. Click **OK**.
20. Click **Start**, point to **Control Panel**, and then click **Display**. Notice that the **Screen Saver** tab is not displayed.
21. Click **OK**.
22. Log on to DEN-CL1 as **Legalmanager** with a password of **Pa$$w0rd**.
23. In **My Computer**, click the **Tools** menu, and then click **Folder Options**. Notice that there is no **Offline Files** tab.
24. Close the **Folder Options** dialog box and close **My Computer**.

► **Create a GPO to reverse a setting in the standard desktop GPO for the legal department**

1. Switch to DEN-DC1 and in the **Group Policy Management** console expand **contoso.msft**. Click the **Legal** OU.
2. Create and link a GPO called **Reverse Offline Files Setting**.
3. Right-click the **Reverse Offline Files Setting** GPO and click **Edit**.
4. Expand **User Configuration, Administrative Templates, Network,** and click **Offline Files**.
5. Double-click **Prohibit user configuration of Offline Files**, and then click **Disabled**. Click **OK**. Close the **Group Policy Object Editor**.
6. Close **Group Policy Management** and then log off of DEN-DC1.
7. Switch back to DEN-CL1 and, from **Run**, type **gpupdate /force**.
8. In **My Computer**, click the **Tools** menu, and then click **Folder Options**. Notice there is an **Offline Files** tab now. **Cancel** and close **My Computer**.
9. Click **Start** and then click **Printers and Faxes**. Notice the **Add Printer** icon is not available. Check the **Screen Saver** tab and the **Internet Settings, Proxy Settings** to see they are still being enforced.
10. Close all windows and log off.

Important Do not shut down the virtual machines.

Lesson: Assigning Scripts with Group Policy

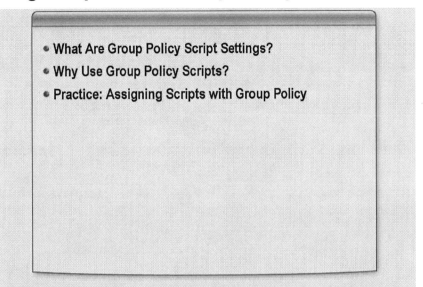

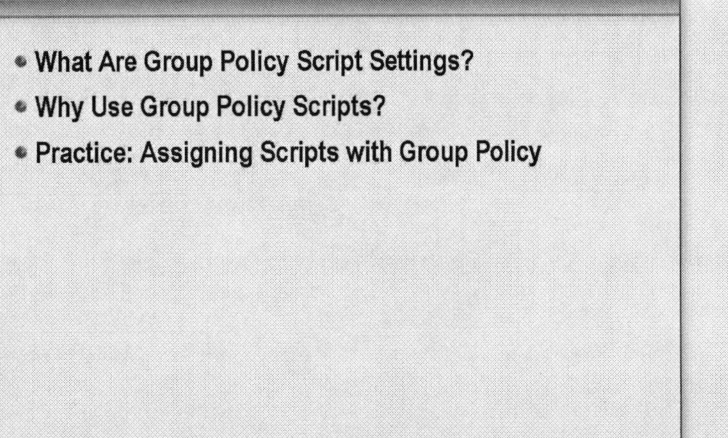
What Are Group Policy Script Settings?
Why Use Group Policy Scripts?
Practice: Assigning Scripts with Group Policy

Introduction

You can use Group Policy to deploy scripts to users and computers. A script is a batch file or a Microsoft Visual Basic® script that can execute code or perform management tasks. You can use Group Policy script settings to automate the process of running scripts.

As with all Group Policy settings, you configure a Group Policy script setting once, and Windows Server 2003 continually implements and enforces it throughout your network.

Lesson objectives

After completing this lesson, you will be able to:

- Explain what Group Policy script settings are.
- Describe the benefits of using Group Policy scripts.
- Assign scripts with Group Policy.

What Are Group Policy Script Settings?

Group Policy script settings can be used to assign:

- For computers
  - Startup scripts
  - Shutdown scripts
- For users
  - Logon scripts
  - Logoff scripts

Introduction

There are script settings under both Computer Configuration and User Configuration in Group Policy. You can use Group Policy to run scripts when a computer starts and shuts down and when a user logs on and logs off. You can specify any script that runs in Windows Server 2003, including batch files, executable programs, JavaScript, Visual Basic, Scripting Edition (VBScript), and any scripts supported by Windows Script Host (WSH).

Computer startup and shutdown scripts

At startup, the computer policy is applied and the startup scripts run. The scripts run synchronously by default and in the following order: local, site, domain, organizational unit, child organizational unit, and so on. Each script must complete or time out before the next one starts. The default time-out is 600 seconds. No user interface appears while computer policies are processed. You can use several policy settings to modify this behavior. Computer startup and shutdown scripts execute under the local system account.

User logon and logoff scripts

At logon, user policy is applied. User logon scripts are processed. Unlike Microsoft Windows NT® 4.0 scripts, Group Policy–based logon scripts are hidden and asynchronous by default. If you run multiple scripts where one script depends on other scripts completing, you will have to change the processing to be synchronous.

Location of scripts

Scripts can be located anywhere on the network, as long as the user or computer receiving the script has network access and Read permission to the location. The preferred location for scripts is in the Sysvol folder. In that way, scripts will be replicated to all domain controllers through the replication of the Sysvol folder. You can add your script to the Scripts folder of the GPO in Sysvol by using the GPMC.

Note In Active Directory Users and Computers, you can assign logon scripts individually to user accounts in the **Properties** dialog box for each user account. However, Group Policy is the preferred method for running scripts, because you can manage these scripts centrally, along with startup, shutdown, and logoff scripts.

Additional reading

For more information about scripting tools, see the TechNet Script Center on the Microsoft TechNet page of the Microsoft Web site.

SCRIPTS IN GROUP POLICY

MUCH MORE FLEXIBLE THAN IN NT.

(1) THERE ARE NOW 4 TRIGGERS ON WHICH YOU CAN RUN A SCRIPT:

- STARTUP (COMPUTER CONFIG)
- LOGON (USER CONFIG)
- LOGOFF (USER CONFIG)
- SHUTDOWN (COMPUTER CONFIG)

ALSO YOU CAN WRITE SCRIPTS IN VBSCRIPT OR JSCRIPT & THEY WILL RUN USING THE BUILT-IN WINDOWS SCRIPT HOST

Why Use Group Policy Scripts?

Group Policy scripts can:

- Perform tasks that cannot be done through other Group Policy settings
- Clean desktops and return computers to their original state
- Provide a secure environment by clearing temp folders and page files

Benefits of Group Policy scripts

To help you manage and configure user environments, you can:

- Run scripts that perform tasks that you cannot perform through other Group Policy settings. For example, you can populate user environments with network connections, printer connections, shortcuts to applications, and corporate documents.
- Clean up desktops when users log off and shut down computers. You can remove connections that you added with logon or startup scripts so that the computer is in the same state as when the user started the computer.
- Shutdown scripts and logoff scripts can be used to delete the contents of temp directories or clear the pagefile to make the environment more secure.

Note Many predefined scripts are available on the Microsoft Technet Script Center.

Practice: Assigning Scripts with Group Policy

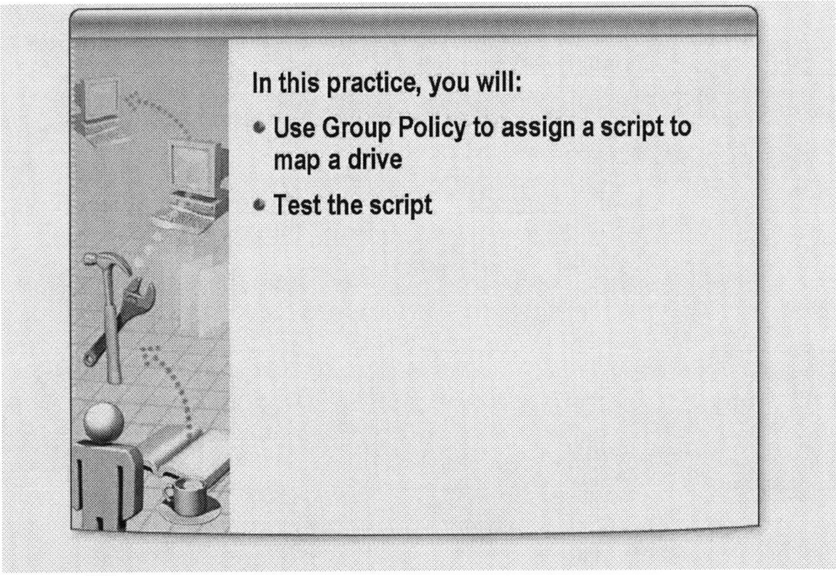

Objective

In this practice, you will:

- Use Group Policy to assign a script to map a drive.
- Test the script.

Instructions

Ensure that the DEN-CL1 and the DEN-DC1 virtual machines are running.

Practice

► **Use Group Policy to assign a script to map a drive**

1. Log on to DEN-DC1 as **Administrator** with the password of **Pa$$w0rd**.
2. Click **Start**, point to **Administrative Tools**, and then click **Group Policy Management**.
3. Create and link a GPO called **Drive Mapping** to the **IT Admin** OU.
4. Right-click and edit the **Drive Mapping** GPO.
5. Expand **User Configuration**, **Windows Settings**, and then click **Scripts (Logon/Logoff)**.
6. Double-click the **Logon** policy.
7. In the **Logon Properties** dialog box, click **Show Files** to display the contents of the **Logon** folder. Notice the path in the **Address** bar.
8. Open **My Computer** and copy the **D:\2274\Labfiles\Admin_Tools\map.bat** file into the **Logon** folder.
9. Close **My Computer** and then close the **Logon** folder.
10. In the **Logon Properties** dialog box, click **Add**.
11. In the **Add a Script** dialog box, click **Browse**.
12. In the **Browse** dialog box, click **map.bat** and click **Open**.
13. Click **OK** twice.
14. Close all open windows and log off.

► **Test the script**

1. Log on to DEN-CL1 as **Judy** with the password of **Pa$$w0rd**.
2. Open **My Computer**. Ensure that you have a J drive that maps to **DEN-DC1\Admin_Tools.**
3. Close all windows and log off of DEN-CL1.

Important Do not shut down the virtual machines.

Lesson: Restricting Group Membership and Access to Software

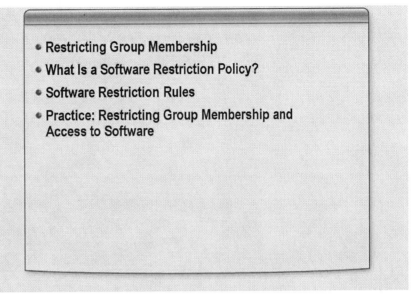

- Restricting Group Membership
- What Is a Software Restriction Policy?
- Software Restriction Rules
- Practice: Restricting Group Membership and Access to Software

Introduction

In a large network environment, one of the challenges of network security is controlling the membership of built-in groups on workstations and member servers. Another concern is preventing access to unauthorized software on workstations.

Lesson objectives

After completing this lesson, you will be able to:

- Configure Group Policy to restrict group membership.
- Explain what Software Restriction policies are.
- Explain the function of Software Restriction rules.
- Restrict group membership and software using group policies.

Restricting Group Membership

Group Policy can control group membership:

- For any group on a local computer
- For any group in Active Directory

Introduction

Built-in groups on workstations and member servers have inherent rights to perform system tasks. Controlling the membership of these groups can be difficult. Group Policy provides settings that allow you to control group membership.

Restricting group membership

You can use the Restricted Groups policy to control group membership. Use the policy to specify what members are placed in a group. If a Restricted Groups policy is defined and Group Policy is refreshed, any current member not on the Restricted Groups policy members list is removed. This can include default members, such as administrators. Although any domain groups can be controlled by assigning Restricted Groups policies to domain controllers, this setting should be used primarily to configure membership of critical groups like Enterprise Admins and Schema Admins. This setting can also be used to control the membership of built-in local groups on workstations and member servers. For example, you can place the Helpdesk group into the local Administrators group on all workstations.

Local users cannot be specified in a domain GPO. Any local users who are currently in the local group that the policy controls will be removed. The only exception is that the local Administrators account will always be in the local Administrators group.

Important The Restricted Groups policy setting does not add to the list of users who have been manually placed in a group. Once a Restricted Groups policy exists, it removes any users who are not specified in the policy.

You can configure the membership of a group by listing the names of the members on the **Members of this group** list. You can also control what groups the group is nested into by adding those groups to the **This group is a member of** list.

What Is a Software Restriction Policy?

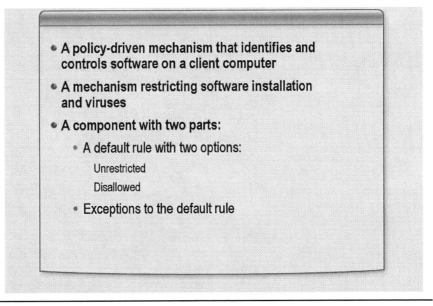

- A policy-driven mechanism that identifies and controls software on a client computer
- A mechanism restricting software installation and viruses
- A component with two parts:
  - A default rule with two options:
    - Unrestricted
    - Disallowed
  - Exceptions to the default rule

Introduction

Software restriction policy provides administrators with a policy-driven mechanism for identifying software and controlling its ability to run on a client computer. Software restriction policies are a part of the Microsoft security and management strategy to assist enterprises in increasing the reliability, integrity, and manageability of their computers.

Restricting access to software

When you assign Group Policy to restrict access to software for a specific computer, it will affect any user who logs on to that computer. When you assign a Group Policy setting to restrict access to software for a specific user, the setting will affect that user regardless of what computer the user logs on to. The setting is configured using the same method for users or computers.

Software Restriction policy is one of many new management features in Windows XP and Windows Server 2003. Software restriction policy can be used to:

- Fight viruses.
- Regulate which ActiveX® controls can be downloaded.
- Run only digitally signed scripts.
- Ensure that only approved software is installed on system computers.
- Lock down the computer.

A Software Restriction policy must be created first. A Software Restriction policy consists of security levels, rules, and settings. There are two rules available, Unrestricted and Disallowed. The default security level is Unrestricted.

- *Unrestricted.* This rule allows all software to be run except for software that is specifically identified as an exception to the rule. The identified software packages are not able to run.

  This policy allows users to install new software programs but still allows an administrator the ability to lock down undesirable software and prevent it from running on client computers. When a new virus or other undesirable software package is identified, the administrator can immediately update the policy to include the new software and prevent it from running on client computers. Users must reboot the computer if the setting is a computer configuration setting, or log off and back on again if the policy is a user configuration setting, before the new software policy will be implemented.

- *Disallowed.* This rule does not allow any software to run on the client computer except for software that has been specifically identified as an exception to the rule. The identified software packages are the only ones that can be run on the client computers affected by the policy. This policy is recommended for use only in very high-security environments or locked-down environments. It can be difficult to manage because each allowed application must be individually identified and because the policy might need to be updated each time a service pack is applied to a software package.

Important Software Restriction policies will only apply when users log on to Windows XP operating systems or later.

Software Restriction Rules

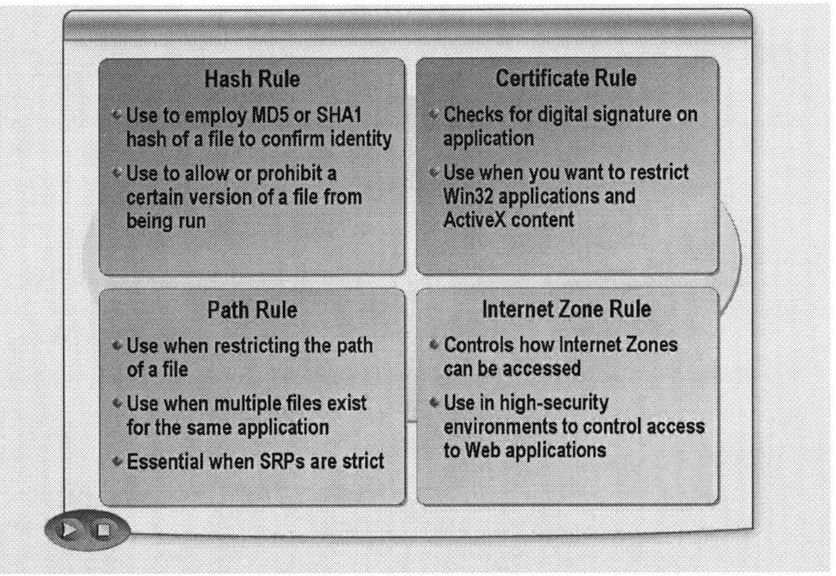

Introduction

Software Restriction policy rules identify whether an application is allowed to run.

When you create a rule, you first identify the application. Then you identify it as an exception to the Unrestricted or Disallowed default setting. Each rule can include comments to describe its purpose. The enforcement engine included in Windows XP queries the rules in the software restriction policy before allowing a program to run.

Software restriction rules

A software restriction policy uses one or more of the following four rules to identify software.

You can designate which applications are allowed or disallowed by creating rules. There are four types of rules that can be created.

- *Hash rule.* A *hash* is a fingerprint that uniquely identifies a software program or executable file, even if the program or executable file is moved or renamed. In this way, administrators can use a hash to track a particular version of an executable file or program that they do not want users to run. This might be the case if a program has security or privacy vulnerabilities or could compromise the stability of the system.

  With a hash rule, software programs remain uniquely identifiable because the hash rule match is based on a cryptographic calculation involving the contents of the file. The hash rule compares the Message Digest 5 (MD5) algorithm or SHA1 hash of a file with the one attempting to run.

  The only file types that are affected by hash rules are those that are listed in the Designated File Types section of the details pane for Software Restriction Policies.

- *Certificate rule.* A certificate rule specifies a signed software publisher's certificate. For example, an administrator can require signed certificates for all scripts and ActiveX controls.
  - When a certificate rule is applied, it checks for a digital signature on the application (for example, Authenticode®). A certificate rule is a strong way to identify software because it uses signed hashes contained in the signature of the signed file to match files regardless of name or location.
  - A certificate rule can be used when you want to restrict both Microsoft Win32® applications and ActiveX content.
  - You can use a hash rule to configure exceptions to a certificate rule, configure the hash rule to identify the executable, and then either allow or restrict the application with the hash rule.
- *Path rule.* A path rule specifies either a folder or a fully qualified program path. When a path rule specifies a folder, the comparison also extends to all subfolders of the folder specified.
  - Path rules support both local and Uniform Naming Convention (UNC) paths.
  - The administrator must define all directories for launching a specific application in the path rule. For example, if the administrator has created a shortcut on the desktop to start an application, in the path rule, the user must have access to both the executable file and the shortcut paths to run the application. Attempting to run the application by using only one part of the path will trigger the Software Restricted warning. Many applications use the %ProgramFiles% variable to install files. If this variable is set to another directory on a different drive, some applications will still copy files to the original C:\Program Files subdirectory. Therefore, it is a best practice to leave path rules defined to the default directory location.
  - Path rules are an essential ingredient of software restriction policy enforcement.
- *Internet zone rule.* Internet zone rules are based on Internet Explorer security zones. You can allow or disallow an application based on the Internet zone from which the application is downloaded. A rule can be created for any of the five zones: Internet, local computer, local intranet, restricted sites, and trusted sites. These rules only apply to software that uses the Windows installer.

Four path rules are configured by default. They are designed to preserve access to the operating system.

Software Restriction settings

There are three settings that can be configured for the Software Restriction policy. They are as follows:

Enforcement Properties determine whether software library files are excluded from the software policy restrictions. Also, you can use this option to prevent software policy restrictions from applying to local administrators.

Designated File Types allow you to add or delete file types from the list of what is considered to be executable code.

Trusted Publishers allow you to define whether end users, local administrators, or enterprise administrators can select trusted publishers. In addition, you can use this option to specify revocation-checking options.

Practice: Restricting Group Membership and Access to Software

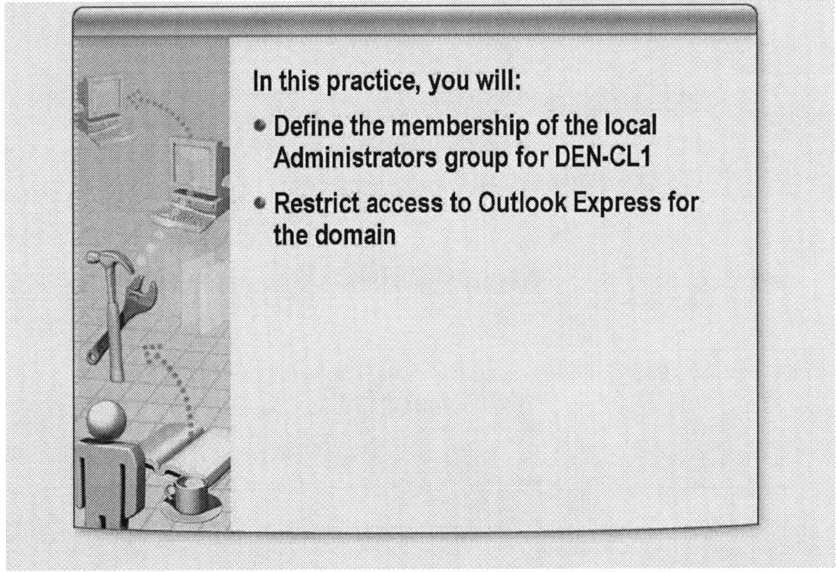
In this practice, you will:
Define the membership of the local Administrators group for DEN-CL1
Restrict access to Outlook Express for the domain

Objectives

In this practice, you will:

- Define the membership of the local Administrators group for DEN-CL1.
- Restrict access to Microsoft Outlook® Express for the domain.

Instructions

Ensure that the DEN-CL1 and the DEN-DC1 virtual machines are running.

Practice

► **Define the membership of the local Administrators group for DEN-CL1**

1. Log on to DEN-DC1 as **Administrator**.
2. Open **Active Directory Users and Computers**.
3. Click the **Computers** container and move the DEN-CL1 computer account into the **IT Admin** organizational unit. Click **Yes** at the Active Directory prompt.
4. Click **Start**, point to **Administrative Tools**, and then click **Group Policy Management**.
5. Create and link a GPO named **Admin Membership** to the **IT Admin** organizational unit.
6. Edit the **Admin Membership** GPO.
7. Expand **Computer Configuration**, **Windows Settings**, **Security Settings** and then click **Restricted Groups**.
8. Right-click **Restricted Groups** and then click **Add Group**.
9. In the **Add Group** dialog box, type **Administrators** and then click **OK**.
10. In the **Administrators Properties** dialog box, in the **Members of this group** section click **Add**.
11. In the **Add Member** dialog box, type **Contoso\G Admins** and then click **OK**.
12. Click **Add** again and locate and add the **Domain Admins** group.

13. Click **OK** twice.
14. Close the **Group Policy Object Editor.**
15. Log on to DEN-CL1 as **Judy** with the password of **Pa$$w0rd.**
16. Click **Start**, click **Run**, and then type **gpupdate /force**. Click **OK.**
17. Right-click **My Computer** and click **Manage** to open **Computer Management** and expand **Local Users and Groups.**
18. Click **Groups** and then open the **Administrators** group.

    Who is in the **Administrators** group?

    ADMIN, DOMAIN ADMINS, G ADMINS

19. Close all open windows.

▶ **Restrict access to Microsoft Outlook® Express for the domain**

1. Switch back to DEN-DC1.
2. Edit the **Default Domain Policy.**
3. Expand **User Configuration, Windows Settings, Security Settings**, and then click **Software Restriction Policies.**
4. Right-click **Software Restriction Policies** and then click **New Software Restriction Policies.**
5. Open the **Security Levels** folder and notice the default setting.
6. Open the **Additional Rules** folder and notice the default rules to allow access to the operating system.
7. Right-click the **Additional Rules** folder and then click **New Path Rule.**
8. In the **New Path Rule** dialog box, click **Browse.**
9. Browse to **C:\Program Files\Outlook Express\msimn.exe** and then click **OK.**
10. Click **OK.**
11. Switch back to DEN-CL1 and, from **Run**, type **gpupdate /force**. Click **OK.**
12. Attempt to open **Outlook Express.** Read the Error message and click **OK.**
13. Close all open windows and log off of both DEN-DC1 and DEN-CL1.

Important Do not shut down the virtual machines.

▶ **To prepare for the next practice**

- Start the DEN-SRV1 virtual machine.

Lesson: Configuring Folder Redirection

- What Is Folder Redirection?
- Folders That Can Be Redirected
- Settings That Configure Folder Redirection
- Security Considerations for Configuring Folder Redirection
- Practice: Configuring Folder Redirection

Introduction

Windows Server 2003 enables you to redirect folders that are included in the user profile from the users' local hard disks to a central server. By redirecting these folders, you can ensure user access to data regardless of the computers to which they log on.

Folder Redirection makes it easier for you to manage and back up data. The folders that you can redirect are My Documents, Application Data, Desktop, and Start Menu. Windows Server 2003 automatically creates these folders and makes them part of the user profile for each user account.

Lesson objectives

After completing this lesson, you will be able to:

- Explain Folder Redirection.
- Explain which folders can be redirected.
- Determine which settings configure Folder Redirection.
- Explain security considerations for configuring Folder Redirection.
- Configure Folder Redirection.

FOLDER REDIRECTION TYPES

BASIC: EVERYONE UNDER THE SCOPE OF THIS POLICY WILL GET THESE FOLDERS REDIRECTED TO THE SAME ROOT PATH.
EX: \\SERVER1\DATA\DAVE
\\SERVER1\DATA\MICHELLE.

ADVANCED: FOLDERS CAN BE REDIRECTED TO DIFFERENT ROOT PATHS BASED ON WINDOWS GROUP MEMBERSHIP.
EX: IF MEMBER OF G SALES → \\SALESSRV1\DATA\JOHN
IF MEMBER OF G ACCOUNTING → \\ACCOUNTINGSRV\FILES\JOAN

What Is Folder Redirection?

Folder Redirection allows:

- Redirection to folders on the local computer or on a network drive
- Folders on a server appear as if they are located on the local drive

Introduction

When you redirect folders, you change the storage location of folders from the local hard disk on the user's computer to a shared folder on a network file server. After you redirect a folder to a file server, it still appears to the user as if it is stored on the local hard disk. You can redirect four folders that are part of the user profile: My Documents, Application Data, Desktop, and Start Menu.

Benefits of Folder Redirection

By storing data on the network, users benefit from increased availability and frequent backup of their data. Redirecting folders has the following benefits:

- The folder data is accessible from any network access point.
- The data in the folders is centrally stored so that the files that they contain are easier to manage and back up.
- Files that are located in redirected folders, unlike files that are part of a roaming user profile, are not copied and saved on the computer that the user logs on to. This means that when a user logs on to a client computer, no storage space is used for these files and that data that might be confidential does not remain on a client computer.
- Data that is stored in a shared network folder can be backed up as part of routine system administration. This is safer because it requires no action on the part of the user.
- As an administrator, you can use Group Policy to set disk quotas that limit the size of special folders.
- Data specific to a user can be redirected to a different hard disk on the user's local computer rather than to the hard disk holding the operating system files. This protects the user's data if the operating system must be reinstalled.

Folders That Can Be Redirected

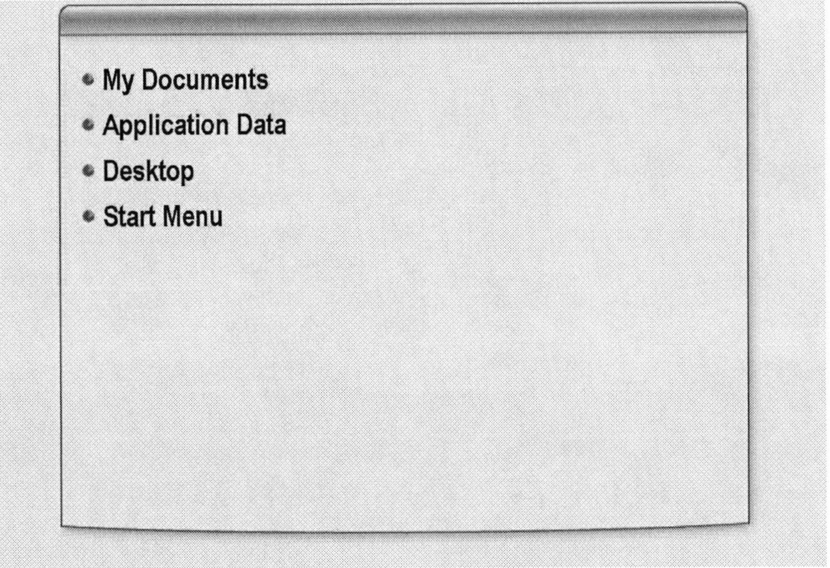

Introduction

You can redirect the My Documents, Application Data, Desktop, and Start Menu folders. An organization should redirect these folders to preserve important user data and settings. There are several advantages to redirecting each of these folders. The advantages vary according to your organization's needs.

Redirected folders

You can use Folder Redirection to redirect any of the following folders in a user profile:

- My Documents

  Redirecting My Documents is particularly advantageous because the folder tends to become large over time.

  Offline Files technology gives users access to My Documents even when the users are not connected to the network. This is particularly useful for people who use portable computers.

- Application Data

  A Group Policy setting controls the behavior of Application Data when client-side caching is enabled. This setting synchronizes application data that is centralized on a server with the local computer. As a result, the user can work online or offline. If any changes are made to the application data, synchronization updates the application data on the client and server.

- Desktop

  You can redirect Desktop and all of its files, shortcuts, and folders to a centralized server.

- Start Menu

  When you redirect Start Menu, its subfolders are also redirected.

Settings That Configure Folder Redirection

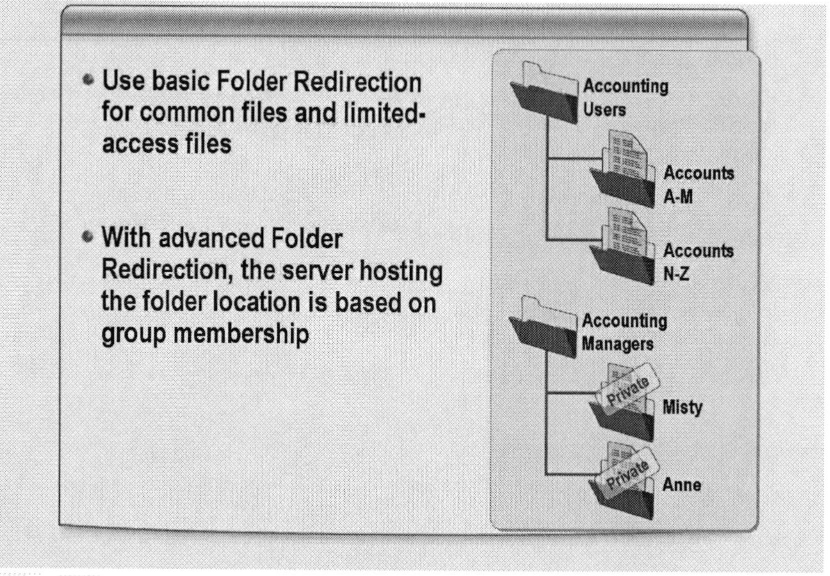

Use basic Folder Redirection for common files and limited-access files
With advanced Folder Redirection, the server hosting the folder location is based on group membership
Accounting Users
Accounts A-M
Accounts N-Z
Accounting Managers
Private
Misty
Private
Anne

Introduction

There are three available settings for Folder Redirection: none, basic, and advanced. Basic folder redirection is for users who must redirect their folders to a common area or users who need their data to be private. Advanced redirection allows you to specify different network locations for different Windows user groups.

Basic Folder Redirection

You have the following basic options for Folder Redirection:

- *Redirect folder to the following location* All users who redirect their folders to a common area can see or use each other's data in the redirected folder. To do this, choose a **Basic** setting and set **Target folder location** to **Redirect folder to the following location**. Use this option for all redirected folders that contain data that is not private. An example of this is redirecting My Documents for a team of Accounts Receivable personnel who all share the same data. The Root Path field allows you to specify the UNC path that the folder will be redirected to.
- *Create a folder for each user under the root path* For users who need their redirected folders to be private, choose a **Basic** setting and set **Target folder location** to **Create a folder for each user under the root path**. Use this option for users who need their data to be private, like managers who keep personal data about employees. The Root Path field allows you to specify the UNC path that the folder will be redirected to. You only need to put in the server name and the share name and Group Policy will append the %username% variable to automatically create a subfolder named for the user and move the redirected folder into it.
- *Redirect to the local userprofile location* This setting will redirect the folder back into the default location of the user's profile on the local hard drive.
- *Redirect to the user's home directory* This setting is only available for the My Documents folder. Use this option only if you have already deployed home folders.

Advanced Folder Redirection

When you select **Advanced – specify locations for various user groups**, folders are redirected to different locations based on the security group membership of the users. After you specify the group whose folders you want to have redirected, you will see the same options that are provided for basic redirection.

Settings

The Settings tab allows you to specify whether the user will be granted exclusive rights to the redirected folder and whether the current contents of the folder will be moved to the new location. You can also specify whether the folder should remain in the network location or be moved back to the local user's profile if the Group Policy is removed.

TO MAKE A ROAMING PROFILE A MANDATORY PROFILE, RENAME THE NTUSER.DAT FILE TO NTUSER.MAN. THIS ESSENTIALLY MAKES THE PROFILE 'READ-ONLY'.

Security Considerations for Configuring Folder Redirection

- NTFS permissions for Folder Redirection root folder
- Shared folder permissions for Folder Redirection root folder
- NTFS permissions for each user's redirected folder

Introduction

Folder Redirection can create folders for you; this is the recommended option. When you use this option, the correct permissions are set automatically. If you manually create folders, you will need to know the correct permissions. The following tables show which permissions to set for Folder Redirection.

Note Although it is not recommended, administrators can create the redirected folders before Folder Redirection creates them.

NTFS permissions required for the root folder

Set the following NTFS permissions for the root folder.

User account	Folder Redirection defaults	Minimum permissions needed
Creator/owner	Full Control, this folder, subfolders, and files	Full Control, this folder, subfolders, and files
Administrators	No permissions	No permissions
Everyone	No permissions	No permissions
Local System	Full Control, this folder, subfolders, and files	Full Control, this folder, subfolders, and files
Security group of users who need to put data on the shared network server	N/A	List Folder/Read Data, Create Folders/Append Data—This folder only

Shared folder permissions required for the root folder

Set the following shared folder permissions for the root folder.

User account	Folder Redirection defaults	Minimum permissions needed
Authenticated Users	Full Control	Change
Security group of users who need to put data on the shared network server	N/A	Change

NTFS permissions required for each user's redirected folder

Set the following NTFS permissions for each user's redirected folder.

User account	Folder Redirection defaults	Minimum permissions needed
UserName	Full Control, owner of folder	Full Control, owner of folder
Local System	Full Control	Full Control
Administrators	No permissions	No permissions
Everyone	No permissions	No permissions

Note When offline folders are synchronized over the network, the data is transmitted in plain text format. The data is then susceptible to interception by network monitoring tools.

Additional reading

For more information about Folder Redirection, see "Best practices for Folder Redirection," on the Microsoft Web site.

Practice: Configuring Folder Redirection

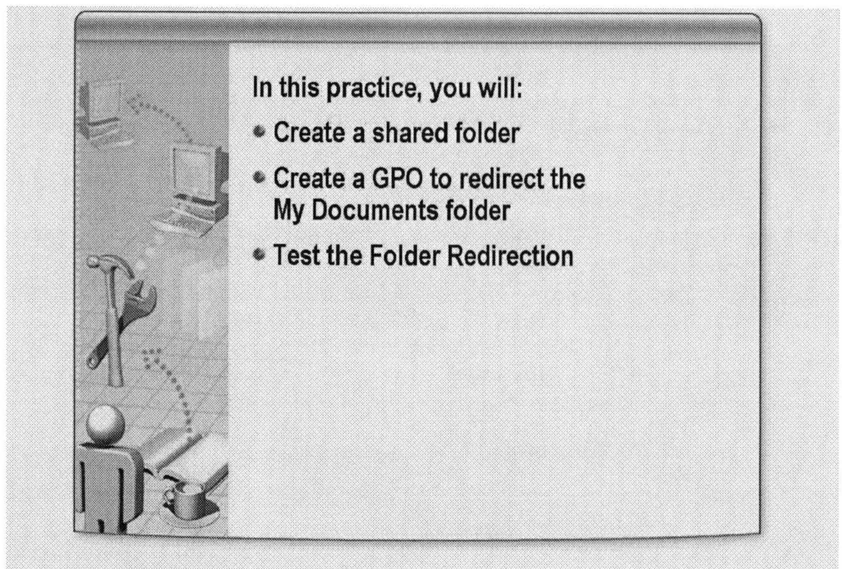

Objective

In this practice, you will:

- Create a shared folder.
- Create a GPO to redirect the My Documents folder.
- Test the Folder Redirection.

Instructions

Ensure that the DEN-CL1, DEN-SRV1 and the DEN-DC1 virtual machines are running.

Practice

► Create a shared folder

1. Log on to DEN-DC1 as **Administrator**.
2. Open Windows Explorer and create a folder named **C:\Redirect**.
3. Share the folder to **Authenticated Users** with **Full Control** permission.
4. Close Windows Explorer.

► Create a GPO to redirect the My Documents folder

1. Open the **Group Policy Management** console and create and link a GPO named **Folder Redirection** to the **Legal** organizational unit.
2. Edit the **Folder Redirection** GPO.
3. Expand **User Configuration, Windows Settings**, and then expand **Folder Redirection.**
4. Right-click the **My Documents** folder and then click **Properties.**
5. In the **My Documents Properties** dialog box, select the setting **Basic-Redirect everyone's folder to the same location.**
6. Ensure that the **Target folder location** is set to **Create a folder for each user under the root path.**
7. In the **Root Path** field, type **\\DEN-DC1\Redirect.**

8. Click the **Settings** tab. Note the default settings for the **My Documents** folder.
9. Click **OK.**
10. Close all open windows and log off of DEN-DC1.

► Test the Folder Redirection

1. Log on to the DEN-CL1 as **Legaluser** with the password of **Pa$$w0rd.**
2. Click **Start**, right-click the **My Documents** folder and click **Properties.**

   What is the path in the Target folder location field?

   ____

   Note It may require two logons to see the results of the GPO.

   ---

3. Click **OK**
4. Open the **My Documents** folder. Create a new document named **legal.txt.** Enter some text and save the document.
5. Close all open windows and log off.
6. Log on to DEN-SRV1 as **Legaluser.**
7. Open the **My Documents** folder and open the **legal.txt** document. You should see the text you entered.
8. Close all open windows and log off.

Important Do not shut down the virtual machines.

Lesson: Determining Applied GPOs

- What Are gpupdate and gpresult?
- What Is Group Policy Reporting?
- What Is Group Policy Modeling?
- What Are Group Policy Results?
- Practice: Determining Applied GPOs

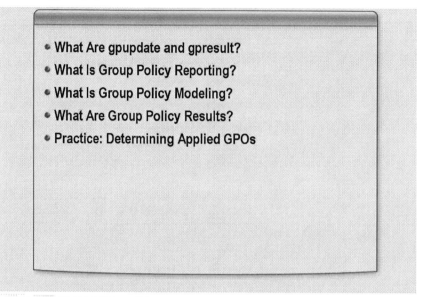

Introduction

Group Policy is the primary administrative tool for defining and controlling the operation of programs, network resources, and the operating system for users and computers in an organization. In an Active Directory environment, Group Policy is applied to users or computers on the basis of their membership in sites, domains, or organizational units. Group Policy is refreshed at regular intervals but can also be refreshed manually. Group Policy also has many reporting features to help you document, test, and troubleshoot Group Policy.

Lesson objectives

After completing this lesson, you will be able to:

- Explain what **gpupdate** and **gpresult** are.
- Explain what Group Policy reporting is.
- Explain what Group Policy modeling is.
- Explain what Group Policy results are.
- Determine applied GPOs.

What Are gpupdate and gpresult?

Use gpupdate to:

- Manually refresh updated Group Policy settings
- Force the refresh of all Group Policy settings
- Force a reboot or logoff if required to refresh the settings

Use gpresult to:

- Display the resulting set of policies for a user or computer
- Redirect the resulting set of policies information to a file

Introduction

The **gpupdate** command-line tool can refresh Group Policy settings, including security settings. By default, Group Policy settings are refreshed every 90 minutes on a workstation or server and every five minutes on a domain controller. You can run **gpupdate** to force Group Policy settings to be refreshed.

Because Group Policies can be applied at multiple levels to any computer or user, Group Policy generates a resulting set of policies at logon. The **gpresult** command displays Group Policy settings and Resultant Set of Policy (RSoP) data for a user or a computer. You can use **gpresult** to see what policy setting is in effect and to troubleshoot problems.

Examples of gpupdate

The following examples show how you can use the **gpupdate** command:

- C:\gpupdate
- C:\gpupdate /force
- C:\gpupdate /boot

Parameters of gpupdate

Gpupdate has the following parameters.

Value	Description
/Target:{**Computer** | **User**}	Specifies that only user or only computer policy settings are refreshed. By default, both user and computer policy settings are refreshed.
/Force	Reapplies all policy settings. By default, only policy settings that have changed are reapplied.
/Wait:{*Value*}	Sets the number of seconds to wait for policy processing to finish. The default is 600 seconds. The value '0' means not to wait. The value '-1' means to wait indefinitely.
/Logoff	Causes a logoff after the Group Policy settings are refreshed. This is required for those Group Policy client-side extensions that do not process policy settings during a background refresh cycle but do process policy settings when a user logs on. Examples include user-targeted Software Installation and Folder Redirection. This option has no effect if there are no extensions called that require a logoff.
/Boot	Causes the computer to restart after the Group Policy settings are refreshed. This is required for those Group Policy client-side extensions that do not process policy during a background refresh cycle but do process policy when the computer starts. Examples include computer-targeted Software Installation. This option has no effect if there are no extensions called that require the computer to restart.
/Sync	Causes the next foreground policy setting to be applied synchronously. Foreground policy settings are applied when the computer starts and when the user logs on. You can specify this for the user, computer, or both by using the **/Target** parameter. The **/Force** and **/Wait** parameters are ignored.

Examples of gpresult

The following examples show how you can use the **gpresult** command:

- C:\gpresult /user *targetusername* /scope computer
- C:\gpresult /s *computer* /u *domain/user* /p *password* /user *targetusername* /scope USER
- C:\gpresult /z >policy.txt

Parameters of gpresult

Gpresult has the following parameters.

Value	Description
/**s** *computer*	Specifies the name or IP address of a remote computer. Do not use backslashes. The default is the local computer.
/**u** *domain/user*	Runs the command with the account permissions of the user that is specified by *User* or *Domain/User*. The default is the permissions of the user who is currently logged on to the computer that issues the command.
/**p** *password*	Specifies the password of the user account that is specified in the /**u** parameter.
/**user** *targetusername*	Specifies the user name of the user whose RSoP data is to be displayed.
/**scope** {**user**|**computer**}	Displays either user or computer policy settings. Valid values for the /**scope** parameter are **user** or **computer**. If you omit the /**scope** parameter, **gpresult** displays both user and computer policy settings.
/**v**	Specifies that the output will display verbose policy information. Use this switch when you want to see the settings applied.
/**z**	Specifies that the output will display all available information about Group Policy. Because this parameter produces more information than the /**v** parameter, redirect output to a text file when you use this parameter (for example, you can type **gpresult /z >policy.txt**).
/?	Displays help in the command prompt window.

EXTRA GROUP POLICY TOOLS

GPRESULT: LETS YOU VIEW THE RSOP DATA FOR A COMPUTER/USER.

GPUPDATE: FORCES AN IMMEDIATE POLICY UPDATE

EXTRA FEATURES OF THE GPMC

- GROUP POLICY REPORTING: HTML REPORT OF ALL POLICY SETTINGS SUITABLE FOR PRINTING
- GROUP POLICY MODELING: ALLOWS YOU TO SIMULATE "WHAT IF" SCENARIOS WITHOUT AFFECTING CURRENT ENVIRONMENT. * REQUIRES W2K3 DC TO PERFORM SIM *
- GROUP POLICY RESULTS

What Is Group Policy Reporting?

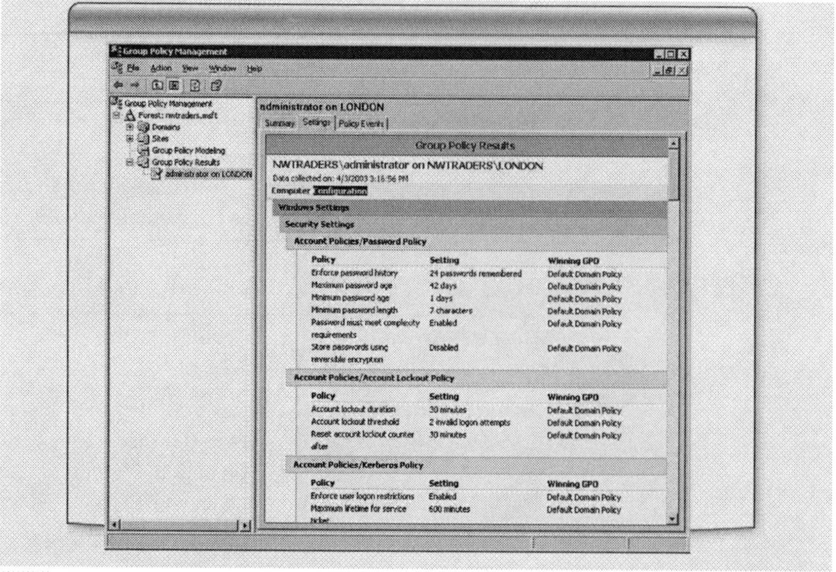

Definition

A systems administrator can make hundreds of changes to a GPO. Group Policy reporting allows you to verify changes made to a GPO without actually opening the GPO and expanding every folder. You can generate a Hypertext Markup Language (HTML) report that lists the items in the GPO that are configured. This report can be printed or saved for documentation purposes.

Settings tab

The **Settings** tab of the details pane for a GPO or GPO link in Group Policy Management shows an HTML report that displays all the defined settings in the GPO. Any user with read access to the GPO can generate this report. If you click **show all** at the top of the report, the report is fully expanded, and all settings are shown. Also, using a context menu, you can print the reports or save them to a file as either HTML or Extensible Markup Language (XML).

Note The new Internet Explorer Enhanced Configuration prompts the user to add the Web site to the list of trusted sites. You should add the site to the list to avoid having the prompt come up every time you view the settings. To add the site you must clear the **Require server verification (https:) for all sites in this zone** and click **Add**.

What Is Group Policy Modeling?

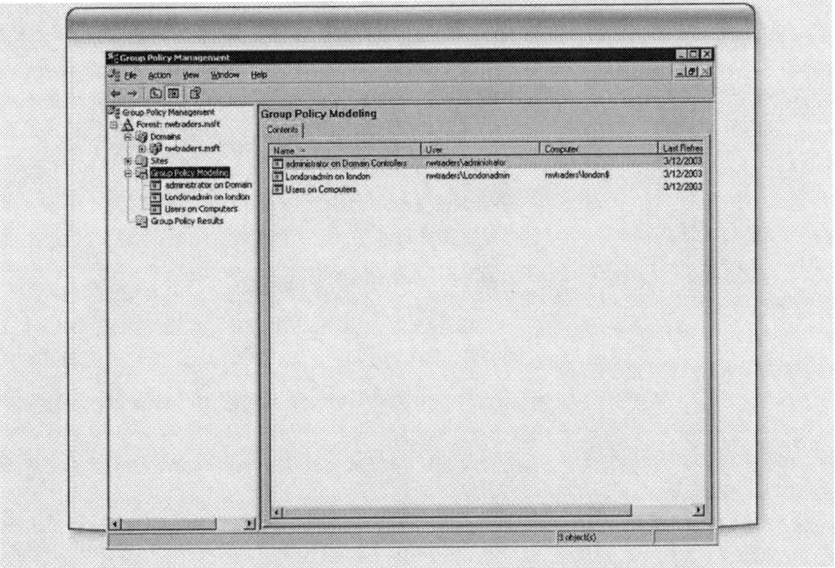

Introduction

Group Policy Modeling enables you to simulate a GPO deployment that is applied to users and computers before you actually deploy the GPO. The simulation creates a report that takes into account the user's organizational unit, the computer's organizational unit, and any group membership and can include Windows Management Instrumentation (WMI) filtering. It also takes into account any Group Policy inheritance issues or conflicts.

Requirements

If you want to use Group Policy Modeling, there must be a Windows Server 2003 domain controller in the forest. This is because the simulation is performed by a service that is only present on Windows Server 2003 domain controllers.

Results of Group Policy Modeling

To perform a Group Policy Modeling query, the user uses the Group Policy Modeling Wizard. After the user completes the Group Policy Modeling Wizard, a new node in the console tree of Group Policy Management appears under **Group Policy Modeling** to display the results. The **Contents** tab in the details pane for Group Policy Modeling displays a summary of all Group Policy Modeling queries that the user has performed.

For each query, Group Policy Management shows the following data:

- **Name**. This is the user-supplied name of the modeling results.
- **User**. This is the user object (or the organizational unit where the user object is located) that the modeling query is based on.
- **Computer**. This is the computer object (or the organizational unit where the computer object is located) that is the subject of the modeling query.
- **Last refresh time**. This is the last time the modeling query was refreshed.

For each query, the details pane for the node contains the following three tabs:

- **Summary**. This contains an HTML report of the summary information, including the list of GPOs, security group membership, and WMI filters.
- **Settings**. This contains an HTML report of the policy settings that were applied in this simulation.
- **Query**. This lists the parameters that were used to generate the query.

What Are Group Policy Results?

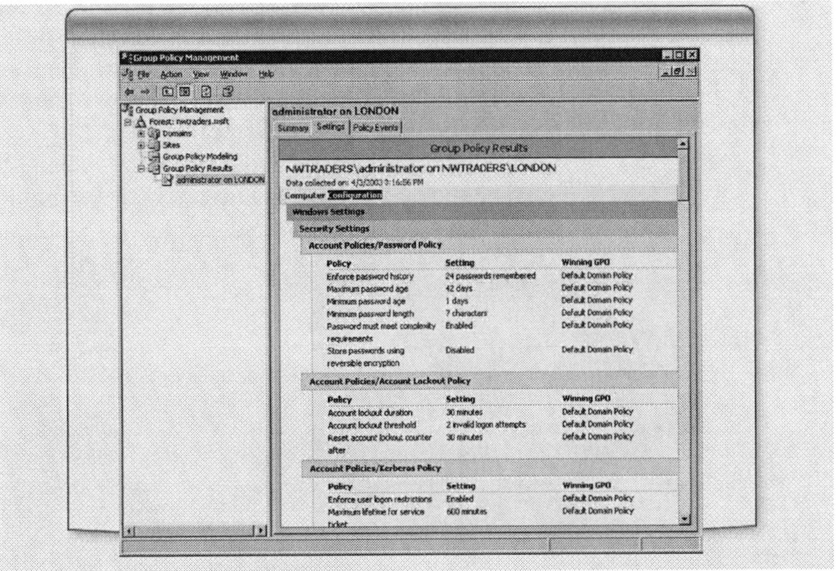

Introduction

The data that is presented in Group Policy Results is similar to Group Policy Modeling data. However, unlike Group Policy Modeling data, this data is not a simulation. It is the actual RSoP data obtained from the target computer.

Requirements

Unlike Group Policy Modeling, the data in Group Policy Results is obtained from the client and is not simulated on the domain controller. Technically, a Windows Server 2003 domain controller is not required to be in the forest if you want to access Group Policy Results. However, the client must be running Windows XP or Windows Server 2003. It is not possible to get Group Policy Results data for a client running Microsoft Windows 2000.

Note By default, only users with local administrator privileges on the target computer can remotely access Group Policy Results data. To gather this data, the user performing the query must have access to remotely view the event log.

Results of Group Policy Results

Each Group Policy Results query is represented by a node under the Group Policy Results container in the console tree of Group Policy Management. The details pane for each node has the following three tabs:

- **Summary**. This contains an HTML report of the summary information including the list of GPOs, security group membership, and WMI filters.
- **Settings**. This contains an HTML report of the policy settings that were applied.
- **Events**. This shows all policy-related events from the target computer.

Windows Firewall settings

The Windows Firewall is enabled by default in Windows XP with SP2 installed. It is designed to block all unsolicited connection attempts. This default setting impacts how RSoP is used across the network. If the Windows Firewall is enabled, then Group Policy should be configured to allow remote administrative tasks in order for RSoP information to be generated. The **Computer Configuration, Administrative Templates, Network Connections, Windows Firewall, Domain Profile** section of Group Policy contains a firewall setting to allow remote administration exceptions. This setting should be enabled to generate RSoP reporting.

Important In order to generate RSoP information for a specific user on a specific computer, the user you are querying on must have a profile on that computer.

Practice: Determining Applied GPOs

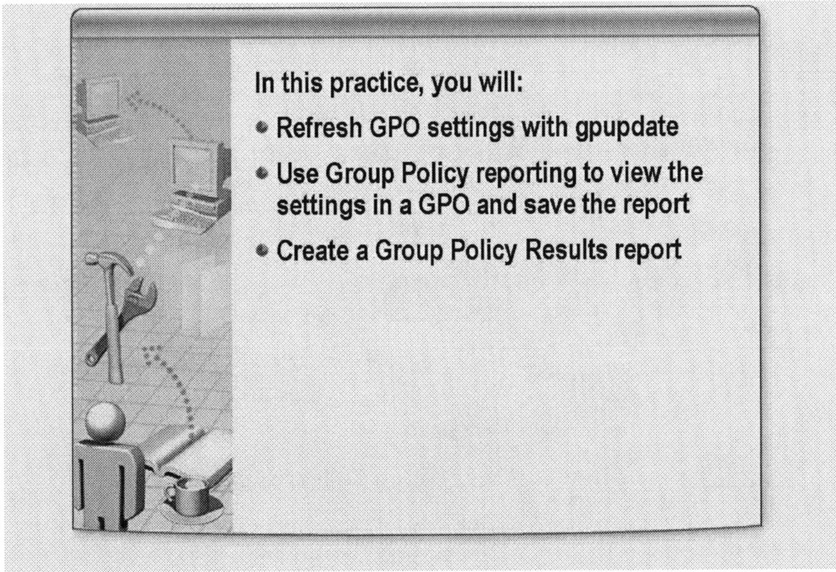

Objectives

In this practice, you will:

- Refresh GPO settings with **gpupdate**.
- Use Group Policy reporting to view the settings in a GPO and save the report.
- Create a Group Policy Results report.

Instructions

Ensure that the DEN-CL1, DEN-SRV1 and the DEN-DC1 virtual machines are running.

Practice

► **Refresh GPO settings with gpupdate**

1. Log on to DEN-DC1 as **Administrator**.
2. Open the **Group Policy Management** console, click the **Group Policy Objects** folder, and edit the **Default Domain Policy**.
3. Expand **User Configuration**, **Administrative Templates**, and then click **Start Menu and Taskbar**.
4. Enable the **Remove Help menu from the Start Menu** setting.
5. Expand **Computer Configuration**, **Administrative Templates**, **Network**, **Network Connections**, **Windows Firewall**, and then click **Domain Profile**.
6. Double-click the **Windows Firewall: Allow remote administration exception** setting.
7. On the **Settings** tab, click **Enabled**, type **localsubnet** in the **Allow unsolicited incoming messages from** field, and click **OK**.
8. Close the **Group Policy Object Editor**.
9. Click the **Start** menu. Notice that **Help and Support** still appears.
10. From **Run**, type **gpupdate /force**.
11. **Help and Support** should no longer appear on the **Start** menu.

► **Use Group Policy reporting to view the settings in a GPO and save the report**

1. Expand the **Group Policy Objects** folder.
2. In the left console pane, click the **Standard Desktop** GPO.
3. In the right pane, click the **Settings** tab.
4. In the **Internet Explorer** dialog box, click **Add.**
5. In the **Trusted Sites** dialog box, clear the **Require server verification (https:) for all sites in this zone** check box, click **Add**, and then click **Close.**
6. View the settings of the GPO.
7. Right-click anywhere on the report and select **Save Report** from the shortcut menu.
8. Save the report as an HTML file in C:\.
9. Close **Group Policy Management.**
10. Browse to C:\ and open the **Standard Desktop.htm** file. Click **OK** at the **Information Bar** prompt.
11. View the report.
12. Close all open windows.

► **Create a Group Policy Results report**

1. Open **Group Policy Management.**
2. Right-click the **Group Policy Results** folder and then click **Group Policy Results Wizard.**
3. In the **Group Policy Results Wizard**, click **Next.**
4. In the **Computer Selection** page, select **Another computer**, type **DEN-SRV1**, and then click **Next.**
5. In the **User Selection** page, select **Contoso\Legaluser** and then click **Next.**
6. In the **Summary of Selections** page, click **Next.**
7. Click **Finish.**
8. Browse through the report information.
9. Close all windows and log off.

Important Do not shut down the virtual machines.

Lab: Managing the User Environment by Using Group Policy

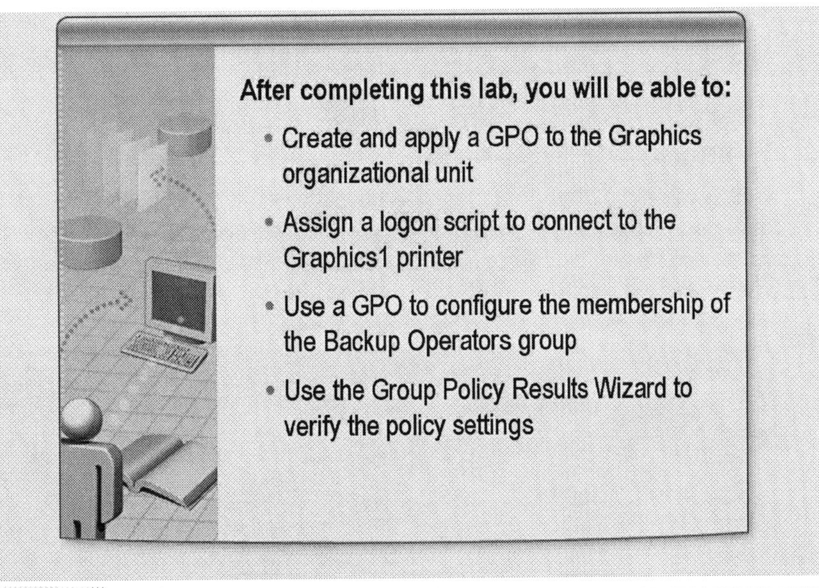
After completing this lab, you will be able to:
Create and apply a GPO to the Graphics organizational unit
Assign a logon script to connect to the Graphics1 printer
Use a GPO to configure the membership of the Backup Operators group
Use the Group Policy Results Wizard to verify the policy settings

Objectives

After completing this lab, you will be able to:

- Create and apply a GPO to the Graphics organizational unit.
- Assign a logon script to connect to the Graphics1 printer.
- Use a GPO to configure the membership of the Backup Operators group.
- Use the Group Policy Results Wizard to verify the policy settings.

Prerequisites

To complete this lab, you must have the following virtual machines:

- DEN-DC1
- DEN-CL1

Estimated time to complete this lab: 40 minutes

Exercise 1
Creating and Applying a GPO to the Graphics Organizational Unit

In this exercise, you will create a GPO to configure the desktop for the Graphics department.

Scenario

Contoso Ltd. has determined the Graphics department needs a more detailed configuration than the Standard Desktop GPO provides. You will create and link a GPO named Graphics Desktop to further configure the users in the Graphics department. You will create a GPO that removes the Run command and populates the home page of Internet Explorer.

Properties	Special Instructions
1. Create and link a GPO.	**a.** Log on to DEN-DC1 as **Administrator** with the password of **Pa$$w0rd**. **b.** Open **Group Policy Management** and create and link a GPO named **Graphics Desktop** to the **Graphics** organizational unit.
2. Edit the policy.	**a.** Right-click and edit **Graphics Desktop**. **b.** Expand **User Configuration**, **Administrative Templates** and configure as follows: • In **Start Menu and Taskbar**, enable the **Remove Run menu from Start Menu** setting. • In **Windows Components**, in **Windows Messenger**, enable the **Do not allow Windows Messenger to be run** setting. • In **Control Panel**, in **Display**, enable the **Prevent changing wallpaper** setting. • In **Desktop**, enable the **Hide and disable all items on the desktop** setting. **c.** Close the **Group Policy Object Editor**.
3. Test the policy.	**a.** Log on to DEN-CL1 as **GraphicsUser** with the password of **Pa$$w0rd**. **b.** Ensure that the desktop has nothing displayed. **c.** Ensure that the **Run** command does not appear on the **Start** menu. **d.** In **Control Panel**, switch to **Classic View**, double-click **Display** and attempt to change the desktop wallpaper. **e.** Attempt to launch Windows Messenger. **f.** Close all open windows and log off.

Exercise 2
Assigning a Logon Script to Connect to the Graphics1 Printer

In this exercise, you will create and assign a logon script that connects users in the Graphics organizational unit to the Graphics1 printer.

Scenario

Contoso Ltd. employees are not allowed to add printers. You must create a GPO that connects the Graphics users to the Graphics1 printer. You will use the Printers.vbs script provided in the Admin_Tools folder.

Tasks	Special instructions
1. Create a GPO.	a. Switch to DEN-DC1 and create and link a GPO named **Map Printer** to the **Graphics** organizational unit. b. Edit the **Map Printer** GPO.
2. Edit the GPO.	a. Expand **User Configuration**, **Windows Settings**, **Scripts**, and then double-click **Logon**. b. In the **Logon Properties** box, click **Show Files** to display the Logon folder window. c. Start Windows Explorer and copy **D:\2274\Labfiles\Admin_Tools\printer.vbs** to the **Logon** folder. d. Close the **Logon** folder, and then click **Add**. e. In the **Add a Script** dialog box, click **Browse**, and then select **printer.vbs**. f. Click **OK** twice. g. Click **OK** to close the **Logon Properties** window. h. Close the **Group Policy Object Editor**.
3. Test the setting.	a. Log on to DEN-CL1 as **GraphicsUser** with the password of **Pa$$w0rd**. b. Open the **Printers and Faxes** folder. c. Ensure that the **Graphics1** printer appears. d. Close all open windows and log off of DEN-CL1.

Exercise 3
Using a GPO to Configure the Members of the Backup Operators Group

In this exercise, you will configure a GPO to place the G Admins global group in the Backup Operators group on all workstations and servers in the domain.

Scenario

Judy Lew has been assigned to back up data on all workstations and servers in the domain. You will create a GPO to ensure that Judy Lew is placed in the Backup Operators group on all workstations and servers. Judy Lew is a member of the G Admins global group.

Tasks	Special instructions
1. Create a GPO.	a. Switch to DEN-DC1 and create and link a GPO named **Backup Operators** to the **contoso.msft** domain. b. Edit the **Backup Operators** GPO.
2. Edit the GPO.	a. Expand **Computer Configuration**, expand **Windows Settings**, and then expand **Security Settings.** Click the **Restricted Groups** folder. b. Right-click the **Restricted Groups** folder and then click **Add Group.** c. In the **Add Group** dialog box, type **Backup Operators**, and then click **OK.** d. In the **Backup Operators Properties** dialog box, click **Add** in the **Members of this group** section, and then type **Contoso\G Admins.** e. Click **OK** twice. f. Close the **Group Policy Object Editor.**
3. Test the setting.	a. Log on to DEN-CL1 as **Administrator.** b. From **Run**, type **gpupdate /force.** c. Open **Computer Management**, and then expand **Local Users and Groups**, and **Groups** and then open the **Backup Operators** group. d. Ensure that the **G Admins** group is a member.

Exercise 4
Using the Group Policy Results Wizard to Verify the Policy Settings

In this exercise, you will use the Group Policy Results Wizard to verify the policy settings for the GraphicsUser user account.

Scenario

You need to document which GPO settings are applied to Graphics department users. You will use the Group Policy Results Wizard to verify the policy settings for the GraphicsUser user account.

Tasks	Special instructions
1. Run the Group Policy Results Wizard.	**a.** Switch to DEN-DC1. **b.** In **Group Policy Management**, right-click **Group Policy Results** and click **Group Policy Results Wizard**. **c.** On the **Group Policy Results Wizard Welcome** screen, click **Next**. **d.** On the **Computer Selection** screen, click **Another computer**, type **DEN-CL1** in the field, and then click **Next**. **e.** On the **User Selection** screen, notice that only users who have logged on to DEN-CL1 are listed. **f.** Select **GraphicsUser**, and then click **Next**. **g.** On the **Summary of Selections** screen, click **Next**. **h.** Click **Finish**.
2. View and save the report.	**a.** Click the **Summary** tab of the report. **b.** In the **Computer Configuration Summary** section, expand **Group Policy Objects** and **Applied GPOs**. What GPOs are being applied to the computer? **c.** In the **User Configuration Summary** section, expand **Group Policy Objects** and **Applied GPOs**. What GPOs are being applied to the user? **d.** Click the **Settings** tab. What GPO is applying the setting that hides the screen saver? What GPO is applying the setting that removes the **Run** command from the **Start** menu? **e.** Right-click the report and then click **Save Report**. Save the report as an HTML file in the **My Documents** folder.
3. Complete the lab exercise.	**a.** Close all programs and shut down all computers. Do not save changes. **b.** To prepare for the next module, start the DEN-DC1 and DEN-CL1 virtual computers.

This page intentionally left blank.

Module 10: Implementing Administrative Templates and Audit Policy

Contents

Overview

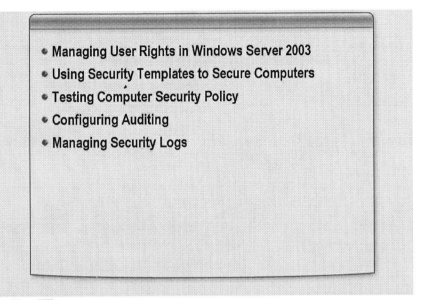

- Managing User Rights in Windows Server 2003
- Using Security Templates to Secure Computers
- Testing Computer Security Policy
- Configuring Auditing
- Managing Security Logs

Introduction

This module will provide a broad overview of security in Microsoft® Windows Server™ 2003. You will learn how to use security templates and test computer security policy. You will also learn how to configure auditing and manage security logs.

Objectives

After completing this module, you will be able to:

- Manage user rights in Windows Server 2003.
- Use security templates to secure computers.
- Test computer security policy.
- Configure auditing.
- Manage security logs.

Lesson: Managing User Rights in Windows Server 2003

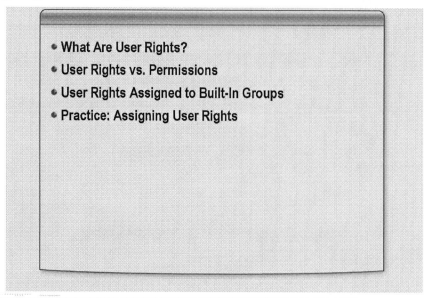

- What Are User Rights?
- User Rights vs. Permissions
- User Rights Assigned to Built-In Groups
- Practice: Assigning User Rights

Introduction

In this lesson, you will learn about user rights, permissions, and user rights assigned to built-in groups. You will also learn how to assign user rights.

Lesson objectives

After completing this lesson, you will be able to:

- Describe user rights.
- Distinguish between rights and permissions.
- Describe the user rights that are assigned to built-in groups.
- Assign user rights.

What Are User Rights?

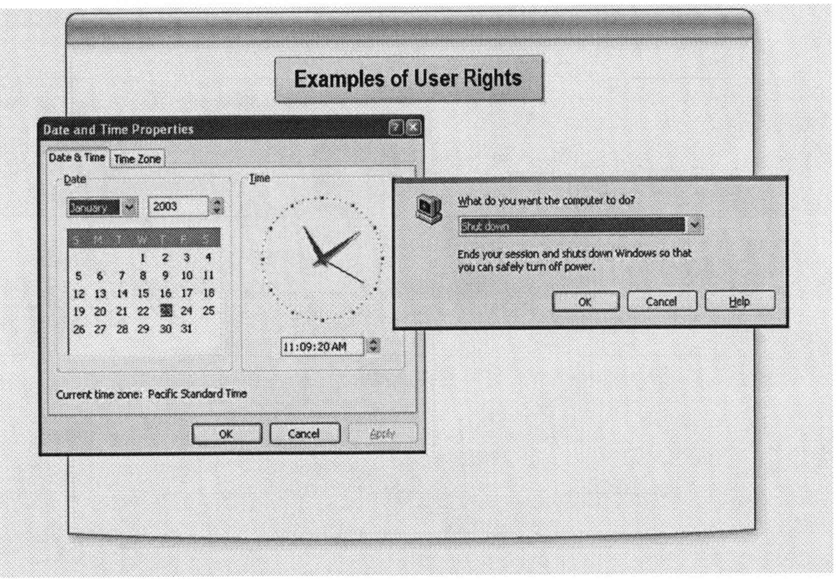

Definition

When a user logs on to a computer or accesses a computer over the network, the user receives an access token on that computer that includes their user rights. A user right authorizes a user who is accessing a computer to perform certain actions on the system. Users who do not have the appropriate rights to perform an action are blocked from performing that action.

Who do user rights apply to?

User rights can apply both to individual users and to groups. However, user rights are best administered when they are assigned to groups. Assigning user rights to groups ensures that a user who logs on as a member of a group automatically receives the rights that are associated with that group. Windows Server 2003 enables an administrator to assign rights to users and groups.

User rights that are assigned to a group are applied to all members of the group while they are members. If a user is a member of multiple groups, the user's rights are cumulative, which means that the user has more than one set of rights. In general, user rights assigned to one group do not conflict with the rights assigned to another group. The only time that rights assigned to one group might conflict with those assigned to another is in the case of certain logon rights. To remove rights from a user, the administrator simply removes the user from the group. The user no longer has the rights assigned to that group.

Common user rights

Common user rights include the following:

- *Allow log on locally*. Enables a user to log on to the local computer or to the domain from a local computer.
- *Change the system time*. Enables a user to set the time of the internal clock of a computer.
- *Shut down the system*. Enables a user to shut down a local computer.
- *Access this computer from a network*. Enables a user to access a computer running Windows Server 2003 from any other computer on the network.

User Rights vs. Permissions

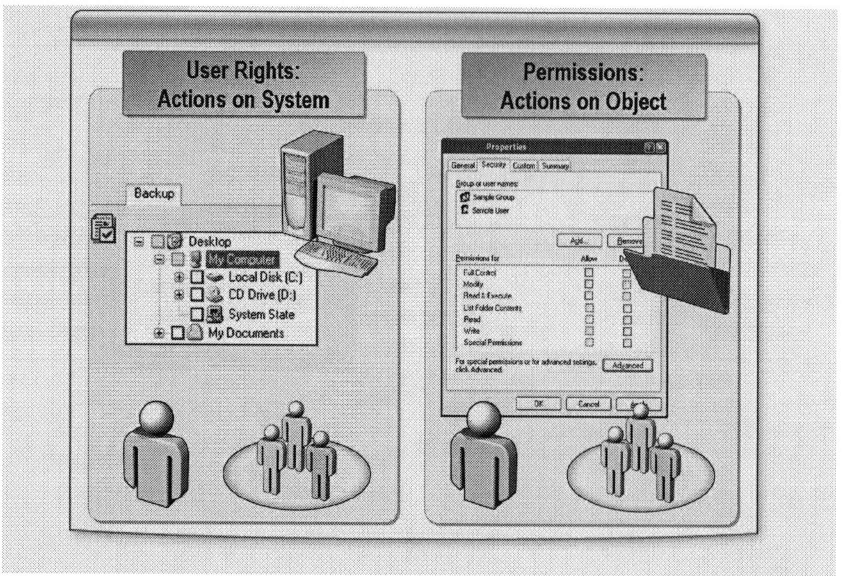

Introduction

Administrators can assign specific user rights to group accounts or to individual user accounts. These rights authorize users to perform specific actions, such as log on to a system interactively or back up files and directories. User rights are different from permissions—user rights are attached to user accounts, and permissions are attached to objects.

What are user rights?

User rights determine which users can perform a specific task on a computer or in a domain. Rights apply to the entire system, rather than to a specific resource, and affect the overall operation of the computer or domain. All users accessing network resources must have certain common rights on the computers they use, such as the right to log on to the computer. Administrators can assign specific common user rights to groups or to individual users. Additionally, Windows Server 2003 assigns certain rights to built-in groups by default.

What are permissions?

Permissions define the type of access granted to a user or group for an object or object property. For example, you can grant Read and Write permissions to the Finance group for a file named Payroll.xls.

You can grant permissions for any secured objects such as files, objects in the Active Directory® directory service, or registry objects. You can grant permissions to any user, group, or computer. It is a good practice to grant permissions to groups.

You can grant permissions for objects to:

- Groups, users, and special identities in the domain.
- Groups and users in any trusted domains.
- Local groups and users on the computer where the object resides.

When you provide access to file resources on a computer running Windows Server 2003, you can control who has access to resources and the nature of their access by granting the appropriate permissions. Permissions define the type of access assigned to a user or group for any resource.

For example, users in the Human Resources department of an organization might need to modify the organization's document describing Human Resources policies. To facilitate this, the administrator must grant the appropriate permission to the members of the Human Resources department.

To grant permissions for individual files and folders, Windows Server 2003 uses the NTFS file system. You can also control the permissions for accessing shared folder resources and network printers.

USER RIGHTS ARE PART OF THE COMPUTER'S SECURITY POLICY WHICH CAN BE SET LOCALLY (IN CONTROL PANEL) OR VIA A GROUP POLICY OBJECT. SAME RULES (IN GENERAL) WILL APPLY: LOCAL - SITE - DOMAIN - OU

EXCEPTION TO THIS IS THE "ACCOUNT POLICIES"

User Rights Assigned to Built-In Groups

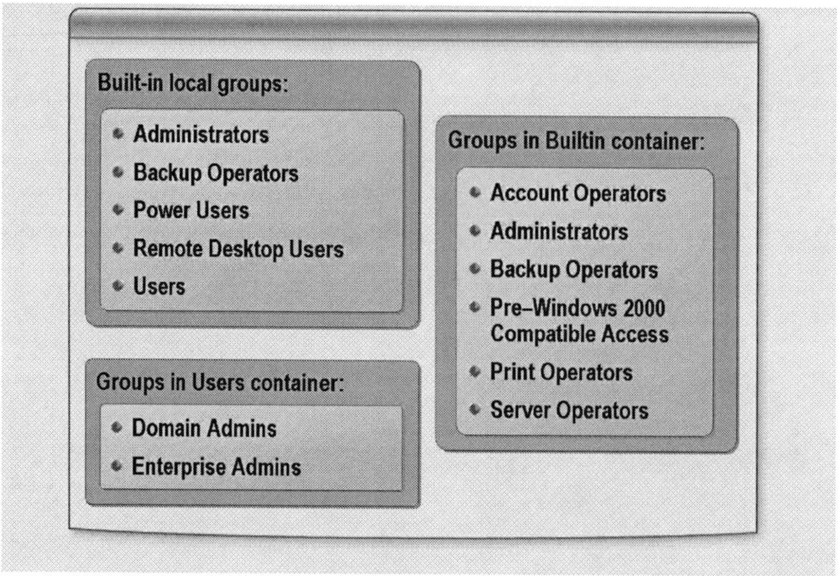

Built-in local groups:
Administrators
Backup Operators
Power Users
Remote Desktop Users
Users
Groups in Builtin container:
Account Operators
Administrators
Backup Operators
Pre–Windows 2000 Compatible Access
Print Operators
Server Operators
Groups in Users container:
Domain Admins
Enterprise Admins

Introduction

By default, Windows Server 2003 assigns certain rights to built-in groups. The built-in groups include local groups, groups in the Builtin container, and groups in the Users container.

Built-in groups and user rights

Use built-in groups to assign rights to users when possible. However, if the built-in group assigns too many rights, you should create a security group for the task and directly assign user rights to that group. For example, if you want to allow users only to back up files and directories, but not to be able to restore them, create a security group and assign it the right to back up files and directories rather than use the Backup Operators built-in group. The Backup Operators group has the right to back up and restore files and directories.

User rights assigned to local groups

Specific user rights are assigned to the following local groups:

- *Administrators*. This group has full rights to the computers in the domain, including the following rights:
  - Access this computer from the network; Adjust memory quotas for a process; Allow log on locally; Allow log on through Terminal Services; Back up files and directories; Bypass traverse checking; Change the system time; Create a pagefile; Debug programs; Force shutdown from a remote system; Increase scheduling priority; Load and unload device drivers; Manage auditing and security log.
- *Backup Operators*. This group has the following rights:
  - Access this computer from the network; Allow log on locally; Back up files and directories; Bypass traverse checking; Restore files and directories; Shut down the system.

- *Power Users*. This group has the following rights:
  - Access this computer from the network; Allow log on locally; Bypass traverse checking; Change the system time; Profile single process; Remove computer from docking station; Shut down the system.
- *Remote Desktop Users*. This group has the following right:
  - Allow log on through Terminal Services.
- *Users*. This group has the following rights:
  - Access this computer from the network; Allow log on locally; Bypass traverse checking.

User rights assigned to groups in the Builtin container

Specific user rights are assigned to groups in the Builtin container:

- *Account Operators*. This group has the following rights:
  - Allow log on locally; Shut down the system.
- *Administrators*. This group has full rights to the computers in the domain, including the following rights:
  - Access this computer from the network; Adjust memory quotas for a process; Allow log on locally; Back up files and directories; Bypass traverse checking; Change the system time; Create a pagefile; Debug programs; Enable computer and user accounts to be trusted for delegation; Force a shutdown from a remote system; Increase scheduling priority; Load and unload device drivers; Manage auditing and security log.
- *Backup Operators*. This group has the following rights:
  - Allow log on locally; Back up files and directories; Restore files and directories; Shut down the system.
- *Pre-Windows 2000 Compatible Access*. This group has the following rights:
  - Access this computer from the network; Bypass traverse checking.
- *Print Operators*. This group has the following rights:

  Allow log on locally; Shut down the system.
- *Server Operators*. This group has the following rights:
  - Allow log on locally; Back up files and directories; Change the system time; Force shutdown from a remote system; Restore files and directories; Shut down the system.

User rights assigned to groups in the Users container

Specific user rights are assigned to groups in the Users container:

- *Domain Admins*. This group has full rights to the computers and other objects in the domain, including the following rights:
  - Access this computer from the network; Adjust memory quotas for a process; Allow log on locally; Back up files and directories; Bypass traverse checking; Change the system time; Create a pagefile; Debug programs; Enable computer and user accounts to be trusted for delegation; Force a shutdown from a remote system; Increase scheduling priority; Load and unload device drivers; Manage auditing and security log.
- *Enterprise Admins*. (Appears only in the forest root domain.) This group has full rights to the computers and other objects in the domain, including the following rights:
  - Access this computer from the network; Adjust memory quotas for a process; Allow log on locally; Back up files and directories; Bypass traverse checking; Change the system time; Create a pagefile; Debug programs; Enable computer and user accounts to be trusted for delegation; Force shutdown from a remote system; Increase scheduling priority; Load and unload device drivers; Manage auditing and security log.

Note The **Properties** dialog box of the user right does not display the users or groups who are assigned the user right by default. You can view this information and an explanation of the function of the user right by clicking Help on the user right shortcut menu.

Additional reading

For more information about user rights and upgrading operating systems, see article 323042, "Required User Rights for the Upgrade from Windows 2000 to Windows Server 2003," in the Microsoft Knowledge Base at the Microsoft Help and Support Web site.

For more information about user rights and service accounts, see article 325349, "HOW TO: Grant Users Rights to Manage Services in Windows Server 2003," in the Microsoft Knowledge Base at the Microsoft Help and Support Web site.

Practice: Assigning User Rights

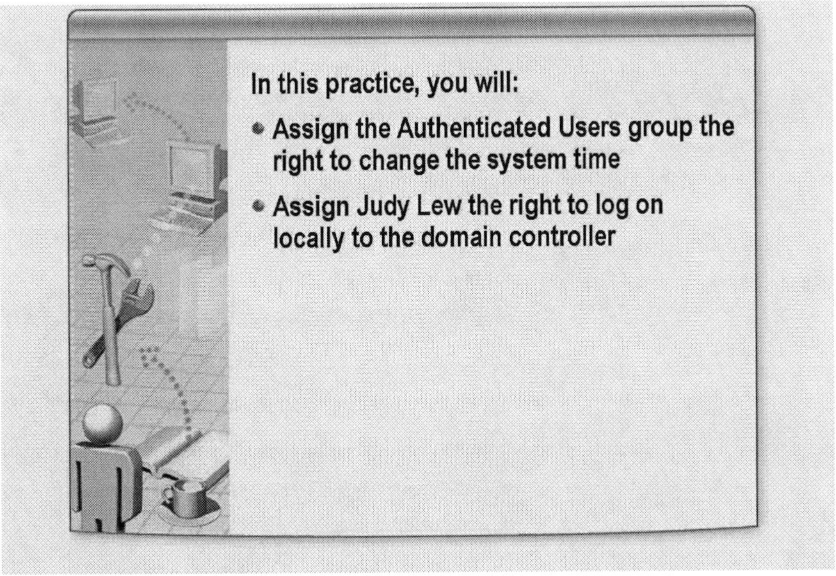

Objectives

In this practice, you will:

- Assign the Authenticated Users group the right to change the system time.
- Assign Judy Lew the right to log on locally to the domain controller.

Instructions

Ensure that the DEN-DC1 and the DEN-CL1 virtual machines are running.

Practice

► **Assign the Authenticated Users group the right to change the system time**

1. Log on to DEN-CL1 as **Don** with the password of **Pa$$w0rd**.
2. Double-click the clock on the taskbar to attempt to change the system time.
3. Read the error message, and then click **OK**.
4. Log on to DEN-DC1 as **Administrator** with the password of **Pa$$w0rd**.
5. Click **Start**, point to **Administrative Tools**, and click **Domain Security Policy**.
6. Navigate to **Security Settings/Local Policies/User Rights Assignment/ Change the system time**, and then right-click and click **Properties**.
7. In the **Change the system time Properties** dialog box, select the **Define these policy settings** check box.
8. Click **Add User or Group**, and then type **Authenticated Users** in the **User and group names** field.
9. Click **OK** twice, and then close the **Default Domain Security Settings** console.
10. Log off of DEN-DC1.

11. Switch to DEN-CL1, and at the **Run** command, type **gpupdate /force**. Click **OK** and then log off DEN-CL1.
12. Log on to DEN-CL1 as **Don**.
13. Double-click the clock on the taskbar to attempt to change the system time. Verify that the **Date and Time Properties** dialog box appears.

Note It may take two logons for the new setting to take effect.

14. Close all programs, and then log off from DEN-CL1.

► **Assign Judy Lew the right to log on locally to the domain controller**

1. Attempt to log on to DEN-DC1 as **Judy** with the password of **Pa$$w0rd**.
2. Read the logon message, and then click **OK**.
3. Log on to DEN-DC1 as **Administrator**.
4. Click **Start**, point to **Administrative Tools**, and then click **Domain Controller Security Policy**.
5. Navigate to **Security Settings/Local Policies/User Rights Assignment/ Allow log on locally**, and then right-click and click **Properties**.
6. Notice the default list of groups that have the right to log on to the domain controller.
7. Click **Add User or Group**, and then type **Contoso\Judy** in the **User and group names** field.
8. Click **OK** twice.
9. To refresh the security settings click **Start**, click **Run**, type **gpupdate /force** and then click **OK**,
10. Log off from DEN-DC1.
11. Attempt to log on to DEN-DC1 as **Judy** with the password of **Pa$$w0rd**. The logon should succeed.
12. Log off DEN-DC1.

Lesson: Using Security Templates to Secure Computers

- What Is a Security Policy?
- What Are Security Templates?
- What Are Security Template Settings?
- Windows Server 2003 Security Guide Templates
- Windows XP Security Guide Templates
- Ways to Deploy Security Templates
- Practice: Using Security Templates to Secure Computers

Introduction

You create security templates to create a security policy and alter a security policy to meet the security needs of your company. You can implement security policies in several different ways. The method you use depends on your organization's size and security needs. Smaller organizations, or those not using Active Directory, can configure security manually on an individual basis. If your organization is large or requires a high level of security, consider using Group Policy objects (GPOs) to deploy security policy.

Lesson objectives

After completing this lesson, you will be able to:

- Describe a security policy.
- Describe security templates.
- Describe security template settings.
- Describe the security templates that are included in the Windows Server 2003 Security Guide.
- Describe the security templates that are included in the Microsoft Windows® XP Security Guide.
- Explain ways to deploy security templates.
- Use security template to secure computers.

What Is a Security Policy?

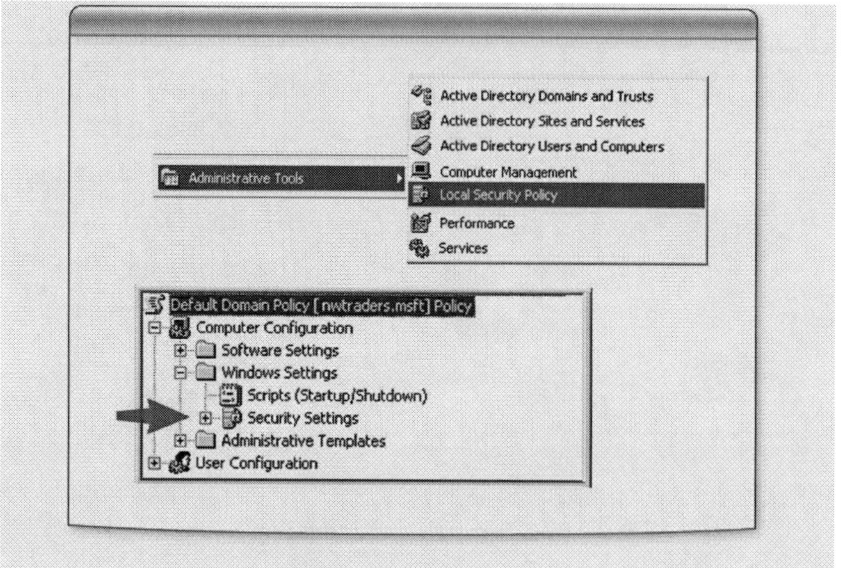

Definition

A security policy is a combination of security settings that affect the security on a computer. You can use a security policy to establish account policies and local policies on your local computer and in Active Directory.

Security policy on a local computer

With a local security policy, you can control:

- Account policies.
- Local policies.
- Public Key policy.
- Software Restriction policy.
- IP Security policies.

If your network does not use Active Directory, you can configure a security policy by using Local Security Policy, which is found on the **Administrative Tools** menu on computers running Windows Server 2003.

Security policies in Active Directory

Security policies in Active Directory have the same security settings as a security policy on local computers plus a number of extra settings to deal with domain configurations. However, administrators of Active Directory–based networks can save considerable administrative time by using Group Policy to deploy the security policy. You can edit or import security settings in a GPO for any site, domain, or organizational unit, and the security settings are automatically deployed to the computers when the computers start. When editing a GPO, expand **Computer Configuration** or **User Configuration** and then expand **Windows Settings** to find the security policy settings.

Additional reading

For more information about default domain user rights, see article 324800, "HOW TO: Reset User Rights in the Default Domain Group Policy in Windows Server 2003," in the Microsoft Knowledge Base at the Microsoft Help and Support Web site.

What Are Security Templates?

Template	Description
Setup security.inf	Default security settings
DC security.inf	Default security settings for a domain controller
Compatws.inf	Modifies permissions and registry settings for application compatibility
Securedc.inf and Securews.inf	Enhances security settings
Hisecdc.inf and Hisecws.inf	Increases the restrictions on security settings
Rootsec.inf	Specifies permissions for the root of the system drive
IESacls.inf	Configures auditing and permissions on registry keys of Internet Explorer

Definition

A security template is a collection of configured security settings. Windows Server 2003 provides predefined security templates that contain the recommended security settings for different situations.

You can use predefined security templates as a base to create security policies that are customized to meet different organizational requirements. You customize the templates with the Security Templates snap-in. After you customize the predefined security templates, you can use them to configure security on an individual computer or thousands of computers.

How security templates are applied

You can configure individual computers with the Security Configuration and Analysis snap-in or the **secedit** command-line tool or by importing the template into Local Security Policy. You can configure multiple computers by importing a template into Security Settings, which is an extension of Group Policy.

You can also use a security template as a baseline for analyzing a system for potential security holes or policy violations by using the Security Configuration and Analysis snap-in. By default, the predefined security templates are stored in *systemroot*/Security/Templates.

Predefined templates

Windows Server 2003 provides the following predefined templates:

- Default security (Setup security.inf)

  The Setup security.inf template is created during installation of the operating system for each computer and represents the default security settings that are applied during installation, including the file permissions for the root of the system drive. It can vary from computer to computer, based on whether the installation was a clean installation or an upgrade. You can use this template on servers and client computers, but not on domain controllers. You can apply portions of this template for disaster recovery.

  Default security settings are applied only to clean installations of Windows Server 2003 on an NTFS partition. When computers are upgraded from Microsoft Windows NT® version 4.0, security is not modified. Also, when you install Windows Server 2003 on a FAT (file allocation table) file system, security is not applied to the file system.

- Domain controller default security (DC security.inf)

  The DC security.inf template is created when a server is promoted to a domain controller. It reflects default security settings on files, registry keys, and system services. Reapplying the template resets these settings to the default values, but doing so might overwrite permissions on new files, registry keys, and system services created by other applications. You can apply the template by using the Security Configuration and Analysis snap-in or the **secedit** command-line tool.

- Compatible (Compatws.inf)

  Default permissions for workstations and servers are primarily granted to three local groups: Administrators, Power Users, and Users. Administrators have the most privileges, and Users have the least.

  Members of the Users group can successfully run applications that take part in the Windows Logo Program for Software. However, they might not be able to run applications that do not meet the requirements of the program. If other applications are to be supported, the Compatws.inf template changes the default file and registry permissions that are granted to the Users group. The new permissions are consistent with the requirements of most applications that do not belong to the Windows Logo Program for Software.

- Secure (Secure*.inf)

  The Secure templates define enhanced security settings that are least likely to affect application compatibility. For example, the Secure templates define stronger password, lockout, and audit settings.

- Highly Secure (hisec*.inf)

  The Highly Secure templates are supersets of the Secure templates. They impose further restrictions on the levels of encryption and signing that are required for authentication and for the data that flows over secure channels and between server message block (SMB) clients and servers.

- System root security (Rootsec.inf)

  By default, Rootsec.inf defines the permissions for the root of the system drive. You can use this template to reapply the root directory permissions if they are inadvertently changed, or you can modify the template to apply the same root permissions to other volumes. As specified, the template does not overwrite explicit permissions that are defined on child objects. It propagates only the permissions that are inherited by child objects.

- Internet Explorer Security (Iesacls.inf)

  Iesacls.inf is designed to establish auditing for registry keys that are associated with Microsoft Internet Explorer. The permissions are set on these keys to allow the Everyone group Full Control access to the keys. Auditing is configured to track when anyone attempts to modify the values of those keys.

Additional reading

For more information about applying security policies, see article 325351, "HOW TO: Apply Local Policies to All Users Except Administrators on Windows Server 2003 in a Workgroup Setting," in the Microsoft Knowledge Base at the Microsoft Help and Support Web site.

For more information about **secedit**, see "Secedit" at the Microsoft TechNet Web site.

What Are Security Template Settings?

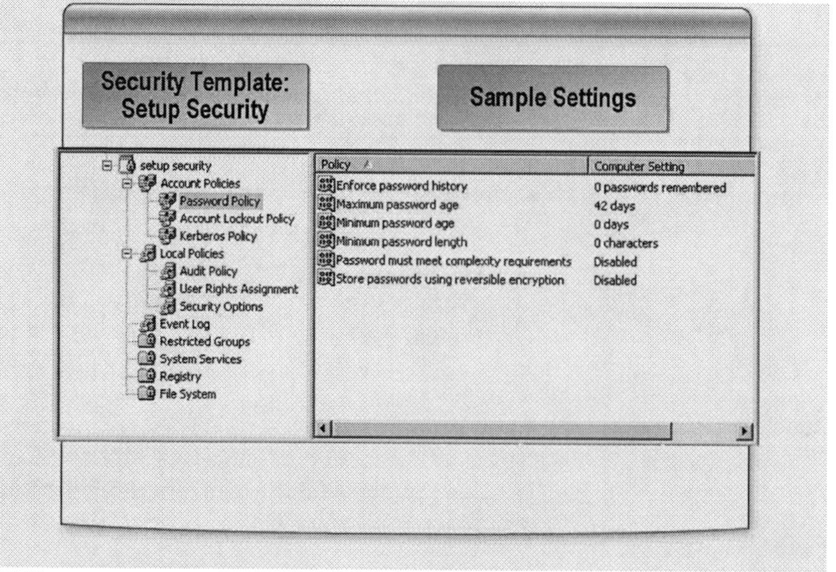

Introduction

Security templates contain security settings for all security areas. You can apply templates to individual computers or deploy them to groups of computers by using Group Policy. When you apply a template to existing security settings, the settings in the template are merged into the computer's security settings.

You can configure and analyze security settings for computers by using the Security Settings Group Policy extension or Security Configuration and Analysis.

Types of security template settings

The following list describes each of the security template settings:

- Account Policies

  You can use account policy settings to configure password policies, account lockout policies, and Kerberos version 5 (V5) protocol policies for the domain. A domain's account policy defines the password history, the lifetime of the Kerberos V5 tickets, account lockouts, and more.

- Local Policies

  Local policy settings, by definition, are local to computers. Local policies include audit policies, the assignment of user rights and permissions, and various security options that can be configured locally.

  It is important not to confuse local policy settings with setting policies locally. As with all of these security settings, you can configure these settings by using Local Security Policy and Group Policy.

- Event Log

  You use event log settings to configure the size, access, and retention parameters for application logs, system logs, and security logs.

- Restricted Groups

  You use restricted group settings to manage the membership of built-in groups that have certain predefined capabilities, such as Administrators and Power Users, in addition to domain groups, such as Domain Admins. You can add other groups to the restricted group, along with their membership information. This enables you to track and manage these groups as part of security policy.

  You can also use restricted group settings to track and control the reverse membership of each restricted group. Reverse membership is listed in the **Members Of** column, which displays other groups to which the restricted group must belong.

- System Services

  You use system services settings to configure security and startup settings for services running on a computer. System services settings include critical functionality, such as network services, file and print services, telephony and fax services, and Internet or intranet services. The general settings include the service startup mode (automatic, manual, or disabled) and security on the service.

- Registry

  You use registry settings to configure security on registry keys.

- File System

  You use file system settings to configure security on specific file paths.

Important When you use the Local Security Policy tool to edit the policies of a member server, only the Account Policies, Local Policies, Public Key Policies, Software Restriction Policies, and IP Security Policies on Active Directory areas are available.

Also, you can assign password settings, account lockout settings, and Kerberos settings at the domain or organizational unit level. However, if you configure the policy at the organizational unit level, the settings affect only the local Security Accounts Manager (SAM) databases of computer objects in the organizational unit, not the domain password policies. Windows Server 2003 does not process any changes that you make to these three settings in a GPO at the site level.

Additional reading

For more information about security template best practices, see the TechNet article “Best practices for Security Templates” at the Microsoft TechNet Web site.

Windows Server 2003 Security Guide Templates

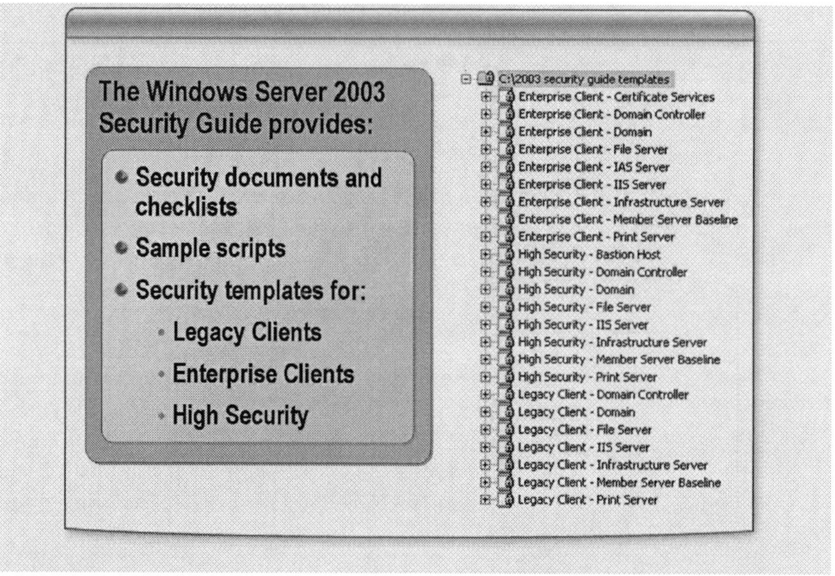

Introduction

The Windows Server 2003 Security Guide provides a set of documents, tools, and templates to help secure Windows Server 2003 in many environments. While Windows Server 2003 is secure after a default installation, there are a number of security options that you can configure based on specific requirements. The material in the Windows Server 2003 Security Guide explains the different requirements to secure three distinct environments. The three environments considered are named Legacy Client, Enterprise Client, and High Security.

Legacy Client settings

The Legacy Client settings are designed to work in an Active Directory domain running on Windows Server 2003 domain controllers with client computers and member servers running Microsoft Windows 98, Windows NT 4.0, and later.

Enterprise Client settings

The Enterprise Client settings are designed to work in an Active Directory domain running on Windows Server 2003 domain controllers with client computers and member servers running Microsoft Windows 2000, Windows XP, and later.

High Security environment

The High Security settings are also designed to work in an Active Directory domain running on Windows Server 2003 domain controllers with client computers and member servers running Windows 2000, Windows XP, and later. However, the High Security settings are so restrictive that many applications might not function, performance of the servers might be noticeably slower, and managing the servers will be more challenging.

Note The Windows Server 2003 Security Guide is included on the Student Materials compact disc and is also available at the Microsoft Download Center Web site.

Windows XP Security Guide Templates

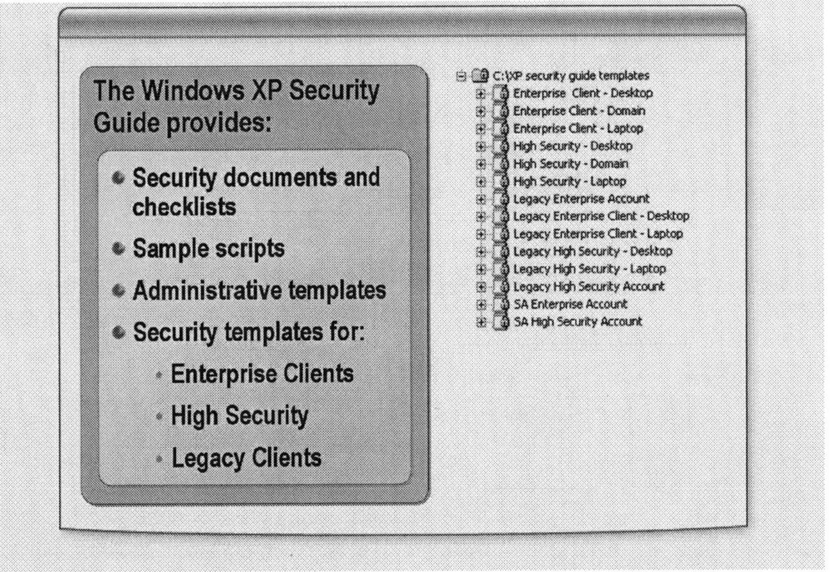

Introduction

The Windows XP Security Guide v2.0 describes the features and recommended settings for Microsoft Windows XP Service Pack 2 (SP2).

New templates

The guide includes tested templates for security settings on these elements and much more:

- Windows Firewall, which replaces Internet Connection Firewall (ICF)
- Remote procedure call (RPC) communications
- Memory protection
- E-mail handling
- Web download controls
- Spyware controls

Administrative templates

The Windows XP Security Guide version 2.0 includes administrative templates that control the settings of Microsoft Office 2003 products. You can configure all options of the Tools menu of any of the Microsoft Office 2003 products through Group Policy by importing the administrative templates into a GPO and modifying the settings. For example, the macro security settings or default file locations can be enforced by adding these administrative templates to a Group Policy. The templates need to be added to each GPO where they need to be applied.

Types of security templates

Enterprise Clients. The enterprise environment consists of a Windows 2000 or Windows Server 2003 Microsoft Active Directory domain. The clients in this environment will be managed using Group Policy that is applied to containers, sites, domains, and organizational units. Group Policy provides a centralized method to manage security policy across the environment.

High Security. The high-security environment consists of elevated security settings for the client. When applying high-security settings, user functionality is limited to specific functions that are required only for the necessary tasks. Access is limited to approved applications, services, and infrastructure environments.

Caution The High Security templates were designed for high-security environments. The High Security templates provide maximum security without regard for functionality of applications. These templates should be fully tested before being deployed.

Legacy Clients. The stand-alone environment consists of those organizations that have some computers that cannot be joined to a domain or computers that are members of a Windows NT 4.0 domain. These clients have to be configured using Local Policy settings. The management of stand-alone machines can be considerably more challenging than using an Active Directory–based domain for management of user accounts and policies.

Note The Windows XP Security Guide is included on the Student Materials compact disc and is also available at the Microsoft Download Center Web site.

Ways to Deploy Security Templates

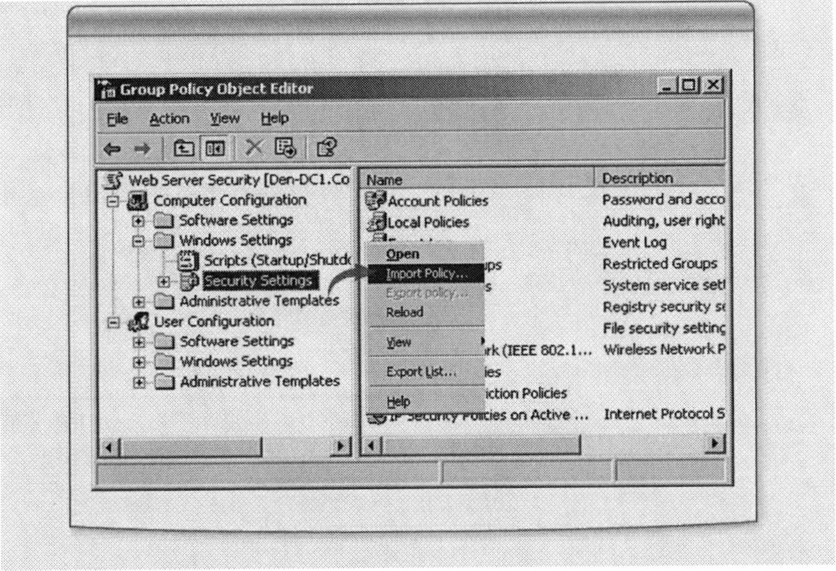

Introduction

In a domain environment, the most efficient way to provide consistent security settings to large numbers of computers is to use a GPO. You can configure templates based on the roles of computers in the organization and import them into GPOs. For example, you can develop a custom template and import it into the GPO used to configure all the organization's Web servers.

In a stand-alone environment, there is no central authority to deliver security settings. You must configure security on an individual basis. Templates become even more valuable in this situation. By configuring a group of templates for computers based on their role, you can provide consistent security settings to those computers. As security needs change, you only need to change the template and reapply it to the computers to get the desired results.

Deploying security templates to GPOs

You can import custom security templates into the security settings section of any GPO. Then you can configure security settings for all the computer accounts in the organizational unit by linking it to the GPO. This requires that your organizational unit structure places computer accounts in organizational units based on their role in the organization. For example, you might have an organizational unit that contains all of your computers running Microsoft SQL Server™. When a new computer running SQL Server is brought on to the network and its computer account is placed in the SQL organizational unit, the security will be automatically configured based on the GPO that is linked to the organizational unit.

Deploying security templates to stand-alone computers

You can import a custom template directly into a stand-alone computer's security settings. By developing custom templates for different computer roles, you can provide consistent security for computers that are not members of your domain. For example, you can create a custom template that will configure identical security settings for all your Microsoft Internet Security and Acceleration (ISA) servers that are stand-alone computers on your perimeter network.

The Security Configuration Wizard

The Security Configuration Wizard (SCW) is an attack-surface reduction tool for members of the Microsoft Windows Server 2003 family with Service Pack 1 (SP1). SCW determines the minimum functionality that is required for a server's role or roles and disables functionality that is not required. SCW guides you through the process of creating, editing, applying, or rolling back a security policy based on the selected roles of the server. The security policies that you create by using SCW are XML files that, when applied, configure services, network security, specific registry values, audit policy, and if applicable, Internet Information Services (IIS). SCW is an optional component included with Windows Server 2003 SP1.You can install and run SCW only on computers running a member of the Windows Server 2003 family with SP1. The computers that you target with SCW must run a member of the Windows Server 2003 family with SP1. SCW is not used with Microsoft Windows Small Business Server 2003.

Note For more information about the Security Configuration Wizard, see Microsoft Course 2275, *Maintaining a Microsoft Windows Server 2003 Environment*.

Practice: Using Security Templates to Secure Computers

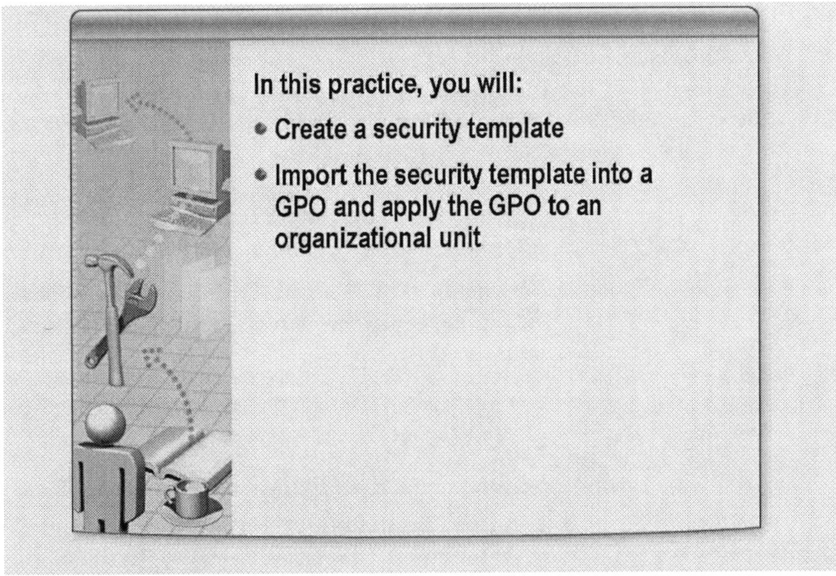
In this practice, you will:
Create a security template
Import the security template into a GPO and apply the GPO to an organizational unit

Objectives

In this practice, you will:

- Create a security template.
- Import the security template into a GPO and apply the GPO to an organizational unit.

Instructions

Ensure that the DEN-DC1 and the DEN-CL1 virtual machines are running.

Practice

► **Create a security template**

1. Log on to DEN-DC1 as **Administrator.**
2. Create a custom Microsoft Management Console (MMC), and then add the Security Templates snap-in.
3. Expand Security Templates, in the console tree, right-click **C:\WINDOWS\security\templates**, and then click **New Template.**
4. In the **C:\WINDOWS\security\templates** dialog box, in the **Template Name** box, type **SecureXP**, and then click **OK.**
5. In the Security Templates MMC, expand **SecureXP**, **Local Policies**, and **Security Options**, and then double-click **Accounts: Rename administrator account.**
6. Select the **Define this policy setting in the template** check box, type **XPAdmin** in the field, and then click **OK.**
7. Double-click **Interactive logon: Do not display last user name.**
8. Select the **Define this policy setting in the template** check box, click **Enabled**, and then click **OK.**
9. Right-click **File System**, and then click **Add File.**
10. Select **C:\Program Files** in the **Add a file or folder** dialog box, and then click **OK.**

11. Click **Add** in the **Database Security for %ProgramFiles%** dialog box, add the **DL Sales Modify** group, and then click **OK.**
12. Assign **Modify** permission to the **DL Sales Modify** group, and then click **OK.**
13. In the **Add Object** dialog box, take note of the settings, and then click **OK** to accept the defaults.
14. Close and save the Security Templates MMC as **Security Templates.**
15. Click **Yes** in the **Save Security Templates** dialog box to save the SecureXP template to the default location.

► **Import the security template into a GPO and apply the GPO to an organizational unit**

1. Open **Group Policy Management** and then create and link a GPO named **XP Security** to the **Sales** organizational unit.
2. Right-click and edit the **XP Security** policy.
3. In the **Group Policy Object Editor**, expand **Computer Configuration, Windows Settings**, and **Security Settings.**
4. Right-click **Security Settings**, and then click **Import Policy.**
5. In the **Import Policy From** dialog box, click **Secure XP.inf**, and then click **Open.**
6. Close the **Group Policy Object Editor** and **Group Policy Management.**
7. Open **Active Directory Users and Computers**, and move **DEN-CL1** from the **Computers** container to the **Sales** organizational unit.
8. Close **Active Directory User and Computers** and then log off of DEN-DC1.
9. Log on to DEN-CL1 as **Administrator.**
10. Click **Start**, click **Shutdown**, and then click **Restart.** Do not shut down the virtual machine.
11. Log on to DEN-CL1 as **Administrator.**
12. Open **Computer Management**, expand **Local Users and Groups** and then click **Users.**

    What is the name of the built-in administrator account?

    XP ADMIN
    ____

13. Close all open windows, and then log off.

Important Do not shut down the virtual machines.

Lesson: Testing Computer Security Policy

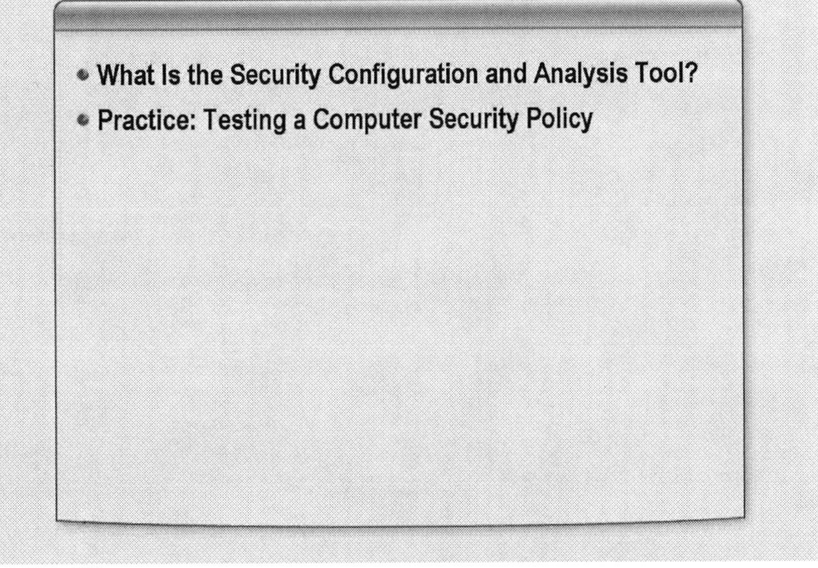

What Is the Security Configuration and Analysis Tool?
Practice: Testing a Computer Security Policy

Introduction

Before you deploy a security template to large groups of computers, it is important to analyze the results of applying a configuration to ensure that there are no adverse effects on applications, connectivity, or security. A thorough analysis also helps you to identify security holes and deviations from standard configurations. You can use the Security Configuration and Analysis snap-in to create and review possible scenarios and adjust a configuration.

Lesson objectives

After completing this lesson, you will be able to:

- Describe the Security Configuration and Analysis tool.
- Test computer security by using the Security Configuration and Analysis tool.

What Is the Security Configuration and Analysis Tool?

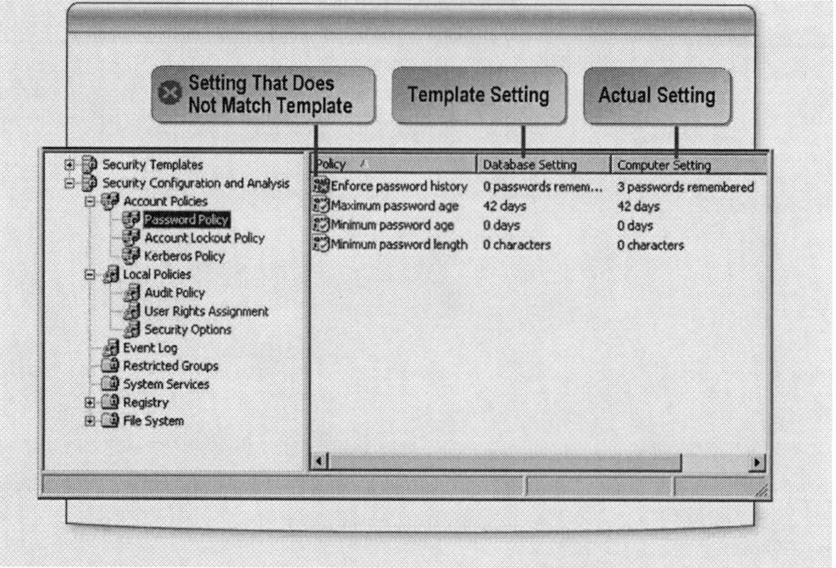

Introduction

The most common tool that you can use to analyze computer security is the Security Configuration and Analysis tool.

Security Configuration and Analysis tool

The Security Configuration and Analysis tool compares the security configuration of the local computer to an alternative configuration that is imported from a template (an .inf file) and stored in a separate database (an .sdb file). When analysis is complete, you can browse the security settings in the console tree to see the results. Discrepancies are marked with a red flag. Consistencies are marked with a green check mark. Settings that are not marked with either a red flag or a green check mark are not configured in the database.

Why use the Security Configuration and Analysis tool?

After analyzing the results by using the Security Configuration and Analysis tool, you can perform various tasks, including:

- Eliminating discrepancies by configuring the settings in the database to match the current computer settings. To configure database settings, double-click the setting in the Details pane.
- Importing another template file, merging its settings, and overwriting settings where there is a conflict. To import another template file, right-click **Security Configuration and Analysis**, and then click **Import Template**.
- Exporting the current database settings to a template file. To export another template file, right-click **Security Configuration and Analysis**, and then click **Export Template**.

- Configuring a computer's security settings with the settings in the template. To configure the computer to match the template settings, right-click **Security Configuration and Analysis**, and then click **Configure Computer Now**. You should use **Configure Computer Now** only to modify security areas *not* affected by Group Policy settings, such as security on local files and folders, registry keys, and system services. Otherwise, when the Group Policy settings are applied, the Group Policy settings from the domain controller will take precedence over local settings. In general, do not use **Configure Computer Now** when you are analyzing security for domain-based clients, since you will have to configure each client individually. In this case, you should return to **Security Templates**, modify the template, and reapply it to the appropriate GPO.

Note You can also use the **secedit** command-line utility to analyze computer security settings. By using the **secedit** tool in a batch file or an automatic task scheduler, you can automatically create and apply templates and analyze system security. You can also run the **secedit** tool dynamically from a command prompt window. The **secedit** tool is useful when you have multiple computers on which you must analyze or configure security and must perform these tasks during off-hours.

Additional reading

For more information about the security tools, see "Security Configuration Manager" and "Best Practices for Security Configuration and Analysis" on the Microsoft TechNet Web site.

Practice: Testing a Computer Security Policy

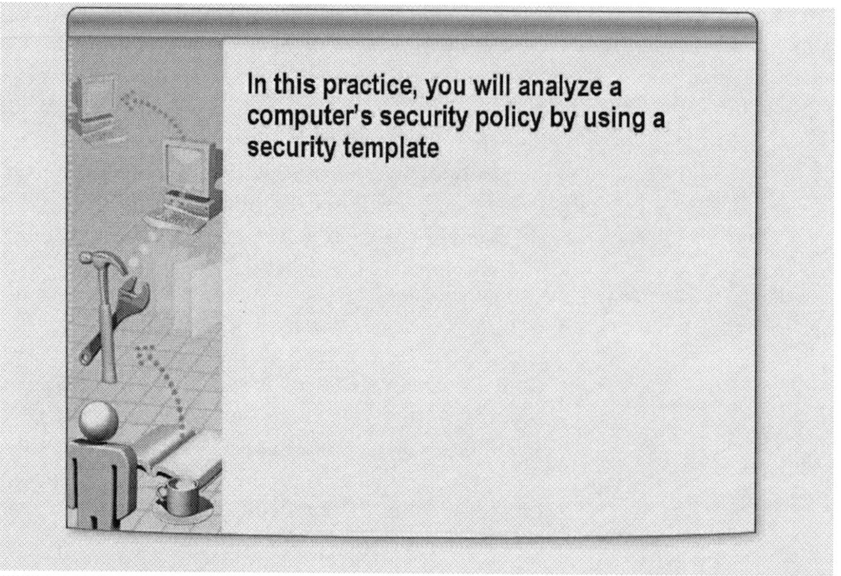
In this practice, you will analyze a computer's security policy by using a security template

Objective

In this practice, you will:

- Analyze a computer's security policy by using a security template.

Instructions

Ensure that the DEN-DC1 and the DEN-CL1 virtual machines are running.

Practice

► **Analyze a computer's security policy by using a security template**

1. Log on to DEN-CL1 as **Administrator**.
2. Create an MMC, and then add the **Security Configuration and Analysis** snap-in.
3. In the console tree, right-click **Security Configuration and Analysis**, and then click **Open Database**.
4. In the **Open Database** dialog box, type **Enterprise Client** in the **File name** field, and then click **Open**.
5. In the **Import Template** dialog box, in the **Look in** field, browse the network to **\\Den-DC1\Admin_Tools\XP security templates**, select **Enterprise Client – Desktop.inf**, and then click **Open**.
6. In the console tree, right-click **Security Configuration and Analysis**, and then click **Analyze Computer Now**.
7. In the **Perform Analysis** dialog box, click **OK** to accept the default path for the log file.

8. When the analysis is complete, expand **Local Polices** and click **Security Options**.

   What are the **Database** and **Computer** settings for **Renaming the administrator account**?

   NOT ANALYZED AND XPADMIN

   Do the Database and Computer settings for **Interactive logon: Do not display last user name** agree?

   YES, BOTH SAY ENABLED

9. Click **File System, C:**.

   What are the **Database** and **Computer** settings for the **Program Files** directory?

   NOT ANALYZED

10. Close all open windows and log off of **DEN-CL1**.

► **To prepare for the next practice**

- Start DEN-SRV1 to prepare for the next practice.

Note Do not shut down the virtual machines.

Lesson: Configuring Auditing

- What Is Auditing?
- What Is an Audit Policy?
- Types of Events to Audit
- Guidelines for Planning an Audit Policy
- Practice: Configuring Auditing
- Best Practices for Configuring Auditing

Introduction

No security strategy is complete without a comprehensive auditing strategy. More often than not, organizations learn this only after they experience a security incident. Without an audit trail of actions, it is almost impossible to successfully investigate a security incident. You must determine as part of your overall security strategy what events you need to audit, the level of auditing appropriate for your environment, how the audited events are collected, and how they are reviewed.

Lesson objectives

After completing this lesson, you will be able to:

- Describe auditing.
- Describe what an audit policy is.
- Describe types of events to audit.
- Identify the guidelines for planning an audit policy.
- Configure auditing.
- Apply best practices while configuring auditing.

What Is Auditing?

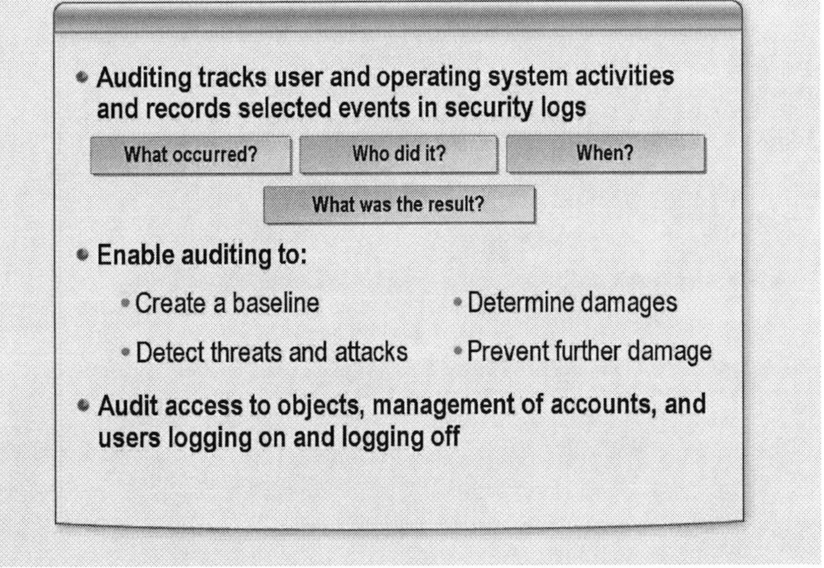

Auditing tracks user and operating system activities and records selected events in security logs
What occurred?
Who did it?
When?
What was the result?
Enable auditing to:
Create a baseline
Determine damages
Detect threats and attacks
Prevent further damage
Audit access to objects, management of accounts, and users logging on and logging off

Definition

Auditing is the process that tracks user and operating system activities by recording selected types of events in the security log of a server or a workstation. Security logs contain various audit entries, which contain the following information:

- The action that was performed
- The user who performed the action
- The success or failure of the event and when the event occurred
- Additional information, such as the computer where the event occurred

Why perform auditing?

Enable auditing and monitor audit logs to:

- Create a baseline of normal network and computer operations.
- Detect attempts to penetrate the network or computer.
- Determine what systems and data have been compromised during or after a security incident.
- Prevent further damage to networks or computers after an attacker has penetrated the network.

The security needs of an organization help determine the amount of auditing that is used. For example, a minimum-security network might choose to audit failed logon attempts to monitor against potential brute-force attacks. A high-security network might choose to audit both successful and failed logon attempts to track any unauthorized users who successfully gain access to the network.

Although auditing might provide valuable information, excessive auditing fills the audit log with unnecessary information. This can potentially affect the performance of your system and make it extremely difficult to find relevant information.

Types of events to audit

The most common types of events to audit are when:

- Objects, such as files and folders, are accessed.
- Managing user accounts and group accounts.
- Users log on to and log off the system.

Additional reading

For more information about auditing, see the TechNet article "Auditing overview" at the Microsoft TechNet Web site.

What Is an Audit Policy?

- An audit policy determines the security events that will be reported to the network administrator
- Set up an audit policy to:
  - Track success or failure of events
  - Minimize unauthorized use of resources
  - Maintain a record of activity
- Security events are stored in security logs

Introduction

Establishing an audit policy is an important part of security. Monitoring the creation or modification of objects gives you a way to track potential security problems, helps to ensure user accountability, and provides evidence in the event of a security breach.

Definition

An audit policy defines the types of security events that computers running Windows Server 2003 record in the security log on each computer. Windows Server 2003 writes events to the security log on the specific computer where the event occurs.

Why set up an audit policy?

Set up an audit policy for a computer to:

- Track the success and failure of events, such as attempts to log on, attempts by a particular user to read a specific file, changes to a user account or group membership, and changes to security settings.
- Minimize the risk of unauthorized use of resources.
- Maintain a record of user and administrator activity.

Use Event Viewer to view events that Windows Server 2003 records in the security log. You can also archive log files to track trends over time. This is useful to determine trends in the use of printers, access to files, and attempts at unauthorized use of resources.

How can you implement an audit policy?

You can set up an audit policy on any single computer, either directly by using the Local Policy snap-in or indirectly by using Group Policy, which is more commonly used in large organizations. After an audit policy is designed and implemented, information begins to appear in the security logs. Each computer in the organization has a separate security log that records local events.

When you implement an audit policy:

- Specify the categories of events that you want to audit. Examples of event categories are user logon, user logoff, and account management. The event categories that you specify constitute your audit policy.
- Set the size and settings of the security log. You can view the security log by using Event Viewer.
- Determine which objects you want to monitor access to and what type of access you want to monitor and whether you want to audit directory service access or object access. For example, if you want to audit attempts by users to open a particular file, you can configure audit policy settings in the object access event category so that successful and failed attempts to read a file are recorded.

Default audit policies

The default auditing settings for servers are configured by administrative templates. The following security templates configure default auditing settings:

- Setup security.inf
- Hisecdc.inf
- Hisecws.inf
- Securedc.inf
- Securews.inf

To view the policy settings that each security template configures, in the Security Templates snap-in, navigate to **Local Policies\Audit Policy** for each administrative template.

Additional reading

For more information about audit policies, see the TechNet article "Auditing policy" at the Microsoft TechNet Web site.

Types of Events to Audit

- Account Logon
- Account Management
- Directory Service Access
- Logon
- Object Access
- Policy Change
- Privilege Use
- Process Tracking
- System

Introduction

The first step in creating a strategy for auditing the operating system is to determine what type of actions or operations that you need to record.

Determining what events to audit

What operating system events should you audit? You do not want to audit every event, because auditing all operating system events requires enormous system resources and might negatively affect system performance. You should work with other security specialists to determine what operating system events to audit. Only audit events that you believe will be useful for later reference.

An effective way to begin determining what events to audit is to gather the relevant group of people and discuss the following issues:

- What actions or operations you want to track
- On what systems you want to track these events

For example, you might decide to track:

- All domain and local logon events on all computers.
- The use of all files in the Payroll folder on the HR server.

The success and failure events

In Windows Server 2003, audit events can be split into two categories:

- Success events

  A success event indicates that the operating system has successfully completed the action or operation. Success events are indicated by a key icon.

- Failure events

  A failure event indicates that an action or operation was attempted but did not succeed. Failure events are indicated by a padlock icon.

Failure events are very useful for tracking attempted attacks on your environment, but success events are much more difficult to interpret. The vast majority of success events are indications of normal activity, and an attacker who accesses a system also generates a success event.

Often, a pattern of events is as important as the events themselves. For example, a series of failures followed by a success might indicate an attempted attack that was eventually successful.

Similarly, the deviation from a pattern might also indicate suspicious activity. For example, suppose that the security logs show that a user at your organization logs on every workday between 8 A.M. and 10 A.M., but suddenly the user is logging on to the network at 3 A.M. Although this behavior might be innocent, it should be investigated.

Events that Windows Server 2003 can audit

The first step in implementing an audit policy is to select the types of events that you want Windows Server 2003 to audit. The following table describes the events that Windows Server 2003 can audit.

Event	Example
Account Logon	An account is authenticated by a security database. When a user logs on to the local computer, the computer records the Account Logon event. When a user logs on to a domain, the authenticating domain controller records the Account Logon event.
Account Management	An administrator creates, changes, or deletes a user account or group; a user account is renamed, disabled, or enabled; or a password is set or changed.
Directory Service Access	A user accesses an Active Directory object. To log this type of access, you must configure specific Active Directory objects for auditing.
Logon	A user logs on to or off a local computer, or a user makes or cancels a network connection to the computer. The event is recorded on the computer that the user accesses, regardless of whether a local account or a domain account is used.
Object Access	A user accesses a file, folder, or printer. The administrator must configure specific files, folders, or printers to be audited, the users or groups that are being audited, and the actions that they will be audited for.
Policy Change	A change is made to the user security options (for example, password options or account logon settings), user rights, or audit policies.
Privilege Use	A user exercises a user right, such as changing the system time (this does not include rights that are related to logging on and logging off) or taking ownership of a file.
Process Tracking	An application performs an action. This information is generally useful only for programmers who want to track details about application execution.
System	A user restarts or shuts down the computer, or an event occurs that affects Windows Server 2003 security or the security log.

Events edited by default

The Setup security.inf template includes default settings that enable auditing of successful account logon events and successful logon events. No other events are audited by default.

Guidelines for Planning an Audit Policy

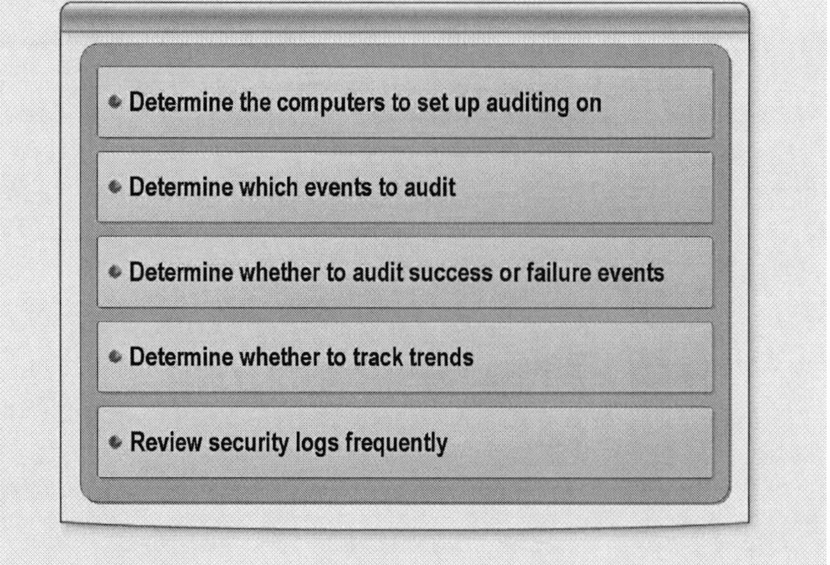
Determine the computers to set up auditing on
Determine which events to audit
Determine whether to audit success or failure events
Determine whether to track trends
Review security logs frequently

Introduction

Auditing too many types of events can create excess overhead, which might result in diminished system performance.

Guidelines

Use the following guidelines when planning an audit policy:

- Determine the computers to set up auditing on. Plan what to audit for each computer, because Windows Server 2003 audits events on each computer separately. For example, you might frequently audit computers used to store sensitive or critical data, but you might infrequently audit client computers that are used solely for running productivity applications.
- Determine the types of events to audit, such as the following:
  - Access to files and folders
  - Users logging on and off
  - Shutting down and restarting a computer running Windows Server 2003
  - Changes to user accounts and groups
- Determine whether to audit success or failure events, or both. Tracking success events can tell you how often Windows Server 2003 or users access specific files or printers. You can use this information for resource planning. Tracking failure events can alert you to possible security breaches.
- Determine whether you need to track trends of system usage. If so, plan to archive event logs. Some organizations are required to maintain a record of resource and data access. For example, a legal firm might need to track who accesses documents.
- Review security logs frequently and regularly according to a schedule. Configuring auditing alone does not alert you to security breaches.

Practice: Configuring Auditing

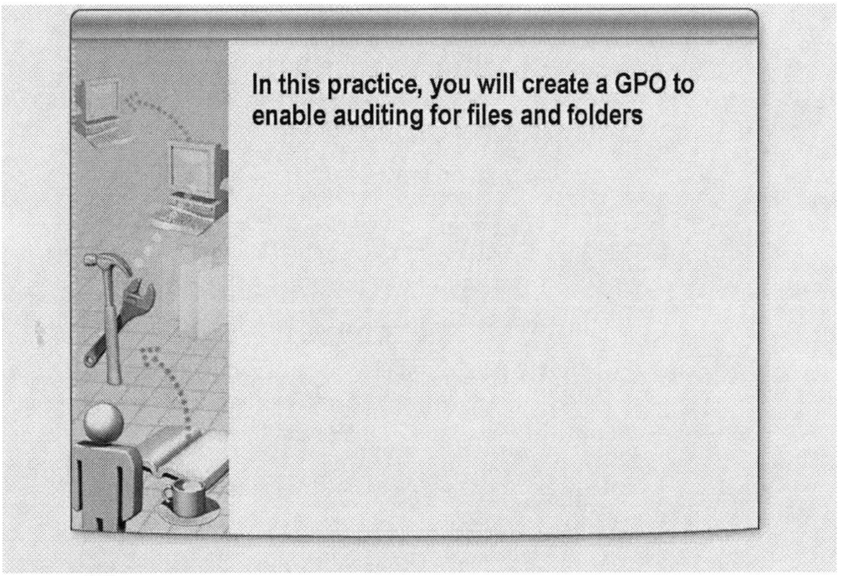
In this practice, you will create a GPO to enable auditing for files and folders

Objective

In this practice, you will:

- Create a GPO to enable auditing for files and folders.

Instructions

Ensure that the DEN-DC1, DEN-SRV1 and the DEN-CL1 virtual machines are running.

Practice

► **Create a GPO to enable auditing for files and folders**

1. Log on to DEN-DC1 as **Administrator**.
2. Open **Active Directory Users and Computers**, and move the **DEN-SRV1** computer account from the **Computers** container into the **Legal** organizational unit.
3. Close **Active Directory Users and Computers**.
4. Open **Group Policy Management**, and create and link a GPO named **Legal Auditing** to the **Legal** organizational unit.
5. Right-click and edit the **Legal Auditing** policy.
6. Expand **Computer Configuration, Windows Settings, Security Settings, Local Polices, Audit Policy**, and double-click **Audit object access**.
7. In the **Audit object access Properties** dialog box, select the **Define these policy settings** check box, select **Success** and **Failure**, and then click **OK**.
8. Close the **Group Policy Object Editor**.
9. Log on to DEN-SRV1 as **Administrator**.
10. Open Windows Explorer, right-click **C:\Legal**, and then click **Sharing and Security**.
11. Share the **Legal** folder with the share name **Legal**, and then assign the Everyone group **Change** permission to the share.
12. Click the **Security** tab, and then assign the **DL Legal Write** group **Write** permission.

13. Click **Advanced**, and then select the **Auditing** tab in the **Advanced Security Settings for Legal** dialog box.
14. Add the **Everyone** group, audit them for **Full Control** of **Successful** and **Failed**, and then click **OK** three times.
15. At the **Run** command prompt, type **gpupdate /force** to refresh the policy. Click **OK**
16. Log on to DEN-CL1 as **Don**, and then connect to **\\DEN-SRV1\Legal**.
17. Attempt to delete the **Briefs** folder. Click **Yes** to confirm the deletion. You will receive an *Error Deleting file or Folder* message. Click **OK** to acknowledge the message.
18. Close all open windows on DEN-CL1 and log off.
19. Return to DEN-SRV1, and then open the **Security** log in Event Viewer. You will see a padlock icon, indicating the failure event. Double-click the entry and examine it.
20. Close all open windows, and then log off all computers.

Important Do not shut down the virtual machines.

Best Practices for Configuring Auditing

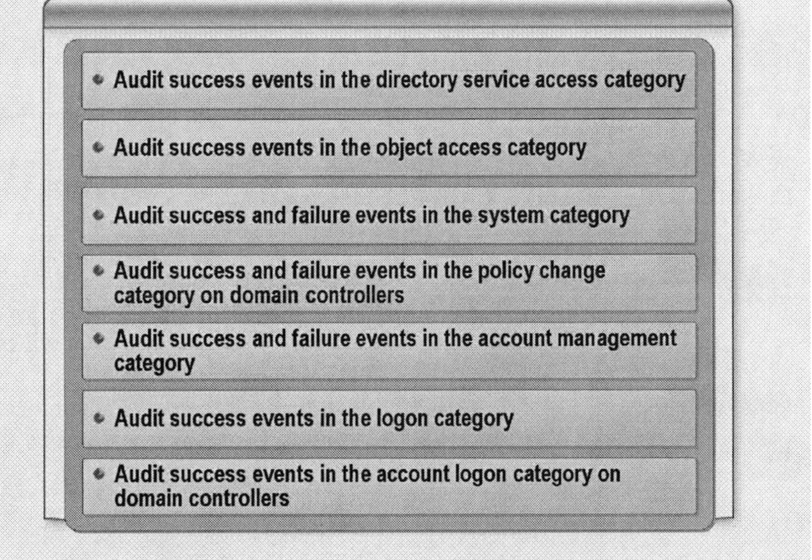
Audit success events in the directory service access category
Audit success events in the object access category
Audit success and failure events in the system category
Audit success and failure events in the policy change category on domain controllers
Audit success and failure events in the account management category
Audit success events in the logon category
Audit success events in the account logon category on domain controllers

Best practices

Apply the following best practices while performing auditing:

- Audit success events in the directory service access category.

  By auditing success events in the directory service access category, you can find out who accessed an object in Active Directory and what operations were performed.

- Audit success events in the object access category.

  By auditing success events in the object access category, you can ensure that users are not misusing their access to secured objects.

- Audit success and failure events in the system category.

  By auditing success and failure events in the system category, you can detect unusual activity that indicates that an attacker is attempting to gain access to your computer or network.

- Audit success and failure events in the policy change category on domain controllers.

  If an event is logged in the policy change category, someone has changed the Local Security Authority (LSA) security policy configuration. If you use Group Policy to edit your audit policy settings, you do not need to audit events in the policy change category on member servers.

- Audit success and failure events in the account management category.

  By auditing success events in the account management category, you can verify changes that are made to account properties and group properties. By auditing failure events in the account management category, you can see whether unauthorized users or attackers are trying to change account properties or group properties.

- Audit success events in the logon category.

  By auditing success events in the logon category, you have a record of when each user logs on to or logs off a computer. If an unauthorized person steals a user's password and logs on, you can find out when the security breach occurred.

- Audit success events in the account logon category on domain controllers.

  By auditing success events in the account logon category, you can see when users log on to or log off the domain. You do not need to audit events in the account logon category on member servers.

- Set an appropriate size for the security log.

  It is important to configure the size of the security log appropriately, based on the number of events that your audit policy settings generate.

Additional reading

For more information about managing audit logs, see article 325898, "HOW TO: Set Up and Manage Operation-Based Auditing for Windows Server 2003, Enterprise Edition," in the Microsoft Knowledge Base at the Microsoft Help and Support Web site.

Lesson: Managing Security Logs

- Types of Log Files
- Common Security Events
- Tasks Associated with Managing the Security Log Files
- Practice: Managing Security Logs

Introduction

You can configure the security logs to record information about Active Directory and server events. These events are recorded in the Windows security log. The security log can record security events, such as valid and invalid logon attempts, as well as events that are related to resource use, such as creating, opening, or deleting files. You must log on as an administrator to control what events are audited and displayed in the security log.

Lesson objectives

After completing this lesson, you will be able to:

- Describe the types of security log files and the information contained in each log file.
- Identify common security events.
- Describe tasks that are associated with managing the security log files.
- Manage security log files.

Types of Log Files

The following logs are available in Event Viewer:
- Application
- Security
- System
- Directory service
- File Replication service

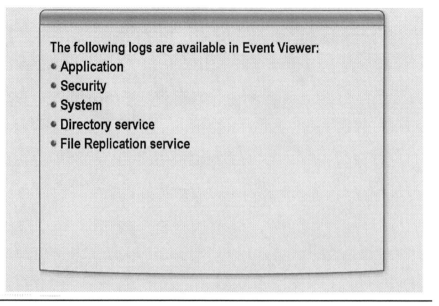

Introduction

The security log records events, such as valid and invalid logon attempts, and events related to resource use, such as creating, opening, or deleting files or other objects. For example, if logon auditing is enabled, attempts to log on to the system are recorded in the security log. After an audit policy is designed and implemented, information begins to appear in the security log.

Each computer in the organization has a separate security log that records local events. Domain controllers hold the security log information about Active Directory.

Logs available in Event Viewer

You can view the following logs in Event Viewer, depending on the type of computer that you are using and the services that are installed on that computer:

- *Application.* Contains events generated by applications installed on the computer, including server applications, such as Microsoft Exchange Server or Microsoft SQL Server, and desktop applications, such as Microsoft Office.
- *Security.* Contains events generated by auditing. These events include logons and logoffs, access to resources, and changes in policy.
- *System.* Contains events generated by components and services in Windows Server 2003.
- *Directory service.* Appears only on domain controllers. The directory service event log contains, for example, Active Directory replication.
- *File Replication service.* Appears only on domain controllers. The file replication service event log contains, for example, events that are related to the replication of Group Policy.

Tip If you decide to use auditing extensively, increase the size of the security log in the Event Log section of the security policy for the Default Domain Controllers GPO.

Security log files format

Security log files are also stored in the *systemroot*/system32/config directory. Security logs can be exported and archived in the following file formats:

- Event log files (.evt; the default)
- Comma-delimited files (.csv)
- Text files (.txt)

Common Security Events

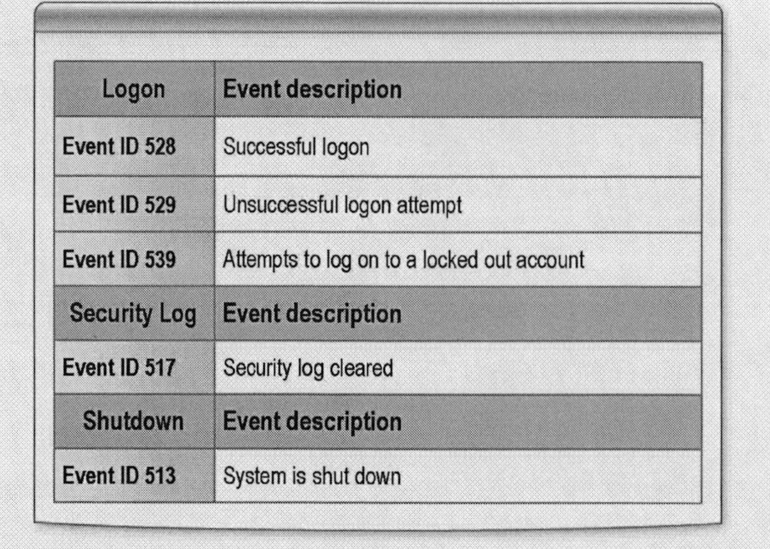

Logon	Event description
Event ID 528	Successful logon
Event ID 529	Unsuccessful logon attempt
Event ID 539	Attempts to log on to a locked out account
Security Log	**Event description**
Event ID 517	Security log cleared
Shutdown	**Event description**
Event ID 513	System is shut down

Introduction

Many events appear in the security log. The following are some common scenarios that might be cause for concern and suggestions for diagnosing problems by using the event log.

Invalid logon attempts and account lockout

A successful logon generates an Event ID 528. When a user attempts to guess another user's password, he or she will likely make several incorrect guesses. Each incorrect guess generates an Event ID 529, which is also generated by a misspelled user name. If an account becomes locked out, subsequent attempts generate an Event ID 539.

Intermittent instances of these events might occur when a user types incorrectly or forgets a password. Repeated instances in a short time period might indicate a password attack.

Change of file ownership

The owner of a file in the NTFS file system can modify the file's permissions to read and modify the file. A user who has the user right to take ownership can access any file by first taking ownership of that file. This change of ownership constitutes the use of a user right and generates an Event ID 578.

Clearing the security log

An unscrupulous administrator with the user right to clear the security log from Event Viewer can clear the log to hide his or her security-sensitive activities.

The security log must always be cleared according to a well-planned schedule and only immediately after a full copy of the log is archived. If the log is cleared under any other circumstances, the administrator must justify his or her actions. Clearing the security log generates an Event ID 517, which is the first event generated in the new log.

System shutdown

Ordinarily, mission-critical servers must be shut down only by administrators. You can prevent others from shutting down a server by assigning or denying the **Shut down the system** user right in the local security policy or by using Group Policy.

To determine whether the **Shut down the system** right was mistakenly assigned, audit the system Event ID 513, which identifies who shut down the computer.

Additional reading

For more information about security events, see article 299475, "Windows 2000 Security Event Description (Part 1 of 2)" and article 301677, "Windows 2000 Security Event Description (Part 2 of 2)" on the Microsoft TechNet Web site.

Tasks Associated with Managing the Security Log Files

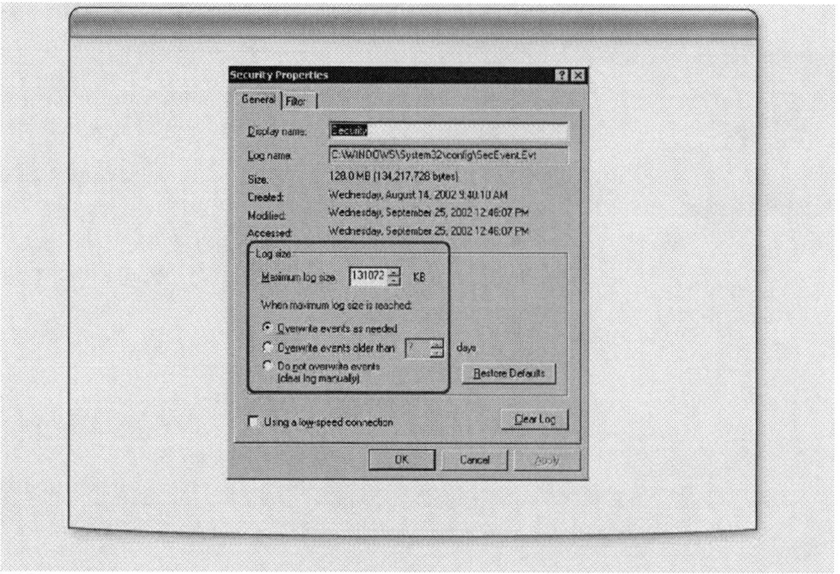

Introduction

All audited events in Windows NT, Windows Server 2003, and Windows XP are recorded in the security log in Event Viewer. Security-related events might also be recorded in the application and system logs.

Evaluate the configuration of the log file

Before you enable audit policies, you must evaluate whether the default configuration of the log files in Event Viewer is appropriate for your organization.

To view the log files settings in Event Viewer:

1. On the **Administrative Tools** menu, click **Event Viewer**.
2. Right-click the Security event log, and then click **Properties**.

Log file location

By default, the security log is stored in the *systemroot*/System32/config directory in a file named SecEvent.evt. In Windows Server 2003, you can change the log file location in the security log **Properties** dialog box. In Windows NT 4.0 and Windows Server 2000, you must edit the registry to change the location of each log file.

By default, only the System account and the Administrators group have access to the security log. This ensures that nonadministrators cannot read, write, or delete security events. If you move the log to a new location, ensure that the new file has the correct NTFS permissions. Because the Event Viewer service cannot be stopped, changes to this setting are not applied until the server is restarted.

Maximum log file size

By default, the maximum size that the security log can grow to before the overwrite settings is initiated is 16,384 KB. Because hard disk space is much more readily available now than it was in the past, you will likely want to increase this setting. The amount by which you increase this setting depends on the overwrite settings configured for the log file, but a good general guideline is to set the maximum size to at least 50 MB. You can change the maximum size of the log file on individual computers in the security log **Properties** dialog box or on many computers by using security templates or editing the registry.

The maximum size that you should set for the combined total size of all event logs is 300 MB. Each security event is 350 to 500 bytes, so a 10 MB event log contains approximately 20,000 to 25,000 security events.

Log file overwrite settings

When you configure the security log settings, you must define the overwrite settings when the maximum log file size is reached. The following list describes the overwrite event options.

- *Overwrite events as needed.* New events continue to be written when the log is full. Each new event replaces the oldest event in the log.
- *Overwrite events older than [x] days.* Events are retained in the log for the number of days you specify before they are overwritten. The default is seven days.
- *Do not overwrite events.* New events are not recorded, and the event log must be cleared manually.

Delegate the right to manage the file

To delegate the rights to manage the security log file, configure the Group Policy setting **Manage auditing and security log**. This setting is found in Computer Configuration/Windows Settings/Security Settings/Local Policies/User Rights Assignment.

Practice: Managing Security Logs

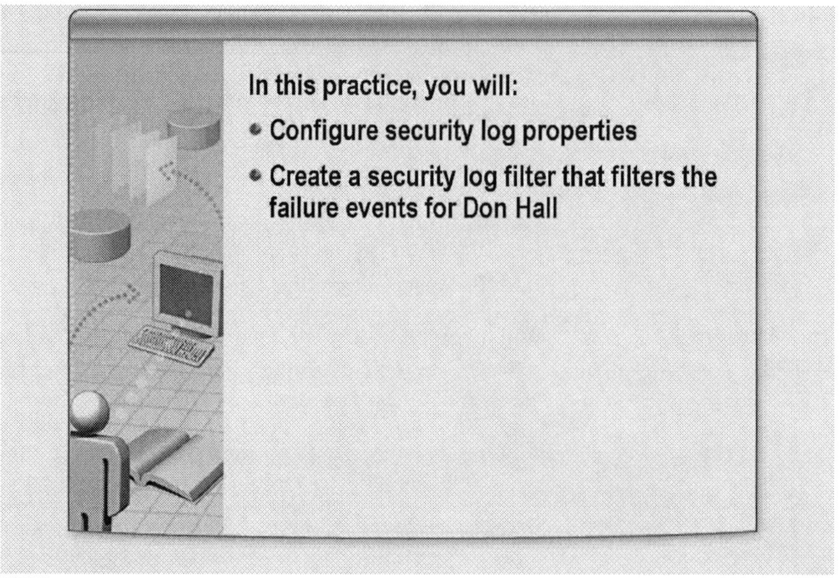

Objectives

In this practice, you will:

- Configure security log properties.
- Create a security log filter that filters the failure events for Don Hall.

Instructions

Ensure that the DEN-DC1, DEN-SRV1 and the DEN-CL1 virtual machines are running.

Practice

► **Configure security log properties**

1. Log on to DEN-SRV1 as **Administrator**.
2. In **Administrative Tools**, open **Event Viewer**.
3. Right-click the **Security** log, and click **Properties**.
4. On the **General** tab, type **30016** in the **Maximum log size** field.
5. Change the overwrite settings to **Do not overwrite events (clear log manually)**, and then click **Apply**.

► **Create a security log filter that filters the failure events for Don Hall**

1. In the **Security Properties** dialog box, click the **Filter** tab.
2. In the **Event types** section, clear all check boxes except **Failure audit**.
3. In the **User** field, type **Don**, and then click **OK**.
4. View the results in the security log. There will be only **Failure Audit events** for **Don**.
5. Close all open windows, and then log off.

Important Do not shut down the virtual machines.

Lab: Managing Security Settings

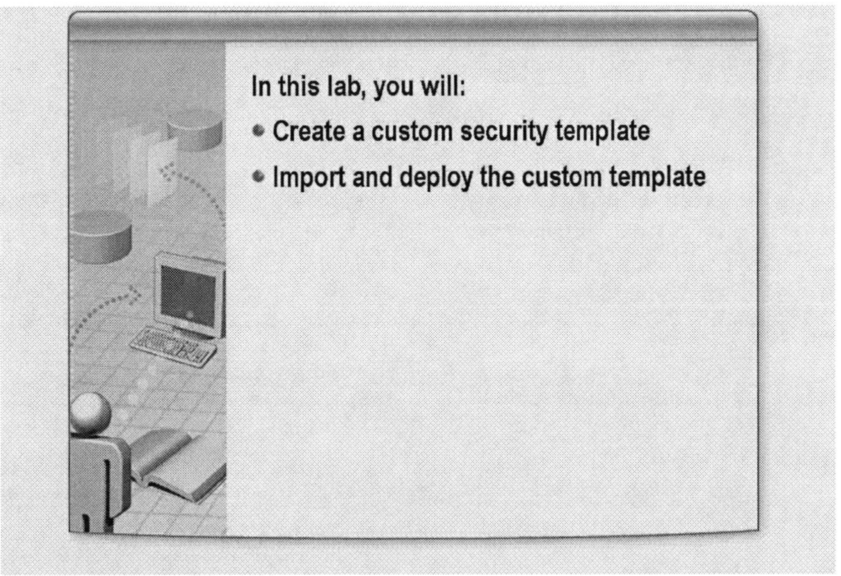
In this lab, you will:
Create a custom security template
Import and deploy the custom template

Objectives

After completing this lab, you will be able to:

- Create a custom security template.
- Import and deploy the custom template.

Prerequisites

To complete this lab, you must have the following virtual machines:

- DEN-DC1
- DEN-SRV1

Estimated time to complete this lab: 20 minutes

Exercise 1
Creating a Custom Security Template

In this exercise, you will create a custom security template.

Scenario

The security team has finished testing the security requirements for Contoso, Ltd. They have given you security requirements that you must use to create a custom security template named Graphics Security Policy.

Tasks	Special instructions
1. Create a new custom security template based on the securews template.	**a.** Log on to DEN-DC1 as **Administrator.** **b.** Open the **Security Templates** MMC. **c.** In the Security Templates snap-in, right-click the **securews** template, and then click **Save As.** **d.** In the **Save As** dialog box, type **Graphics Security Policy** in the **File name** field, and then click **Save.**
2. Enable audit, security policies, and event log properties.	**a.** Expand the **Graphics Security Policy** template. **b.** Expand **Local Policies**, and click **Audit Policy**. Notice that some auditing policies are enabled because this template was copied from the securews template. **c.** Enable **Audit object Access** for **Success** and **Failure**, and then click **OK.** **d.** Click **Security Options.** Notice that many security policies are enabled because this template was copied from the securews template. **e.** Configure the **Accounts: Rename administrator account** to set **Graphics Admin** as the name of the built-in administrator account. **f.** Change the **Interactive logon: Do not display last user name** from **Disabled** to **Enabled**, and then click **OK.** **g.** In the **Security Templates** tree, click **Event Log.** **h.** Double-click **Maximum security log size,** configure the log to be **99,840 KB**, and then click **OK.** **i.** Double-click the **Retain security log** setting, configure the period to be **7 days**, and then click **OK.** **j.** Click **OK** to accept the suggested value for the retention method.
3. Save the Graphics Security Policy template.	**a.** Right-click the **Graphics Security Policy** template, and then click **Save.** **b.** Close the Security Templates MMC. Click **No** to save console settings.

Exercise 2
Importing and Deploying the Custom Template

In this exercise, you will import the Graphics Security Policy template to a GPO that is linked to the Graphics organizational unit.

Tasks	Special instructions
1. Import the Graphics Security Policy template into a GPO.	a. On DEN-DC1, open **Group Policy Management**, and create and link a GPO named **Graphics Security** to the **Graphics** organizational unit. b. Right-click and edit the **Graphics Security Policy**. c. Expand **Computer Configuration**, **Windows Settings**, and then click **Security Settings**. d. Right-click **Security Settings**, and then click **Import Policy** to import the **Graphics Security Policy** template. e. Close the **Group Policy Object Editor**, and close **Group Policy Management**. f. Open **Active Directory Users and Computers**, and move **the DEN-SRV1** computer account from the Legal OU into the **Graphics** OU.
2. Test the settings.	a. Log on to DEN-SRV1 as **Administrator**. b. At the **Run** command prompt, type **gpupdate /force**. Click **OK**. c. In **Computer Management**, expand **Local Users and Groups**, and then click the **Users** folder. What is the name of the built-in administrators account?
3. Complete the lab exercise.	▪ Close all programs and shut down all computers. Do not save changes.

Course Evaluation

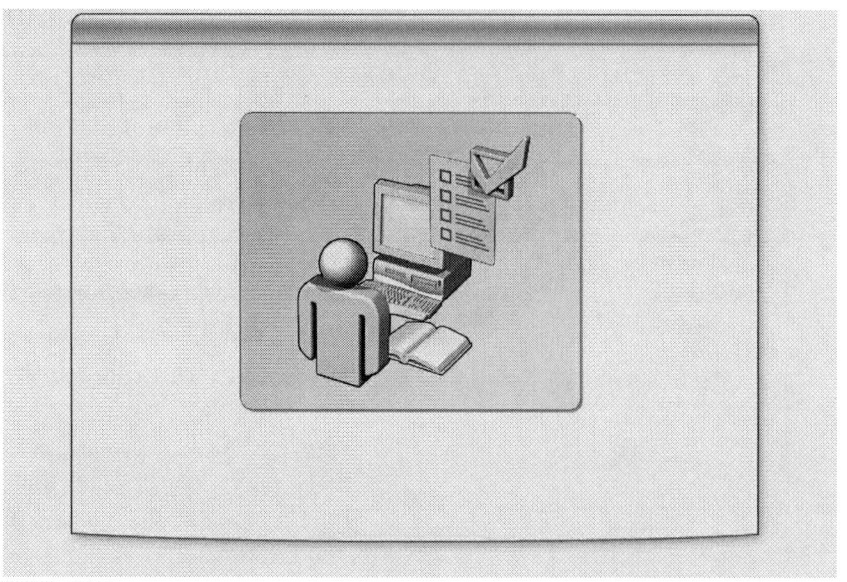

Your evaluation of this course will help Microsoft understand the quality of your learning experience.

To complete a course evaluation, go to the Metrics That Matter page of the Knowledge Advisors Web site at http://www.metricsthatmatter.com/MTMStudent/ClassListPage.aspx?&orig=6&VendorAlias=survey.

Microsoft will keep your evaluation strictly confidential and will use your responses to improve your future learning experience.

Index

Note: Numbers preceding the hyphens indicate the module in which the entry can be found.

Special Characters

A

B

C

D

E

F

H

I

L

M

N

O

Q

R

S

T

U

W

Notes

Notes

Notes

Notes

Notes

Notes

Notes

Notes

EMAIL DPIEHL@SYSBRC.COM

2274 GIVES PARTIAL PREP FOR EXAM 70-290

WWW.TRAN

MSM2274CCP/C90-04719

0 99751 08980 8

G0925060912